AS & A-Level
Psychology

Exam Board: AQA

Psychology raises some deep questions. How does the mind work? Why do we conform to social roles? Does the word "institutionalisation" really *need* to have so many letters in it?

CGP doesn't have definitive answers, but we can help you ace your AS and A-Level exams. This book is packed with no-nonsense study notes for everything on the AQA course, stacks of psychological studies to back up the theory <u>and</u> exam-style questions for every topic.

What more could you ask for — a free online edition? Oh, all right then.

How to access your free Online Edition

This book includes a free Online Edition to read on your PC, Mac or tablet.
You'll just need to go to **cgpbooks.co.uk/extras** and enter this code:

2262 6434 8106 0987

By the way, this code only works for one person. If somebody else has used this book before you, they might have already claimed the Online Edition.

A-Level revision? It has to be CGP!

Published by CGP

Editors:
Luke Bennett, Katherine Faudemer, Ceara Hayden, Kirstie McHale, Rachael Rogers, Camilla Sheridan

Contributors:
Lauren Burns, Richard Carciofo, Elisa Grey, Nigel Holt, Christine Johnson, Tracey Jones, Kate Robson, Denise Say, Stuart Wilson

ISBN: 978 1 78294 330 3

With thanks to Mark Billingham, Lauren Burns and Glenn Rogers for the proofreading.
With thanks to Laura Jakubowski for the copyright research.

Cover image © iStock.com/enot-poloskun

With thanks to Science Photo Library for permission to reproduce the image on page 86.

Critical values tables on page 125 and page 126 from Significance Testing of the Spearman Rank Correlation
Coefficient, Jerrold H Zar, Journal of the American Statistical Association, Sep 1 1972, Taylor & Francis.
Reprinted by permission of the publisher (Taylor & Francis Ltd, http://www.tandfonline.com).

Critical values tables on page 127 and page 129 abridged from FC Powell, Cambridge Mathematical and Statistical
Tables, Cambridge University Press (1979). Reproduced with permission of the Licensor through PLSclear.

Critical values table on page 128 from Extended Tables of the Wilcoxon Matched Pair Signed Rank Statistic,
Robert L McCornak, Journal of the American Statistical Association, Sep 1 1965, Taylor & Francis.
Reprinted by permission of the publisher (Taylor & Francis Ltd, http://www.tandfonline.com).

Clipart from Corel®
Printed by Elanders Ltd, Newcastle upon Tyne.

Based on the classic CGP style created by Richard Parsons.

Contents

If you're revising for the **AS exams**, you'll need the topics marked with an AS stamp.
If you're revising for the **A-Level exams**, you'll need the **whole book**.
Further information about what's required for AS is given on some pages.

We deliberately haven't put any answers in this book, because they'd just be saying what's already in the book. So instead, here's how to write answers and do well.

Conformity

Social psychology looks at how people interact and influence each other. Social influence means people change their behaviour to fit the situation or who they're with — for example, you might act differently with a parent than with a friend.

There's **More Than One Type** of **Conformity**

The influence of others can cause individuals to change their behaviour — this is **social influence**.
Conformity is when the behaviour of an individual or small group is **influenced** by a larger or dominant group.
There are **three** different types of conformity:

Internalisation means accepting the majority's views as your own

1) **Internalisation** is going along with the majority and **believing** in their views —
   you've accepted and **internalised** them so they're now your own too.

2) This might happen if you're in an unfamiliar situation, where you don't know what
   the 'correct' way to behave is. In this situation, you'd look to others for **information**
   about how to behave. This type of influence is called **informational social influence**.

Compliance is going along with things even if you disagree with them

1) **Compliance** is where you go along with the majority, even if you don't share their views.

2) You do this just to appear '**normal**' — going against the majority might lead to exclusion
   or rejection from the group. This type of influence is called **normative social influence**.

Identification means doing what's expected of you to fulfil a role

1) **Identification** is conforming to what's expected of you to fulfil a **social role**.

2) This means changing your behaviour because you want to fit a specific **role in society** (e.g. a nurse),
   or trying to imitate the behaviour of a **role model**. There's more about social roles on pages 5-6.

Sherif (1935) Tested the Effects of **Informational Social Influence**

Sherif researched whether people are influenced by others when they're doing an **ambiguous task**
(one where the answer isn't clear).

Sherif (1935) — Conformity and the autokinetic effect

Method:	This was a **laboratory experiment** with a **repeated measures** design. Sherif used a visual illusion called the **autokinetic effect**, where a stationary spot of light, viewed in a dark room, appears to move. Participants were falsely told that the experimenter would move the light. They had to estimate how far it had moved. In the first phase, individual participants made repeated estimates. They were then put into groups of 3 people, where they each made their estimate with the others present. Finally, they were retested individually.
Results:	When they were alone, participants developed their own stable estimates **(personal norms)**, which varied widely between participants. Once the participants were in a group, the estimates tended to **converge** and become more alike. When the participants were then retested on their own, their estimates were more like the **group estimates** than their original guesses.
Conclusion:	Participants were influenced by the estimates of other people, and a **group norm** developed. Estimates converged because participants used information from others to help them — they were affected by **informational social influence**.
Evaluation:	This was a **laboratory experiment**, so there was strict control of the variables. This means that the results are unlikely to have been affected by a third variable, so it should be possible to establish **cause and effect**. It also means that the method could be **replicated**. The **repeated measures** design meant that **participant variables** that could have affected the results were kept constant. However, the method is flawed because the participants were being asked to judge the movement of a light that wasn't moving — this rarely happens in real life. Because it created an **artificial situation**, the study can be criticised for lacking **ecological validity**. As well as this, the **sample** used was quite limited — all of the participants were male, so the results can't be **generalised** to everyone. An **ethical problem** with this study was **deception** — the participants were told the light was moving when it wasn't.

Conformity

Asch (1951) Looked at the Effects of **Normative Social Influence**

Asch designed an experiment to see whether people would conform to a majority's incorrect answer in an **unambiguous task** (one where the answer is obvious).

Asch (1951) — Conformity on an unambiguous task

Method: Asch carried out a **laboratory experiment** with an **independent groups** design. In groups of 8, participants judged line lengths (shown below) by saying out loud which comparison line (1, 2 or 3) matched the standard line. Each group contained only one real participant — the others were confederates (who acted like real participants but were really helping the experimenter). The real participant always went last or last but one, so that they heard the others' answers before giving theirs. Each participant did 18 trials. On 12 of these (the **critical trials**) the confederates all gave the same wrong answer. There was also a **control group**, where the participants judged the line lengths in isolation.

Lines used in Asch's study.

Standard Line   1   2   3

Seating plan for Asch's study. The real participant was always in position 7 or 8 and the others were confederates.

Stimulus Display

Results: In the control trials, participants gave the wrong answer **0.7%** of the time. In the critical trials, participants **conformed** to the majority (gave the same wrong answer) **37%** of the time. **75%** conformed at least once. Afterwards, some participants said they didn't really believe their answers, but didn't want to look different.

Conclusion: The control condition showed that the task was easy to get right. However, 37% were wrong on the critical trials — they conformed to the majority due to **normative social influence**.

Evaluation: This was a **laboratory experiment**, so there was **good control** of the variables. This minimises the effects of **extraneous variables**. Strict control of the variables also means that you could easily **repeat** the study to see if you get the same results. However, because the participants weren't in a **natural situation**, the study lacks **ecological validity**. Whether they were right or wrong didn't really matter to the participants — they might have been less likely to conform if their answer had had real-life consequences. In terms of **ethics**, the participants were **deceived** and might have been embarrassed when they found out the true nature of the study.

Asch's Participants were Influenced by **Situational Factors**

Sometimes we're influenced by others and conform, but sometimes we resist these influences and behave **independently**. There are **situational** and **dispositional** factors that affect conformity. Situational factors are due to the **social situation** a person is in, whereas dispositional factors are due to the person's **internal characteristics**. Asch investigated **situational factors**:

1) Group Size

You might expect that the bigger the majority is, the more influential it will be. If that was the case, it would be easier to resist conforming when there were fewer people to influence you. To test this, Asch (1956) conducted his conformity experiment with different numbers of confederates as the majority.

With only two confederates, the real participant conformed on only 14% of the critical trials. With three confederates, conformity rose to 32%. There was little change to conformity rates after that — no matter how big the majority group got. So, very small majorities are easier to resist than larger ones. But influence doesn't keep increasing with the size of the majority.

2) Unanimity / Social Support

Asch absolutely loved doing his conformity experiment, so he ran yet another version of it to test the effect of having a **supporter** in the group. Rather than the confederates forming a **unanimous majority**, one of the confederates **agreed** with the **participant**.

Having a fellow **dissenter** (someone who disagrees with the majority) broke the **unanimity** of the group, which made it easier for the participant to **resist** the pressure to conform — the rate of conformity **fell** to **5.5%**.

3) Task Difficulty

When Asch made the task **more difficult** by making the lines more similar, conformity levels increased.

People are more likely to conform if they're less **confident** that they're correct — there's more about this on the next page.

Conformity

Dispositional factors also affect conformity...

Confidence and Expertise Might Affect Conformity

When Asch **debriefed** his participants, he found a common factor of **confidence** in the people who hadn't conformed. If someone felt confident in their judgements, they were more able to **resist** group pressure.

1) **Wiesenthal et al (1976)** found that if people felt **competent** in a task, they were **less likely** to conform.

2) **Perrin and Spencer (1980)** replicated Asch's study with participants who were engineering students. Conformity levels were much **lower**. This could have been due to the fact that engineers had **confidence** in their skills in making accurate observations.

Gender Might Also be a Factor

Until the mid-1970s, the dominant view was that **females conform more than males**. Then **Eagly and Carli** did a load of research that suggests it might not be as simple as all that...

> **Eagly and Carli (1981)** did a **meta-analysis** of conformity research, where they re-analysed data from a number of studies. They did find some sex differences in conformity, but the differences were **inconsistent**. The clearest difference between men and women was in **Asch**-like studies where there was **group pressure** from an **audience**.

> **Eagly (1987)** argued that men and women's **different social roles** explain the difference in conformity — women are more concerned with **group harmony**, so are more likely to agree with others. **Assertiveness** and **independence** are valued male attributes, so maintaining your own opinion under pressure fits with the perceived male social role.

Warm-Up Questions

Q1 What is normative social influence?

Q2 What type of social influence did Sherif's study investigate?

Q3 Outline the strengths and weaknesses of the research method in Asch's study.

Q4 What situational factors did Asch identify that affected conformity levels?

Exam Questions

Q1 Which of the terms A, B, C, D or E best matches the statement below?

> Looking to others for guidance because you lack knowledge of how to behave.

A conformity
B informational social influence
C internalisation
D normative social influence
E compliance   [1 mark]

Q2 Explain what is meant by identification.   [3 marks]

Q3 Discuss **two** variables that affect conformity.   [6 marks]

Q4 Briefly outline and evaluate **two** studies of conformity.   [8 marks]

Do like every psychology student and learn about conformity...

Social influence just means changing your behaviour because of what other people are doing or saying. Conformity is also known as majority influence — it means changing your behaviour to fit in with the rest of the group (the majority). Conformity might not happen in all situations, and some people are more likely to conform than others. Asch showed this in different versions of his study — make sure you know what effect these different set-ups had on conformity.

Conformity to Social Roles

People adopt different behaviours depending on the role they want to play in society. Where it gets interesting is that people conform to roles by adopting the behaviour associated with them, even if the roles are randomly assigned...

Social Roles are the Behaviours that Society Expects from You

1) People hold different **positions** in society, such as teenager, grandparent, manager, priest, etc. Most people occupy several positions at the same time — e.g. student, waiter, brother and son.

2) **Social roles** are the sets of **behaviours** and **expectations** that come with holding these positions.

3) For example, in our society a woman who has a baby might be expected to look after and love her child — these are the behaviours that fulfil the social role of '**mother**'.

4) The expectations of a role are held by society. When we accept a role, we **internalise** these expectations so that they shape our behaviour.

Zimbardo et al (1973) Studied Conformity to Social Roles

Zimbardo et al set up a mock prison to see if people would conform to the **assigned roles** of prisoner or guard.

Zimbardo et al (1973) — Stanford prison experiment

Method:	Male students were recruited to act as either guards or prisoners in a mock prison. They were randomly given the roles of prisoner or guard, and their behaviour was observed. The prisoners were 'arrested' as they went about their day, taken to 'prison' and given uniforms and numbers. The guards also wore uniforms and mirrored sunglasses.
Results:	Initially, the guards tried to assert their authority and the prisoners resisted by sticking together. The prisoners then became more passive and obedient, while the guards invented nastier punishments. The experiment was abandoned early because some prisoners became very distressed.
Conclusion:	Guards and prisoners adopted their social roles quickly. Zimbardo claims this shows that our **social role can influence our behaviour** — seemingly well-balanced men became unpleasant and aggressive in the role of guard.
Evaluation:	This was a **controlled observation**, so there was **good control** of variables. However, because it was an artificial environment, the results can't really be **generalised** to real-life situations. In terms of **ethics**, some participants found the experience very distressing. There's also a problem with **observer bias**, as Zimbardo ran the prison himself, and later admitted that he became too personally involved in the situation. The conclusion Zimbardo reached doesn't explain why only some of the participants acted according to their assigned roles.

Studies can help Explain how Social Roles Affect People in the Real World

1) No one has ever replicated Zimbardo's prison study exactly. This has been down to design problems, such as making it an **ethical** experiment.

2) However, there have been other similar studies into **assigned roles**. One of these was done by **Orlando (1973)**.

> Psychologists have to design their experiments to meet ethical guidelines, otherwise they can't be carried out — see pages 108-109 for the guidelines produced by the British Psychological Society.

Orlando (1973) set up a **mock psychiatric ward** in a hospital for three days. 29 staff members of the hospital volunteered to be 'patients', and were held in the ward. Another 22 staff members were involved, but they were just asked to carry out their normal daily roles.

It only took a little while for the 'patients' to start **behaving** like real patients of the hospital. It became very difficult to tell them apart — they seemed to be **conforming** to the roles that had been assigned to them. Many showed signs of depression and withdrawal, and six even tried to escape from the ward.

After the study, the mock patients reported that they had felt frustrated, anxious and despairing. Some felt that they'd **lost their identity**, that their feelings weren't important, and that they weren't being treated as people.

3) Studies like this can give really useful information about how **real patients** might feel in a hospital. Orlando's (1973) study led to more of an effort by the staff to respect the patients, and improved the relationship and cooperation between them.

Conformity to Social Roles

Zimbardo's study has never been exactly replicated, but similar studies have tried to find out more about conformity...

Reicher and Haslam (2006) Developed the Ideas in Zimbardo's Study

1) In the **Holocaust** during World War Two, approximately 6 million Jews were horrifically murdered by the Nazis.

2) Psychologists had different theories about the soldiers who'd carried out the killings. Some thought they must be 'evil', but others thought they were 'normal' people who'd committed atrocities because of their **social role**.

3) **Zimbardo's** (1973) study showed that normal people will shape their behaviour to fit into a social role, even if it's only been randomly assigned.

4) It seemed that the participants' behaviour was **situational**, rather than **dispositional**.

5) **Reicher and Haslam** (2006) recreated a similar situation to Zimbardo's experiment, but they were particularly interested to see how the group dynamics changed over time.

Reicher and Haslam (2006) — The BBC prison study

Method: This was a **controlled observation** in a mock prison, which was filmed for television. The participants were 15 male volunteers who had responded to an advert. They were randomly assigned to 2 groups — 5 were guards and 10 were prisoners. They had daily tests to measure levels of depression, compliance with rules, and stress. The prisoners knew that one of them, chosen **at random**, would become a guard after 3 days. An independent **ethics committee** had the power to stop the experiment at any time in order to protect the participants.

Results: The guards failed to form a united group and identify with their role. They didn't always exercise their power and said they felt uncomfortable with the inequality of the situation. In the first 3 days, the prisoners tried to act in a way that would get them promoted to guard status. After one was promoted, they became a much **stronger group** because they knew there were no more chances of promotion. The unequal system collapsed due to the **unwillingness of the guards** and the **strength of the prisoner group**. On Day 6 the prisoners rebelled and the participants decided to live in a democracy, but this also collapsed due to tensions within the group. Some of the former prisoners then wanted to set up a stricter regime with them as leaders. The study was **abandoned** early on the advice of the ethics committee, as the participants showed signs of stress.

Conclusion: The participants didn't fit into their expected social roles, suggesting that these roles are **flexible**.

Evaluation: In contrast to Zimbardo's findings, Reicher and Haslam's prisoners were a strong group, and the guards were weak. However, it's possible that this was because Reicher and Haslam's guards were not as empowered as Zimbardo's, who were actively encouraged to maintain order. This study has been criticised for being made for TV — many people (including Zimbardo) argued that elements of it were staged and the participants played up to the cameras. Because this was an artificial situation, the results can't be **generalised** to real life. The **ethics** of this study were good — the participants were not **deceived**, so they were able to give **informed consent**. The participants were **protected** by the ethics committee and the study was abandoned as soon as they appeared to be becoming stressed. They were also **debriefed** and offered counselling afterwards.

Warm-Up Questions

Q1 What is a social role?

Q2 What's the difference between situational and dispositional behaviour?

PRACTICE QUESTIONS

Exam Questions

Q1 Briefly outline and evaluate identification with social roles as an explanation for conformity. [4 marks]

Q2 Describe and evaluate the findings of one study on conformity to social roles. [8 marks]

Who knew role-play was so popular?

Conformity's handy because it means you don't have to make any decisions for yourself... It's all about wanting to fit in with a group, even if you think it's actually a bit rubbish. Personally I reckon joining a group that involves being arrested and put in a fake prison isn't really ideal. I'd probably just say thanks but I'm washing my hair that week.

Obedience to Authority

Atteeennnnnnnnnnnnshun! Obedience means acting in response to a direct order, usually from an authority figure.

Milgram (1963) Studied Obedience

Milgram (1963) — Obedience to Authority

Method:	Milgram conducted a number of **laboratory experiments** to test factors thought to affect obedience. This condition tested whether people would obey orders to shock someone in a separate room. It took place at the prestigious Yale University. **40 men** participated, responding to newspaper adverts seeking **volunteers** for a study on 'learning and memory'. They received payment for attending, which didn't depend on them proceeding with the experiment. The experimenter wore a grey technician's coat. Each participant was introduced to a **confederate** (acting like a participant, but who was really part of the experimental set-up). They drew lots to see who would act as 'teacher' and 'learner', but this was fixed so the participant was always the teacher. The participant witnessed the confederate being strapped into a chair and connected up to a shock generator in the next room. It didn't actually give electric shocks, but the participants thought it was real. The switches ranged from 15 volts (labelled 'Slight Shock') to 450 volts (labelled 'XXX'). The participant taught the learner word-pairs over an intercom. When the learner answered incorrectly, the participant had to administer an **increasing level of shock**. After the 300 V shock, the learner pounded on the wall and made no further responses. If participants hesitated during the process, the experimenter told them to continue. **Debriefing** included an interview, questionnaires and being reunited with the 'learner'.
Results:	**26 participants (65%)** administered **450 V** and **none stopped before administering 300 V** (when the learner banged on the wall). Most participants showed obvious signs of stress like sweating, groaning and trembling.
Conclusion:	**Ordinary people** will **obey orders** to hurt someone else, even if it means acting against their conscience.

Milgram's Experiment had Good and Bad Points

1) **Internal validity**: It's possible that participants didn't really believe they were inflicting electric shocks — they were just going along with the **experimenter's expectations** (showing **demand characteristics**). But Milgram claimed participants' **stressed reactions** showed they believed the experiment was real.

2) **Ecological validity**: Milgram's participants did a task that they were unlikely to encounter in real life (shocking someone). So the study **lacks ecological validity**. However, because it was a **laboratory experiment** there was good control of the variables, so it's possible to establish **cause and effect**.

3) **Ethical issues**: The participants were **deceived** as to the true nature of the study. This means they couldn't give **informed consent**. They weren't informed of their **right to withdraw** from the experiment. In fact, they were prompted to continue when they wanted to stop. The participants showed signs of stress during the experiment, so they weren't **protected**. However, they were extensively **debriefed** and 84% of them said they were pleased to have taken part. As well as this, at the time of the experiment there weren't any formal ethical guidelines in place, so technically Milgram didn't breach any. There's more general stuff on ethics on pages 108-110.

Milgram Identified Situational Factors that Affected Obedience

Milgram carried out his experiment in loads of slightly different ways to investigate the effect that certain conditions would have on the results.

1) **Presence of allies** — When there were 3 teachers (1 participant and 2 confederates), the real participant was **less likely to obey** if the other two refused to obey. Having **allies** can make it easier to resist orders.

2) **Proximity of the victim** — Milgram's results suggest an important factor was the **proximity (closeness)** of the learner. In the condition described above, 65% gave the maximum shock. This dropped to 40% with the learner in the **same room**, and 30% when the participant had to put the learner's hand onto the shock plate. Proximity made the learner's suffering harder to ignore.

3) **Proximity of the authority** — When the authority figure gave prompts by **phone** from another room, obedience rates dropped to 23%. When the authority figure wasn't close by, orders were **easier to resist**.

4) **Location of the experiment** — When the participants were told the study was being run by a private company, and the experiment was moved to a set of **run-down offices** in a nearby town, the proportion of people giving the maximum shock fell to 48%. When his association with a prestigious university (Yale) was removed, the authority of the experimenter seemed **less legitimate**, so the participants were more likely to question it. (There's more about legitimate authority on the next page.)

Obedience to Authority

There are lots of explanations for why people obey authority...

Milgram's **Agency Theory (1973)** Explains **Obedience**

1) When people behave on behalf of an **external authority** (do as they're told), they're said to be in an **agentic state**. This means they act as someone's **agent**, rather than taking personal responsibility for their actions.

2) The opposite of this is behaving **autonomously** — not following orders.

3) Milgram's **agency theory** stated that when we feel we're acting out the wishes of another person (being their agent), we feel **less responsible** for our actions.

4) This effect is seen in Milgram's studies. Some participants were concerned for the **welfare** of the learner and asked who would take **responsibility** if the learner was harmed. When the experimenter (authority) took responsibility, often the participant would continue.

5) This **agentic state** was also encouraged by the experiment's set-up. The participants voluntarily entered a **social contract** (an obligation) with the experimenter to take part and follow the procedure of the study.

6) People can start off acting in an **autonomous** way (thinking for themselves), but then become obedient. This is known as an **agentic shift**. When Milgram's participants arrived for the experiment they were in an **autonomous state**, but as soon as they started following orders they underwent an **agentic shift**, and entered an **agentic state**.

7) Milgram claimed that there were some **binding factors** that might have kept his participants in the **agentic state**:

   - **Reluctance** to **disrupt the experiment** — participants had already been paid, so may have felt **obliged** to continue.
   - The **pressure** of the **surroundings** — the experiment took place in a prestigious university (see previous page). This made the experimenter seem like a **legitimate authority** (see below).
   - The **insistence** of the **authority figure** — if participants hesitated they were told that they **had** to continue the experiment.

Milgram's **Agency Theory** is **Supported** by his **Results**

Before his studies, Milgram believed that people were **autonomous** and could **choose** to resist authority. His **agency theory** shows Milgram's findings changed his mind about how much impact authority figures have.

Evaluation of Agency Theory

1) There's lots of experimental evidence to support agency theory — Milgram's participants often claimed they wouldn't have gone as far by themselves, but they were just following orders.

2) Sometimes people resist the pressure to obey authority. This can be because of the situation, or because of individual differences (see page 10). Agency theory doesn't explain why some people are more likely to exhibit independent behaviour (i.e. resist pressure to conform or obey) than others.

Obedience Can Depend on the **Legitimacy** of the **Authority**

1) We're socialised to recognise the authority of people like parents, police officers, doctors, teachers, etc.

2) These kinds of people are legitimate authorities — they're given the right to tell us what to do. This means we're more likely to obey them.

3) Legitimate authority comes from having a defined social role which people respect — usually because it implies knowledge or comes with legal power.

4) When Milgram re-ran his study in some run-down offices, obedience rates were lower than when the study was run in the university (see previous page).

5) He argued that the experimenter's authority was higher in the university situation because of the status of the university.

6) Bickman (1974) conducted a field experiment where researchers ordered passers-by to do something like pick up a bit of litter. They were dressed either in a guard's uniform, as a milkman, or just in smart clothes. People were much more likely to obey the person in a guard's uniform. This was because he seemed to be the most legitimate authority figure.

Obedience to Authority

The **Authoritarian Personality** Can Also Explain **Obedience**

1) Adorno's theory of the **authoritarian personality** is a **dispositional** (personality) explanation of obedience.

2) **Adorno et al (1950)** proposed that **over-strict parenting** results in a child being socialised to **obey authority unquestioningly**, because they learn strict obedience to their parents.

3) Adorno expanded on this idea to argue that strict parenting also resulted in **prejudice**:
   - Strict parenting means the child feels **constrained**, which creates **aggression**.
   - But the child is afraid they'll be **disciplined** if they express this aggression towards their parents, so instead they're hostile to people they see as weak or **inferior** to them — usually minority groups.

4) Adorno et al defined the collection of traits that they thought resulted from over-strict parenting as the **authoritarian personality**. As well as **aggression** to people of perceived **lower status**, and **blind obedience**, the identifying traits included being **conformist** and having **rigid moral standards**.

| The F-scale | Adorno et al (1950) developed a scale to measure how strongly people express **authoritarian traits**, called the **F-scale**. *The 'F' stands for fascism.* |

Adorno et al (1950) developed a scale to measure how strongly people express **authoritarian traits**, called the **F-scale**. *The 'F' stands for fascism.*

This research began shortly after the end of the Second World War — Adorno's team were trying to find out if there are characteristics of individuals which could explain the persecution of Jews and other minority groups by the Nazis in the 1930s and 40s.

Evaluation of Adorno's Authoritarian Personality Theory

1) **Elms and Milgram (1966)** found that participants who scored higher on the **F-scale** (so had more authoritarian traits) had been willing to administer bigger shocks in Milgram's experiment.

2) However, this doesn't necessarily mean that a strict upbringing or having authoritarian traits **causes** people to be obedient — other factors such as **education** could cause both authoritarian traits and obedience.

3) Also, Milgram found that **situational factors** like proximity and location (see page 7) had a bigger effect on obedience.

4) The theory also doesn't explain how **whole societies** can become obedient — not everybody has this personality type.

Warm-Up Questions

Q1 Outline the method of Milgram's (1963) experiment.

Q2 In Milgram's 1963 experiment, what percentage of participants gave the maximum shock?

Q3 Why was the validity of Milgram's study criticised?

Q4 What is meant by 'proximity' and why is it a factor in obedience?

Q5 What is meant by an 'agentic shift'?

Q6 Why might obedience rates have dropped when Milgram's study took place in run-down offices?

Q7 What does the F-scale measure?

Exam Questions

Q1	Evaluate Milgram's (1963) study of obedience in terms of ethical issues.	[6 marks]
Q2	Outline **two** situational variables that may affect obedience.	[4 marks]
Q3	Discuss explanations for obedience to authority.	[16 marks]

Pretty shocking results, don't you think?

Milgram crops up all the time, so you need to learn this stuff well. You've got to admit it's pretty incredible that people would give someone a 450 V shock just because they were told to. Everyone thinks that they wouldn't have done it if they were one of the participants, but really it's impossible to know. I definitely would have though. I love electricity.

Resistance to Social Influence

So why, you might ask, do some people resist social influence where others don't? It's an intriguing question...

Having **Social Support** Can Make People **More** Resistant

1) More of Milgram's participants resisted orders if there were **other participants present** who refused to obey (see page 7). This suggests that people find it easier to stand up to authority if they have support from others, because they no longer have to take full responsibility for rebelling.

2) This ties in with Asch's research on conformity. He found that participants were more likely to resist the pressure to conform if one of the confederates **agreed** with them (page 3). It seems that people are more likely to display independent behaviour if they've got **support** from others.

3) It doesn't really make sense to call this behaviour **independent**, seeing as it depends on having someone else there to agree with you... But just go with it...

Aspects of **Personality** May Influence **Independent Behaviour**

Your resistance to social influence might also be affected by a personality characteristic called **locus of control**. This indicates how much **personal control** you believe you have over events in your life.

The idea is that people who feel they're generally in control of what happens in their life are more likely to resist — this is a **dispositional explanation** for resistance.

1) **Rotter (1966)** developed a **questionnaire** to **measure locus of control**.

2) The questionnaire involved choosing between **paired statements** like these ones:

> A: Misfortune is usually brought about by people's own actions.
>
> B: Things that make us unhappy are largely due to bad luck.

If you agree with the first statement, you have an internal locus of control. This is categorised by a belief that what happens in your life results from your own behaviour or actions. E.g. if you did well in a test you might put it down to how much work you did for it.

If you agree with the second statement, you have an external locus of control. This is a belief that events are caused by external factors, like luck or the actions of others. E.g. if you did well in a test you might put it down to good questions coming up, or a lenient examiner.

3) People with an **internal locus of control** feel a stronger sense of control over their lives than people with an **external locus of control**. This means that they're more likely to exhibit **independent behaviour** — i.e. they're less likely to conform or obey.

4) People with an **external locus of control** may be more likely to conform or obey.

Warm-Up Question

Q1 What's the difference between an internal and an external locus of control?

Exam Question

Q1 Which **two** of the following are factors which may make resistance to social influence more likely?

    A the agentic state   **B** an internal locus of control   **C** unanimity of the group
    D social support   **E** an external locus of control   [2 marks]

Q2 Explain how an individual's personality can make them more likely to resist social influence.   [4 marks]

Resisting social pressure to stop making terrible jokes is really hard. Seriously.

Some things make resisting social influence easier — social support and having an internal locus of control are the key ones. A lot of it's common sense really — people are more likely to do what everybody else is doing if they're the only one that's different, but if you see yourself as in control or you feel responsible then you might be able to resist.

Minority Influence and Social Change

So far most of this social influence stuff has been about majority influence, but that's not the only type of social influence. Minorities can have social influence too — funnily enough this is called minority influence.

Minority Influence Can be Quite Powerful

1) Obviously people don't always go along with the majority — if they did, nothing would ever change.

2) Sometimes **small minorities** and even **individuals** gain influence and change the way the majority thinks.

3) In **minority influence**, it seems that a form of **internalisation** (see page 2) is taking place. Members of the majority actually take on the beliefs and views of a **consistent minority** — rather than just complying.

Minority Influence is Stronger if the Minority...

... is Consistent

Moscovici et al (1969) did some research into **minority influence** that compared **inconsistent** minorities with **consistent** minorities.

	Moscovici et al (1969) — Minority influence
Method:	This was a laboratory experiment into **minority influence** using 192 women. In groups of 6 at a time, participants judged the colour of 36 slides. All of the slides were blue, but the brightness of the blue varied. Two of the six participants in each group were **confederates**. In one condition the confederates called all 36 slides 'green' (consistent) and in another condition they called 24 of the slides 'green' and 12 of the slides 'blue' (inconsistent). A control group was also used which contained no confederates.
Results:	In the **control group** the participants called the slides 'green' **0.25%** of the time. In the **consistent** condition **8.4%** of the time participants adopted the minority position and called the slides 'green', and **32%** of the participants called the slides 'green' at least once. In the **inconsistent** condition the participants moved to the minority position of calling the slides 'green' only **1.25%** of the time.
Conclusion:	The confederates were in the **minority** but their views appear to have influenced the real participants. The use of the two conditions illustrated that the minority **had more influence** when they were **consistent** in calling the slides 'green'.
Evaluation:	This study was a laboratory experiment, so it **lacked ecological validity** because the task was artificial. The participants may have felt that judging the colour of the slide was a **trivial** exercise — they might have acted differently if their principles were involved. Also, the study was only carried out on women, so the results can't be generalised to men. However, owing to the use of a **control** group, we know that the participants were actually influenced by the minority rather than being independently unsure of the colour of the slides. In a similar experiment, participants were asked to **write down** the colour rather than saying it out loud. In this condition, even more people agreed with the minority, which provides **more support** for minority influence.

... is Flexible

Nemeth et al (1974) repeated Moscovici's experiment, but instructed participants to answer with **all of the colours** they saw in the slide, rather than a single colour. For example, they could answer 'green-blue' rather than 'green'. They ran **three variations** — where the two confederates:

1) said **all** of the slides were 'green'
2) said the slides were 'green' or 'green-blue' at **random**
3) said the **brighter** slides were 'green-blue' and the **duller** slides were 'green' or vice versa

When the confederates always answered 'green', or varied their response randomly (so were **inconsistent**), they had no effect on the participants' responses. But in the condition where the confederates responses **varied** with a feature of the slides (the brightness), the confederates had a **significant effect** on the participants' responses.

The confederates had most influence when they were **consistent but flexible** — Nemeth proposed that rigid consistency (always answering 'green') wasn't effective because it seemed **unrealistic** when more subtle responses were allowed.

Minority Influence and Social Change

There are different theories about how minority influence works — some people think it can be explained by the same process as majority influence, but some people think it's a completely different kettle of fish...

Moscovici's **Conversion Theory** Says **Minority Influence** Works **Differently**

Moscovici's **conversion theory** (1980) suggests that majority and minority influence are **different processes**:

Majority Influence	Minority Influence
People **compare their behaviour** to the majority (social comparison), and change their behaviour to **fit in** without considering the majority's views in detail.	When a minority is consistent people may actually examine the minority's beliefs in detail because they want to understand why the minority sees things differently.
So majority influence involves **compliance** — it doesn't always cause people to change their private feelings, just their behaviour.	This can lead to people privately accepting the minority view — they convert to the minority position.
	Social pressure to conform may mean their behaviour doesn't actually change, at least at first.

Minorities Can Change Views When They're Committed

In his conversion theory Moscovici described the **factors** that he thought enabled minority influence to happen — the main factor was **consistency**, which shows **commitment**:

1) Initially, minority views can be seen as **wrong**, because they don't match up with what's considered the **norm**.

2) But by being **consistent** the minority group shows that it has a clear view which it's **committed** to, and isn't willing to compromise (i.e. the minority isn't willing to give in to the pressure to conform).

3) This creates a **conflict** — when you're faced with a consistent minority you have to seriously consider whether they might be right, and if you should change your view. Moscovici called this the **validation process**.

4) If there's no reason to **dismiss** the minority view (there doesn't seem to be an error in their perception or reasoning, they're not acting out of self-interest, and so on), then you begin to see things as the **minority** does.

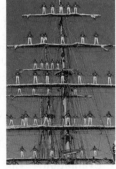

The longer Ron stayed on the mast, the more people joined him.

Social Impact Theory Outlines Three Influential Factors

Latané and Wolf's **social impact theory** (1981) argued that social influence occurs when the **combined** effects of **three factors** are significant enough:

1) **Strength** — how powerful, knowledgeable, and consistent the group appear to be.

2) **Numbers** — how many people are in the group.

3) **Immediacy** — how close the source of influence is to you (physically, or in terms of a relationship).

Latané and Wolf's theory says that **minority influence** happens through the same process as **majority influence** — it's just the **balance** of factors that create the social influence that's different.

The number of people in a minority is relatively small, but if the minority has strength and immediacy they can still exert **social influence** — a majority doesn't need as much strength or immediacy, because they have the numbers.

Lots of studies have provided **support** for social impact theory. However, Mullen (1985) conducted a **meta-analysis** of studies investigating social impact theory and found that lots of them relied on **self report** rather than observable behaviour. He argued that support for social impact theory could actually be a result of **demand characteristics** (see page 106). A **field experiment** by Sedikides and Jackson (1990) did provide support for social impact theory though, which contradicts Mullen's findings.

Minority Influence and Social Change

Minorities Can Become Majorities through the Snowball Effect

Whatever the process (conversion theory or social impact theory), minority influence is necessary for **social change** to take place...

1) If some people in a group start to agree with a minority view then the minority becomes more **influential**. This results in more and more people converting to the minority view. Eventually the minority becomes a majority. **Van Avermaet (1996)** described this as the **snowball effect**.

2) For this to happen people need to go from **privately** accepting the minority view to **publicly** expressing it.

3) One explanation of why this might happen is **social cryptoamnesia** — this means public opinion changes gradually over time, until the minority view is **accepted as the norm**, but people forget where the view originally came from.

Minorities Can Cause Social Change

There are many examples in history of things changing because the ideas of a few have taken hold. Try these for starters:

Martin Luther King

1) In the 1950s in America, black people did not have the same **rights** as white people. For example, in parts of America, buses were **segregated** and black people had to give up their seats to white people.

2) **Reverend Martin Luther King** challenged the views of the majority to bring about **political and social rights** for black people. He and other activists used **peaceful** protests like marches and sit-ins. This was known as the **Civil Rights Movement**. His ideas were so unpopular that during this time his home was bombed by activists, he was subjected to personal abuse, and he was **arrested**.

3) In the end though, the actions of civil rights activists influenced the **majority**. Nowadays there are **laws** that ensure people are given equal rights regardless of racial origin, and in 1964 Martin Luther King was awarded the **Nobel Peace Prize**.

Suzie was confident that it was only a matter of time before everyone started dressing like her.

Gay Rights Movements

1) Homosexuality used to be **illegal** in the UK. It was **decriminalised** in England and Wales in 1967 — but the age of consent was 21 (higher than for heterosexual people) and homosexuals were still treated **negatively**.

2) Over the last few decades, there have been moves towards equality as a result of **Gay Rights Movements**. These **minorities** have successfully **changed attitudes**. For example, the Equality Act (Sexual Orientation) 2007 made it **illegal to discriminate** against gay men and women in the provision of goods and services, and **same-sex marriage** was legalised in the UK in 2014.

Warm-Up Questions

Q1 According to Moscovici et al's (1969) study, how does consistency affect minority influence?

Q2 What is social cryptoamnesia?

PRACTICE QUESTIONS

Exam Questions

Q1 Briefly outline and evaluate one study into minority influence. [4 marks]

Q2 Discuss how social influence can lead to social change. [16 marks]

Who knew snowflakes could be so influential...

So minority influence can be a big deal. Here's an example: I think you should learn the stuff on this page. Most people probably don't agree — but you will, won't you? I've really got under your skin, haven't I? Power to the minority!

Types of Memory

Cognitive psychologists are interested in mental processes, and one of their big areas of research is memory.

Memory is a **Process** in Which Information is **Retained** About the Past

Most psychologists agree that there are three types of memory — the **sensory register**, **short-term memory (STM)** and **long-term memory (LTM)**. The three memory stores differ in **duration** (how long a memory lasts), **capacity** (how much can be held in the memory) and **coding** (how information is stored, creating a 'trace').

Sensory Register

1) The sensory register temporarily stores information from our senses (sight, sound, touch, taste and smell) — it's constantly receiving information from around us.

2) Unless we pay attention to it, it disappears quickly through spontaneous decay — the trace just fades.

3) The sensory register has a limited capacity, and a very limited duration (i.e. we can remember a little information for a very short time).

4) Information is coded depending on the sense that has picked it up — e.g. visual, auditory or tactile.

Short-Term Memory

1) Short-term memory has a limited capacity and a limited duration (i.e. we can remember a little information for a short time).

2) Coding is usually acoustic (sound).

Long-Term Memory

1) Long-term memory has a pretty much unlimited capacity and is theoretically permanent (i.e. it can hold lots of information forever). Coding is usually semantic (the meaning of the information).

2) There are different types of long-term memory:

- Episodic memory stores information about events that you've actually experienced, such as a concert or a visit to a restaurant. It can contain information about time and place, emotions you felt, and the details of what happened. These memories are declarative — this means they can be consciously recalled.

- Semantic memory stores facts and knowledge that we have learnt and can consciously recall, such as capital cities and word meanings. It doesn't contain details of the time or place where you learnt the information — it's simply the knowledge.

- Procedural memory stores the knowledge of how to do things, such as walking, swimming or playing the piano. This information can't be consciously recalled.

Studies Have Looked at the **Duration** of Memory

Sperling (1960) Investigated the Sensory Register Using Very Brief Displays

	Sperling (1960) — An investigation of the sensory register
Method:	In a **laboratory experiment**, participants were shown a grid with three rows of four letters for **50 milliseconds** (0.05 seconds). They then had to **immediately recall** either the **whole grid**, or a randomly chosen **row** indicated by a tone (high, medium or low) played straight after the grid was shown.
Results:	When participants had to recall the **whole grid**, they only managed to recall **four or five letters** on average. When a particular **row** was indicated, participants could recall an average of **three items**, no matter which row had been selected.
Conclusion:	The participants didn't know which row was going to be selected, so it could be concluded that they would have been able to recall three items from **any** row, therefore almost the whole grid was held in their sensory register. They couldn't report the whole grid because the trace **faded** before they could finish recall.
Evaluation:	Because this was a laboratory experiment, it was highly scientific. The **variables** could be controlled, and it would be easy for someone to **replicate** the study. However, the **artificial** setting of the study means that it lacks **ecological validity** — people don't normally have to recall letters in response to a sound, so the results might not represent what would happen in the real world.

Types of Memory

Peterson and Peterson (1959) Investigated STM Using Trigrams

Peterson and Peterson (1959) — The duration of STM

Method: Participants were shown **nonsense trigrams** (3 random consonants, e.g. CVM) and asked to recall them after either 3, 6, 9, 12, 15 or 18 seconds. During the pause, they were asked to count backwards in threes from a given number. This was an '**interference task**' to prevent them from repeating the letters internally.

Results: After **3 seconds**, participants could recall about **80%** of trigrams correctly.
After **18 seconds**, only about **10%** were recalled correctly.

Conclusion: When rehearsal is prevented, **very little** can stay in STM for longer than about **18 seconds**.

Evaluation: The results are likely to be reliable — it's a **laboratory experiment** where the variables can be tightly controlled. However, nonsense trigrams are artificial, so the study lacks **ecological validity** (see pages 100-101 for more about reliability and validity). Meaningful or 'real-life' memories may last longer in STM. Only one type of **stimulus** was used — the duration of STM may depend on the type of stimulus. Also, each participant saw **many different trigrams**. This could have led to confusion, meaning that the first trigram was the only realistic trial.

Bahrick et al (1975) Investigated LTM in a Natural Setting

Bahrick et al (1975) — Very long-term memories (VLTMs)

Method: 392 people were asked to list the names of their ex-classmates. (This is called a '**free-recall test**'.) They were then shown photos and asked to recall the names of the people shown (**photo-recognition test**) or given names and asked to match them to a photo of the classmate (**name-recognition test**).

Results: Within 15 years of leaving school, participants could **recognise** about **90%** of names and faces. They were about **60%** accurate on **free recall**. After 30 years, **free recall** had declined to about **30%** accuracy. After 48 years, name-recognition was about **80%** accurate, and photo-recognition about **40%** accurate.

Conclusion: The study is evidence of **VLTMs** in a '**real-life**' setting. Recognition is better than recall, so there may be a huge store of information, but it's not always easy to **access** all of it — you just need help to get to it.

Evaluation: This was a field experiment and so had **high ecological validity**. However in a 'real-life' study like this, it's hard to **control** all the variables, making these findings less reliable — there's no way of knowing exactly **why** information was recalled well. It showed better recall than other studies on LTM, but this may be because **meaningful** information is stored better. This type of information could be rehearsed (if you're still in touch with classmates, or if you talk to friends about memories of classmates), increasing the rate of recall. This means that the results can't be generalised to other types of information held in LTM.

Studies Have Looked at the **Capacity** of Memory

STM and LTM Have Very **Different Capacities**

Jacobs (1887) — The capacity of STM

Method: Participants were presented with a string of letters or digits. They had to repeat them back in the same order. The number of digits or letters increased until the participant failed to recall the sequence correctly.

Results: The majority of the time, participants recalled about **9 digits** and about **7 letters**. This capacity increased with **age** during childhood.

Conclusion: Based on the range of results, Jacobs concluded that STM has a **limited storage capacity** of **5-9 items**. Individual differences were found, such as STM increasing with age, possibly due to use of memory techniques such as **chunking** (see the next page). Digits may have been easier to recall as there were only 10 different digits to remember, compared to 26 letters.

Evaluation: Jacobs' research is **artificial** and **lacks ecological validity** — it's not something you'd do in real life. Meaningful information may be recalled better, perhaps showing STM to have an even greater capacity. Also, the previous sequences recalled by the participants might have confused them on future trials.

Types of Memory

Miller Reviewed Research into the Capacity of STM

1) **Miller (1956)** reviewed research into the capacity of STM. He found that people can remember about seven items.

2) He argued that the capacity of STM is **seven, plus or minus two** — 'Miller's magic number'.

3) He suggested that we use '**chunking**' to combine individual letters or numbers into larger, more meaningful units.

People find numbers easier to remember than letters.

> For example, **2,0,0,3,1,9,8,7** is about all the digits STM can hold.
> 'Chunked' into the meaningful recent years of **2003** and **1987**, it's much easier to remember.

STM could probably hold about seven such pieces of chunked information, increasing STM's capacity.

Coding is About the Way Information is Stored in Memory

1) In **STM**, we sometimes try to keep information active by repeating it to ourselves. This means it generally involves **acoustic** coding.

2) In **LTM**, coding is generally **semantic** — it's more useful to code words in terms of their meaning, rather than what they sound or look like (although coding in LTM **can** also be visual or acoustic).

Acoustic coding is about how the information sounds. Semantic coding is about the meaning of the information.

Baddeley (1966) — Investigating coding in STM and LTM

Method: Participants were given four sets of words that were either **acoustically similar** (e.g. man, mad, mat), **acoustically dissimilar** (e.g. pit, cow, bar), **semantically similar** (e.g. big, large, huge) or **semantically dissimilar** (e.g. good, hot, pig). The experiment used an **independent groups** design (see page 98) — participants were asked to recall the words either immediately or following a 20-minute task.

Results: Participants had problems recalling acoustically similar words when recalling the word list immediately (from **STM**). If recalling after an interval (from **LTM**), they had problems with semantically similar words.

Conclusion: The patterns of confusion between similar words suggest that **LTM** is more likely to rely on **semantic** coding and **STM** on **acoustic** coding.

Evaluation: This is another study that **lacks ecological validity**. Also, there are **other types** of LTM (e.g. episodic memory, procedural memory) and **other methods** of coding (e.g. visual) which this experiment doesn't consider. The experiment used an **independent groups** design, so there wasn't any control over participant variables.

Warm-Up Questions

Q1 What is coding?
Q2 Outline Sperling's (1960) study.
Q3 What is Miller's magic number?

Exam Questions

Q1 Identify and outline **two** types of long-term memory. [4 marks]

Q2 Describe and evaluate research into the differences between short-term and long-term memory. [16 marks]

Remember the days when you didn't have to remember stuff like this...

So already you can probably see that there's more to memory than what you can remember and what you can't. But don't worry — if... oh, hang on, what was I saying... Ah yes, if you make sure you know what the sensory register, short-term memory and long-term memory are, and how they differ, then you'll be on the road to collecting marks.

Models of Memory

Before you start reading this page, make sure you've got to grips with what short-term memory, long-term memory and the sensory register are. If you've even got the slightest niggling doubt, head back to page 14 to remind yourself.

Atkinson and Shiffrin (1968) Created the **Multi-Store Model**

1) The multi-store model proposes that memory consists of three stores — a **sensory register**, a **short-term store** and a **long-term store**, and information has to move through these stores to become a memory.

2) Information from our environment (e.g. visual or auditory) initially goes into the **sensory register**. You don't really notice much of this stuff. However, if you pay attention to it, or think about it, the information will pass into **short-term memory**.

3) Short-term memory has a **finite** capacity and duration. But if information is processed further (rehearsed) then it can be transferred to **long-term memory**. In theory, the information can then remain there forever. (Unless you really, really need to remember it, in which case it'll probably stay there until something more interesting comes along, like a bee or a cloud.)

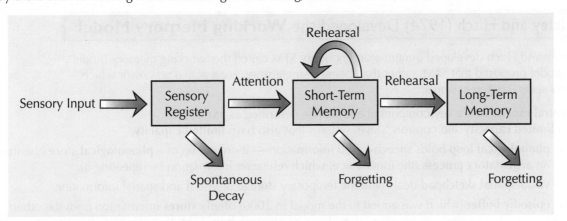

Many Studies **Support** the Multi-Store Model...

Several studies have been carried out that show that memory is made up of separate stores.

1) The **Primacy Effect** — Research shows that participants are able to recall the first few items of a list better than those from the middle. The multi-store model explains this because **earlier** items will have been **rehearsed** better and transferred to **LTM**. If rehearsal is prevented by an **interference task**, the effect disappears.

2) The **Recency Effect** — Participants also tend to remember the **last few** items better than those from the middle of the list. As STM has a capacity of around 7 items, the words in the middle of the list, if not rehearsed, are **displaced** from STM by the last few words heard. These last words are still in **STM** at the end of the experiment and can be **recalled**.

3) People with **Korsakoff's Syndrome** (amnesia that's mostly caused by chronic alcoholism) provide support for the model. They can recall the **last** items in a list (unimpaired recency effect), suggesting an unaffected **STM**. However, their **LTM** is very poor. This supports the model by showing that STM and LTM are **separate stores**.

4) **Milner et al (1957)** carried out a **case study** into a patient called HM who had suffered from severe and frequent epilepsy. His seizures were based in a brain structure called the hippocampus. Doctors decided to surgically remove part of the brain around this area. The operation reduced his epilepsy, but led to him suffering **memory loss**. He could still form **short-term memories**, but was unable to form **new long-term memories**. This case study supports the idea that different types of memory are **separate systems** in the brain.

Models of Memory

...But There Are Also Many **Limitations** of the Model

Although there's lots of support for the model, there's plenty of criticism too.

1) In the model, information is transferred from the STM to LTM through **rehearsal**. But in **real life** people don't always spend time rehearsing, yet they still transfer information into LTM. Rehearsal is not always needed for information to be stored and some items can't be rehearsed, e.g. smells.

2) The model is **oversimplified**. It assumes there is only one long-term store and one short-term store. This has been disproved by evidence from **brain damaged** patients, suggesting several **different** short-term stores, and other evidence suggesting different long-term stores.

Baddeley and Hitch (1974) Developed the **Working Memory Model**

Baddeley and Hitch developed a multi-store model of STM called the 'working memory model'. Their model proposed that STM, rather than being a single store, is an active processor which contains several different stores.

The **central executive** is a key component and can be described as attention. It has a **limited capacity** and controls 'slave' systems that also have **limited capacity**:

1) The **phonological loop** holds speech-based information — it's made up of a **phonological store** (the inner ear) and an **articulatory process** (the inner voice, which rehearses information by repeating it).

2) The **visuo-spatial sketchpad** deals with the temporary storage of visual and spatial information.

3) The **episodic buffer** (which was added to the model in 2000) briefly **stores** information from the other subsystems and **integrates** it together, along with information from LTM, to make complete scenes or '**episodes**'.

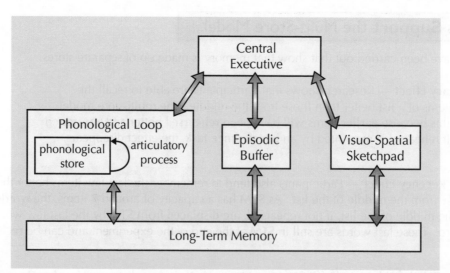

The **Working Memory Model** Came From **Experimental Evidence**

Baddeley and Hitch based their model on results from studies that used '**interference tasks**':

1) If participants are asked to perform two tasks simultaneously that use the **same system**, their performance will be **affected** — e.g. saying 'the the the' while silently reading something is very difficult.

2) According to the working memory model, both these tasks use the **phonological loop**. This has **limited capacity**, so it can't cope with both tasks. Performance on one, or both tasks, will be affected.

3) However, if the two tasks involve **different systems**, performance **isn't affected** on either task (e.g. saying 'the the the' whilst tracking a moving object).

Models of Memory

As Usual the Model has **Strengths**...

1) **Shallice and Warrington (1974)** found **support** for the working memory model through their case study of KF.

> KF was a brain-damaged patient who had an impaired STM. His problem was with immediate recall of words presented **verbally**, but not with visual information. This suggested he had an **impaired articulatory loop** but an intact visuo-spatial sketchpad, therefore providing evidence for the working memory model's view of STM. This finding could not have been explained using the multi-store model of memory, which proposed that short-term memory was just one system.

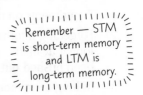

Remember — STM is short-term memory and LTM is long-term memory.

2) **Gathercole and Baddeley (1993)** reported on a laboratory study which **supports** the model:

> Participants were split into **two groups**. All of the participants had to carry out a task where they had to follow a moving spot of light. This would use the **visuo-spatial sketchpad**. At the same time, one group of participants also had to describe the angles on a letter — another task involving the **visuo-spatial sketchpad**. The other group of participants were given a second task that would use the **phonological loop** — they had to do a **verbal** task whilst following the light. Gathercole and Baddeley found that performance was much **better** in the participants doing tasks which used **separate systems**.

3) The model has **less emphasis** on **rehearsal** than the multi-store model of memory. Rather than being the key process, rehearsal is just **one possible** process in the working memory model. This can therefore help to explain why, in real life, some things end up in our long-term memory even though we haven't rehearsed them — it suggests that other processes are at work.

... and **Weaknesses**

The working memory model is currently the main model of short-term memory, but some psychologists have **criticised** it. For example:

1) They think that Baddeley and Hitch's idea of a central executive is **simplistic** and **vague**. Their model doesn't really explain exactly what the central executive is, apart from being involved in attention. However, it's difficult to design tasks to test the central executive.

2) The model only explains how information is dealt with in **short-term memory**. It doesn't explain how information is **transferred** to long-term memory.

3) Much of the research which has supported the working memory model has been **laboratory studies**. This reduces the **ecological validity** of the evidence, as highly controlled studies might not be representative of what happens in the real world.

Warm-Up Questions

Q1 What is the primacy effect?

Q2 Who came up with the working memory model?

Q3 How did the study of KF provide support for the working memory model?

PRACTICE QUESTIONS

Exam Questions

Q1 Which of these is **not** a component of the working memory model?
   A central executive   **B** phonological loop   **C** visuo-spatial sketchpad   **D** sensory register   [1 mark]

Q2 Describe and evaluate the multi-store model of memory.   [16 marks]

My friend does shoots for all the high street shops — she's a multi-store model...

These pages might not have the excitement factor of electric shocks and general nastiness, but it's good solid psychology, and I'm afraid you need to know it. As well as knowing their features, make sure you know the strengths and weaknesses of the models so that you can evaluate them. And have a few studies up your sleeve for support.

Forgetting

This page is all about why you can't remember the last page. Maybe you didn't rehearse it enough, or maybe you only looked at the letters instead of trying to understand the facts. Or maybe you spilt tea on it and couldn't read the words...

Forgetting is When Learnt Information **Can't be Retrieved**

1) Experiments on memory assume that if you **can't retrieve** a memory, it's forgotten.

2) Forgetting information from STM is thought to be down to an **availability problem** — the information is no longer available because of the **limited capacity** or the **limited duration** of STM. The information may have been **pushed out (displaced)** or simply have **faded away (decayed)**.

3) In **long-term memory** forgetting can be caused by **decay** (an availability problem), but it can also be because:

   - The information was stored, but is hard to **retrieve** — an **accessibility** problem, e.g. you read something once, a long time ago, and now need a lot of help to recall it.

   - The information is **confused** — there is an **interference** problem, e.g. two pieces of learnt information are too similar, and you can't tell them apart easily.

Interference is One **Explanation** for **Forgetting**

One theory about forgetting is that your **ability to remember** a particular thing you've learnt can be affected by having learnt something similar **before** or **since**. This is known as **interference** — there are two types:

Retroactive Interference

Retroactive interference is where **new information** interferes with the ability to recall **older information**.

> **Underwood and Postman (1960)** carried out a study which supported **retroactive interference**. In a lab experiment, participants were split into two groups. Both groups were given a list of **paired words** to learn, e.g. **cat–tree**. The experimental group was then given a **second list** of words to learn, where the **first** of the words in each pair was the **same** as in the first list, e.g. **cat–dirt**. The control group wasn't given a second word list. Both groups were then tested on their **recall** of the **first word list**, by being given the first word from each pair. Recall was better in the **control group**, suggesting that **retroactive interference** of the second word list had affected recall for the experimental group.

Proactive Interference

Proactive interference is where **older information** interferes with the ability to recall **new information**.

> **Underwood (1957)** studied proactive interference by looking at the results of studies into forgetting over a 24-hour period. He found that if people had previously learnt 15 or more word lists during the same experiment, a day later their recall of the last word list was around 20%. If they hadn't learnt any earlier lists, recall a day later was around 80%. Underwood concluded that proactive interference from the earlier lists had affected the participants' ability to remember later ones.

Jasper couldn't quite recall what his mother had told him about these things.

The Interference Theory Has **Strengths** and **Weaknesses**

1) Proactive and retroactive interference are **supported** by loads and loads of **studies**, many of which were highly controlled **laboratory experiments**.

2) As well as in laboratory experiments, there is evidence for interference existing in **real-world settings** too. For example, you might struggle to remember your French vocabulary if you later start learning German.

3) However, interference effects seem much greater in **artificial** laboratory settings than they do in real life, so it may not be **as strong** a theory as once thought.

4) The theory gives us an explanation for **why** we forget, but it doesn't go into the cognitive or biological **processes** involved — it doesn't fully explain why or how interference happens.

Forgetting

Recall Can Depend on Getting the Right Cues

Another theory of memory states that being able to recall a piece of information depends on getting the **right cue**. In this theory, forgetting is treated as a **retrieval failure** — the information still exists in memory but it isn't **accessible**.

We have more chance of retrieving the memory if the **cue** is **appropriate**. Cues can be **internal** (e.g. your mood) or **external** (e.g. context, like surroundings, situation, etc.). We remember more if we are in the same **context/mood** as we were in when we coded the information originally. This is known as **cue-dependent learning**.

	Tulving and Psotka (1971) — Forgetting in LTM
Method:	Tulving and Psotka compared the theories of **interference** and **cue-dependent forgetting**.
	Each participant was given either 1, 2, 3, 4, 5 or 6 lists of 24 words. Each list was divided into 6 categories of 4 words. Words were presented in category order, e.g. all animals, then all trees etc. After the lists were presented, in one condition, participants had to simply recall all the words — **total free recall**. In another condition, participants were given all the category names and had to try to recall words from the list — **free cued recall**.
Results:	In the **total free recall** condition, there seemed to be evidence of **retroactive** interference. Participants with 1 or 2 lists to remember had higher recall than those with more lists to remember, suggesting the later lists were **interfering** with remembering the earlier lists.
	However, in the **cued recall** test, the effects of retroactive interference **disappeared**. It didn't matter how many lists a participant had — recall was still the same for each list (about **70%**).
Conclusion:	The results suggest that interference had not caused forgetting. Because the memories became accessible if a cue was used, it showed that they were available, but just inaccessible. Therefore, the forgetting shown in the total free recall condition was **cue-dependent forgetting**.
Evaluation:	Tulving and Psotka's study was a **laboratory experiment** so will have been highly **controlled**, reducing the effect of **extraneous variables** (page 97). However, laboratory experiments lack **ecological validity** as the setting and task are **artificial**. The study only tested memory of words, so the results can't reliably be **generalised** to information of other types.

As usual, the theory has strengths and weaknesses:

1) Cue-dependent forgetting is thought to be the best explanation of forgetting in LTM, as it has the **strongest** evidence. Most forgetting is seen to be caused by **retrieval failure**. This means that virtually all memory we have is available in LTM — we just need the right cue to be able to access it.

2) However, the evidence is **artificial** (e.g. recalling word lists), lacking meaning in the real world. Also, it would be difficult, if not impossible, to test whether all information in LTM is accessible and available, and just waiting for the right cue.

3) The theory might not explain **all types** of memory. For example, cues might not be relevant to procedural memory (see page 14), such as remembering how to ride a bike or play a musical instrument.

Warm-Up Questions

Q1 What is retroactive interference?
Q2 What is proactive interference?
Q3 Give one weakness of the interference theory of forgetting.

PRACTICE QUESTIONS

Exam Question

Q1 In a study, participants learned a word list in either a room painted red or a room painted yellow.
They were then tested either in the same room, or in the other coloured room.
Recall was better when participants were tested in the same room that they had learned in.
Outline and evaluate a theory of forgetting that could explain why this occurred. [8 marks]

Remember, remember the 5th of October...

Make up some word lists and get your friends to read them. Give them an interference task, then test them. I'm always doing experiments on my friends... well, I was until that incident with the misplaced electrode anyway.

Eyewitness Testimony

If you witness a crime or an accident, you might have to report what you saw, and your version of events could be crucial in prosecuting someone... But your memory isn't as accurate as you might think...

Eyewitness Testimony Can Be **Inaccurate** and **Distorted**

1) Eyewitness testimony (EWT) is the evidence provided by people who witnessed a particular event or crime. It relies on recall from memory.

2) EWT includes, for example, descriptions of criminals (e.g. hair colour, height) and crime scenes (e.g. time, date, location).

3) Witnesses are often inaccurate in their recollection of events and the people involved. As you can probably imagine, this has important implications when it comes to police interviews.

4) Many cognitive psychologists focus on working out what factors affect the accuracy of eyewitness testimony, and how accuracy can be improved in interviews.

Eyewitness Testimony Can Be Affected by **Misleading Information**

Loftus and Palmer (1974) investigated how EWT can be **distorted**.
They used **leading questions**, where a certain answer is implied in the question.

For example, the question, "How much will prices go up next year?" is leading, because it implies that prices **will** go up. A better question would be, "What do you think will happen to prices next year?"

Loftus and Palmer (1974) — A study into eyewitness testimony

Loftus and Palmer carried out two experiments in their study.

Experiment 1:

Method:	Participants were shown a film of a multiple car crash. They were then asked a series of questions including 'How fast do you think the cars were going when they **hit**?' In different conditions, the word 'hit' was replaced with '**smashed**', '**collided**', '**bumped**' or '**contacted**'.
Results:	Participants given the word '**smashed**' estimated the **highest speed** (an average of 41 mph); those given the word '**contacted**' gave the **lowest** estimate (an average of 32 mph).

Experiment 2:

Method:	The participants were split into three groups. One group was given the verb 'smashed', another 'hit', and the third, control group wasn't given any indication of the vehicles' speed. A week later, the participants were asked '**Did you see any broken glass?**'.
Results:	Although there was no broken glass in the film, participants were more likely to say that they'd seen broken glass in the '**smashed**' condition than any other.
Conclusion:	**Leading questions** can affect the **accuracy** of people's memories of an event.
Evaluation:	This has implications for questions in **police interviews**. However, this was an artificial experiment — watching a video is not as **emotionally arousing** as a real-life event, which potentially affects recall. In fact, a later study found that participants who thought they'd witnessed a **real** robbery could give an **accurate** description of the robber. The experimental design might lead to **demand characteristics**, where the results are skewed because of the participants' expectations about the purposes of the experiment. For example, the leading questions might have given participants **clues** about the nature of the experiment (e.g. they could have realised that the experiment was about susceptibility to leading questions), and so participants might have acted accordingly. This would have reduced the **validity** and **reliability** of the experiment.

Eyewitness Testimony

Loftus and Zanni (1975) also Looked at Leading Questions

Loftus and Zanni (1975) investigated how altering the wording of a question can produce a **leading question** that can distort EWT.

Loftus and Zanni (1975) — A study into leading questions

Method:	Participants were shown a film of a car crash. They were then asked either 'Did you see **the** broken headlight?' or 'Did you see **a** broken headlight?'. There was no broken headlight shown in the film.
Results:	17% of those asked about 'the' broken headlight claimed they saw one, compared to 7% in the group asked about 'a' broken headlight.
Conclusion:	The simple use of the word '**the**' is enough to affect the accuracy of people's memories of an event.
Evaluation:	Like the study by Loftus and Palmer (previous page), this study has implications for eyewitness testimony. This study was a **laboratory study**, which made it possible to control any **extraneous variables** (p.97) This means it's possible to establish **cause and effect**. However, the study was **artificial** (participants were shown a film of a car crash, not an actual car crash), so the study lacked **ecological validity**.

Post-Event Discussion Can Affect the Accuracy of Recall

Studies where a confederate has been used to feed other participants with **misleading post-event information** have shown that this can affect recall. For example:

Shaw et al (1997) paired participants with a confederate (who pretended to be another participant). The pairs were shown videos of a **staged robbery** and were interviewed together afterwards. The participant and the confederate alternated who answered the questions first. When the **participant** responded **first**, recall was accurate 58% of the time. When the **confederate** answered first and gave **accurate** answers, the recall of the participants was 67%. If the confederate gave **inaccurate** answers, correct recall for the participants fell to 42%.

If the misleading information is received through a **conversation**, the effects can be just as big, if not bigger. For example:

Gabbert et al's (2004) study involved two groups of participants — young adults (17-33 years old) and older adults (58-80 years old). Both groups watched a staged crime and were then exposed to misleading information in one of two ways — through conversation with a confederate who was pretending to be another participant, or reading a written report of the crime, supposedly written by another participant. The participants were then given a recall test about the event they'd witnessed. It was found that both groups of adults were more likely to report inaccurate information after a conversation with a confederate than after reading the report.

Warm-Up Questions

Q1 What is eyewitness testimony?
Q2 What are leading questions?
Q3 What leading question was used in Loftus and Zanni's (1975) study?
Q4 How can post-event discussion affect the accuracy of recall?

Exam Question

Q1 Discuss research into the effect of misleading information on eyewitness testimony. [8 marks]

Do you remember the fun time you had reading this page...?*

If you witness something dead important, remember that not everything you think you remember did definitely happen. Leading questions can, for example, mislead people into thinking they saw something they didn't. So little brother, what colour was the dog that you saw eating all Mum's luxury chocolate biscuits? Burp.

Eyewitness Testimony

The **Age** of the **Witness** Can Affect the **Accuracy of Eyewitness Testimony**

Studies have shown that the **age** of the witness is a factor in whether they're affected by leading questions.

Valentine and Coxon (1997) — The effect of age on EWT

Method:	3 groups of participants (children, young adults and elderly people) watched a video of a kidnapping. They were then asked a series of leading and non-leading questions about what they had seen.
Results:	Both the elderly people and the children gave more incorrect answers to non-leading questions. Children were misled more by leading questions than adults or the elderly.
Conclusion:	Age has an effect on the accuracy of eyewitness testimony.
Evaluation:	This has **implications** in law when children or elderly people are questioned. However, the experiment was **artificial** and so wasn't as emotionally arousing as the same situation would have been in real life — the study **lacks ecological validity**. The results may only show how well people remember things from **TV**, rather than showing the accuracy of memories of real-life situations.

Anxiety Can Affect **Focus**

Psychologists tend to believe that **small increases** in anxiety and arousal may **increase the accuracy** of memory, but **high levels** have a **negative effect** on accuracy.

In **violent crimes** (where anxiety and arousal are likely to be high), the witness may focus on **central details** (e.g. a weapon) and neglect other peripheral details (e.g. what the criminal was wearing).

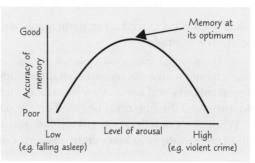

Eyewitnesses recall seeing fair weather and blue skies, but nothing else remarkable.

Loftus (1979) — Weapon focus in EWT

Method:	In a study with an **independent groups** design, participants heard a discussion in a nearby room. In one condition, a man came out of the room with a pen and grease on his hands. In the second condition, the man came out carrying a knife covered in blood. Participants were asked to identify the man from 50 photographs.
Results:	Participants in condition 1 were 49% accurate. Only 33% of the participants in condition 2 were correct.
Conclusion:	When anxious and aroused, witnesses focus on a weapon at the expense of other details.
Evaluation:	The study has **high ecological validity**, as the participants weren't aware that the study was staged. However, this means that there are also **ethical** considerations, as participants could have been very distressed at the sight of the man with the knife.

Misleading Questions and Anxiety **Don't Always** Affect EWT

1) A **field study** by **Yuille and Cutshall (1986)** showed that witnesses of a **real** incident (a gun shooting) had **remarkably accurate memories** of the event.

2) A thief was shot and killed by police and witnesses were interviewed. Thirteen of them were invited to be **re-interviewed five months later**. Recall was found to be **highly accurate**, even after this time period.

3) The researchers had included two **misleading questions** in the study but these were found to have **no effect** on the subjects' answers.

4) This study had **high ecological validity** as it was based on a real-life event. However, the witnesses who experienced the **highest levels of stress** were also **closest** to the event — it's difficult to determine whether **proximity** or **stress** contributed to the accuracy of their recall.

Eyewitness Testimony

The **Cognitive Interview** was Developed to **Increase Accuracy**

Cognitive psychologists have played a big part in helping to **increase the accuracy** of eyewitness testimony. As you've seen, research shows that the accuracy of eyewitness testimony is affected by many factors. The **cognitive interview technique (CIT)** was developed by **Geiselman et al (1984)** to try to increase the accuracy of witnesses' recall of events during police questioning.

Here's basically what happens in cognitive interviews:

1) The interviewer tries to make the witness **relaxed** and tailors his/her **language** to suit the witness.
2) The witness mentally recreates the **environmental context** (e.g. sights and sounds) and **internal context** (e.g. mood) of the crime scene.
3) The witness reports absolutely **everything** that they can remember about the crime, even if it feels irrelevant.
4) The witness is asked to recall details of the crime in **different orders**.
5) The witness is asked to recall the event from various **different perspectives**, e.g. from the eyes of other witnesses.
6) The interviewer avoids any **judgemental** and **personal comments**.

There is **Research** to **Support** the Cognitive Interview

Research has shown that people interviewed with the cognitive interview technique are much more **accurate** in their recall of events. For example:

Geiselman et al (1986) — The effect of the cognitive interview

Method: In a staged situation, an intruder carrying a **blue** rucksack entered a classroom and stole a slide projector. Two days later, participants were questioned about the event. The study used an **independent groups** design — participants were either questioned using a standard interview procedure or the cognitive interview technique. Early in the questioning, participants were asked 'Was the guy with the **green** backpack nervous?'. Later in the interview, participants were asked what colour the man's rucksack was.

Results: Participants in the cognitive interview condition were less likely to recall the rucksack as being green than those in the standard interview condition.

Conclusion: The cognitive interview technique **reduces the effect of leading questions**.

Evaluation: The experiment was conducted as though a real crime had taken place in the classroom — it had **high ecological validity**. The experiment used an **independent groups** design. The disadvantage of this is that the participants in the cognitive interview condition could have been naturally less susceptible to leading questions than the other group (due to individual differences).

The CIT has been shown to increase the accuracy of EWT. This means the police can work more efficiently, so public money is better spent, which in turn is beneficial for the economy.

Warm-Up Questions

Q1 What did Valentine and Coxon's (1997) study show about the effect of age on eyewitness testimony?
Q2 What did the study by Yuille and Cutshall (1986) show about the effect of misleading questions on recall?
Q3 Who developed the cognitive interview technique?

Exam Questions

Q1 Briefly outline the effect that anxiety can have on the accuracy of eyewitness testimony. [4 marks]

Q2 Outline the techniques used in a cognitive interview. [4 marks]

A tall, thin man, quite short, with black, fair hair — great fat bloke she was...

Well, now I haven't a clue what I've really experienced in my life. Did that man I saw shoplifting really have stubble, scars and a ripped leather jacket, or is that just my shoplifter stereotype kicking in? In fact, come to think of it, I couldn't actually tell you whether my granny has a hairy chin or not. I think she does, but then I think all grannies do...

Attachment

These pages deal with the different features of attachments and how they develop between infants and their carers. Simple eh — you'd think, but this is psychology after all...

Attachment is a Strong Emotional Bond

Attachment is a close emotional relationship between an infant and their caregiver.
'Securely attached' infants will show a desire to be **close** to their **primary caregiver** (usually their biological mother). They'll show **distress** when they're **separated**, and **pleasure** when they're **reunited**.

Features of Caregiver-Infant Interaction

There are common **caregiver-infant interactions** which are seen in attachments.
These are thought to be involved in **developing** and **maintaining** the attachment.

1) **Sensitive responsiveness** — The caregiver responds appropriately to signals from the infant.
2) **Imitation** — The infant copies the caregiver's actions and behaviour. For example, Meltzoff and Moore (1977) found that infants between 2 and 3 weeks of age appeared to imitate the facial expressions and hand movements of the experimenter.
3) **Interactional synchrony** — Infants react in time with the caregiver's speech, resulting in a 'conversation dance'. Condon and Sander (1974) provided evidence for this concept, by showing how babies do appear to move in time with adult conversations.
4) **Reciprocity/turn-taking** — Interaction flows back and forth between the caregiver and infant.
5) **Motherese** — The slow, high-pitched way of speaking to infants. However, there is no evidence that this influences the strength of an attachment between parent and infant.

Baby Juanita took 'imitating Mummy' quite literally.

Schaffer Identified Stages in Attachment Formation

1) The **pre-attachment (or asocial) phase** — During the first **0 to 3 months** of life, the baby learns to **separate** people from objects but doesn't have any strong preferences about who cares for it.

2) The **indiscriminate (or diffuse) attachment phase** — Between **6 weeks and seven months** the infant starts to clearly **distinguish** and **recognise** different people, smiling more at people it knows than at strangers. However, there are still no strong preferences about who cares for it.

3) The **discriminate (or single) attachment phase** — From **seven to eleven months** the infant becomes able to form a **strong attachment** with an **individual**. This is shown by being content when that person is around, distressed when they leave and happy when they return. It may be scared of strangers and avoid them.

4) The **multiple attachment phase** — From about **nine months** the infant can form **attachments to many different people**. Some attachments may be stronger than others and have **different functions**, e.g. for play or comfort, but there doesn't seem to be a limit to the number of attachments it can make. Although Schaffer found that after 18 months, approximately **32%** of babies had **at least five** attachments, the original attachment is still the strongest.

Schaffer and Emerson (1964) — Evidence for attachment stages

Method:	60 babies were observed in their homes in Glasgow every four weeks from birth to about 18 months. Interviews were also conducted with their families.
Results:	Schaffer's stages of attachment formation were found to occur. Also, at 8 months of age about 50 of the infants had more than one attachment. About 20 of them either had no attachment with their mother or had a stronger attachment with someone else, even though the mother was always the main carer.
Conclusion:	Infants form attachments in **stages** and can eventually attach to **many people**. **Quality of care** is important in forming attachments, so the infant may not attach to their mother if other people respond more accurately to its signals.

Attachment

Evaluation of Schaffer and Emerson (1964)

There is now a lot of evidence to support Schaffer and Emerson's results and their stages of attachment formation, but there are also criticisms of the study. For example, Schaffer and Emerson used a **limited sample**, and evidence from interviews and observations may be **biased** and **unreliable**.

Additionally, there are some cross-cultural differences that should be considered. **Tronick et al (1992)** found that infants in Zaire had a strong attachment with their mother by six months of age but didn't have strong attachments with others, even though they had several carers.

The **Father** Plays an Important **Role** Too

Schaffer and Emerson (1964) found that the attachment between caregiver and infant varied across the infants. Their **mother** was the primary attachment for only **half** of the infants. A **third** of the infants preferred their **father**, whilst the **rest** had their strongest attachment with their **grandparents** or **siblings**.

A lot of the initial research into caregiver-infant attachment focused on the mother being the primary caregiver. But that ignores the role of the father.

- **Goodsell and Meldrum (2009)** conducted a large study into the relationship between infants and their fathers. They found that those with a secure attachment to their mother are also more likely to have a secure attachment to their father.

As research has suggested that the primary caregiver can be the father, or even other substitutes, more mothers are returning to work after childbirth. This has a positive impact on the economy.

- **Ross et al (1975)** showed that the number of nappies a father changed was positively correlated to the strength of their attachment. This was supported by a study by **Caldera (2004)** who investigated 60 fathers and mothers and their 14-month-old infants. Caldera found that when the father was involved in care-giving activities, they were much more likely to develop a strong attachment with their child.

- But there is research which suggests the **role** a mother and father plays can be **different**. **Geiger (1996)** suggested that a mother's relationship is primarily **nurturing** and **caring**, but a father's relationship is more focused around **play**.

Warm-Up Questions

Q1 What is 'attachment'?

Q2 What are the four stages of attachment described by Schaffer and Emerson (1964)?

Q3 Give one criticism of Schaffer and Emerson's (1964) research into the attachment of children.

PRACTICE QUESTIONS

Exam Questions

Q1 Read the extract, then answer the question that follows.

> At 6 months, whenever Selby got upset he was more than happy to be comforted by the nearest person. He smiled more at his mother, but was generally a very happy baby to be around. Three months later, he started to experience separation anxiety. He began to cry a lot when his mother left the room and wouldn't settle without his regular night-time routine.

Outline the **two** stages of attachment identified by Schaffer which are shown by Selby. [4 marks]

Q2 Which of these terms best describes the act of a child reacting in time with their caregiver's speech?
A imitation   B motherese   C interactional synchrony   D sensitive responsiveness [1 mark]

Multiple attachments sound great — if Mum says no, ask Dad...

There's lots of really useful info on these pages to get you excited about attachment. It's really relevant too. As times have started to change, and the role of the primary caregiver is shifting, it's a good idea to think about how fathers develop attachments with their children too. But, first things first — learn those stages of attachment formation.

Animal Studies of Attachment

Some psychologists have studied animals to try to uncover more about attachment. So next time you see a baby chicken hatching from an egg — be warned. It may become attached to you, and then there's no going back...

Lorenz Studied Imprinting in Geese

1) Konrad Lorenz (1935) found that geese automatically 'attach' to the first moving thing they see after hatching, and follow it everywhere (I bet this gets quite annoying). This is called imprinting.

2) He randomly divided a clutch of greylag goose eggs into two groups. He left one group with the mother and incubated the other eggs.

3) Lorenz observed that the goslings from the incubator eggs followed him around in exactly the same way that the goslings from the other eggs would follow their mother.

4) He put both sets of goslings together and observed that when they were released, the two groups quickly re-formed as the goslings went off in search of their respective 'mothers'. Both sets of goslings had imprinted on the first moving object that they had seen.

Lorenz wasn't an experienced father, but his geese loved him.

5) After further experiments, Lorenz determined that imprinting was most likely between 13 and 16 hours after hatching.

6) As such, he concluded that imprinting seems to occur during a 'critical period'. It's a fast, automatic process.

7) He also noted that after this critical period, it was too late for the young birds ever to imprint.

8) It's unlikely to occur in humans. Our attachments take longer to develop and we don't automatically attach to particular things — quality care seems more important in human attachment formation. However, Bowlby's theory (page 30) is based on the same principles.

Harlow Showed That Comfort is Important in Attachment

Just because babies spend most of their time either eating or sleeping, it doesn't mean they automatically attach to the person who feeds them. Good quality interaction with the baby seems more important — the baby will attach to whoever is the most sensitive and loving. This is also shown in Harlow's study:

Harlow (1959) — The need for 'contact comfort'

Method:	Harlow aimed to find out whether baby monkeys would prefer a source of **food** or a source of **comfort** and **protection** as an attachment figure. In **laboratory experiments** rhesus monkeys were raised in isolation. They had two 'surrogate' mothers. One was made of wire mesh and contained a feeding bottle, the other was made of cloth but didn't contain a feeding bottle.
Results:	The monkeys spent most of their time clinging to the cloth surrogate and only used the wire surrogate to feed. The cloth surrogate seemed to give them **comfort** in new situations. When the monkeys grew up they showed signs of **social** and **emotional disturbance**. The females were bad mothers who were often violent towards their offspring.
Conclusion:	Infant monkeys formed more of an attachment with a figure that provided comfort and protection. Growing up in isolation affected their development.
Evaluation:	This was a **laboratory experiment**, so there was strict control of the variables. This means that it's unlikely the results were affected by an unknown variable. However, it can be argued that you can't **generalise** the results of this study to human beings, because humans and monkeys are **qualitatively different**. There were also **ethical problems** with this study — the monkeys were put in a stressful situation, and later they showed signs of being psychologically damaged by the experiment. Monkeys are social animals, so it was unfair to keep them in isolation. The fact that they were in isolation also means that the study lacked **ecological validity** — the monkeys weren't in their natural environment, so the results can't be reliably applied to real life. Laboratory experiments can usually be **replicated**, but ethical guidelines now in place mean that you couldn't repeat this study today to see whether you'd get the same results.

Mummy?

Animal Studies of Attachment

Harlow Continued His Research with Monkeys

Harlow's (1959) study concluded that rhesus monkeys developed **stronger** attachments with a cloth surrogate than a wire surrogate. He carried out further studies with different conditions.

Harlow's further research

Harlow and Zimmerman (1959) added in a **fearful** stimulus. When a fearful object (such as an oversized toy) was placed in the cage, the monkey would cling to the **cloth surrogate** first before exploring the object. Monkeys in cages with only a **wire surrogate** would remain frozen or run wildly around the cage. The researchers concluded that a **strong** attachment with a primary caregiver is therefore highly **important** in the development of an infant.

Harlow and Sumoi (1970) investigated other factors in generating a strong attachment. When they placed a cloth surrogate **with food** and a cloth surrogate **without food** in the cage, they found that the one **with food** was **preferred**. They concluded that **food** may still be a **significant** factor in developing attachments.

Psychologists Often Use Animals in Research

1) When animals are used in psychological research, the findings of the studies should be interpreted **carefully**. It is **hard to generalise** the findings from one species to another because the behaviour of an animal can often be very different to that of a human.

2) Lorenz used **precocial** species — these are species that have their eyes open and can walk right from birth. So they are very different from human infants, who cannot walk until a lot later.

   Precocial species want to stay close to the caregiver to avoid wandering off and getting eaten.

3) Although the results of animal studies might not always be generalisable to human populations, they can often **influence policies** and **theories** in different areas of research.

Researchers Have to Think About Ethics

See pages 108-110 for more about ethics in general.

Although animal studies have provided valuable information for developmental research, there's debate about whether they're ethical or not.

Advantage — Some research designs couldn't have been conducted on humans ethically — e.g. Harlow's study of attachment, where young monkeys were separated from their mothers (see previous page).

Disadvantage — Some see it as unethical to inflict suffering on animals, especially when they can't give consent.

Warm-Up Questions

Q1 What species did Lorenz (1935) use in his research on attachment?

Q2 What did Lorenz (1935) conclude from his study?

Q3 Why might researchers choose to use animals in their studies?

Exam Questions

Q1 Outline Lorenz's research investigating attachment. [4 marks]

Q2 Briefly outline and evaluate Harlow's study into attachment. [4 marks]

Monkey lovin'...

Hanging around a pond waiting for the geese to hatch seems like a nice idea. I'd love to have some instant gosling children following me round. But I guess it wouldn't be so much fun when you have to regurgitate worms into their beaks at four in the morning. Then they break your arm with their wings. Or is that swans...

Explanations of Attachment

There are several different theories of attachment, from learning theory to Bowlby's monotropic theory.
Take a look at these two pages to learn all about them. It's exciting stuff. Really, it is.

Learning Theory Links Attachment to Pleasure

Learning theory is also known as the **behaviourist theory**, and focuses on the baby wanting its needs fulfilled.
Conditioning is given as an explanation for how attachments form.

See pages 54-59 for loads more on learning theory.

Classical Conditioning. This is about learning **associations** between different things in our environment. Getting food naturally gives the baby **pleasure**. The baby's desire for food is fulfilled whenever its mother is around to feed it. So an **association is formed between mother and food**. So, whenever its mother is around, the baby will feel pleasure — i.e. 'attachment'.

Operant Conditioning. Dollard and Miller (1950) claimed that babies feel discomfort when they're hungry and so have a desire to get food to **remove the discomfort**. They find that if they cry, their mother will come and feed them — so the discomfort is removed (this is '**negative reinforcement'**). An easy life. The mother is therefore associated with food and the baby will want to be close to her. This produces 'attachment behaviour' (distress when separated from the mother, etc.).

Learning Theory Has Strengths and Weaknesses

Some comments on the learning theory of attachment include:

- The learning theory of attachment has lots of **support** from **scientific research**.
- But it is **reductionist** — it tries to explain complex attachment using simple stimulus-response processes.
- Lots of the evidence for learning theory uses **animal research**, so the findings aren't always **generalisable**.
- Schaffer and Emerson's (1964) findings don't fully support learning theory. In their study, half of the infants didn't have their mother as the primary attachment.
- There are **other theories** of attachment which also have support, such as Bowlby's theory (see below).

John Bowlby's Monotropic Theory of Attachment is an Evolutionary Theory

Bowlby (1951) argued that something like imprinting (p.28) occurs in humans.
He went on to develop several main claims:

1) Attachment Can Be Explained by Evolution

We have evolved a biological need to attach to our main caregiver.
This biological need has developed through natural selection to ensure the survival of the child to maturity.

2) We Create One Special Attachment

Bowlby's idea of monotropy is that we form one main attachment — usually to our biological mother.
Forming this attachment has survival value, as staying close to the mother ensures food and protection.
A strong attachment provides a 'safe base', giving us confidence to explore our environment.

3) We Create an Internal Working Model of Attachment

Bowlby's theory also says that forming an infant attachment gives us a 'template' for all future relationships — we learn to trust and care for others. This forms an internal working model for all later attachments.

The model is a 'working' model because it can change and develop over time, depending on how the person's relationships change. See page 38 to see how it helps to explain the formation of adult relationships.

The primary caregiver provides the foundations for the child's future relationships.
This is called the continuity hypothesis.

Explanations of Attachment

4) There is a Critical Period for Attachment

The first three years of life are the **critical period** for attachment to develop — otherwise it might never do so.

If the attachment doesn't develop (e.g. because of separation or death), or if it's broken, it might seriously damage the child's social and emotional development (see pages 34-37).

Bowlby's **'maternal deprivation hypothesis'** (p.34) assumes if the relationship between the primary caregiver (often mother) and infant is disrupted or stopped during the critical period, there are long-term consequences.

It was critical that Jimmy bonded with Terrence from the moment they first met.

Comments on **Bowlby's** Theory

1) There is some **evidence** for his claims. **Harlow's** study supports the idea that we have evolved a need to attach. It also suggests that social and emotional development might be damaged if an attachment isn't formed. See page 38 for another study that supports Bowlby's theory.

2) **Schaffer and Emerson (1964)** provided evidence against Bowlby's claims about monotropy. They found that, rather than one main attachment, many children form **multiple attachments**, and may not attach to their mother (see page 26).

3) **Harlow's** study of monkeys raised in isolation (p.28) also goes against the idea of **monotropy**. Other monkeys who didn't have a mother, but who grew up together, didn't show signs of social and emotional disturbance in later life. They didn't have a primary caregiver, but seemed to attach to each other instead.

4) There is **mixed evidence** for claims of a **critical period** for attachments to develop (see above, page 28 and page 38).

5) The effect of attachment not developing, or being broken, may not be as bad as Bowlby claimed (see p.35).

6) Bowlby's report in the 1950s led to an **increase** in **'stay at home'** mothering. This had a subsequent **impact on the economy** as fewer women were going to work.

Warm-Up Questions

Q1 How can classical conditioning be used to explain attachment?

Q2 What is 'monotropy'?

Q3 What is Bowlby's internal working model?

Q4 How long does Bowlby's critical period for attachment last for?

PRACTICE QUESTIONS

Exam Questions

Q1 Read the report, then answer the question that follows.

> Sadia's mother rejected her from an early age and she was brought up by various family members. Sadia is now six, and struggles to maintain her own friendships or develop any attachments with her peers.

Suggest how Bowlby's internal working model of attachment might explain Sadia's current relationships. [4 marks]

Q2 Evaluate Bowlby's theory of attachment. [4 marks]

Q3 Outline the learning theory of attachment. [6 marks]

I'm really quite attached to that giant piece of lemon drizzle cake...

There's more than one explanation of attachment, but don't get overwhelmed. Just think of the two on these pages as two main perspectives. Learning theory suggests our attachments are created from our experiences, whereas Bowlby's theory suggests there is some biological and natural drive causing us to develop attachments. Exciting stuff...

Types of Attachment

If you enjoyed the last two pages, then you're gonna love these ones. As you know, an 'attachment' is a strong, emotional bond between two people. Psychologists are interested in how our first attachments form and what influences them.

Attachments Can Be **Secure** or **Insecure**

Secure Attachments

In a secure attachment, there's a **strong bond** between the child and its caregiver. If they're separated, the infant becomes **distressed**. However, when they're reunited, the child is **easily comforted** by the caregiver. The majority of attachments are of this type. Secure attachments are associated with a healthy cognitive and emotional development.

This might also be called 'Type B'.

Insecure Attachments

Attachments can also be insecure. Here, the bond between child and caregiver is **weaker**. Ainsworth et al came up with **two types** of insecure attachment:

Insecure-avoidant

If they're separated from their caregiver, the child **doesn't** become particularly distressed, and can usually be comforted by a **stranger**. This type of insecure attachment is shown by children who generally **avoid** social interaction and intimacy with others.

This is also known as 'anxious-avoidant' or 'Type A'.

There are many ways to form a strong attachment with your child.

Insecure-resistant

The child is often **uneasy** around their caregiver, but becomes **upset** if they're separated. Comfort can't be given by strangers, and it's also often **resisted** from the caregiver. Children who show this style of attachment both **accept** and **reject** social interaction and intimacy.

This is also known as 'anxious-resistant' or 'Type C'.

An Infant's **Reaction** in a **Strange Situation** Shows if It's **Securely** Attached

Ainsworth came up with the concept of the **strange situation**. She used it to assess how children react under conditions of **stress** (by separation from the caregiver and the presence of a stranger) and also to **new situations**.

	Ainsworth et al (1978) — The strange situation
Method:	In a **controlled observation**, 12-18 month old infants were left in a room with their mother. Eight different scenarios occurred, including being approached by a stranger, the infant being left alone, and the mother returning. The infant's reactions were constantly observed.
Results:	About 15% of infants were **'insecure-avoidant' (type A)** — they ignored their mother and didn't mind if she left. A stranger could comfort them. About 70% were **'securely attached' (type B)** — they were content with their mother, upset when she left, and happy when she returned. They also avoided strangers. About 15% were **'insecure-resistant' (type C)** — they were uneasy around their mother and upset if she left. They resisted strangers and were also hard to comfort when their mother returned.
Conclusion:	Infants showing different reactions to their carers have different types of attachment.
Evaluation:	The research method used allowed control of the variables, making the results reliable. However, the laboratory-type situation made the study artificial, **reducing** the ecological validity. The parents may have changed their behaviour, as they knew that they were being observed. This could have had an effect on the children's behaviour. Also, the new situation in the experiment may have had an effect on the children's behaviour — the study might not accurately represent their behaviour in real life. Another problem is that the mother may not have been the child's **main attachment figure**.

Types of Attachment

Similar Studies Have Taken Place in **Different Cultures**

Ainsworth et al's (1978) findings have been shown many times in the **USA**, but it wasn't then known whether they could be applied to other **cultures**. **Cross-cultural studies** have since taken place:

Van Ijzendoorn and Kroonenberg (1988) — Cross-cultural studies

Method:	Van Ijzendoorn and Kroonenberg carried out a meta-analysis of 32 studies of 'the strange situation' in different countries (e.g. Japan, Britain, Sweden, etc.). They were analysed to find any overall patterns.
Results:	The percentages of children classified as secure or insecure were **similar** across the countries tested — there were more differences within the actual countries than between them. Secure attachments were the most common type of attachment in the countries studied. Some differences were found in the distribution of insecure attachments. In Western cultures, the dominant type of insecure attachment was **avoidant**, with the highest proportion of insecure-avoidant children coming from Germany. However, in non-Western cultures, the dominant type of insecure attachment was **resistant**. Here, Japan had the highest proportion of insecure-resistant children.
Conclusion:	There are cross-cultural similarities in raising children, with common reactions to the 'strange situation'.
Evaluation:	Children are brought up in different ways in different cultures. This might result in different types of attachment in different cultures. Because of this, the 'strange situation' might not be a suitable method for studying cross-cultural attachment. Using a **different type** of study may have revealed different patterns or types of attachment in different cultures. Also, the study assumes that different **countries** are the same thing as different **cultures**. One problem with the research method is that meta-analyses can **hide** individual results that show an unusual trend.

There are Important **Findings** from Strange Situation Research

1) **Some cultural differences are found.** Grossman et al (1985) claimed that more 'avoidant' infants may be found in Germany because of the value Germans put on independence — so 'avoidance' is seen as good.

2) **The causes of different attachment types are debatable.**
   The causes may be the sensitivity of their carers and/or their inborn temperament.

3) **The strange situation experiment doesn't show a characteristic of the child.** The experiment only shows the child's relationship with a specific person, so they might react differently with different carers, or later in life.

4) **Attachment type may influence later behaviours.** Securely attached children may be more confident in school and form strong, trusting adult relationships (p.38). 'Avoidant' children may have behaviour problems in school and find it hard to form close, trusting adult relationships. 'Resistant' children may be insecure and attention-seeking in school and, as adults, their strong feelings of dependency may be stressful for partners.

Warm-Up Questions

Q1 What is a secure attachment?

Q2 What are the two types of insecure attachment?

Q3 Who came up with the 'strange situation'?

Q4 What have cross-cultural studies shown about attachments?

PRACTICE QUESTIONS

Exam Questions

Q1 a) Briefly outline and evaluate Ainsworth et al's (1978) 'strange situation' study. [4 marks]

    b) Explain **two** disadvantages of using the 'strange situation' in a study of attachment. [4 marks]

Try to get all these ideas firmly attached to the inside of your head...

Next time you're in trouble at school and your parents are called in to 'discuss your behaviour', try sobbing gently under your breath, 'I think it's all my insecure-resistant attachment formation — it's left me insecure and needy of attention'. It's a desperate attempt, but it might just make your parents feel bad enough to let you off.

Disruption of Attachment

The attachments we form are pretty important — there can be serious consequences if they're broken...

Attachment Can Be Disrupted by **Separation** or **Deprivation**

Separation is where a child is away from a **caregiver** they're attached to (such as their mother). The term's used when it's a **relatively short** time, just hours or days — not a longer or permanent separation.

Deprivation describes the loss of something that is **wanted or needed**. So, 'maternal deprivation' is the loss of the mother (or other attachment figure). A more **long-term** or even **permanent** loss is implied.

John Bowlby (1953) Studied Longer-Term **Maternal Deprivation**

John Bowlby argued that long-term **deprivation** from an attachment figure could be harmful. He produced his **maternal deprivation hypothesis**:

1) Deprivation from the main carer during the **critical period** (the first 3 years) will have harmful effects on a child's emotional, social, intellectual and even physical development. Not so good.

2) Long-term effects of deprivation may include **separation anxiety** (the fear of another separation from the carer). This may lead to problem behaviour, e.g. being very clingy, and avoiding going to school. Future relationships may be affected by this emotional insecurity. Bowlby's research showed evidence for this.

Bowlby (1944) — The 44 juvenile thieves

Method:	**Case studies** were completed on the backgrounds of 44 adolescents who had been referred to the clinic where Bowlby worked because they'd been stealing. There was a **control group** of 44 'emotionally disturbed' adolescents who didn't steal.
Results:	17 of the thieves had experienced frequent separations from their mothers before the age of two, compared with 2 in the control group. 14 of the thieves were diagnosed as 'affectionless psychopaths' (they didn't care about how their actions affected others). 12 of these 14 had experienced separation from their mothers.
Conclusion:	Deprivation of the child from its main carer early in life can have very **harmful long-term consequences**.
Evaluation:	The results indicate a link between deprivation and criminal behaviour. However, it can't be said that one **causes** the other. There may be **other factors** (e.g. poverty) that caused the criminal behaviour. Although case studies provide a lot of **detailed information**, the study relied on **retrospective data**, which may be unreliable.

Evidence of **Maternal Deprivation** from **Separation** Studies

Studies which have investigated the effects of short-term separation can also support the idea of Bowlby's **maternal deprivation hypothesis**:

Robertson and Robertson (1968) — A separation study

Method:	In a naturalistic observation, several children who experienced short separations from their carers were observed and filmed. For example, a boy called John aged around 18 months stayed in a residential nursery for nine days while his mother had another baby.
Results:	For the first day or two, John **protested** at being separated from his mother. He then started trying to get attention from the nurses, but they were busy with other children so he gave up trying. After another few days, he began to show signs of **detachment** — he was more active and content than he had been previously at the nursery. But, when his mother came to collect him, he was reluctant to be affectionate.
Conclusion:	The short-term separation had very **bad effects** on John, including possible **permanent damage** to his attachment with his mother.
Evaluation:	John's reaction might not have been due to separation — it could have been down to his new environment or the fact that he was getting much less attention than he was used to. There will have been little control of **variables**, and it would be difficult to replicate each **individual situation**. However, as the study took place in a natural setting, the results will have **ecological validity** but will be less **reliable**.

Disruption of Attachment

Bowlby's **Maternal Deprivation Hypothesis** has **Strengths** and **Weaknesses**

Strengths:
Other evidence **supports** Bowlby's claims. **Goldfarb (1943)** found that orphanage children who were socially and maternally deprived were later less intellectually and socially developed.

Weaknesses:
The **evidence** can be criticised. Bowlby linked the thieves' behaviour to maternal deprivation, but **other things were not considered**, e.g. whether the poverty they grew up in led them to steal. The children in Goldfarb's study may have been most harmed by the **social deprivation** in the orphanage rather than the maternal deprivation.

The **Effects** of **Disruption of Attachment** Can be **Reversed**

One of Bowlby's **assumptions** of his maternal deprivation hypothesis was that the consequences were **not** reversible. However, further research has shown that even when deprivation has harmful effects, these may be reversed with appropriate, **good-quality care**.

Skeels and Dye (1939) found that children who had been socially deprived (in an orphanage) during their first two years of life quickly **improved** their **IQ scores** if they were transferred to a school where they got one-to-one care.

Koluchova (1976) — The Case of the Czech Twin Boys

This is the case of **twin boys** whose mother died soon after they were born. Their father remarried and their stepmother treated them very cruelly. They were often kept locked in a cellar, had no toys and were often beaten.

They were found when they were seven with rickets (a bone development disease caused by a lack of vitamin D), and **very little social or intellectual development**.

They were later adopted and made **much progress**. By adulthood they had above average intelligence and had normal social relationships.

Warm-Up Questions

Q1 What does Bowlby's maternal deprivation hypothesis propose?

Q2 Give one weakness of Bowlby's maternal deprivation hypothesis.

Q3 Give one example of when the effects of a disruption of attachment have been reversed.

Exam Questions

Q1 Outline one study that supports Bowlby's theory of maternal deprivation. [4 marks]

Q2 Describe and evaluate Bowlby's theory of maternal deprivation. [16 marks]

So if you're left alone for a while at age 2, you may become a bank robber...

Sounds like a pretty poor excuse to me, but there you go. This is all certainly interesting stuff. Just make sure you learn it all. Including all the studies. If you know the details, you can pick up extra marks in the exam.

Effects of Institutionalisation

It's really easy to get privation and deprivation confused. But it's a good idea to make sure you know the difference between the two — institutionalisation often refers to privation rather than deprivation.

There's a **Difference** Between **Privation** and **Deprivation**

Rutter criticised Bowlby's **maternal deprivation hypothesis**, saying that Bowlby was confused with the term 'deprivation'. He used it to refer to several things — separation from the mother, loss of the mother, and failure to develop an attachment with the mother. These things are now split into deprivation and privation.

When Sophie was deprived of her blanket things got ugly.

Privation is where a child has never had an attachment to its mother or caregiver.

Deprivation is where an attachment was once formed but is now broken.

In reality, it is very **difficult** to distinguish between them.

A **Case Study** of **Privation**

Rutter (1981) claimed that the effects of **maternal privation** are more likely to be **serious** than the effects of **maternal deprivation**. Evidence for this comes from **case studies** of children who have suffered through difficult conditions or cruel treatment. A nasty case study coming up...

Curtiss (1977) — The Case of Genie

This reported the case of a girl who suffered extreme cruelty from her parents, and never formed any attachments. Her father kept her strapped to a high chair with a potty in the seat for most of her childhood. She was beaten if she made any sounds, and didn't have the chance to play with toys or with other children.

She was finally discovered when she was 13 years old. She was physically underdeveloped and could only speak with animal-like sounds. After a lot of help she later learned some language, but her social and intellectual skills never seemed to fully develop.

Romanian **Orphan** Studies

The fall of the communist regime in Romania during the early 1990s allowed the world to see the vast overcrowding in their orphanages. The orphans were fed, clothed and looked after, but they lacked any form of **sensitive care** or any opportunity to form an **emotional attachment**.

Since then, various studies of Romanian orphans have enabled psychologists to look directly at the impacts of **privation**.

Studies of children raised in **institutions** (e.g. orphanages) may provide **more reliable data** than case studies, as sample sizes are so much bigger.

	Rutter et al (2007) — A longitudinal study of Romanian orphans
Method:	111 Romanian orphans who were adopted by British families were compared with a group of 52 UK adoptees and followed over a prolonged period. Some of the orphans were adopted before they were 6 months old and some were older than 6 months. Each child was assessed at ages 4, 6 and 11.
Results:	The children who were **younger** than 6 months when they were adopted had the same level of emotional development as other UK children who were adopted at the same age. However, the Romanian orphans who were **older** than 6 months at adoption showed signs of insecure attachments and social problems. The **UK children** who were older than 6 months at adoption didn't show the same problems.
Conclusion:	The effects of privation can be **reversed** if an attachment starts to form **before** the age of 6 months. **Long-term** effects are more **permanent** if attachment doesn't start to occur within 6 months. Maternal deprivation on its own doesn't cause permanent effects because the UK adopted children had been separated but didn't show any problems.
Evaluation:	The results with the older children may be due to a lack of any stimulation in the orphanage. As a **longitudinal study**, Rutter was able to investigate the children over a long period of time, meaning the results provide a better insight into the long-term effects of privation. However, they collected mainly **qualitative** data which, although detailed, is more difficult to create **generalised laws** or **theories** from.

Effects of Institutionalisation

Hodges and Tizard (1989) Studied Early Institutional Care

Rutter et al's research into institutionalisation built upon the research by **Hodges and Tizard (1989)**.

Hodges and Tizard (1989) — Children raised in institutions.

Method: This was a **longitudinal** (long-term) study of 65 children who had been placed in a residential nursery before they were four months old. They hadn't had the opportunity to form close attachments with any of their caregivers. By the age of four, some of the children had returned to their birth mothers, some had been adopted, and some had stayed in the nursery.

Results: At 16 years old, the **adopted** group had **strong** family relationships, although compared to a control group of children from a 'normal' home environment, they had weaker peer relationships. Those who stayed in the **nursery** or who returned to their **mothers** showed **poorer** relationships with family and peers than those who were adopted.

Conclusion: Children can **recover** from early maternal privation if they are in a good **quality**, **loving** environment, although their social development may not be as good as children who have never suffered privation.

Evaluation: This was a **natural experiment**, so it had **high ecological validity**. However, the sample was quite **small** and more than 20 of the children couldn't be found at the end of the study, so it's hard to **generalise** the results. Because lots of institutionalised children are unfortunately often **underfed** and **malnourished**, with a lack of stimulation, it could be these factors that influence their behaviour, rather than the lack of attachment itself.

Studies Have Suggested Long-Term Effects of Institutionalisation...

Bowlby's study of the **44 juvenile thieves**, Rutter et al's (2007) study on **Romanian orphans** and others on institutionalisation and hospitalisation, have suggested that long-term effects of disrupted attachments can include:

1) **Affectionless psychopathy** (as seen in the 44 juvenile thieves study).
2) **Anaclitic depression** — involving appetite loss, sleeplessness and impaired social and intellectual development.
3) **Deprivation dwarfism** — infants are physically underdeveloped due to emotional deprivation.
4) **Delinquency** — minor crimes committed by youths.
5) **Reduced intelligence** — infants don't develop intellectually as fast as their peers.

Warm-Up Questions

Q1 What is the difference between privation and deprivation?
Q2 What research method did Rutter et al (2007) use in their Romanian orphan study?
Q3 Outline the strengths and weaknesses of Hodges and Tizard's (1989) study.

Exam Questions

Q1 Discuss, with reference to research, the effects of institutionalisation on young children. [8 marks]

Q2 Read the item below, then answer the question that follows.

> Meryl was a troubled teenager. Her school report continued to outline her struggle to form social relationships with her peers, her failing results and her turn to petty crime. Meryl had been adopted from an orphanage at the age of 6.

With reference to Meryl's behaviour, outline **two** effects of institutionalisation. [4 marks]

Developmental problems — enough to make you develop mental problems...

There are some pretty grisly studies on these pages. It may not be the nicest of topics, but it is interesting to see how these theories of privation and deprivation fit within developmental psychology. My advice would be to get the theories and studies in your head quickly and move on to the next bit. Maybe make yourself a hot chocolate too...

Early Attachment and Later Relationships

It kind of makes sense that our early attachments and relationships will influence the relationships we might have as adults. But psychologists like to study these things in depth anyway. So take a look at these pages...

The **Internal Working Model** Helps Explain **Adult** Relationships

Bowlby's **internal working model** (page 30) looked at how our childhood attachments influence adult relationships.

Examples

- If a child has a **secure attachment** to a **sensitive** caregiver, they are likely to see themselves as **worthy** of being loved. They are then likely to form future **secure relationships**.

- If a child has an **insecure attachment** with a caregiver who rejects them, they are likely to see themselves as **unworthy** of being loved. They are then likely to form future **insecure relationships**.

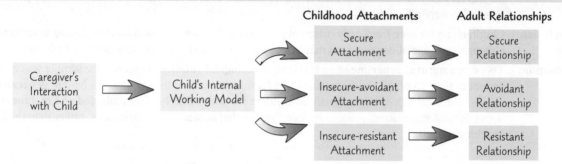

Hazan and Shaver (1987) developed a study to explore how early attachment can predict adult relationships.

Hazan and Shaver (1987) — The influence of early attachments

Method:	Hazan and Shaver conducted a 'love quiz' in a local newspaper. The quiz had two parts. The first part assessed the attachment type of each person with their parents. The second part involved questions asking about their current beliefs about romantic love.
Results:	The first 620 responses were analysed. They found that there was a correlation between the type of childhood attachment and people's later views on romantic love. Secure children were more likely to have happy and trustworthy relationships. Insecure-avoidant children ended up fearing intimacy and insecure-resistant children were more likely to be worried that they weren't loved in their relationships.
Conclusion:	Hazan and Shaver concluded that their findings provided **support** for Bowlby's **internal working model** — that early attachments **do** influence adult relationships.
Evaluation:	The quiz relied on people thinking back to their childhood, which isn't always accurate. Additionally, the study used a **volunteer sample**, so a certain type of person might be more likely to respond. Also, people may have answered untruthfully to show themselves in a better light. However, they did repeat the study in 2003, and found similar results.

The **Adult Attachment Interview** Explored the Role of **Early Attachments**

Psychologists developed a way to try to scientifically assess the relationship between early childhood attachments and later adult attachments. They came up with the **adult attachment interview**.

It's based on the idea that it doesn't really matter exactly **what** the childhood attachment was — it's **how** it was remembered. This again supports the **internal working model**.

Main et al (1985) — The Adult Attachment Interview

This **semi-structured interview** involves a series of questions about childhood attachment relationships, and how these were seen to influence later relationships. The interviewee is asked to give **five adjectives** explaining their relationship with each of their parents. They're then asked to explain why they chose each adjective. Other questions are then asked about times they got upset, if they ever felt rejected, and how they believe their early experiences influenced their adult attachments. The results are then **classified** by trained coders into a category — **secure, dismissing, preoccupied** or **unresolved/disorganised**.

Main et al (1985) went on to show that the categories of adult relationships could be predicted from people's recall of their childhood attachments.

Early Attachment and Later Relationships

Research Suggests Two **Long-Term Effects** of **Privation**

The **Cycle of Privation**

Some studies suggest that children who experience **privation** go on to have difficulties caring for their own children:

Quinton et al (1984) compared 50 women who had experienced institutional care as children with 50 women who hadn't. They found that the women who had been raised in institutions were more likely to have parenting difficulties later in life. This suggests that there is a **cycle of privation** — children who have experienced privation later go on to become less caring parents. Therefore, their children are deprived of a strong maternal attachment and may then be less caring to their children, and so on.

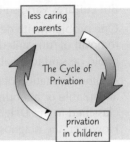

less caring parents

The Cycle of Privation

privation in children

Reactive Attachment Disorder — Parker and Forrest (1993)

Parker and Forrest (1993) outlined this rare but serious condition, which occurs in children who have been **permanently damaged** by early experiences such as **privation** of attachment. Symptoms include:

1) an inability to give or receive affection
2) dishonesty
3) poor social relationships
4) involvement in crime

But It's Not All **Bad**...

Freud and Dann (1951) showed that privation might not necessarily lead to detrimental outcomes.

Freud and Dann (1951) studied six children who were rescued after WWII. They had been orphaned during the war at a few months old, and raised within a deportation camp. Although they were looked after by the Jewish people 'passing through' to the concentration camps, the children didn't have time to form any adult attachments, instead forming bonds amongst themselves. When the war ended, the children were adopted by British families and have since shown few signs of a troubled upbringing, having a normal level of intelligence and maintaining normal relationships.

Warm-Up Questions

PRACTICE QUESTIONS

Q1 Give an example of a study which supports Bowlby's internal working model.
Q2 What useful assessment tool did Main et al (1985) develop?
Q3 What is the 'cycle of privation'?
Q4 Describe Freud and Dann's (1951) case study of the German orphans.

Exam Question

Q1 Read the item below, then answer the question that follows.

As an infant, Norman was often uneasy around his mother, but when he was dropped off at school, he would cry and wail all day. When Norman grew up and went to university, he was fearful of forming any romantic relationships and any time he did get feelings for anyone, he became anxious and overwhelmed.

Use Bowlby's internal working model to explain Norman's behaviour towards others. [4 marks]

My mum is a bit bonkers — what does that mean I'll be like as a parent...?

As with everything in psychology, there are studies that support and refute the main theories. So, although some studies say that early attachments do affect later relationships, there are also those that don't. Gah... nothing is simple these days. But — on a side note, once you've learnt these pages, you're done with attachment. For now.

Defining Abnormality

Defining what's abnormal is easy — it's just what's not normal. But what's normal...?

Abnormality Can be Described as **Deviation from Social Norms**

1) All societies have their **standards** of behaviour and attitudes. Deviating from these can be seen as abnormal.

2) But **cultures vary**, so there isn't one universal set of social 'rules'.

3) One problem with defining abnormality as deviation from social norms is that it can be used to **justify** the removal of 'unwanted' people from a society. For example, people opposing a particular political regime could be said to be abnormal.

4) Another limitation of defining abnormality as deviation from social norms is that what is considered acceptable or abnormal can **change over time**. For example, as recently as 1974, homosexuality was classified in the **Diagnostic and Statistical Manual of Mental Disorders (DSM)** (see page 42) as a **disorder**. However, the diagnosis was dropped because it was found that homosexuality **wasn't as infrequent** as previously thought, and that homosexuals don't differ from heterosexuals in terms of **psychological well-being**.

Abnormality Can also be Described as **Deviation from Statistical Norms**

Abnormality can also be seen as statistically rare behaviour — this can be expressed in terms of the **normal distribution**:

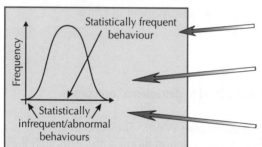

People who behave in the average way make up the middle of the bell-shaped curve.

Those people who behave 'abnormally' make up the tail ends of the bell curve — this behaviour is rare (statistically infrequent).

This axis shows a numerical measure of the behaviour, e.g. the number of hand washes per week.

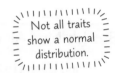

Not all traits show a normal distribution.

However, there are **problems** with defining abnormality simply in terms of statistical infrequency:

1) It doesn't take account of the **desirability of behaviour**, just its frequency. For example, a very high IQ is abnormal, as is a very low one, but having a high IQ is desirable whereas having a low IQ is undesirable.

2) There's **no distinction** between **rare**, **slightly odd** behaviour and **rare**, **psychologically abnormal** behaviour.

3) There's **no definite cut-off point** where normal behaviour becomes abnormal behaviour.

4) Some behaviours that are considered psychologically abnormal are quite common, e.g. mild depression. **Hassett and White (1989)** argue that you cannot use statistical infrequency to define abnormality because of this. Using the statistical infrequency idea, some disorders would not be classed as anything unusual.

Failure to Function Adequately is Another Definition of **Abnormality**

You can't function adequately if you can't cope with the demands of day-to-day life.

Various **criteria** are used for diagnosis, including:

1) **Dysfunctional behaviour** — behaviour which goes against the accepted standards of behaviour.

2) **Observer discomfort** — behaviour that causes other individuals to become uncomfortable.

3) **Unpredictable behaviour** — impulsive behaviour that seems to be uncontrollable.

4) **Irrational behaviour** — behaviour that's unreasonable and illogical.

5) **Personal distress** — being affected by emotion to an excessive degree.

If you can tick the box for **more than one** of the criteria above, the person's behaviour is considered to be **abnormal**. It does seem a bit unfair though — we've probably all done stuff that could fit under these categories at some point. People are always uncomfortable around me, but that could be because I've got fleas.

Defining Abnormality

Jahoda (1958) Identified Six Conditions Associated with Ideal Mental Health

Jahoda's six conditions were:

1) **Positive self-attitude**
2) **Self-actualisation** (realising your potential, being fulfilled)
3) **Resistance to stress**
4) **Personal autonomy** (making your own decisions, being in control)
5) **Accurate perception of reality**
6) **Adaptation to the environment**

As far as Doug was concerned, he was in control of everything he needed in life.

However, it can be **hard to meet** all the standards set in this list, and they're **subjective** (ideas of what is required for each will differ from person to person).

Also, a violent offender, for example, may have a positive self-attitude and be resistant to stress, etc. — yet society wouldn't consider them to be in good mental health.

The Idea of Ideal Mental Health Varies Across Time and Between Cultures

What's considered mentally 'healthy' at one time, wouldn't necessarily be at another.
For example, in some cultures today, it's considered **abnormal** for women to **enjoy sex** — they may be forced to have their clitoris surgically removed to prevent their enjoyment. In Victorian times here, women who enjoyed sex were deemed abnormal and hence Freud coined the term '**nymphomania**'. There's still influence from this today — there are still **double standards** about male and female sexual activity.

But the idea of 'ideal' mental health can be a useful one because it moves away from focusing on mental 'illness'.

Some Symptoms are Associated with Mental Illness

The Department of Health provides a guide to assess symptoms associated with mental illness.
To be classified as a mental illness, there should be **one or more** of the following (**not temporary**) symptoms:

1) Impairment of intellectual functions, such as memory and comprehension.
2) Alterations to mood that lead to delusional appraisals of the past or future, or lack of any appraisal.
3) Delusional beliefs, such as of persecution or jealousy.
4) Disordered thinking — the person may be unable to appraise their situation or communicate with others.

Warm-Up Questions

Q1 Define abnormality using the deviation from social norms explanation.

Q2 What does Jahoda (1958) say are the six conditions associated with mental health?

Q3 Give three of the symptoms that the Department of Health uses to classify mental illness.

Q4 If someone's forgotten their trousers, should they be allowed on the bus?

PRACTICE QUESTIONS

Exam Questions

Q1 Outline the problems with defining abnormality in terms of deviation from social norms. [3 marks]

Q2 Outline the key features of the idea of abnormality as the failure to function adequately. [6 marks]

Q3 Discuss definitions of abnormality. [8 marks]

I'm not abnormal — I'm just a little socially deviant...

Ah, wouldn't it be easier to just be a fish... Nobody minds if you're abnormal when you're under the sea — you can swim around any way you like. You could befriend a manatee and have an adventure. The kindly sea cow — he'd never judge you for your dysfunctional and unpredictable behaviour. Unless you were a blobfish, nobody wants to be one of those...

Depression, Phobias and OCD

Depression, phobias and OCD are all examples of mental health disorders. The defining characteristics of mental health disorders such as these can be found in the DSM...

Psychologists Try to **Classify** Mental Disorders

The **DSM** is the American Psychiatric Association's Diagnostic and Statistical Manual of Mental Disorders. It contains mental health disorders, and is systematically reviewed and modified in line with new research.

1) The DSM is used to classify disorders using defined **diagnostic criteria**. This includes a list of symptoms which can be used as a **tool** for diagnosis.
2) The DSM makes diagnosis **concrete and descriptive**.
3) Classifications allow data to be collected about a disorder. This can help in the development of new **treatments** and medication.
4) This type of classification has been criticised for **stigmatising** people and ignoring their 'uniqueness' by putting them in **artificial groups**.

Both Dr. Heath and Dr. Sun would defend their diagnoses to the death.

Depression is a **Mood Disorder**

Mood disorders are characterised by **strong emotions**, which can influence a person's ability to **function normally**. A mood disorder can affect a person's **perceptions**, **thinking** and **behaviour**.

Depression is one of the most **common** mood disorders. There are many types, including:

1) **Major depression (unipolar disorder)** — an **episode** of depression that can occur **suddenly**.
   - Major depression can be **reactive** — caused by **external factors**, e.g. the death of a loved one.
   - Or, it can be **endogenous** — caused by **internal factors**, e.g. neurological factors.
2) **Manic depression (bipolar disorder)** — **alternation** between two **mood extremes** (**mania** and **depression**).
   - The change in mood often occurs in regular **cycles** of days or weeks.
   - Episodes of **mania** involve **overactivity**, **rapid speech** and feeling extremely **happy** or **agitated**.
   - Episodes of **depression** involve the symptoms covered below.

Depression has Lots of **Clinical Characteristics**

People with depression can experience a **range** of possible **symptoms**:

Physical / behavioural symptoms

- **Sleep disturbances** — **insomnia** (being unable to sleep) or **hypersomnia** (sleeping a lot more than usual).
- Change in **appetite** — people may eat **more** or **less** than **usual**, and gain or lose **weight**.
- **Pain** — especially **headaches**, **joint ache** and **muscle ache**.
- Lack of **activity** — **social withdrawal** and loss of **sex drive**.

Cognitive symptoms

- Experiencing persistent **negative beliefs** about **themselves** and their **abilities**.
- **Suicidal** thoughts.
- **Slower** thought processes — **difficulty concentrating** and **making decisions**.

Affective / emotional symptoms

- Extreme feelings of **sadness**, **hopelessness** and **despair**.
- **Diurnal mood variation** — changes in mood throughout the day, e.g. feeling worse in the morning.
- **Anhedonia** — no longer **enjoying** activities or hobbies that **used** to be **pleasurable**.

For a person to be diagnosed with **major depression**, the DSM (see above) states that at least **five symptoms** must have been present nearly every day for at least **two weeks**.

Depression, Phobias and OCD

A **Phobia** is an **Irrational Fear**

A phobia is an example of an **anxiety disorder** — it's an **extreme**, **irrational fear** of a particular **object** or **situation**. The **DSM** classifies several types of phobia:

1) Specific phobias

This is a fear of specific **objects** or **situations**. There are **five** subtypes:

1) **Animal** type (also called **zoophobia**, e.g. fear of spiders)
2) **Environmental dangers** type (e.g. fear of water)
3) **Blood-injection-injury** type (e.g. fear of needles)
4) **Situational** type (e.g. fear of enclosed spaces or heights)
5) **'Other'** (any phobia that isn't covered in the categories above)

2) Agoraphobia

1) This is a fear of **open spaces**, **using public transport**, being in an **enclosed space**, **waiting in line** or **being in a crowd**, or **not being at home**.
2) It's specifically linked to the **fear** of not being able to escape or find help if an embarrassing situation arises.
3) It often involves the sufferer **avoiding the situation** in order to avoid distress.
4) It may develop as a **result** of **other phobias**, because the sufferer's afraid that they'll come across the **source** of their **fear** if they leave the house.

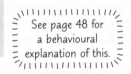
See page 48 for a behavioural explanation of this.

3) Social anxiety disorder (social phobia)

This is the fear of **being** in **social situations** (e.g. eating in public or talking in front of a group of people). It's usually down to the possibility of being **judged** or being **embarrassed**.

Phobias have Several **Clinical Characteristics**

The different types of phobia all have very **similar** clinical characteristics.

Cognitive symptoms	**Irrational beliefs** about the **stimulus** that causes fear. People often find it **hard** to **concentrate** because they're **preoccupied** by **anxious thoughts**.
Behavioural symptoms	**Avoiding** social situations because they cause **anxiety**. This happens especially if someone has **social anxiety disorder (social phobia)** or **agoraphobia**.
	Altering behaviour to **avoid** the feared object or situation, and trying to **escape** if it's encountered. People are often generally **restless** and **easily startled**.
Physical symptoms	Activation of the **fight or flight** response when the feared object or situation is encountered or thought about. This involves release of **adrenaline**, **increased heart rate** and **breathing**, and **muscle tension** (see page 81).
Emotional symptoms	**Anxiety** and a feeling of **dread**.

There are Various **Diagnostic Criteria** for **Phobias**

The **DSM** classifies a fear as a phobia if you can put a tick next to these criteria:

1) There's **significant prolonged fear** of an object or situation which lasts **more than 6 months**.
2) People experience an **anxiety response** (e.g. increased heart rate) if they're exposed to the phobic stimulus.
3) Phobias are **out of proportion** to any actual danger.
4) Sufferers go out of their way to **avoid** the phobic stimulus.
5) The phobia **disrupts** their **lives**, e.g. they avoid social situations.

Sophie did everything she could to hide her parrotophobia.

Depression, Phobias and OCD

Not quite done yet... Obsessive-compulsive disorder (OCD) is up next. Most of us have the odd obsessive thought (like checking your phone's off ten times before the exam starts) — but in OCD it's taken to extremes and affects daily life.

OCD has Two Parts

1) Obsessive-compulsive disorder has two parts — **obsessions** and **compulsions**. Most people with OCD experience obsessions and compulsions that are **linked** to each other. For example, excessive worrying about catching germs (an obsession) may lead to excessive hand-washing (a compulsion).

2) Obsessions are the **cognitive** aspect of OCD, and compulsions are the **behavioural** aspect. OCD also has an **emotional** aspect — the obsessions tend to cause people **anxiety**, and their compulsions are an attempt to relieve this.

3) Obsessive-compulsive disorder affects about **2%** of the world's population. Sufferers usually develop the disorder in their **late teens** or **early 20s**. The disorder occurs **equally in men and women** and in all **ethnic groups**.

Obsessions are the Cognitive Part of the Disorder

Obsessions are **intrusive** and **persistent thoughts**, **images** and **impulses**. They are the **internal** aspect of OCD. They can range from worrying that you left the oven on to worrying that you might kill your parents. For thoughts like these to be **classified** as obsessions, the **DSM** (see page 42) outlines the following criteria:

- **Persistent** and **reoccurring** thoughts, images or impulses that are **unwanted** and cause **distress** to the person experiencing them. For example, imagining that you've left the door unlocked and burglars are rampaging through your house.

  In most people, these thoughts cause anxiety and distress.

- The person actively tries to **ignore** the thoughts, images or impulses but is **unable to**.

- The obsessions have not been caused by **other physiological substances**, such as drugs.

Compulsions are Repetitive Actions

- Compulsions are **physical** or **mental repetitive actions**. They are the **external** aspect of OCD.

- For example, **checking** the door is locked nine times or repeating a certain **phrase** or **prayer** to **neutralise** an unwanted thought.

- The problem is that the action only reduces the anxiety caused by an obsession for a **short time**, which means that the obsession starts up again.

- The **DSM** uses the following diagnostic criteria:

  1) The person repeats physical behaviours or mental acts that relate to an obsession. Sometimes the person has rules that they must follow strictly. For example, a rule that you must check the door is locked ten times before you can leave home.

  2) The compulsions are meant to reduce anxiety or prevent a feared situation — in reality they're excessive or wouldn't actually stop a dreaded situation.

  3) The compulsions have not been caused by other physiological substances, such as drugs.

No matter how many times he checked, the doctor still couldn't prove who'd eaten his stash of lollipops.

The DSM states that if the obsessions or compulsions last **at least one hour each day** this is an indication of a **clinical case** of OCD. Another indication of OCD is if the obsessions and compulsions **interfere** with a person's ability to maintain a relationship, hold down a job or take part in social activities.

Depression, Phobias and OCD

There are **Several Types** of **OCD Behaviours**

There are several common types of OCD behaviours. Here are four:

1) **Checking** — includes checking that the lights are off or that you have your purse or wallet.

2) **Contamination** — this involves a fear of catching germs by, say, going to a restaurant, touching door handles, shaking hands or using public toilets.

3) **Hoarding** — keeping useless or worn-out objects, such as old newspapers or junk mail.

4) **Symmetry and orderliness** — getting objects lined up 'just right', such as having all the tins in your food cupboard facing exactly the same way, or everything on your desk arranged in a neat order in the right places.

Warm-Up Questions

Q1 What's the difference between major depression and manic depression?

Q2 What is anhedonia?

Q3 What are the five subtypes of specific phobias?

Q4 Outline the diagnostic criteria for phobias.

Q5 Give an example of an obsession.

Q6 Give an example of a compulsion.

PRACTICE QUESTIONS

Exam Questions

Q1 Read the item below and answer the questions that follow.

> Since Jonathan lost his job six months ago he has had low moods and has been having difficulty sleeping.
> He describes how he is feeling:
>> 'I don't get any pleasure from things any more. I used to go to the cinema or meet up with friends at the weekend, but now I don't want to go out because I know I won't enjoy it and I'll just drag other people down. I'm looking for a new job but I don't have the right skills for the jobs that are advertised. I don't think I'll ever find anything.'

    a) Outline **two** emotional characteristics of depression that you can identify in Jonathan's description. [2 marks]

    b) Outline one cognitive characteristic of depression that is **not** mentioned in Jonathan's account. [1 mark]

Q2 Outline one cognitive characteristic and one emotional characteristic of phobias. [2 marks]

Q3 Read the item below, then answer the questions that follow.

> Peter suffers from intrusive thoughts that he will cause an accident while driving his car. Before driving he repeatedly checks that his seat belt is correctly fastened. Peter feels he must begin his drive to work at a precise time, and he is unable to leave the house if he misses this departure time.

    a) Outline a cognitive characteristic of OCD that you can identify from the description of Peter's experience. [1 mark]

    b) With reference to the item above, discuss the interaction between the behavioural, emotional and cognitive characteristics of OCD. [6 marks]

Doctor, Doctor, I'm having unwanted thoughts about revision...

OCD isn't all about checking and straightening — intrusive thoughts can be violent and upsetting, and they often cause anxiety. This anxiety is the emotional aspect of OCD, along with obsessions (cognitive) and compulsions (behavioural). On top of that, you also need to know the emotional, cognitive and behavioural aspects of depression and of phobias. Chin up...

The Cognitive Approach to Depression

The cognitive explanation of depression basically rests on the idea that disorders happen because of faulty thinking. There are other explanations for depression, and other treatments, but you just need to know the cognitive stuff. Phew.

The **Cognitive** Model of Abnormality Concentrates on **Thoughts** and **Beliefs**

The **cognitive approach** assumes that behaviours are controlled by **thoughts** and **beliefs**. So, irrational thoughts and beliefs cause abnormal behaviours.

The cognitive approach is covered in detail in Section Five.

There are several models that explain how **faulty cognitions** can lead to depression. For example:

Ellis's ABC model

1) **Ellis (1962)** proposed the '**ABC model**'.

2) The model claims that disorders begin with an **activating event (A)** (e.g. a failed exam), leading to a **belief (B)** about why this happened.

3) This may be rational (e.g. 'I didn't prepare well enough'), or irrational (e.g. 'I'm too stupid to pass exams').

4) The belief leads to a **consequence (C)**. Rational beliefs produce adaptive (appropriate) consequences (e.g. more revision). Irrational beliefs produce maladaptive (bad and inappropriate) consequences (e.g. getting depressed).

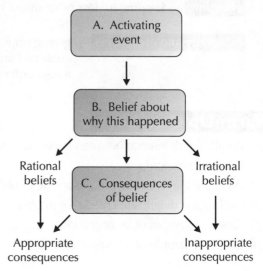

A. Activating event

B. Belief about why this happened

Rational beliefs — C. Consequences of belief — Irrational beliefs

Appropriate consequences — Inappropriate consequences

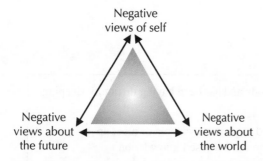

Negative views of self

Negative views about the future — Negative views about the world

Beck's negative triad

Beck (1963) identified a '**negative triad**' of automatic thoughts linked to **depression** — negative views about:

1) **themselves** (e.g. that they can't succeed at anything),

2) the **world** (e.g. that they must be successful to be a good person),

3) the **future** (e.g. that nothing will change).

The **Cognitive** Explanation of **Depression** Has **Strengths** and **Weaknesses**

Strengths:

1) The cognitive model offers a **useful** approach to depression because it considers the role of **thoughts** and **beliefs**, which are greatly involved in problems like depression.

2) Hollon and Kendall (1980) developed the **Automatic Thoughts Questionnaire (ATQ)** to measure the **negative thinking** associated with depression. **Harrell and Ryon (1983)** used the ATQ to compare negative thinking in 114 depressed and non-depressed participants. The **depressed** participants scored **significantly higher** (more negative thinking) than the other groups, supporting a **correlation** between negative thinking and depression.

3) Cognitive therapies have often **successfully treated** depression (see next page).

Weaknesses:

1) Faulty cognitions may simply be the **consequence** of depression rather than its cause. For example, depression may be caused by a chemical imbalance in the brain, which causes people to think very negatively.

2) The person could begin to feel like he or she is to **blame** for their problems.

Strengths:
Looks good in pink.

Weaknesses:
Only has half a pair of trousers.

The Cognitive Approach to Depression

CBT Tries to Change Faulty Cognitions

Cognitive therapies are used to treat a range of conditions, but they're particularly helpful for things like depression.

Cognitive behaviour therapy (CBT) aims to **identify** and **change** the patient's **faulty cognitions**.
The idea is that patients learn how to **notice** negative thoughts when they have them, and **test** how accurate they are.
This is generally what happens during CBT:

1) The therapist and client **identify** the client's faulty **cognitions** (thoughts and beliefs).

2) The therapist then tries to **help** the client see that these cognitions aren't true, e.g. that the client doesn't always fail at what they do.

3) Together, they then set **goals** to think in more positive or adaptive ways, e.g. focusing on things the client has succeeded at and trying to build on them.

4) Although the client may occasionally need to look back to past experiences, the treatment mainly focuses on the **present situation**.

5) Therapists sometimes encourage their clients to keep a **diary** — they can record their thought patterns, feelings and actions.

Stuart's faulty cognition had led to a disastrous footwear decision.

Advantages of CBT

- CBT **empowers** patients — it puts them in charge of their own treatment by teaching them **self-help strategies**. This means there are **fewer ethical issues** than with other therapies like drug therapy.

- **DeRubeis et al (2005)** compared **CBT** and **drug therapy** as depression treatments in a placebo-controlled trial. Both treatments were **more effective than the placebo** after 8 weeks. Generally the two therapies were similarly effective, but CBT may have been **less effective than drug therapy** in cases where therapists **lacked experience**.

- **Hollon et al (2005)** compared participants from DeRubeis et al's (2005) study after they were **withdrawn** from treatment (CBT and drug treatment), with participants who **continued** drug treatment. Participants **withdrawn from CBT** were **significantly less likely** than patients **withdrawn from drug treatment** to have **relapsed** after one year, and **no more likely** to have relapsed than patients who **continued** drug treatment.

- **Brandsma et al (1978)** found that **CBT** is particularly effective for people who put a lot of **pressure** on themselves and feel **guilty** about being **inadequate**.

CBT might be expensive initially, but if it reduces relapse then it may cost less overall. Also, if people need less time off work and are able to contribute more to society, it's better for the economy in the long run (see page 91).

Disadvantages of CBT

- Cognitive therapies may take a long **time** and be **costly**. They may be more effective when **combined** with other approaches, e.g. drug therapy.

- As **DeRubeis et al (2005)** found, CBT may only be effective if the therapist is **experienced**. Patients whose therapists are still gaining this experience may be better off with **drug therapy**.

- The person could begin to feel like he or she is to **blame** for their problems.

Warm-Up Questions

Q1 Outline Ellis's ABC model.

Q2 What three factors make up Beck's 'negative triad'?

Q3 What is the main aim of CBT?

PRACTICE QUESTIONS

Exam Questions

Q1 Outline the assumptions of the cognitive explanation of depression. [4 marks]

Q2 Evaluate the cognitive explanation of depression. [6 marks]

Q3 Describe and evaluate the cognitive approach to treating depression. [16 marks]

I think, therefore I am. Depressed...

So that was the cognitive approach to depression. You need to know the explanation, the treatment, and the strengths and weaknesses of both. It's a wonder the psychologists who come up with these theories don't get more depressed themselves. You'd think having thousands of students saying their ideas are a bit weak might upset them slightly...

The Behavioural Approach to Phobias

There are various explanations for how phobias develop, and how to treat them, but you only need to learn the behavioural approach. Which is great — it's my favourite. Although I'm not too keen on the picture at the bottom of the next page...

The Behavioural Model of Abnormality says **Behaviours** are all **Learnt**

Behaviourists argue that **phobias** are learnt in the same way that all behaviours are learnt — through **classical** and **operant conditioning**.

The behavioural approach is covered in detail in Section Five.

Classical Conditioning

See page 55 for more on classical conditioning.

1) In **classical conditioning** a natural reflex is produced in response to a previously neutral stimulus — **phobias** can be created when the **natural fear** response becomes associated with a particular stimulus.

A certain stimulus, e.g. a loud noise (unconditioned stimulus — UCS)	triggers →	a natural reflex, e.g. fear (unconditioned response — UCR)
UCS repeatedly presented with another stimulus, e.g. a rat (conditioned stimulus — CS)	triggers →	fear (unconditioned response — UCR)
Over time, the rat presented by itself	triggers →	fear (conditioned response — CR)

2) Phobias can **generalise** to similar stimuli (see page 55). For example, **Watson and Rayner (1920)** conditioned a phobia in Little Albert using the method above (see page 57). Albert's resulting phobia of white rats was generalised to fluffy white objects.

Operant Conditioning

See page 56 for more on operant conditioning.

1) **Operant conditioning** is learning from the **consequences** of actions. Actions which have a good outcome through **positive reinforcement** (reward) or **negative reinforcement** (removal of something bad) will be repeated. Actions which have a bad outcome (**punishment**) will not be repeated.

2) Operant conditioning is important in **maintaining** phobias (see below).

The **Two-Process Model** Explains how **Phobias** are **Produced** and **Maintained**

Mowrer's **two-process model** (1947) explains how classical and operant conditioning produce and maintain phobias.

1) People develop phobias (usually specific phobias) by **classical conditioning** — a CS (conditioned stimulus) is paired with an UCS (unconditioned stimulus) to produce the CR (conditioned response).

2) Once somebody has developed a phobia, it's maintained through **operant conditioning** — people get anxious around the phobic stimulus and avoid it. This prevents the anxiety, which acts as **negative reinforcement**.

Operant conditioning can also explain how **social phobia** and **agoraphobia** develop from a specific phobia — people are anxious that they'll experience a **panic attack** in a social situation or an open place (because of their specific phobia), so they avoid these situations.

Social phobia or agoraphobia can develop on their own through classical conditioning (if the anxiety-inducing situations have been paired with an unconditioned stimulus).

The **Behavioural** Explanation of **Phobias** Has **Strengths** and **Weaknesses**

Strengths:

1) **Barlow and Durand (1995)** showed that in cases of individuals with a severe fear of driving, **50%** of them had actually been involved in a road accident. Through **classical conditioning**, the road accident (an UCS) had turned driving into a CS for those now with the phobia.

2) Behavioural **therapies** are very **effective** at treating phobias by getting the person to **change** their **response** to the **stimulus** (see next page). This suggests that they treat the **cause** of the problem.

Weakness:

1) **Davey (1992)** found that only **7%** of spider phobics recalled having a **traumatic experience** with a spider.

2) This suggests that there could be **other explanations**, e.g. biological factors. (But just because they couldn't remember the experience, this doesn't mean it didn't happen.)

The Behavioural Approach to Phobias

Phobias Can be Treated Using Behavioural Therapies

Behavioural treatment for **phobias** is based on **classical conditioning** — there are **two techniques**:

Systematic desensitisation

1) Systematic desensitisation works by using **counter-conditioning** so that the person learns to **associate** the **phobic stimulus** with **relaxation** rather than **fear**.

2) First, the phobic person makes a '**fear hierarchy**'. This is a list of feared events, showing what they fear least (e.g. seeing a picture of a spider) through to their most feared event (e.g. holding a spider).

3) They are then taught **relaxation techniques** like deep breathing.

4) The patient then **imagines** the anxiety-provoking situations, starting with the least stressful. They're encouraged to use the **relaxation techniques**, and the process stops if they feel anxious.

Real-life situations can also be used (rather than just the imagination), for example actually looking at a spider.

5) Relaxation and anxiety can't happen at the same time, so when they become relaxed and calm, they're no longer scared. This is repeated until the feared event is only linked with **relaxation**.

6) This whole process is repeated for each stage of the fear hierarchy, until they are **calm** through their **most feared** event.

Flooding

1) This involves exposing the patient to the phobic stimulus straight away, without any relaxation or gradual build-up. This can be done in real life, or the patient can be asked to visualise it. For example, someone who was afraid of heights might imagine standing on top of a skyscraper.

2) The patient is kept in this situation until the anxiety they feel at first has worn off. They realise that nothing bad has happened to them in this time, and their fear should be extinguished.

Advantages

- **Behavioural therapy** is very effective for treating **specific phobias**. **Zinbarg et al (1992)** found that **systematic desensitisation** was the **most effective** of the currently known methods for treating phobias.

- It works very **quickly**, e.g. **Ost et al (1991)** found that anxiety was reduced in **90%** of patients with a specific phobia after just **one session** of **therapy**.

Disadvantages

- There are **ethical issues** surrounding behavioural therapy — especially **flooding**, as it causes patients a lot of anxiety. If patients **drop out** of the therapy **before** the fear has been extinguished, then it can end up causing **more anxiety** than before therapy started.

- **Behavioural therapy** only treats the **symptoms** of the disorder. **Other therapies** try to tackle the **cause** of it, e.g. cognitive behaviour therapy.

Warm-Up Questions

Q1 How might a specific phobia develop through classical conditioning?

Q2 What is the behavioural therapy, flooding?

Q3 Give one strength of the behavioural approach to treating phobias.

Exam Questions

Q1 Outline systematic desensitisation as a treatment for phobias. [4 marks]

Q2 Discuss the behavioural explanation of phobias. [16 marks]

So, you're scared of spiders — oooh, look what I have here...

Hmmm... you wouldn't be able to use the excuse of 'phobia of revision' if your teacher was a behaviourist. So I guess you'd better just get on with it just in case. Doing well in your exam will be a positive reinforcement — or something...

The Biological Approach to OCD

There's more than one approach to explaining and treating OCD, but you just need to know about the biological one. Shame really — it's all interesting stuff. Ah well, can't win them all. Best just get stuck into this biological stuff. Read on...

The Biological Model Assumes Psychological Disorders are **Physical Illnesses**

The **biological approach** assumes that psychological disorders are **physical illnesses** with physical causes. In principle they're no different from physical illnesses like flu, except they have major psychological symptoms. There are several **biological explanations** for **OCD**:

The biological approach is covered in detail in Section Five.

1) **Genetic** Factors

Some researchers think that **genetics** plays a part in OCD. Studies have looked at OCD rates among people with a relative who has OCD, to see if having a relative with OCD **significantly** increases your chances of developing it.

EVIDENCE FOR

1) **Billet et al (1998)** did a **meta-analysis** of twin studies that had been carried out over a long period of time. They found that for **identical twins**, if one twin had OCD then **68%** of the time both twins had it, compared to **31%** for **non-identical twins**.

2) **Pauls et al (2005)** found that **10%** of people with an **immediate relative** (i.e. parents, offspring or siblings) with OCD also suffered from the disorder. This is compared to around **2%** of people in the general population.

EVIDENCE AGAINST

1) No study has found a **100%** concordance rate, so **genetics can't** be the full story in OCD. It's possible that children **imitate** the obsessive and compulsive behaviour of their relatives.

2) Concordance rates don't prove that OCD is **caused** by genetics. It may be that **general anxiety** is genetic and that going on to develop OCD itself has **other contributing factors**, e.g. biochemical or psychological factors.

Concordance means how likely it is that both people in a pair will have a certain characteristic, given that one of them does.

2) **Biochemical** Factors

PET scans have shown that levels of the **neurotransmitter serotonin** are lower in OCD sufferers.

See page 79 for more on serotonin and other types of neurotransmitter.

EVIDENCE FOR

1) **Insel (1991)** found that a class of drugs called SSRIs, which increase levels of serotonin, can reduce symptoms of OCD in **50 to 60%** of cases. There's more about this on the next page.

2) **Zohar et al (1996)** also found that SSRIs alleviated symptoms in **60%** of patients with OCD.

EVIDENCE AGAINST

1) SSRIs appear to offer some relief to sufferers of OCD. However, as this is not true in **100%** of cases, there must be more to understanding OCD.

2) The link with serotonin is correlational, so it doesn't show cause and effect. It may be that decreased serotonin levels are a symptom of OCD, rather than a cause of it.

3) **Neurological** Factors

Some research using **PET scans** has found that **abnormality** in the **basal ganglia** within the brain may be linked to OCD.

EVIDENCE FOR

1) **Max et al (1995)** found **increased rates** of OCD in people after **head injuries** that caused brain damage to the **basal ganglia**.

2) Other researchers have found **increased activity** in this area during OCD-related thoughts and behaviours.

3) OCD is often found in people with **other diseases** which involve the basal ganglia, e.g. **Parkinson's** and **Huntington's disease**.

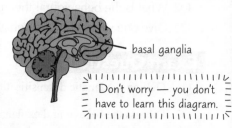

— basal ganglia

Don't worry — you don't have to learn this diagram.

EVIDENCE AGAINST

1) **Aylward et al (1996)** didn't find a significant difference in **basal ganglia impairment** between OCD patients and controls.

2) Basal ganglia damage **hasn't** been found in **100%** of people with OCD, so it can't be the full story.

The Biological Approach to OCD

The **Biological** Explanation of **OCD** Has **Strengths** and **Weaknesses**

Strengths:

1) It has a **scientific** basis in biology — there's evidence that low serotonin and damage to the basal ganglia **correlate** with cases of OCD, though this doesn't necessarily show a **causal** relationship.

2) **Twin studies** have shown that genetics have at least some effect on the likelihood of developing OCD.

3) It can be seen as **ethical** — people **aren't blamed** for their disorders; they just have an illness.

Weaknesses:

1) The explanation doesn't take into account the effect of the **environment, family, childhood experiences** or **social influences** — psychologists taking other approaches consider these sorts of things important factors.

2) Biological therapies raise **ethical** concerns. Drugs can produce addiction and may only suppress symptoms rather than cure the disorder.

OCD Can be **Treated** Using **Biological Therapy**

1) The **biological** approach to treating OCD involves **drug therapy**.

2) Drug treatments usually work by increasing levels of **serotonin** in the brain using **selective serotonin reuptake inhibitors (SSRIs)**. These are a type of **antidepressant** drug that **increase** the availability of **serotonin**.

3) SSRIs **prevent the reuptake** of serotonin in the **synaptic cleft** (the gap between two neurons — see page 78). This means there's **more serotonin** available to the next neuron.

Advantages

- Several researchers have found SSRIs to be **effective** in treating OCD. **Thoren et al (1980)** found that use of an SSRI was significantly better at **reducing obsessional thoughts** than a placebo.

- Research has found that using **other antidepressants** that don't affect serotonin levels is **ineffective** at reducing OCD symptoms.

> OCD affects lots of people in the UK. If sufferers can have the most appropriate treatment, they can maintain a better quality of life and remain effective members of society.

Disadvantages

- Up to **50%** of patients with OCD **don't** experience any improvement in their symptoms when taking SSRIs. Out of those that do improve, up to **90%** have a **relapse** when they stop taking them.

- SSRIs have to be taken for **several weeks** before the patient experiences an improvement in their symptoms.

- **Side effects** of using these types of drugs include **nausea** and **headaches**, and sometimes increased levels of **anxiety**. This can cause people to **stop taking** their medication.

Warm-Up Questions

Q1 What is the main idea behind the biological approach to explaining psychological disorders?

Q2 Outline a study that shows that OCD has a genetic factor.

Q3 Outline the link between serotonin levels and OCD.

Q4 Give one piece of evidence for the neurological explanation of OCD.

Q5 What are SSRIs?

Exam Questions

Q1 Briefly outline one weakness of the biological approach to treating OCD. [2 marks]

Q2 Discuss the biological explanation of OCD. [16 marks]

And there was me thinking basal ganglia was a sub-genre of reggae...

So there are several biological factors that might explain OCD, and there's evidence for and against all of them. Oh well. Make sure you've learnt them all, and you can evaluate each of them, as well as the biological explanation of OCD as a whole. You need to be able to explain and evaluate drug therapy for OCD too. Then you can have a little lie down...

The Origins of Psychology

Once upon a time (around 1879), there was a man called Wilhelm who lived in a pleasant German city. He decided to set up a psychology lab. And from there, modern psychology as we know it was born...

Psychology is a Science with **Lots of Theories** and **Few Facts**

Psychology is "**the scientific study of the mind and behaviour**".
This basically means that psychologists look at what people and animals do, why they do it, and how they feel.

A lot of psychology sounds like **common sense**, but it's a science, so everything's got to be investigated.
You've got to come up with a **theory** about something and then **scientifically test** it.

It's difficult to prove things in psychology, so there are loads of disagreements and a lot of theories that sound rubbish. But you can't just say they're rubbish in your exam — that'd be too easy. No, you've got to use other theories and experiments to support your answer.

The different schools of thought are called **approaches**. Each approach has its own explanation for why we do what we do. You'll be looking at the **behavioural**, **cognitive**, **biological**, **psychodynamic** and **humanistic** approaches.

If you're doing <u>AS Level</u>, you only need to know about the behavioural, cognitive and biological approaches.

Wundt was the **Father** of **Experimental Psychology**

Structuralism breaks down human thoughts and experiences into basic components.

Wilhelm Wundt (1832 – 1920)

In 1879, **Wilhelm Wundt** opened an **Institute for Experimental Psychology** in Germany.
He separated psychology from philosophy and focused on studying the mind in a much more structured and scientific way. Using a **structuralist** and **reductionist** (see below) approach, Wundt used methods such as **introspection** to try to uncover what people were thinking and experiencing.

Introspection Involves Looking into Your Mind

Introspection is a psychological method which involves analysing your own thoughts and feelings internally.

In the 1800s, there were no brain scans or computers to enable people to explore the inside workings of the brain. So, as a way to investigate people's consciousness, Wundt used **introspection** to study **sensation** and **perception**. Participants were asked to describe their experiences when presented with a set of stimuli, and often their reaction times were recorded.

Introspection allowed Wundt to analyse the quality of the sensations people experienced.

Problems with Introspection

- It doesn't explain **how** the mind works. It relies on people describing their thoughts and feelings, which usually isn't **objective**.
- It doesn't provide data that can be used **reliably**. Because people are reporting on their experiences, their accounts can't be confirmed.

Even though Wundt's method of introspection wasn't that objective, his experimental approach to psychology did influence other areas of the subject. These include the beginnings of the **behavioural**, **cognitive** and **biological** approaches.

Shaun's experience of wearing a onesie was slightly different to others'.

Wundt Believed in **Reductionism**

There's more on reductionism on page 141.

Reductionism is the idea that things can be reduced to simple cause-and-effect processes. Wundt came from a biological background, and so he believed that the underlying structure of human experience could be broken down into smaller, **measurable** parts. He used introspection to measure these parts.

The Origins of Psychology

But is Psychology a **Science?**

Wundt's founding of experimental psychology kicked psychology into the scientific world. It could now be taken much more seriously. But there is still a lot of **controversy** around the idea that it is a **true science**.

There are several features that make something a science:

1) Objectivity — scientific observations should be recorded without bias and not influenced by any other factors, or any other people.

2) Control — scientific observations should take place under controlled conditions.

3) Predictability — scientists should be able to use the results and knowledge gained from experiments to predict future behaviour.

4) Hypothesis testing — theories generate predictions (hypotheses) which can be tested to either strengthen the support for the theory, or else disprove it.

5) Replication — each experiment should be able to be replicated exactly so people can have confidence in the results.

See page 96 for more on hypotheses.

There are Arguments **For** and **Against** Psychology as a Science

The debate around whether psychology can be called a science continues to the present day.

Arguments For:

- **Allport (1947)** said psychology has the same aims as science — to **predict**, **understand** and **control**.
- Behaviourist, cognitive and biological approaches to psychology all use **scientific procedures** to investigate theories. They are usually controlled and unbiased.

Arguments Against:

- There are other approaches in psychology which don't use objective methods to study behaviour. They use **unreliable** methods — e.g. interview techniques which can be **biased** and interpreted differently by different researchers.
- It's very hard to get a **representative** sample of the population for a study, so findings can't reliably be **generalised**.
- Psychological experiments are also open to **extraneous variables**, such as **demand characteristics** (when participants try to guess the aim of the study), which can be hard to control.

Warm-Up Questions

Q1 What role did Wilhelm Wundt play in the development of psychology?

Q2 What is 'introspection'?

Q3 What is 'reductionism'?

Q4 Describe five features of a science.

PRACTICE QUESTIONS

Exam Questions

Q1 What did Wundt study using introspection?
    A Brain waves   **B** Memory   **C** Sensation   **D** Attachment   [1 mark]

Q2 Outline how psychology has emerged as a science.   [6 marks]

Q3 Is psychology a science? Discuss this statement using what you know about the origins of psychology.   [8 marks]

Wundt's da Daddy...

It all started long ago... well, actually not really that long ago. Psychology is a relatively new discipline, but it has a lot going for it. When Wundt first started his Institute for Experimental Psychology, little did he know how we'd all be revising away for our Psychology exams over 100 years later. He must be so proud.

Behaviourism — Classical and Operant Conditioning

There are lots of different approaches to the study of psychology — up first is the behaviourist approach...

Behaviourism is Also Known as 'Learning Theory'

1) Behaviourism ('**Learning Theory**') started in America in the early 1900s, mainly through the ideas of **John Watson**.

2) Watson felt that earlier psychological research wasn't as scientific as it should be.

3) For example, Wilhelm Wundt tried to study consciousness using **introspection**. This involves analysing your own experiences. However, there's no way of finding out whether what a person said is true or not, so introspection can never be properly scientific.

4) Watson came up with some assumptions on which to base a **scientific** approach to psychology.

There are **Three** Main **Assumptions** of Behaviourism

Remember — this is theory, not fact.

1) **Nearly all behaviour is learnt.**

   The only exceptions are a few inborn **reflexes** (e.g. blinking when we get dirt in our eyes) and a few inborn **instincts** (e.g. instinctively running when in some types of danger).

   However, evidence now shows that **genetics** can influence psychological features, e.g. genetics may contribute to the development of schizophrenia. Behaviourism still claims, though, that learning, and not genetics, is the cause of the **majority** of behaviours, even if some vague genetic causes can be found.

2) **Animals and humans learn in the same ways.**

   Humans can do much more complex things than other animals, but the **principles** by which we learn are the **same**. So, we learn to drive a car through the same principles as a cat learns to use a cat-flap. This is based on the idea that we can form **stimulus-response associations** between stimuli and our actions. However, although we may both use conditioning, humans can be said to use other forms of learning as well, such as **social learning** (see pages 58-59).

3) **The 'mind' is irrelevant.**

   We can't directly observe and measure a person's thinking. So we can only obtain **measurable data** by studying behaviour.

   However, although **cognitive abilities** cannot be directly, scientifically measured, they may give a more complete explanation of behaviour — as shown by **social learning theory** (see pages 58-59).

'All learnt through stimulus-response associations.' Pretty impressive, but it does beg the question 'why?'

Behaviourists Use Their **Assumptions** to Design **Research Methods**

The research methods used by behaviourists follow directly from their **assumptions**, as follows:

1 — Nearly all behaviour is learnt.
So, understanding the principles of **learning** is the main research goal.

2 — Animals and humans learn in the same ways.
Animals can be used as research subjects because what is true for them should also be true for humans. Using animals has **practical advantages**, e.g. they are easy to keep, in many circumstances they don't know they are being studied and so behave 'naturally', and procedures can be used with them which would be illegal with humans (e.g. administering shocks as punishment to see the effect on learning).

3 — The 'mind' is irrelevant.
Behaviourists only observe **quantifiable behaviour** — e.g. how many times a lever is pressed, or how long it takes to solve a puzzle. Typical research therefore involves **laboratory experiments** on animals, to see how they learn.

Behaviourism — Classical and Operant Conditioning

Behaviourists Proposed **Two Types** of Conditioning:

1) **Classical Conditioning**

In early 1900s Russia, **Ivan Pavlov** was studying how dogs' salivation helps them to digest food, when he noticed that they would sometimes salivate **before** they got food. Instead of just thinking they were hungry, he realised they had **associated** food with another stimulus, such as the sound of the door opening. Pavlov started to experiment...

1) Whenever Pavlov gave his dogs some food, he would also ring a bell. After repeating this procedure several times, Pavlov then tried ringing the bell without giving the dogs any food. The bell alone caused salivation.

2) When dogs see food, they salivate. This is an automatic, unlearned response — a reflex. The food is an **unconditioned stimulus (UCS)** and salivation is an **unconditioned response (UCR)**.

3) The bell had become a **conditioned stimulus (CS)**, and salivation had become a **conditioned response (CR)**.

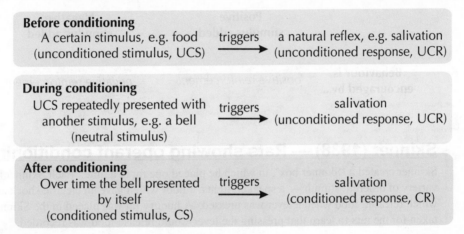

He later made the dogs associate food with lights and other abstract stimuli. This process of learning can be applied to human development:

Having its needs dealt with and gaining comfort naturally makes a baby happy. It hasn't **learnt** to be happy. It's an **inborn reflex**.

So, comfort is an **unconditioned stimulus (UCS)** that produces happiness — an **unconditioned response (UCR)**.

The baby's mother will talk to it while she feeds it and changes its nappy, etc. So, the baby hears its mother's voice every time it's made comfortable and happy.

The sound of its mother's voice is paired with having needs met and being comfortable (UCS), so the mother's voice becomes a **conditioned stimulus (CS)**.

Eventually the sound of the mother's voice alone will make the baby feel happy, even when it isn't paired with having its needs met. The CS (voice) now causes a **conditioned response (CR)** — the baby has **learnt** to be pleased at the sound of its mother's voice.

There are Several **Principles** of Classical Conditioning

- **Generalisation** — when stimuli similar to the original CS (e.g. a bell with a different pitch) produce the CR (e.g. salivating).
- **Discrimination** — when stimuli similar to the original CS don't produce the CR. This can be achieved by withholding the UCS (e.g. food) when the similar stimulus is used.
- **Extinction** — when the CR (e.g. salivating) isn't produced as a result of the CS (e.g. bell). This happens when the CS is repeatedly presented without the UCS (e.g. food) following it.
- **Spontaneous recovery** — when a previously extinct CR is produced in response to the CS. This happens when the CS is presented again after a period of time during which it's not been used.
- **Higher order conditioning** — when a new CS (e.g. a light) produces the CR because the animal associates it with the original CS. This can be achieved by consistently presenting the new CS before the original CS.

Behaviourism — Classical and Operant Conditioning

2) Operant Conditioning

Classical conditioning only applies to reflexive responses. **B.F. Skinner** studied how animals can learn from the **consequences of their actions**. Consequences can be classified as follows:

1) **Positive reinforcement**. This is when something 'desirable' is obtained in response to doing something. E.g. giving a chocolate bar to a well-behaved child to encourage future good behaviour.

2) **Negative reinforcement**. This is when something 'undesirable' (the negative reinforcer) is removed when something happens. E.g. being told by the teacher that you'll have no extra homework if you pass your test.

	Positive stimulus added	**Negative** stimulus added
Behaviour is encouraged by...	*positive reinforcement*	*negative reinforcement*

	Skinner (1938) — Rats showing operant conditioning
Method:	Skinner created a 'Skinner box', in which he placed one rat at a time. Each Skinner box contained a variety of different stimuli — a speaker, lights, a floor which gave an electric shock and a food dispenser which released food when a lever was pressed. A hungry rat was placed in the Skinner box. The time taken for the rats to learn that pressing the lever would release food was recorded.
Results:	Initially, the rat would run around the cage until it accidentally pressed the lever and it was rewarded with food. The more the rat was put back into the box, the quicker they got at learning where the lever was.
Conclusion:	Rats can learn behaviour through operant conditioning. A behaviour such as pressing a lever can be positively reinforced by receiving food.
Evaluation:	Skinner's experiment has been hugely influential in promoting the idea of behavioural psychology. However, his experiment did use animals, which means the results might not be generalisable to humans. His sample size was also small, reducing the reliability of his results.

Skinner carried out other variations of this study to test **negative reinforcement**.
E.g. he showed that a rat could learn to **prevent** an electric shock by pressing the lever when a light came on.

Conditioning Has **Strengths** and **Weaknesses**

- There's a lot of evidence to show that animals and humans can learn by conditioning, but conditioning can't explain all human behaviour. We also learn by observation, as shown by **social learning theory** (p.58-59).

- Most research into conditioning has involved animals. This means generalising to humans is difficult. More research into human conditioning would be useful.

- Different species have different capacities for learning by conditioning. Some may also learn by simple observation, with no reinforcement involved.

- Genetics seem to influence and limit what different species can learn by conditioning.

- Lots of experiments into learning in animals may be seen as unethical. Nowadays, researchers have to conduct a cost-benefit analysis of whether it's acceptable to use animals, and they must ensure that any animals are well looked after.

Behaviourism — Classical and Operant Conditioning

Behaviourist Research Has Provided Great **Insights** into Learning

1) Along with Pavlov's research into classical conditioning using dogs, and Skinner's research into operant conditioning using rats, research has been carried out using humans.

2) One experiment which involved humans was Watson and Rayner's experiment on '**Little Albert**':

Watson and Rayner (1920) — Little Albert learned fear

Method:	The participant was an 11-month-old boy called 'Little Albert'. He showed no fear of white fluffy objects such as rats or rabbits. The researchers tried to create a conditioned response to these objects. A white rat was placed in front of Little Albert. As he reached out for it, a metal bar was struck loudly behind his head. This was repeated twice at first, then 5 more times a week later.
Results:	When Little Albert was shown a rat, he would start to cry. This also extended to other white fluffy objects, such as a white Santa Claus beard.
Conclusion:	A fear response to white fluffy objects had been **conditioned** in Little Albert, showing that abnormal behaviour can be **learned**.
Evaluation:	The experiment was very **unethical** — such an experiment couldn't be repeated today. **Not everyone** goes on to develop a fear or phobia after a negative situation, so learning theory can't be the full story. It was a laboratory study, so it **lacks ecological validity** as the situation was artificial. However, the results **support** Pavlov's idea of classical conditioning.

Behaviourists are often criticised for focusing research on animals.
Plenty of research has been done on humans, which has shown things like:

- our **genes** influence our behaviour
- we can **learn in ways other than conditioning**
- **mental, cognitive processes are relevant** to understanding behaviour.

Ionie didn't like Santa's beard either, but it was worth it for a present.

Warm-Up Questions

Q1 What are the three main assumptions of behaviourism?

Q2 Describe the principles of classical conditioning.

Q3 What is 'positive reinforcement'?

Q4 Give an example of negative reinforcement.

Q5 What device did Skinner use to illustrate operant conditioning?

Q6 Outline Watson and Rayner's (1920) method.

PRACTICE QUESTIONS

Exam Questions

Q1 Describe Pavlov's influence on behavioural psychology. [4 marks]

Q2 Read the item, then answer the question that follows.

> After crying, an infant's dirty nappy is removed.
> The child is likely to cry the next time the nappy needs changing.

What type of reinforcement is shown by the infant? [1 mark]

Learn like a dolphin — lob live fish in the air and catch them in your mouth...

The behaviourists assume that humans and animals learn the same way. Still, I've never met an animal that was scared of Santa. Apart from reindeer, of course — they can't stand him. But that's because there's no pension scheme — once those reindeer can't fly any more, that's it. He sends 'em off to the glue factory and uses their antlers as shoehorns.

Behaviourism — Social Learning Theory

Behavioural psychologists came up with another idea on top of classical and operant conditioning. It's called the social learning theory — and there's a juicy study for you to read all about here. Happy days.

Social Learning Theory (SLT) Expands on Behaviourist Theories

A guy called **Bandura** developed SLT in the 1960s. It agrees with the idea that people can learn by conditioning but also claims that they learn a lot from role models. Some mediational (cognitive) processes are also involved between the stimulus and the response.

People must focus their **attention** on the role model, **perceive** what they do and **remember** it in order to learn how to do it too.

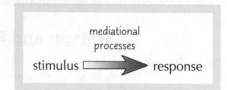

Behaviour is Learnt Through Different **Processes**...

SLT proposes that several processes take place for learning to happen:

Modelling involves observing and imitating another person (the model). It also requires identification with the model — where certain attractive qualities and characteristics are picked up on. If you identify with the model, you can copy and learn from their behaviour. The model will often be someone who is significant to the observer (e.g. a parent, a celebrity, a peer).

Behaviour can also be learnt through:

- **Reinforcement** — **Positive** and **negative** reinforcement makes the behaviour more likely to happen again in the future.

- **Vicarious Reinforcement** — Seeing others being rewarded for a behaviour influences someone in whether they choose to imitate the behaviour.

... and **Mediated** Through Cognitive Processes

For effective learning, **mediational processes** need to happen. These are cognitive processes:

1) Attention

To learn a behaviour from others, you have to pay **attention**. Once you notice your role model, you have to give your full attention and **attend** to their behaviour.

2) Retention

Not only do you need to pay attention at the time, but you need to remember what you observed to be able to model it.

'Retention' might also be called 'encoding'.

3) Reproduction

You then judge whether you have the **ability** to reproduce the behaviour. If you think you **can** reproduce the behaviour, you're far more likely to do it. (E.g. if you think you can't juggle with fire, you're unlikely to copy a fire-juggler.)

Jessie modelled her behaviour on 'girl stuck in box'.

4) Motivation

Finally, you **evaluate** the direct or indirect results of imitating the behaviour. If the behaviour results in a good reward, you're more likely to imitate it.

Social Learning Theory is Reductionist

SLT is a **reductionist theory** — it explains things through very basic cause-and-effect mechanisms. For example, it explains all behaviour as a result of **learning** from others, and **ignores** any biological explanations.

Behaviourism — Social Learning Theory

Bandura Studied Imitation of Aggression

Bandura et al (1961) showed successfully how children **imitate** and can be **influenced by** adult role models.

Bandura et al (1961) — Imitation of aggressive models

Method: 36 girls and 36 boys with a mean age of 52 months took part in the study. The study had a **matched participants design** (children were matched on ratings of aggressive behaviour shown at their nursery school) and had **three conditions**. In the first condition, children observed **aggressive adult models** playing with a Bobo doll (an inflatable figure with a weight in the bottom) — e.g. hitting it with a mallet. In the second, children observed **non-aggressive models** playing with other toys and ignoring the Bobo doll. The third condition was a **control condition** in which children had no exposure to the models. The children's behaviour was then observed for 20 minutes in a room containing aggressive toys (e.g. a Bobo doll, a mallet) and non-aggressive toys (e.g. a tea set, crayons).

Results: Children exposed to aggressive models imitated a lot of their aggressive behaviour. Children in the non-aggressive and control conditions showed barely any aggressive behaviour. Aggressive behaviour was slightly higher in the control condition than in the non-aggressive condition.

Conclusion: Aggressive behaviour is learned through **imitation** of others behaving aggressively.

Evaluation: This study provides evidence for **social learning theory**. There was **strict control** of the variables, meaning that the results are likely to be **reliable** and the study can be **replicated**. However, it has **low ecological validity** because the participants weren't in a natural situation. It's also difficult to **generalise** the results because a limited sample was studied — the children were all from the same school. The study encouraged aggression in children — this could be an **ethical problem**.

Some Comments on SLT, Behaviourism and Bandura's Research:

1) Bandura's study shows that reinforcement is not needed for learning. We can learn just by observing. However, the reinforcement the model is seen to receive may have an effect — for example, if you see a model punished for an action, you're unlikely to copy it.

2) Bobo dolls are designed for 'aggressive' play — you're supposed to hit them. As well as this, the children were shown how to play with the doll, so this study might actually be a test of obedience (see page 7) rather than observational learning.

3) Behaviourism and SLT emphasise learning as the cause of behaviour and so are on the 'nurture' side of the nature-nurture debate (see page 142). This has implications for society. For example, children may imitate aggression from media role models. However, potential genetic influences are not taken into account.

4) It can often be difficult to conclude that observational learning has taken place. Sometimes, behaviours can be repeated a long time after they've been observed.

Warm-Up Questions

Q1 What is 'vicarious reinforcement'?
Q2 What did Bandura et al (1961) find in their study of imitation?
Q3 Give one limitation of social learning theory.

PRACTICE QUESTIONS

Exam Questions

Q1 Which of these is a not a mediational process proposed by social learning theory?
  A reproduction **B** reductionism **C** retention **D** motivation   [1 mark]

Q2 Briefly describe and evaluate research into social learning theory.   [8 marks]

My dad's just given me a really big slice of chocolate cake for revising...

Hopefully this'll act as some form of vicarious reinforcement to kick-start you into revising these pages. Learning Psychology is all about engaging your mediational processes. You just have to remember what they are first.

The Cognitive Approach

Welcome to the cognitive approach. A fine approach if ever I saw one. A real rollicking riotous romp of an approach — full of mystery and intrigue, with a few exciting twists and turns along the way. So get comfy on your bedroom floor, line up your miniature highlighters, and saddle up the revision pony, cos the next stop's Examsville, Arizona...

Cognitive Psychology Looks at How We **Interpret** the World

1) Whilst the behavioural approach studies observable behaviour, the cognitive approach does the opposite — it looks at the internal workings of the mind and explains behaviour through **cognitive processes**. It is all about **how** we think.

2) Cognitive psychologists try to **explain behaviour** by looking at our **perception**, **language**, **attention** and **memory**.

3) Cognitive psychology uses experimental procedures and methods to test behaviour scientifically.

4) The mind can be compared to a computer, so it is a **reductionist** approach — see p.141.

Cognitive psychology is sometimes called the information processing approach.

5) **Computers** and computer models are often used to explain how we think and behave. Humans are treated as **information processors** (computers) and behaviour is explained in terms of **information processing** (how computers deal with information).

6) **Computer** and **theoretical models** are used to **explain** and make **inferences** about the mental processes that lead to particular behaviours, since they can't be observed directly.

7) For example, cognitive psychologists have deduced that memory can be divided into short-term memory and long-term memory based on studies that show primacy and recency effects (see page 17). These experiments have lead to **theoretical models**, such as the multi-store model of memory (page 17).

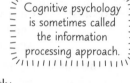

You've been experiencing downtime due to access problems with your communication software. I'll need to reboot you.

Cognitive Psychologists Use **Three** Main Research Methods

Here's a snappy little phrase to remind yourself with before you read on: '**ecological validity**' — it's the measure of how much the result of an experiment reflects what would happen in **natural settings**. If a result has **low** ecological validity, it might work fine in the lab. But try to use it to explain real-life behaviour, and you'll find yourself up the creek without a paddle. And no one wants that.

1 — Laboratory Experiments

A lot of research in cognitive psychology happens in laboratories. This is very scientific and reliable as it is possible to have great control over variables in a lab. However, often this type of research doesn't tell us much about the real world — it has low ecological validity.

2 — Field Experiments

Field experiments take place in a natural situation (e.g. studies of memory or attention in a school environment), so they have more ecological validity, but there's less control of most of the variables.

3 — Natural Experiments

Natural experiments involve making observations of a naturally occurring situation. The experimenter has little control of the variables, and participants can't be randomly assigned to conditions. Natural experiments have high ecological validity, but they're not massively reliable, as uncontrolled (or confounding) variables can affect the results.

The **Principles** of the Cognitive Approach

Cognitive psychologists have outlined several general principles:

- **Our mental systems have a limited capacity** — The amount of information that can be processed will be influenced by how demanding the task is and how much other information is being processed.

- **A control mechanism oversees all mental processes** — This will require more processing power for new tasks, leaving less available for everything else.

- **There is a two-way flow of information** — We take in information from the world, process it, and react to it. We also use our knowledge and experiences to understand the world.

The Cognitive Approach

Cognitive Psychology Developed as the **Computer Age Developed**

As computers developed in the 1950s and 1960s, the analogy between the human brain and a computer was formed.

1) People began to see similarities in how computers and humans make sense of information.

2) Computer terms are often used in cognitive psychology.
   Cognitive psychologists use **computer models** to represent particular features of the human mind.

> *As well as computer models, theoretical models are used to explain and predict behaviour.*

- The brain is described as a **processor** (the thing that makes things happen) — it has data **input** into it, and **output** from it.
- Some parts of the brain form **networks** (interconnected parts).
- Some parts can work **sequentially** (info travels along just one path). This means one process must finish before another starts. This occurs in more demanding, or unknown tasks.
- And they can work in **parallel** too (info travels to and fro along lots of paths at the same time). This is more likely to happen for tasks which are familiar.

3) The computer and human systems follow the **same** route — data input, processing and data output.
   For example:

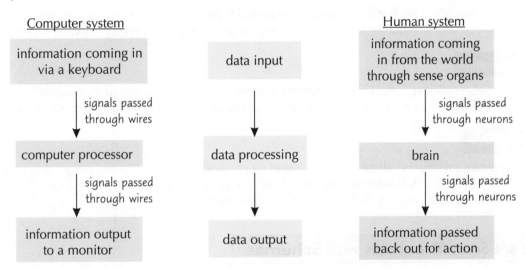

Be careful though... there are **differences** between humans and computers that make computer models less useful:

- Humans are often influenced by **emotional** and **motivational** factors — something computers aren't affected by.
- Humans have an **unlimited** but **unreliable** memory, whereas computers have a limited but reliable memory.
- Humans also have **free will** (the ability to choose between decisions) which computers don't.

Warm-Up Questions

Q1 Outline three research methods that cognitive psychologists might use.

Q2 Outline the principles of the cognitive approach.

PRACTICE QUESTIONS

Exam Question

Q1 Discuss the use of computer and theoretical models to explain mental processes. [8 marks]

Overloaded with information? Processor running slowly? Time to reboot...

It's a big ol' technical world out there, so it kind of makes sense that cognitive psychologists compare our brains to a computer. But just be wary of ignoring all our emotional stuff. If a computer started to cry, it'd electrocute itself...

The Cognitive Approach

More on the cognitive approach? It really is your lucky day...

A **Schema** Helps You **Organise** All the Information You Know

A **schema** contains all the information you know about an object, action or concept — e.g. the schema of a human face contains the information that a face has two eyes, a mouth and a nose, and the schema of riding a bike contains all the movements you'd need to make. Schemas help you to **organise** and **interpret** information and experiences.

- When information is **consistent** with a schema, it is **assimilated** into the schema. For example, a child's schema for an apple may be an edible, green, hard sphere. Everytime the child sees a green apple, the experience is assimilated and the schema is strengthened.
- When information is **inconsistent** with a schema, **accommodation** occurs and the schema has to **change** in order to **resolve** the problem. So if a child sees a red apple, their apple schema has to **accommodate** this new information — it becomes an edible, hard sphere that is either green or red.

There are lots of different **types** of schema:

Role Schemas

These are ideas about the behaviour which is expected from someone in a certain role, setting or situation. E.g. your schema for a doctor might be someone who is intelligent, respectable, sensible, etc.

Event Schemas

These are also called scripts. They contain information about what happens in a situation. E.g. when you go to a restaurant you know you'll usually need to read a menu and place an order.

Self Schemas

These contain information about ourselves based on physical characteristics and personality, as well as beliefs and values. Self schemas can affect how you act — e.g. if your self-schema says that you are health-conscious, you are likely to eat well and exercise regularly.

There are Some **Problems** with **Schemas**

Sometimes schemas can **stop** people from **learning** new information.

For example, **prejudice** and **stereotypes** can be an **outcome** of schemas. A schema which holds expectations or beliefs about a certain subgroup of people may bias the way we process incoming information. This means we may be more likely to **pay attention** to information we can **easily assimilate**, and ignore information that would involve changing our schemas to **accommodate**.

Bartlett Investigated **Schemas**

Bartlett (1932) was one of the first psychologists to test and illustrate the idea of schemas.

Bartlett (1932) — The War of the Ghosts

Method:	English participants were asked to read a Native American folk tale, called 'The War of the Ghosts'. It was an **unfamiliar** story, full of strange and unusual names, ideas and objects. It also had a different structure to your average English story. The participants were asked to **recall** the story after different lengths of time.
Results:	All of the participants changed the story to fit their own schemas. The details in the story became more English, the story started to contain elements of English culture, and details and emotions were added. As the length of time between hearing and recalling the story increased, the amount of information remembered became a lot less.
Conclusion:	People use their own schemas to help interpret and remember the world around them.
Evaluation:	This study was conducted in a laboratory, so it lacks **ecological validity**. But it was highly influential at the time as it paved the way for further cognitive research.

The Cognitive Approach

The Emergence of **Cognitive Neuroscience**

Hari was super excited to hear about developments in cognitive neuroscience.

1) Although the cognitive approach started in the 1950s and 1960s, it wasn't until the 1970s that the influence of neuroscience really took hold. With modern brain imaging techniques and procedures, **cognitive neuroscience** started to emerge.

2) Cognitive neuroscience is an approach in psychology which **maps** human **behaviour** to **brain function**. Brain-imaging techniques allow psychologists to discover when and where things happen in the brain in relation to people's behaviour at the time.

Cognitive Neuroscience Uses Lots of **Different** Methods

Cognitive neuroscientists use a variety of methods to study cognition. They include:

- **lesion studies** — looking at people with brain damage to see how behaviour is affected (see pages 66-67).
- **electrophysiology** — using electric and magnetic fields to measure brain activity and brain waves (see page 66).
- **neuroimaging** — pinpointing areas of the brain which are active when a task is performed. For example, PET scans (p.66) have been used to show the brain areas that are most active during memory tasks.

The Cognitive Approach Has **Strengths** and **Weaknesses**

Strengths

- It considers mental processes which are often overlooked in the other approaches.
- It has had a big influence on the development of therapies, e.g. cognitive behaviour therapy (page 47).

Weaknesses

- Research is often carried out in artificial situations (laboratories, using computer models) and the role of emotion and influence from other people is often ignored. For these reasons some argue that the results aren't valid in the real world.
- Cognitive psychology fails to take individual differences into account by assuming that all of us process stuff in exactly the same way.

Warm-Up Questions

Q1 What is a 'schema'?

Q2 Describe two types of schema.

Q3 Give one research method used in cognitive neuroscience.

Exam Questions

Q1 What is cognitive neuroscience? Illustrate your answer with an example. [4 marks]

Q2 Read the item and then answer the question that follows.

> Jo took her daughter to the zoo. When her daughter saw the zebras, she pointed and said "horse".

Use schemas to explain how Jo's daughter made this mistake. [2 marks]

The next thing you'll know, they'll be reading minds...

Cognitive neuroscience is making a big impact in the world of psychology. So be careful — there'll soon be an app on your phone which will know what you're thinking. But when that happens, remember one thing. You saw it here first. CGP — leading the way in cognitive neuroscience and technology. Sort of.

The Biological Approach — The Role of Genetics

The biological approach is all about looking at how genes, neurotransmitters and other squidgy bits cause behaviour. It's kind of a bit like Biology at school, except you won't have to dissect anything...

There are Three Basic Assumptions of the Biological Approach

1) Human behaviour can be explained by looking at biological stuff such as **hormones**, **genetics**, **evolution** and the **nervous system**.

2) In theory, if we can explain all behaviour using **biological causes**, unwanted behaviour could be **modified** or **removed** using **biological treatments** such as medication for mental illness.

3) Experimental research conducted using **animals** can inform us about human behaviour and biological influences, because we share a lot of biological similarities.

Genetics is Used to Explain Behaviour

First of all, here's a speedy recap of the basic genetic knowledge that will be handy to know:

1) At conception, the egg and sperm join up to give a total of **46 chromosomes**.
2) Each chromosome is made up of a coil of **DNA**, which in turn is made up of loads and loads of **genes**.
3) The genes contain the information that make us **unique** in appearance (e.g. hair, skin and eye colour).
4) However, genes are also relevant in psychology, as they are important in the **development** of the **brain**, and therefore have a role in our **behaviour**.

> **Darwin's theory of evolution** suggests that over time, individuals who are better adapted to their environment through having better genes are more likely to survive to reproduce and pass on their useful genes. Those who are less well-adapted will be less likely to survive to reproduce and pass on their genes. Eventually, their less useful genes will be eliminated from the gene pool for that species. Through this process of natural selection, early humans became better adapted to their environments. For instance, behaviours such as phobias and aggression may have evolved because of the survival advantage they gave.

5) The **genotype** of a person is the genes they have. The **phenotype** of a person is the characteristics their genes produce — for example, hair colour, eye colour, etc.

Genetics Can Explain Psychological Traits

Faulty genes are known to cause some diseases that have psychological effects, e.g. Huntington's disease that leads to a deterioration of mental abilities.

Biological psychologists reckon that **genetics** can explain **"psychological traits"**. These are things like gender behaviour (things that men and women do differently), intelligence, personality and sexual orientation.

Declan was not happy to learn that 'genes' and 'jeans' were very different things.

They also study genetics to see which genes make some people **more likely** to develop things like **mental illness** or **addictions**.

Twin studies and adoption studies are useful for investigating these areas.

The Biological Approach — The Role of Genetics

Research Has Looked at the **Genetic Basis** of **Mental Illnesses**

Schizophrenia is a mental illness which has been studied a lot in psychology.
Twin studies and **adoption studies** have highlighted the possible role of genetics.

There's loads more about schizophrenia on pages 176-185.

Twin Studies

Identical twins share **100%** of their genes. So in theory, if schizophrenia has a purely **genetic basis** and if one twin suffers from schizophrenia, then the other twin will too. **Non-identical twins** share **50%** of their genes, so the risk of both suffering should be lower.

Gottesman (1991) — A meta-analysis of twin studies

Method: Gottesman carried out a meta-analysis of approximately 40 twin studies.

Results: It was found that having an **identical twin** with schizophrenia gave you a **48%** chance of developing the condition. This reduced to **17%** in **non-identical twins**.

Conclusion: Schizophrenia has a strong **genetic basis**.

Evaluation: The meta-analysis was carried out on field studies, giving the research **high ecological validity**. Because identical twins share 100% of their genes, it might be expected that both twins would always suffer from the same conditions. The fact that both twins had developed schizophrenia in only about half of the cases means that **another factor** must also be involved. Identical twins tend to be treated more similarly than non-identical twins, and so the **family environment** might play a large role.

Adoption Studies

Adoption studies have also provided evidence for a **genetic basis** of schizophrenia.

Heston (1966) — An adoption study of schizophrenia

Method: 47 adopted children whose biological mothers had schizophrenia were studied. The control group consisted of 50 adopted children whose biological mothers didn't suffer from schizophrenia. The children were followed up as adults and were interviewed and given intelligence and personality tests.

Results: Of the experimental group, 5 of the 47 became schizophrenic, compared to 0 in the control group. Another 4 of the experimental group were classified as borderline schizophrenic by the raters.

Conclusion: The study supports the view that schizophrenia has a **genetic basis**.

Evaluation: Interview data can be unreliable and affected by **social desirability bias**. However, interviews are a good way of getting data in a **naturalistic way**. The adopted children whose mothers didn't suffer from any conditions might have not shown any symptoms of schizophrenia **yet** — it can't be completely ruled out.

Warm-Up Questions

Q1 Define 'genotype' and 'phenotype'.

Q2 Describe one study which supports the argument for the genetic basis of mental illness.

Exam Questions

Q1 Complete the following sentence:

The biological model assumes behaviour can be determined by

A genetics   **B** role models   **C** operant conditioning   **D** classical conditioning   [1 mark]

Q2 Discuss the role of genetics within the biological approach.   [8 marks]

Flares, skinny, straight leg, boyfriend fit... it's all about the genes...

Your genes help make you who you are. And not just someone with a keen fashion sense. Don't forget that there are lots of different types of jeans, for every different shape and size. So find the ones that suit you best.

The Biological Approach — Brain Structure

Biological psychologists also reckon that behaviour can be determined by brain structure. Nowadays they use scanning techniques to look at people's brains and try to link structures and activity to various behaviours.

At First it was **Trickier** to **Investigate Brain Structure** and **Function**

Before brain-scanning techniques were developed, psychologists relied on **case studies** of people who had experienced a **brain injury** or had **brain operations**. If the person had brain damage in a **specific area** and also a **change in behaviour**, the assumption could be made that the two were related.

> For example, in 1848 Phineas Gage had damage to part of his frontal lobe after an explosion at work resulted in an iron bar going straight through his head (ouch). After the accident he was less organised, and more impulsive, and experienced personality changes including increased aggression. This led to the belief that this area of the brain is responsible for these behaviours. However, this is a case study of only one person, and so isn't representative of the population, which leads to problems with generalising the results.

But psychologists can't just sit around waiting for people with brain injuries to turn up so they can study them. For one thing, studies like that aren't conducted in **controlled** circumstances, so they're less **scientific**. And **ethically** we can't **deliberately** inflict this type of brain injury on humans. **Non-human animals** have been used to study brain structure and behaviour, but the differences between non-human animal brains and human brains mean that the results may not be that useful when we apply them to **human behaviour** (and there are still **ethics** to be considered when animals are used in research). So ideally psychologists could do with another way of studying brain structure and behaviour — ah-ha, that leads us nicely on to **brain scans**...

Brain Scans Can Help Examine Patterns of Brain Activity and Anatomy

There are five basic techniques used:

1) **PET scans** (positron emission tomography — not what happens in the vets) show which parts of the brain are **active** during different tasks. By studying PET scans, we can link certain areas of the brain with particular **functions**. They also allow us to see where the brain is most active when we are **thinking** about certain things. They show average activity over a 60-second period, not moment by moment.

2) **CAT scans** detect **damaged** parts of the brain, tumours and blood clots. Brain **structure** is shown, not function.

3) **MRI scans** detect small tumours and provide **detailed** information about **structure**.

4) **Functional MRI scans** provide **structural** and **functional** information — see page 86 for more detail.

5) **SQUID magnetometry** produces accurate images of brain **activity** by measuring the magnetic fields generated when neurons are activated. However, outside sources of magnetism can affect measurements.

There's Evidence from **MRI** Scans to Show **Changes** in Brain Structure

Maguire et al (2000) — A study of taxi drivers' brains

Method:	In a **natural experiment**, MRI scans from 16 licensed male London taxi drivers were compared with a control group who had never driven taxis. All of the participants were in good general, neurological and psychiatric health, and had an average age of 44. All of the taxi drivers had been working for at least 18 months.
Results:	The average size of the right posterior hippocampus was **significantly larger** in the taxi driver group compared to the control group. Additionally, the increased size was relative to the length of time the taxi driver had been working — the **longer** they'd been working, the **larger** their right posterior hippocampus.
Conclusion:	The hippocampus is responsible for storing a spatial representation of the environment — it seems that the specific navigational demands on the taxi drivers have resulted in physical change.
Evaluation:	The findings of the study could be used to help those with brain injuries as it shows that the size of structures within the brain can be influenced through cognitive activity. This means **rehabilitation** could be tailored to the specific needs of individuals and their injuries. The study had a good level of **control** and could be **replicated**, which increases its **reliability**. The **sample size** is small though, and the results can only be **generalised** to male taxi drivers in London. Also, the results can't be generalised to **other areas** of the brain.

The Biological Approach — Brain Structure

Brain Structure Has Been Investigated in **Several Areas** of Psychology

1) **Aggression** — Bard and Mountcastle (1948) found that lesioning (i.e. damaging) areas of the brains of **cats** led to changes in levels of **aggression**. Their research suggests that the **hypothalamus** and **amygdala** are involved in aggression.

2) **Memory** — in a case study, Milner et al (1957) found that **HM** was unable to use his long-term memory effectively, suggesting that the **hippocampus** has an important role here (see page 17).

3) **Psychopathology** — Szeszko et al (1995) found differences in the **prefrontal cortex** when comparing people with and without **schizophrenia**, suggesting a relationship between them.

Neurochemistry Might Also Influence Behaviour

Neurochemistry is all about the **nervous system** and **neurotransmitters**.
The **biological approach** looks at the role they might play in explaining behaviour.

- Too much or too little of a particular neurotransmitter may produce psychological disorders, e.g. an increased level of dopamine is linked to schizophrenia. Drugs like cocaine, which increase dopamine levels, can lead to schizophrenia-like symptoms.
- Some biological psychologists investigate the impact neurotransmitters have on behaviour. You can read more about what they do on pages 76 and 79.

The Biological Approach Has **Strengths** and **Weaknesses**

Strengths:
1) The approach can provide **evidence** to support or disprove a theory — it's a very **scientific** approach.
2) If a biological cause can be found for mental health problems or for unwanted behaviour such as aggression, then **biological treatments** can be developed to help individuals.

Weaknesses:
1) The approach doesn't take into account the influence of people's **environment**, their **family**, **childhood experiences** or their **social situation**. Other approaches see these as being important factors in explaining behaviour.
2) Using a biological explanation for negative behaviour can lead to individuals or groups avoiding taking **personal** or **social responsibility** for their behaviour.

Warm-Up Questions

Q1 What research method did Maguire et al (2000) use?

Q2 Name one area of psychology which has been investigated by looking at brain structure.

Q3 Which brain structures did Bard and Mountcastle (1948) suggest are involved in aggression?

Exam Questions

Q1 Read the item and then answer the question that follows.

> Alicia suffered a stroke last year that caused some damage to part of her brain. She has since become more careless, irritable and confused.

Discuss how a biological psychologist might explain Alicia's behaviour. [2 marks]

Q2 Describe the influence of neurochemistry on behaviour. [4 marks]

Imagine what your brain will look like when it's full of all this goodness...

There are lots of approaches in psychology, which is why there's a whole section on them. And I'm afraid you're not done yet. But keep at it — it's an important section as it makes all the other bits of psychology make much more sense.

The Psychodynamic Approach

Psychodynamic theories like to explain behaviour by talking about the unconscious — it all gets a bit weird here...

Freud Developed The **Psychodynamic** Approach

'**Psycho**' refers to the mind and '**dynamic**' refers to change or activity.
So, this approach emphasises the **active nature** of mental processes and their role in **shaping personality** and **behaviour**. This approach was developed by **Sigmund Freud** (1856-1939), in the 18th/early 19th centuries.
It assumes that:

1) Human behaviour has **unconscious causes** that we're not aware of.
2) From birth, humans have a need to fulfil basic biological **motivations** — for food, sleep, warmth etc.
3) **Childhood experiences** are a really important influence on the development of adult personality and psychological disorders.

Bert's main motivation
in life was to sleep. Lots.

Freud Said There Are Three **Levels of Consciousness**

Freud was interested in '**hysteria**', a disorder involving physical symptoms such as headaches, paralysis and blindness, but with no apparent physical cause. As his patients couldn't give any **conscious** reasons, Freud concluded they had an **unconscious** mind and that's where the cause of the hysteria was. He identified three levels of consciousness:

1) **Conscious**. This is what we are **aware** of at any given time, e.g. what we are seeing, hearing, smelling or thinking.

2) **Preconscious**. This is made up of **memories** that we can recall when we want to, e.g. we can recall our address, phone number, childhood memories or what we did at the weekend.

3) **Unconscious**. This is made up of memories, desires and fears which cause us extreme anxiety and have therefore been '**repressed**' or forced out of conscious awareness. However, the unconscious still influences behaviour. For example, it causes 'Freudian slips' and influences the content of our dreams. This part of our mind can be accessed with the help of a **psychoanalyst**, using the methods that Freud developed.

Freudian slips are slips of the tongue believed to reveal a person's secret thoughts — e.g. calling your boyfriend/girlfriend by your ex's name.

Freud Said There Are **Three Parts** of the **Personality**

Freud claimed that the three main parts of the personality are the **id**, the **ego** and the **superego**, and these represent different levels of consciousness.

1) The id is the basic animal part of the personality that contains our innate, aggressive and sexual instincts. It wants to be satisfied by whatever means possible, and obeys the 'pleasure principle'. It accounts for unreasonable behaviour and appears at birth.

2) The ego exists in both the conscious and unconscious parts of the mind and acts as a rational part known as the 'reality principle'. It develops within the first three years after birth and balances the id and the superego to keep our behaviour in line.

3) The superego is in both the conscious and unconscious parts of the mind. This is the part of the mind that takes our morals into consideration and is involved in making us feel guilty. It develops around four to five years of age. It includes ideas about how to behave that we adopt from our parents.

The ego and the superego develop as the child goes through **five stages** of **psychosexual development** — the **oral, anal, phallic, latent,** and **genital** stages (more on this on page 70). Is anyone starting to think Freud was a bit nuts...?

The Psychodynamic Approach

Conflicts Can Develop Between the Parts of the Personality

1) So, as you know, the id, ego and superego represent different levels of **consciousness** and govern the way we **think** and **act**.

2) A way to see the relationships between these three aspects of the personality is by thinking of an **iceberg**. The **tip** of the iceberg is the **conscious** part of the mind made up of part of the ego and part of the superego. But the majority of personality comes from the **unconscious** mind, below the surface. It's made up of the id, a little of the ego and the rest of the superego.

3) Freud believed that these three different parts of consciousness can be in **conflict**. For example, there can be a conflict between the id and the superego because the id wants **instant satisfaction**, whilst the superego tries to impose **morals**.

4) These conflicts can lead to **anxiety**. It's then the ego's job to mediate between the id and the superego to **reduce** this anxiety.

5) It does this using one of several **unconscious** defence mechanisms:

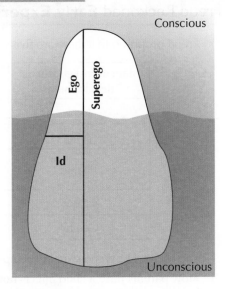

Repression

Repression involves the ego stopping **unwanted** and possibly **painful thoughts** from becoming **conscious**. For example, someone who experienced a **traumatic incident**, such as being mugged, may not recall it later. This is because they have **repressed** the memory.

Denial

Denial is where a threatening event or an unwanted reality is simply **ignored** and **blocked** from conscious awareness. For example, a drug addict might deny that they have a problem, or someone suffering from a bereavement might deny that their loved one has died.

Displacement

Displacement happens when a **negative impulse** is **redirected** onto something else. This could be another person or an object. For example, if your boss has made you angry at work, you might redirect your anger towards something else by kicking a door at home.

Warm-Up Questions

Q1 Who developed the psychodynamic approach?

Q2 What are the three parts of the personality?

Q3 Give the three levels of consciousness outlined by Freud.

Q4 Which part of the personality obeys the pleasure principle?

Q5 What is displacement?

Exam Questions

Q1 Which one of these is **not** a defence mechanism?
   A denial   B repression   C conflict   D displacement   [1 mark]

Q2 Outline the structure of personality as explained by the psychodynamic approach.   [6 marks]

I won't really have to go and get a filling at the dentist...

I'm in denial, you say...? Oh well. Must be a conflict of the different parts of my personality. Or something. Anyway, enough about me. As you can see from these two pages, Freud had some funny old ideas, and as you'll see over the page, his methodology wasn't the most reliable... When you're ready, take a deep breath, and plough on.

The Psychodynamic Approach

If the id, the ego and superego weren't baffling enough, just wait until you read about Freud's psychosexual stages.

Freud Reckoned **Early Experiences** Influence Development

1) Freud proposed that there are **five** stages of development:

Stage of psychosexual development	Age	Characteristics
Oral	0 – 18 months	sucking behaviour
Anal	18 months – 3.5 years	keeping or discarding faeces
Phallic	3.5 – 6 years	genital fixation — Oedipus and Electra complex (see page 162)
Latent	6 years – puberty	repressed sexual urges
Genital	puberty – adult	awakened sexual urges

2) Each stage of psychosexual development focuses on **obtaining pleasure** through a certain part of the body.

3) How parents raise a child affects **how much** pleasure is obtained through that stage (e.g. how strict they are when potty training, and what type of role models they are).

4) If a child doesn't receive enough **pleasure**, or they receive too much, during a stage of development, they will become '**fixated**' at that stage.

> For example, during the oral stage, a conflict could occur when being weaned off breast feeding. This could lead to a fixation in later life, characterised by traits such as nail biting, smoking or abnormal eating behaviours.

5) This experience is all **repressed into the unconscious**, but influences adult personality. Severe fixation could lead to a psychological **disorder**.

Freud Carried Out **Case Studies**

As part of **psychoanalysis**, Freud did **case studies** on his patients using several **methods** to reveal the **conflicts**, **fears** and **desires** buried in their unconscious mind. These problems could then be faced, allowing the patient to understand and resolve them.

Freud (1909) — The case study of Little Hans

Method: Freud carried out a **case study** of a child called Hans who had a phobia of horses. Hans was observed by his father, who made notes of Hans's dreams and stuff he said, and passed them on to Freud for analysis.

Results: Hans was afraid of horses because he thought they might bite him or fall on him. During the study he developed an interest in his 'widdler' (penis). His mum had told him not to play with it or she'd cut it off. Hans told his dad about a dream where he was married to his mum and his dad was now his grandfather.

Conclusion: Freud's interpretation was that Hans had reached the **phallic stage** of development and showed evidence of the '**Oedipus complex**' — he wanted to have an exclusive relationship with his mother and was jealous of his father. Hans had sexual feelings for his mother, shown partly by his dream of marrying her. The horse symbolised Hans's father because, to him, they both had big penises. His fear of horses is an example of **displacement** (page 69) — a **defence mechanism** that protected him from his real fear of his father. Hans suffered from **castration anxiety**. He was afraid that he would be castrated by his father if he found out about his feelings for his mother. This was symbolised by Hans's fear that a horse would bite him.

Evaluation: This was a **case study**, meaning that it provided lots of **detailed data** about one subject, but it does mean the results can't be **generalised**. The findings provided evidence to support Freud's theories. However, the results were based entirely on observation and interpretation. This means a cause and effect relationship **can't** be established. There could be **other explanations** — for example, Hans's anxiety may have come from his mother threatening to cut his penis off. Also, before the study Hans had been frightened by a horse falling down in the street, which could explain his fear of them. Freud analysed information from Hans's father, so the results could be **biased**.

The Psychodynamic Approach

The **Psychodynamic Approach** Has **Strengths** and **Weaknesses**

Like every approach in psychology, the psychodynamic approach has some strengths and weaknesses.
A lot of its **weaknesses** are related to the **research methods** used by Freud.

Strengths

1) The psychodynamic approach was the first theory to focus on **psychological causes** of disorders. Before this, the focus had been on **physical causes** or things like possession by **evil spirits**.

2) It was also one of the first approaches to suggest that mental health disorders may be linked to **unresolved conflicts** related to **biological needs**.

3) It offers methods of **therapy** (such as psychoanalysis) which may also uncover unconscious conflicts. Patients can then **understand** the causes of their problems and so **resolve** them and release their anxieties.

4) Freud's theory places emphasis on how experiences in early childhood can affect **later development**. This has formed the basis for lots of other important theories.

So... hearing voices. Ever get pushed out of the sand pit at school...?

Weaknesses

1) Freud's claims are based on his subjective interpretations of his patients' dreams, etc. Therefore they're often **unreliable** and **open to bias**.

2) Freud's theories are related to the unconscious mind, which can't be accessed. As such, his theories are **unfalsifiable** (i.e. they can't be proved wrong).

3) **Psychoanalysis** may take a long time and so be very expensive. The childhood conflicts that are 'uncovered' may be emotionally distressing and possibly inaccurate, depending on the reliability of the patient's memory, the techniques used to uncover them and the analyst's interpretations.

4) The focus is on the patient's **past**, rather than on the problems that they are **currently suffering**.

5) The approach is based on case studies of people in 'distress', so the findings can't be **generalised** to everyone else.

6) The unscientific research methods mean it's not possible to establish **cause and effect**.

Warm-Up Questions

Q1 Identify the five stages of psychosexual development.

Q2 Give an example of behaviour seen in the first psychosexual stage.

Q3 Outline the method and results of Freud's case study of Little Hans.

PRACTICE QUESTIONS

Exam Questions

Q1 Read the item below and then answer the question that follows.

> As an adult, Ke Jia bites his fingernails and smokes. He has put on lots of weight because he overeats.

Explain how Ke Jia's personality could be explained using the psychodynamic approach to psychology. [4 marks]

Q2 Describe and evaluate the psychodynamic approach to psychology. [16 marks]

I've always wondered if Little Hans had little hands...

Right, so you should now have a good idea of what the psychodynamic approach is all about. Make sure you remember to learn the strengths and weaknesses of the approach — examiners love asking you to evaluate things, and they might even be sneaky enough to get you to contrast the psychodynamic approach with another approach.

Humanistic Psychology

Last up — the humanistic approach to psychology. This approach was developed mainly by Carl Rogers and Abraham Maslow during the 1950s. It's an interesting one, and has influenced counselling today.

Humanistic Psychology Focuses on the Individual

1) Humanistic psychology focuses on the person as a **whole**.

2) Humanistic psychologists believe that all people are **inherently good** and that they're **driven** to achieve their **full potential**.

3) Unlike other types of psychology, it takes into account the **feelings** of the individual rather than just their observable behaviour. It treats every person as being **unique**.

4) Because of this, it has an **idiographic** approach rather than a **nomothetic** approach (see page 144) — it focuses on studying the **individual** rather than producing general rules which come from summarising a group of people.

5) Humanistic psychology assumes that a person's behaviour is caused by their **subjective feelings** and their thoughts about **themselves** (their **self-concept**), especially about how they can become **better people** and **learn** new things.

6) It disagrees with the strictly deterministic ideas of other approaches, which assume that human behaviour occurs in cause and effect relationships. Instead, it believes that human behaviour is determined by **free will**. People can **choose** how to behave — and their behaviour isn't caused by external or biological factors, or even the past.

Maslow Developed a Hierarchy of Needs

1) Humanistic psychology suggests that people are **motivated** to use their own free will to allow them to reach their **fullest potential**.

2) People can be motivated by lots of things — some needs are shared, and others are individual. For example, we're **all** motivated to find food and water, but we **differ** in whether we're motivated to do things like learn a new language or become a football star.

3) **Maslow (1943)** came up with a 'need theory' of motivation — he devised a **hierarchy** to show how human needs can be **categorised** and **prioritised**. This is known as **Maslow's hierarchy of needs**:

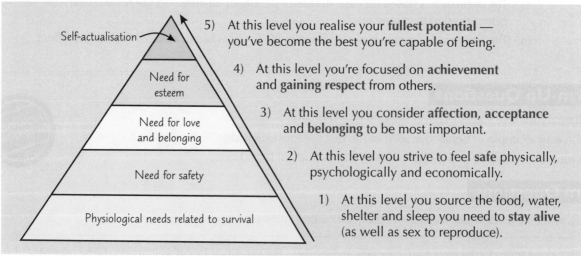

Self-actualisation
Need for esteem
Need for love and belonging
Need for safety
Physiological needs related to survival

5) At this level you realise your **fullest potential** — you've become the best you're capable of being.

4) At this level you're focused on **achievement** and **gaining respect** from others.

3) At this level you consider **affection, acceptance** and **belonging** to be most important.

2) At this level you strive to feel **safe** physically, psychologically and economically.

1) At this level you source the food, water, shelter and sleep you need to **stay alive** (as well as sex to reproduce).

4) In a nice change from psychologists trying to explain what has happened when something has gone wrong with someone, Maslow was more interested in explaining how people try to make themselves the best that they can be. He believed that we spend our lives trying to reach the **top** of the hierarchy, but that **hardly anyone** ever gets there. Sad. He also stated that until **lower level needs** are met, you **can't** attempt to satisfy higher level needs.

5) This seems to make sense in some cases of **real life** — e.g. who'd be interested in reading a psychology book if they were extremely hungry or in immediate physical danger...

6) However, humanistic psychology is quite a **westernised concept**, i.e. western culture encourages individual growth, rather than prioritising the needs of the social group.

7) Also, humanistic psychology assumes that everyone has the ability to self-actualise. But this could be **incorrect**, as self-actualisation may be limited to the most intelligent, well-educated people.

Humanistic Psychology

Self-Actualised People Have Certain Characteristics

According to Maslow, once people have **achieved** all their **previous needs** in the hierarchy, they are ready for **self-actualisation**. He came up with a list of **characteristics** that a self-actualised person might show. These include:

1) A strong sense of self-awareness.
2) A fully accepting view of themselves and others for who they are.
3) The ability to deal with uncertainty and the unknown.
4) A strong sense of creativity.

Maslow believed that self-actualisation could be measured using what he called '**peak experiences**'. These are times where the person feels **wonder** and **euphoria** towards the world around them. After these experiences, people often feel **inspired**, with a renewed sense of **self-awareness**.

There is Limited Evidence for Maslow's Hierarchy of Needs

There is **little evidence** or research to support the hierarchical nature of Maslow's hierarchy of needs. Maslow supported his hierarchy with biographical evidence of famous 'self-actualisers'. However, the hierarchy doesn't explain why some people with the characteristics of a self-actualised person **deprive** themselves of basic needs such as food and shelter (e.g. Mother Teresa).

Despite the limited evidence, a study by **Aronoff (1967)** tested whether the higher levels of the hierarchy are only satisfied once the lower levels have been satisfied and found support for this idea:

Aronoff (1967) — Job demands and the hierarchy of needs

Method:	Aronoff compared people in two jobs in the British West Indies — **fishermen** and **cane cutters**. Cane cutters got paid according to how much cane was cut by the whole group, even when they were off sick. So they had high **job security**, although wages were low. In contrast, fisherman worked alone, doing more challenging work. So they were **less secure** in their job, although they earned more overall. Both groups of people were assessed to see which level they were at on Maslow's hierarchy of needs.
Results:	More **cane cutters** were at the **lower levels** of the hierarchy, still trying to achieve safety and security than **fishermen**, many of whom had satisfied the lower levels of the hierarchy.
Conclusion:	Only those men who had satisfied lower levels of the pyramid would chose to become fishermen, allowing them to develop high self esteem. This suggests that people **cannot reach** the **higher levels** of Maslow's hierarchy until they have **satisfied** the **lower levels**.
Evaluation:	The study supports Maslow's hierarchy of needs theory, and it has **ecological validity** as it studied people in their natural environment. However, it only studied people from one **culture**, so the results can't be **generalised** to the wider population.

Warm-Up Questions

Q1 What does humanistic psychology assume that people are driven to do?
Q2 What is the lowest level in Maslow's hierarchy of needs?
Q3 What is self-actualisation?
Q4 What is meant by a 'peak experience'?

Exam Questions

Q1 Which is these is **not** associated with humanistic psychology?
   A free will   **B** psychosexual stages   **C** determinism   **D** self-actualisation   [1 mark]

Q2 Briefly outline and evaluate Maslow's hierarchy of needs.   [8 marks]

I need my duvet, a cup of tea, a book to read — and that'll do for now...

Humanistic psychologists believe that it's no good studying a load of people and then coming up with a 'one size fits all' rule. They acknowledge that everyone is unique, and that behaviour is more likely to be a result of individual feelings and thoughts. Maslow was one humanistic psychologist, and you'll find out all about Rogers over the page...

Humanistic Psychology

Rogers Also Talked About Self-Actualisation

1) Like Maslow, Rogers believed that all people try to achieve **self-actualisation**. He also claimed that all people are **inherently good** and that they're **motivated** to achieve their **fullest potential**.

2) However, Rogers didn't believe the route to self-actualisation was as **strict** as Maslow had described. Instead of working their way up a hierarchy of needs, Rogers thought that people move towards self-actualisation depending on their own **thoughts** about themselves and the way that they're **treated** by others.

3) From this, he believed that you'll develop in a **psychologically healthy way** if your path to self-actualisation is not blocked. Blockages (e.g. being raised in a difficult environment) can lead to **psychological problems**.

4) Rogers believed that everyone has a **need** to be regarded by others in a good light, and to be shown love, affection and respect. This is particularly important for children, who want to **seek approval** from their parents. They'll be more psychologically **happy** if they get this approval, or **unhappy** if they feel that their parents are **disappointed** or **displeased** with them.

Rogers Described Two Parts of the Self

1) Rogers outlined the differences between how someone **sees themselves** (their **self-concept**) and how they would **like to be** (their **ideal self**).

2) He suggested their self-concept is created and develops in a way which depends on whether they receive **unconditional positive regard** or whether **conditions of worth** are set for them.

Unconditional Positive Regard

- This is where the person gets affection and support no matter what their behaviour is like.
- We need unconditional positive regard to have a positive self-concept.

Conditions of Worth

- This is where approval and affection is given as a result of behaving in a certain way.
- Although this treatment can help someone learn to fit in with the rules of social life, Rogers believed that it could stop them from reaching self-actualisation. This is because the person may focus on keeping other people happy rather than developing their own personality.

3) If they have unconditional positive regard and then receive **love** and **acceptance** for their behaviour, they will experience **congruence** — and become a **fully-functioning person**.

4) However, if they are set conditions of worth then their **ideal self** becomes something different to the **self-concept**, and the person will experience **incongruence** (see below).

Rogers Developed His Ideas Into a Form of Therapy

1) Rogers believed that many people's psychological problems were caused by **incongruence**.

2) This is where there is a **mismatch** between someone's **self-concept** and their **ideal self**. His therapy aimed to remove this incongruence by making it possible for the person to become their ideal self.

3) His therapy was known as **client-centred therapy**, also known as **person-centred therapy**.

4) As the name suggests, the therapy focuses on the **client** — they're **in charge** of what is talked about, and it's their responsibility to eventually **solve** their own problems.

5) The therapist's job is to try and make the client **aware** of their thoughts, actions and behaviours. They can do this by carefully **rephrasing** the client's sentences and **repeating** them back.

For example, a conversation might go like this:
Client: I find my parents really annoying. They're always going on at me and won't let me do what I want.
Therapist: So, you're feeling quite frustrated. Your parents treat you like you're still a child and not an adult.

6) **Unconditional positive regard** (i.e. not judging), **genuineness** and **empathy** are really important in person-centred therapy. The therapist is **supportive** of the client no matter what they do or say, with the aim that the client will come to **value** themselves.

Humanistic Psychology

Rogers's Therapy Seems to **Work**

There's quite a bit of **evidence** that Rogers's person-centred therapy is effective.

> **For example...**
>
> **Gibbard and Hanley (2008)** studied the impact of person-centred therapy on a group of patients suffering from common mental health disorders such as anxiety and depression. They studied almost **700 people** over **five years**. A **questionnaire** was used to measure the extent of their condition **before and after** therapy. It was found that nearly **70%** of the participants showed a **significant improvement** in their mental health after taking part in person-centred therapy.

Humanistic Psychology has **Strengths** and **Weaknesses**

Strengths

1) Humanistic psychology is a very **positive** approach, which states that people are striving to be better.

2) **Free will** is a major part of humanistic psychology, which is less restrictive than more deterministic approaches (see page 140). Humanistic psychologists believe that a deterministic approach is no good for understanding the **complex nature** of human behaviour.

3) The approach treats people as **individuals** and takes the **whole person** into account, rather than reducing individual behaviours to cause and effect responses.

4) Research in this approach gathers **qualitative data** (see page 111) which is **rich in detail**. Rogers **recorded** many of his therapy sessions so they could be **analysed**, making it possible to observe the **successes** as a result of the therapy.

5) The **counselling techniques** which have come from the approach have been shown to be **effective**.

Weaknesses

1) The approach places **less emphasis** on factors such as the role of **genes**, etc. than the **biological** approach.

2) The humanistic approach **lacks objectivity** — it's largely based on feelings and **subjective** reports, and so it's hard to test in a scientific way. It also features things that are hard to **measure**, such as self-actualisation.

3) The approach is **idiographic**, which means it doesn't create generalised laws which can be applied to everyone, making it a **less scientific** approach.

o Maslow's hierarchy is v western + individualistin in other cultures — needs of group prioritised

Warm-Up Questions

o self actualisation only 4 intelligent + well educated?

Q1 What is meant by congruence?
Q2 What was Rogers' therapy called?
Q3 How has humanistic psychology influenced counselling?
Q4 Give one strength and one weakness of the humanistic approach.

PRACTICE QUESTIONS

Exam Questions

Q1 Outline the role that conditions of worth may play in achieving self-actualisation. [2 marks]

Q2 Discuss how humanistic psychology contributes to understanding and explaining psychological problems in people. [16 marks]

So, you're feeling unhappy about having to do this revision...

Has that helped? Has it made you more aware of yourself? Hmm, I'll try again. "So, you're feeling unhappy about having to do this revision, and you just can't believe the teachers are being this mean to you. What rotters." Any better? Well it's tough — you're just going to have to get on with it. I'm not sure I'd make a very good therapist...

Section Six — Biopsychology

The Nervous System

*Biopsychology is really quite exciting. Biology **and** psychology. I know, right — what more could you want...*

Biopsychology Uses Biology to Explain Behaviour

Biopsychology is all about how **biology** influences **behaviour**. Biopsychologists study things like the **nervous system**, **neurotransmitters** and **hormones** — and that means you should too. Sorry about that. First up, the **nervous system**...

The Nervous System Has Two Key Parts

1) Your nervous system is what allows you to **respond** to changes in your **environment** (stimuli). It also allows you to **coordinate** your actions.

2) **Receptors** detect stimuli and **effectors** bring about a response to a stimulus. **Effectors** include **muscle cells** and cells found in **glands**, e.g. the pancreas.

3) Receptors **communicate** with effectors via the **nervous** or **endocrine systems** (see p.80-81), or sometimes both.

4) The nervous and endocrine systems **coordinate** the response.

5) The nervous system has two parts, the **central nervous system (CNS)** and the **peripheral nervous system (PNS)**:

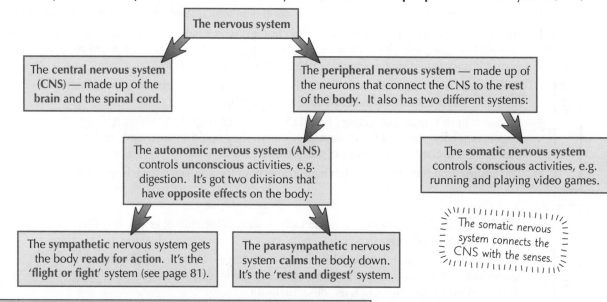

The nervous system

The **central nervous system (CNS)** — made up of the **brain** and the **spinal cord**.

The **peripheral nervous system** — made up of the neurons that connect the CNS to the **rest** of the **body**. It also has two different systems:

The **autonomic nervous system (ANS)** controls **unconscious** activities, e.g. digestion. It's got two divisions that have **opposite effects** on the body:

The **somatic nervous system** controls **conscious** activities, e.g. running and playing video games.

The **sympathetic** nervous system gets the body **ready for action**. It's the '**flight or fight**' system (see page 81).

The **parasympathetic** nervous system **calms the body down**. It's the '**rest and digest**' system.

The somatic nervous system connects the CNS with the senses.

The Cells of the Nervous System are Called Neurons

1) Neurons transmit information as **electrical impulses** around the body.

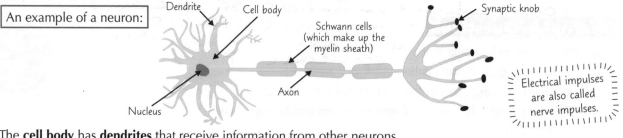

An example of a neuron:

Dendrite
Cell body
Schwann cells (which make up the myelin sheath)
Synaptic knob
Axon
Nucleus

Electrical impulses are also called nerve impulses.

2) The **cell body** has **dendrites** that receive information from other neurons.

3) This info passes along the **axon** in the form of an **electrical impulse** that ends up at a **synaptic knob**. The **myelin sheath** insulates the axon to speed up nervous transmission.

4) There's a small gap before the next neuron called a **synapse**.

5) **Neurotransmitters** are chemicals that are released from the synaptic knob. They pass across the synapse, to pass on the signal to the dendrites of the next neuron. (See page 78 for more on synapses.)

Biopsychologists spend loads of time working out what different neurotransmitters do and how they can be influenced by things like diet, exercise and drugs. They also work out how to manipulate neurotransmitters with medications, to control different behaviours.

For example, if a medication or diet was developed to reduce the neurotransmitters that signal stress, this could help people who get stressed out too easily.

There's more about neurotransmitters on page 79.

The Nervous System

Different **Types** of **Neurons** Have Different **Roles**

Different types of neuron are involved in the transfer of information **to** and **from** the CNS.
The **structure** of these neurons differs:

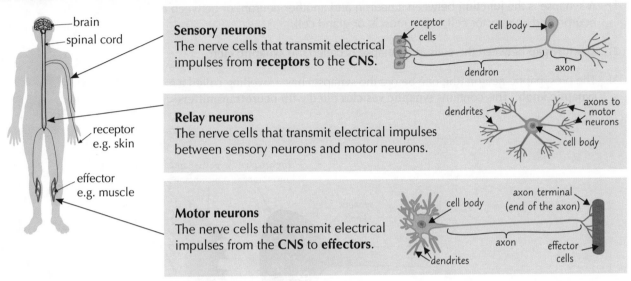

Sensory neurons
The nerve cells that transmit electrical impulses from **receptors** to the **CNS**.

Relay neurons
The nerve cells that transmit electrical impulses between sensory neurons and motor neurons.

Motor neurons
The nerve cells that transmit electrical impulses from the **CNS** to **effectors**.

The **transmission** of information to and from the CNS is shown below:

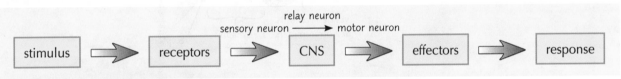

Reflexes Help Prevent **Injury**

Reflexes are fast, automatic responses to certain stimuli. They **bypass** your **conscious** brain completely — instead they go through the **spinal cord** or through an **unconscious** part of the brain. These **rapid responses** help us to **avoid damage**.

Warm-Up Questions

Q1 What does the central nervous system (CNS) consist of?

Q2 Which branch of the autonomic nervous system (ANS) is known as the 'rest and digest' system?

Q3 Outline how information is transmitted to and from the central nervous system (CNS).

Exam Questions

Q1 Label the neuron below by putting the correct letter in each box.

 A synaptic knob

 B nucleus

 C dendrite

 D cell body

 E axon

 [3 marks]

Q2 Which of the following are controlled by the somatic nervous system?
 A digestion   **B** breathing   **C** conscious activities   **D** unconscious activities   [1 mark]

Q3 Outline the function of sensory, relay and motor neurons. [3 marks]

Take a deep breath and let your parasympathetic nervous system kick in...

There's a lot of biology stuff on these pages, but... DON'T PANIC. THERE IS NOTHING TO WORRY ABOUT.
(Sorry — my sympathetic nervous system took over there.) Must remember... parasympathetic means calm. Ahhhh...

The Nervous System

You met neurotransmitters and synapses on page 76. Well, here's a bit more about them. It's your lucky day...

A **Synapse** is a **Junction** Between a Neuron and the Next Cell

1) A synapse is the **junction** between a neuron and another neuron, or between a neuron and an effector cell, e.g. a muscle or gland cell.

2) The tiny **gap** between the cells at a synapse is called the **synaptic cleft**.

3) The presynaptic neuron (the one before the synapse) has a swelling called a **synaptic knob**. This contains **synaptic vesicles** filled with **neurotransmitters**.

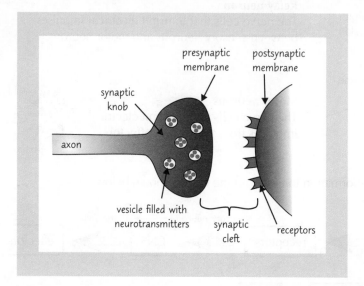

4) When an **electrical impulse** reaches the end of a neuron it causes **neurotransmitters** to be **released** into the synaptic cleft. They **diffuse across** to the **postsynaptic membrane** (the one after the synapse) and **bind** to **specific receptors**.

5) When neurotransmitters bind to receptors they might **trigger** an **electrical impulse** (in a neuron), cause **muscle contraction** (in a muscle cell), or cause a **hormone** to be **secreted** (from a gland cell).

6) Here's what happens when an electrical impulse **arrives** at a **synapse** between **two neurons**:

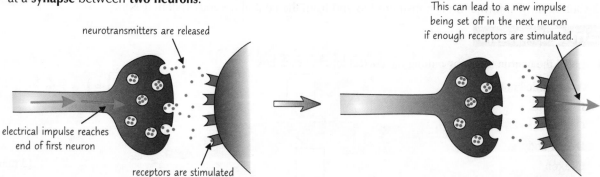

This can lead to a new impulse being set off in the next neuron if enough receptors are stimulated.

7) Because the receptors are **only** on the postsynaptic membranes, synapses make sure **impulses** are **unidirectional** — the impulse can only travel in **one direction**.

What happens at the next neuron depends on the type of neurotransmitter (see the next page).

8) Neurotransmitters are **removed** from the **cleft** so the **response** doesn't keep happening, e.g. they're taken back into the **presynaptic neuron** or they're **broken down** by **enzymes** (and the products are taken into the neuron).

The Nervous System

Neurotransmitters are **Excitatory** or **Inhibitory**

- Excitatory neurotransmitters **increase** the likelihood that an electrical impulse will be triggered in the postsynaptic neuron.

- Inhibitory neurotransmitters **decrease** the likelihood that an electrical impulse will be triggered in the postsynaptic neuron.

Mum couldn't help wishing Harry had a few more inhibitory neurotransmitters.

Some **Neurotransmitters** Come Up a Lot in **Psychology**

There are lots of different neurotransmitters, but some play a larger role than others in **human behaviour**:

Acetylcholine

This **excitatory** neurotransmitter is involved in voluntary **movement**, **memory**, **learning** and **sleep**. Too much is linked to **depression** and too little may result in **dementia**.

Dopamine

Dopamine is a neurotransmitter that helps with **movement**, **attention** and **learning**. Too much is linked to **schizophrenia**, and too little could result in **depression** and **Parkinson's disease**.

Noradrenaline

Noradrenaline is closely related to **adrenaline**. It is often associated with the 'fight or flight' response (see page 81). Too much is linked to **schizophrenia** and too little may result in **depression**.

Serotonin

Serotonin is involved in emotion, mood, sleeping and eating. Too little is linked to **depression**.

GABA

GABA is an **inhibitory** neurotransmitter. Too little GABA is linked to **anxiety disorders**.

Warm-Up Questions

Q1 What is a synapse?

Q2 How do synapses ensure that nerve impulses are unidirectional?

Q3 Give one way that neurotransmitters are removed from the synaptic cleft.

Q4 Explain the difference between an excitatory and inhibitory neurotransmitter.

Q5 Name four different neurotransmitters.

Exam Questions

Q1 Outline how information is transmitted between two neurons. [6 marks]

Q2 Look at the synapse to the right and answer the following questions.

a) What is the name of Structure X?

  A synaptic knob
  B synaptic cleft
  C receptor
  D vesicle
  E postsynaptic membrane [1 mark]

b) What is released from Structure X? [1 mark]

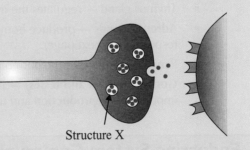

Structure X

Talk about being a bit of a noradrenaline junkie...

Yep, that's me. Someone who truly loves rollercoasters, extreme ironing and Psychology revision. Give me a dose of noradrenaline any day. In fact, some days, my heart gets racing just at the thought of those joyful exams which'll be here before you know it. Hmmm... maybe you should start to learn some of this stuff now. Go on — it won't bite...

The Endocrine System

Some days you might wake up and not want to do any Psychology revision. Don't blame it on Psychology. Blame it on your hormones — they can account for a lot you know...

The **Endocrine System** Sends Information as **Chemical Signals**

1) The **endocrine system** (also known as the hormonal system) involves **glands** and **hormones**:

> A **gland** is a group of cells that are specialised to **secrete** a useful substance, such as a **hormone**. E.g. the **pancreas** secretes **insulin**.
>
> **Hormones** are 'chemical messengers'. Many hormones are **proteins** or **peptides**, e.g. **insulin**. Some hormones are **steroids**, e.g. **progesterone**.

2) **Hormones** are **secreted** when a **gland** is **stimulated**:

> Glands can be stimulated by a change in concentration of a specific substance (sometimes another hormone).
>
> They can also be stimulated by electrical impulses.

3) Hormones **diffuse directly into** the **blood**, then they're **taken** around the body by the **circulatory system**.

4) They **diffuse out** of the blood **all over** the **body**, but each hormone will only **bind** to **specific receptors** for that hormone, found on the membranes of some cells (called **target cells**).

> *An organ that contains target cells is called a target organ.*

5) The hormones trigger a **response** in the **target cells** (the **effectors**).

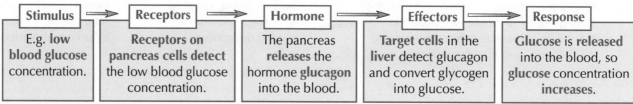

Stimulus	Receptors	Hormone	Effectors	Response
E.g. **low blood glucose** concentration.	**Receptors on pancreas cells detect** the low blood glucose concentration.	The pancreas **releases** the hormone **glucagon** into the blood.	**Target cells** in the **liver** detect glucagon and convert glycogen into glucose.	**Glucose** is **released** into the blood, so **glucose** concentration **increases**.

6) The **endocrine system** is responsible for regulating a large number of **bodily functions**, such as **growth**, **metabolism**, **sleep**, **reproduction**, etc. There are several major glands:

- Hypothalamus — it produces hormones that control the pituitary gland.
- Pituitary gland — known as the 'master gland' because it releases hormones to control other glands in the endocrine system.
- Pineal gland — responsible for the production of melatonin, which plays a role in the control of sleep patterns.
- Thyroid gland — produces hormones such as thyroxine. The thyroid is responsible for controlling the body's metabolic rate, as well as regulating growth and maturation.
- Parathyroid glands — produce a hormone called the parathyroid hormone. This helps control the levels of minerals such as calcium within the body.
- Thymus gland — regulates the immune system.
- Adrenal glands — produce hormones such as adrenaline. Responsible for the 'fight or flight' response (see next page).
- Pancreas — releases the hormones insulin and glucagon, which regulate blood sugar level.
- Gonads (ovaries and testes) — produce sex hormones, e.g. testosterone and oestrogen. These are important in reproduction and the development of sex organs and secondary sexual characteristics.

Endocrine System Communication is **Slower, Long-lasting** and **Widespread**

- Hormones **aren't** released directly onto their target cells — they must **travel** in the **blood** to get there. This means that chemical communication (by hormones) is **slower** than electrical communication (by nerves).
- They **aren't broken down as quickly** as neurotransmitters, so the **effects** of hormones can **last** for much **longer**.
- Hormones are transported **all over** the **body**, so the response may be **widespread** if the target cells are widespread.

The Endocrine System

The Hypothalamus Prepares You for 'Fight or Flight'

When the body is **threatened** (e.g. by a danger such as a giant face-licking millipede) it responds by **preparing for action** (e.g. for fighting or running away). This response is called the '**fight or flight**' response. The **hypothalamus** helps coordinate this response. Here's how...

The activation of the 'fight or flight' response

1) In the **initial shock response**, the **hypothalamus** triggers activity in the **sympathetic branch** of the **autonomic nervous system (ANS)**.

2) This stimulates the **adrenal medulla** within the **adrenal glands**, which releases **adrenaline** and **noradrenaline** into the bloodstream.

3) These hormones affect the body in several ways, including:

- **Blood pressure** and **heart rate** increase to get blood quickly to areas of the body where it's needed for activity.
- **Digestion decreases** so that blood can be directed to the brain and muscles.
- **Muscles** become more **tense** so that the body is physically responsive.
- **Perspiration increases** so that the body can cool down.
- **Breathing rate increases** so that more oxygen can be sent to the muscles.
- **Pupil size increases** so more light can enter the eye to allow for clearer vision.
- **Salivation decreases** as the digestive system isn't needed.

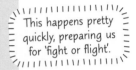
This happens pretty quickly, preparing us for 'fight or flight'.

4) The result of these changes is that the body is **ready to use energy** to deal with the stressful situation, e.g. running away from the rhino that's escaped from the zoo.

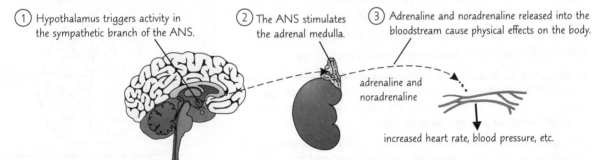

1) Hypothalamus triggers activity in the sympathetic branch of the ANS.

2) The ANS stimulates the adrenal medulla.

3) Adrenaline and noradrenaline released into the bloodstream cause physical effects on the body.

adrenaline and noradrenaline

increased heart rate, blood pressure, etc.

Warm-Up Questions

Q1 What is the endocrine system also known as?

Q2 Describe the role of the pituitary gland.

Q3 Which endocrine gland is responsible for regulating blood sugar level?

PRACTICE QUESTIONS

Exam Questions

Q1 Outline how hormones allow communication within the body. [6 marks]

Q2 Read the item below, then answer the question that follows.

> When Anita saw a spider, her heart rate increased, she started to sweat and she began breathing rapidly.

Discuss how adrenaline can explain Anita's reaction. [6 marks]

Make sure you don't choose 'flight' when you're faced with an exam...

If you've ever had that panicky feeling just before going into an exam, or whilst paragliding over a bubbling volcano (you never know), that'll be your hypothalamus kicking into action. It's kind of nice that it gets you ready for these sorts of things. Isn't your body a marvellous thing? It's always good to be prepared, as the Scouts might say...

Localisation of Function

Yep, it's a page about brains. Ever really thought about what's going on up there...? Nah, me neither. Luckily for you, biopsychologists have and it's pretty interesting stuff. Lots of tricky names coming up though, so brace yourself...

Localisation of Function — Certain Bits of the Brain Do Certain Things

Certain areas of the brain are thought to be responsible for particular functions, e.g. vision, language, coordination... This is known as **localisation of function**:

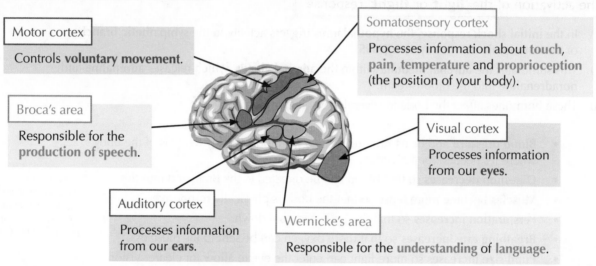

Motor cortex
Controls **voluntary movement**.

Somatosensory cortex
Processes information about **touch**, **pain**, **temperature** and **proprioception** (the position of your body).

Broca's area
Responsible for the **production of speech**.

Visual cortex
Processes information from our **eyes**.

Auditory cortex
Processes information from our **ears**.

Wernicke's area
Responsible for the **understanding** of **language**.

The **Brain** is Divided into **Two Hemispheres**

1) The brain is split into **two hemispheres** (halves) — the **right hemisphere** and the **left hemisphere**.

2) The two hemispheres are **connected** by the **corpus callosum**.

3) Different **functions** are **dominant** in each hemisphere.

4) In most people, **Broca's** and **Wernicke's areas** are only found in the **left hemisphere** — so it handles the bulk of **language** functions. The left hemisphere is also generally responsible for **logic**, **analysis** and **problem solving**.

5) The **right** hemisphere is more concerned with things like **spatial** comprehension, **emotions** and **face recognition**.

6) This is known as **hemispheric lateralisation of function**.

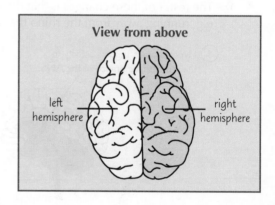

View from above

left hemisphere

right hemisphere

The **Two Hemispheres** Can **Communicate** via the **Corpus Callosum**

In general, each **hemisphere** deals with **information** from the **opposite side** of the body.

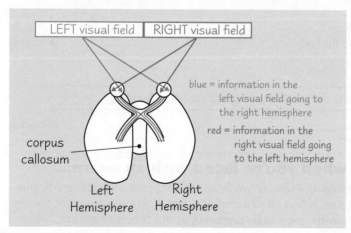

LEFT visual field   RIGHT visual field

blue = information in the left visual field going to the right hemisphere

red = information in the right visual field going to the left hemisphere

corpus callosum

Left Hemisphere

Right Hemisphere

For example...

1) Information from the **right visual field** (that's the right half of what you see) goes to the **visual cortex** in the **left hemisphere**.

2) Information from the **left visual field** goes to the **visual cortex** in the **right hemisphere**.

3) Information passes through the **corpus callosum** to whichever side of the brain needs to deal with it.

Localisation of Function

Split Brain Surgery Gives an Opportunity for Research

1) In very severe cases of **epilepsy**, the only treatment available is to **sever** the **corpus callosum**. This stops seizures spreading across the brain.

2) But a **side effect** of splitting the hemispheres is that **information** can no longer move between them.

3) Scientists have used **split brain surgery patients** to study the different roles of the two hemispheres — take a look at Sperry's study...

Sperry (1968) — Effects of split brain surgery

Method: The study involved a combination of **case studies** and **experiments**. The 11 participants had undergone split brain surgery as a result of epilepsy that couldn't be controlled by medication. A control group was used who had no hemisphere disconnection. In one of the experiments, participants covered one eye and looked at a fixed point on a projection screen. Pictures were projected onto the **right** or **left** of the screen at high speeds so that there was no time for eye movement.

Results: If the picture was shown in the **right visual field**, all of the participants could say or write what it was without a problem. But if the image was flashed onto the **left** the split brain participants couldn't say or write what they'd seen. They could however select a corresponding object with their left hand, which represented what had been shown to their left eye (right hemisphere), even though they didn't know why they had selected this object.

Conclusion: This shows that **different areas** of the brain specialise in **different functions**. The **left** hemisphere (which receives visual information from the right visual field) can **convert** sight into spoken and written language. Usually information entering the right hemisphere can cross over to be processed in the left. As the results show, this **can't** happen in **split brains**, so the information going to the right hemisphere can't be converted into language at all. However, the right hemisphere can still produce a non-verbal response.

Evaluation: Using case studies as well as experiments meant that Sperry obtained both **qualitative** and **quantitative** data. Also, using both research methods meant that the **reliability** and the **validity** of the study were increased. However, the study only used 11 participants, which is a very **small sample** size for being able to generalise the results to others. But, it would have been difficult to find a large number of split brain patients to study. Epilepsy is usually caused by **brain damage** and the patients had also been on **medication** which may have affected their brains. Therefore, it is hard to conclude that the ways they processed information would be the same as for people **without** epilepsy or split brain treatment. The study has also been criticised in terms of **ecological validity** — the experimental situation was artificial, so it's difficult to **generalise** the results to real-life situations.

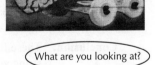

Warm-Up Questions

Q1 What is the function of the somatosensory cortex?

Q2 Which hemisphere does information from the right visual field go to?

Q3 What is split brain surgery?

What are you looking at?

Exam Questions

Q1 Look at the diagram of the left hemisphere below.

Area X

    a) Name the area labelled X in the diagram. [1 mark]

    b) Complete the following sentence. The area labelled X is responsible for
    A voluntary movement.   **B** vision.
    C speech production.   **D** proprioception. [1 mark]

Q2 a) Outline one study which provides evidence for hemispheric lateralisation of function. [4 marks]

    b) Evaluate the study described in part a). [4 marks]

Brings a whole new perspective to being in two minds about things...

It's all a bit confusing this split brain stuff, so don't panic if you don't get it straight away. Just take your time and draw out some diagrams to help you — it'll click eventually. Nightmare stuff, this, if you get your left and right muddled up...

Plasticity

Brain engaged — it's about to get deep...

The Brain is **Constantly Reorganising** Itself

1) The brain has the ability to **alter** its **structure** and **function** in response to changes in the environment.

2) This is known as **plasticity**. Here's how it works:

- Information takes a pathway through the brain, travelling from one **neuron** to the next via synapses.
- When we're presented with new **information**, new neural pathways begin to form.
- Using a neural pathway strengthens it — the more a pathway is used, the stronger the connections between the neurons become.
- If a neural pathway is not used it becomes weaker.

Harold was fully aware that 'practice would make perfect'.

3) This constant **rewiring** and **reorganisation** of the brain is the basis of how we **learn** and **adapt to changes** in our **environment**. For example, when we first carry out a new action, we are not very good at it. If we **repeat** the action over and over again (i.e. **practise** it), the pathways **strengthen** and we **get better** at the action.

4) Plasticity was previously thought to only occur in **babies** and **children**. Although plasticity is **greatest** in the **developing brain**, it is now widely accepted that plasticity occurs **throughout adult life** too.

There's Lots of **Evidence** for Plasticity

Different areas in the **somatosensory cortex** and the **motor cortex** of the brain represent different **parts of the body**. This is known as **cortical representation**. For example, one area of the somatosensory cortex processes sensory information from your lips and another area processes sensory information from your toes.

Lots of studies providing support for plasticity have focused on changes in cortical representation — this is known as **cortical reorganisation**.

Elbert et al (1995) — Plasticity in musicians

Method:	**Nine musicians** who played either the violin, cello or guitar were compared to **six non-musicians**. A technique called **magnetic source imaging** was used to measure the area of the **somatosensory cortex** representing the **digits of the left hand** of each participant.
Results:	The area of the somatosensory cortex representing the digits of the left hand was **larger** in the stringed instrument players than in the controls.
Conclusion:	These findings suggest that the **increased** amount of **sensory processing** required from the left hands of stringed instrument players results in **structural changes** in the brain, providing support for plasticity.
Evaluation:	Other researchers argue that the increased representation of the left hand digits in the musicians may have been **genetic** rather than as a result of playing an instrument. In other words, they may have been good musicians because of a natural trait. The study used a fairly **small sample size** so may not be representative.

The left hand carries out lots of fast, fine movements when playing a stringed instrument. A large amount of sensory information is also processed, for example, to detect the amount of pressure being applied to the strings.

Studies have also provided **evidence** of plasticity in the **motor cortex**.

- Karni et al (1995) used fMRI (see p.86) to show that learning and practising a sequence of finger movements over a period of four weeks led to activation of a larger area of the motor cortex when carrying out the sequence. This suggests that some reorganisation had occurred.

- Nudo et al (1996) mapped the motor cortex of adult monkeys before and after training in a task which mainly required use of the digits. They found that the representation of the digits in the motor cortex increased. They then carried out training in a task that mainly used the forearm. They found that the forearm representation increased and the digit representation decreased. This suggests that plastic changes are continuous and reversible (at least in monkeys).

Plasticity

Plasticity Can Allow Functional Recovery After Brain Damage

1) **Brain damage** can be caused by serious head injuries, strokes, tumours, infections, etc.

2) This **brain damage** can result in **loss of function**. For example, damage to Broca's area can result in the loss of speech, damage to the auditory cortex can cause loss of hearing, etc.

3) The brain has the potential to **recover** some of this lost function.

4) This is thought to be due to **plasticity** — the brain begins to **rewire** itself.

5) There is evidence that **healthy areas** of the brain located **near** the damaged area begin to **take over** the function of the damaged area.

Using the Affected Area Can Encourage Functional Recovery

After a stroke which has caused loss of function on one side of the body (e.g. the right arm), some patients are prevented from using their non-affected side (e.g. their left arm). This forces them to 're-learn' how to use their affected arm. This method is known as **constraint-induced movement therapy** (**CIMT**).

Advantages

- Numerous studies have shown that CIMT produces cortical reorganisation which results in regained or improved function.

- The principles of CIMT can also be applied to patients who suffer from aphasia as a result of stroke damage. Instead of communicating in other ways, e.g. drawing pictures, using sign language, etc. they play a game which requires them to try and speak a word presented on a card. Studies have shown that this therapy caused dysfunctional areas near the damaged area to become functional again.

> People with aphasia struggle to speak correctly, for example, they may use the wrong word or use the wrong sounds in the word.

Disadvantages

- CIMT can be very **frustrating** for the patient.

- CIMT needs to be very **intensive** to be effective. Patients are often required to train the affected limb for several hours a day, for consecutive weeks and have their unaffected limb restrained for 90% of the time that they are awake.

- It is most effective in treating patients who have suffered **mild** to **moderate** strokes. If there's lots of damage to the brain, it can be much harder to regain function.

Warm-Up Questions

Q1 What is meant by cortical representation?

Q2 Outline the findings of Elbert et al's (1995) study.

Q3 What brain scanning method did Karni et al (1995) use in their study?

Q4 What does CIMT stand for?

Q5 Give one disadvantage of CIMT.

Exam Questions

Q1 Esi has recently had a stroke which has caused loss of function in her left arm. Describe how the brain's plasticity could allow her to regain function in her left arm. [2 marks]

Q2 Outline and evaluate evidence for plasticity within the brain. [8 marks]

I think I'm going to need an electrician...

Crikey. Isn't the brain amazing? It's constantly reorganising to learn, adapt and even fix itself. I know it's tricky to get your head round all of this, but read these pages through a couple more times and you'll soon get those neural pathways strengthened up — use it or lose it, my friend.

Studying the Brain

As you've probably gathered by now, biopsychologists really like the brain, and they've got a few tricks up their lab coat sleeves for studying it. First up, fMRI, which you should remember from page 66...

fMRI Scans Show Brain Activity

Functional magnetic resonance imaging (fMRI) scans are **3D** scans providing **structural** and **functional** information. They show **changes** in **brain activity** as they actually happen, by using a really strong magnetic field and radio waves:

1) **More oxygenated blood** flows to **active areas** of the brain (to supply the neurons with oxygen and glucose).

2) Molecules in **oxygenated blood respond differently** to a **magnetic field** than those in deoxygenated blood.

3) So the **more active areas** of the brain can be **identified** on an fMRI scan.

See p.66 for other ways of scanning the brain.

Uses of fMRI

1) fMRI scans are used to research the function of the brain as well as its structure. If a participant carries out a task whilst in the scanner, the part of the brain that's involved with that function will be more active. (It's often coloured by the computer so that it shows up more easily.)

2) For example, a participant might be asked to move their left hand when in the fMRI scanner. The areas of the brain involved in moving the hand will show up on the fMRI scan.

3) fMRI scans can be used to diagnose medical problems because they can also show damaged or diseased areas of the brain.

4) They are also used to study abnormal activity in the brain. For example, Shegrill et al (2001) used fMRI to show which areas of the brain were active during hallucinations in a patient with schizophrenia.

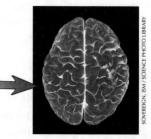

This fMRI scan looks down on the brain from above. The red area is active when the person moves their left hand.

fMRI scans are a really useful tool for biopsychologists, as they provide a **non-invasive** way of studying the brain. However the machines are very **expensive** to buy and run. They also require people to lie very still in an enclosed space for a period of time, which can be a problem for people who suffer from **claustrophobia** (fear of confined spaces). They have **poor temporal resolution** — this means they don't show changes over **time** accurately.

EEGs Show Electrical Activity

1) An **electroencephalogram (EEG)** shows the **overall electrical activity** of the brain. It picks up the signal of many neurons firing together — not individual neurons.

2) Multiple **electrodes** are placed on the **scalp** and the electrical activity in the brain is recorded for a period of time.

3) This produces a **pattern of waves**. These patterns represent different levels of **arousal** or **consciousness**. For example, the different stages of sleep each have their own typical wave patterns.

Uses of EEGs

1) EEGs are commonly used in **sleep studies**.

2) They have also been used in the study of conditions such as **depression** and **schizophrenia**. E.g. a meta-analysis by Boutros et al (2008) showed that patients suffering from schizophrenia displayed **abnormal EEG wave patterns** compared to controls.

3) **Abnormal EEGs** have also been identified in patients suffering from eating disorders such as **anorexia nervosa**.

4) This means EEGs have the potential to be used as a **diagnostic tool**.

Stage 1	
Stage 2	
Stage 3	
Stage 4	
REM Sleep (active sleep)	

These EEG wave patterns show brain activity during the different stages of sleep.

EEGs and ERPs (see next page) are also **non-invasive**, and they are **cheaper** to carry out than fMRI scans. Although they have a **good temporal resolution**, they have **poor spatial resolution** — this means it's hard to work out which area of the brain the waves originate from.

Studying the Brain

ERPs Show Electrical Activity in the Brain in Response to a Stimulus

1) Biopsychologists can also look at how an EEG wave pattern **changes** in **response** to a **stimulus**.
2) This change is known as an **event-related potential (ERP)**.
3) If a **specific stimulus** is presented, it produces a **specific change** in the wave pattern:

> It's important to remember that the EEG represents the activity of the whole brain — not individual neurons.

normal wave pattern

stimulus

4) Biopsychologists have identified **different ERPs** which are produced in response to **different stimuli**.

Uses of ERPs

1) ERPs have been used a lot in memory research, as they give biopsychologists lots of clues about information processing in the brain.
2) Research has shown differences in the ERPs of people suffering from certain psychiatric disorders compared to healthy individuals. For example, Miltner et al (2000) found that people with phobias had an ERP of a greater amplitude in response to images of the objects they feared, compared to non-phobic individuals.

Post-mortem Examinations Show the Structure of the Brain

1) **Post-mortem examinations** involve **dissecting** (cutting up) the brain of a person who has **died**.
2) This allows researchers to physically look at the **internal structure** of the brain.

> Before modern techniques such as brain scanning were invented, post-mortems were one of the only ways of studying the brain.

Uses of Post-mortem Examinations

1) If a person had a **medical condition** when they were alive, a post-mortem could show up any **structural abnormalities** that could **explain their condition**. For example, a study by Brown et al (1986), which used post-mortem examinations, showed that patients who had suffered from **schizophrenia** had **enlarged ventricles** in their brains.
2) Post-mortems have provided **evidence** for **localisation of function** in the brain. For example, **Paul Broca** carried out post-mortem examinations on two patients who developed **speech problems** as a result of **brain damage**. Both patients had damage to the **same area** of the brain, so Broca concluded this area (which we now know as **Broca's area**) was involved in **speech production**.

An obvious **disadvantage** of post-mortem examinations is that the person has to have **died** before the examination can be carried out, so they will **not benefit** from any of the findings.

A **disadvantage** of **all** of these methods of studying the brain, is that although they do give us information about what's going on in the brain, they **don't** allow **cause and effect** to be established. For example, the enlarged ventricles in people with schizophrenia **haven't** necessarily been **caused** by schizophrenia.

Warm-Up Questions

Q1 Give one problem with functional magnetic resonance imaging (fMRI).
Q2 What does an electroencephalogram (EEG) show?

PRACTICE QUESTIONS

Exam Questions

Q1 Briefly outline how functional magnetic resonance imaging (fMRI) works. [4 marks]

Q2 Briefly explain one advantage and one disadvantage of using electroencephalography to study the brain. [4 marks]

I wonder what level of arousal your EEG would show right now...

I don't know about you but I think all this stuff is pretty neat. In fact, there are whole areas of research in psychology that just wouldn't have been possible without these techniques, so hats off to the scientists who came up with them.

Biological Rhythms

The Beatles. Whitney Houston. Elvis. They all had rhythm, and so do you. You don't have to write a song on it (unless you really want to) but you do need to know about it. And these lovely pages are here to help.

Biological Rhythm Cycles **Vary** in **Length**

Biological rhythms can be classified according to how long their cycle lasts.

Living together had led to more than just Kim and Mia's menstrual cycles synchronising.

1) Circadian rhythms — have cycles that generally occur once every 24 hours. For example, we will usually go through the sleep-wake cycle once every day.

2) Infradian rhythms — have cycles that occur less than once every day. For example, the menstrual cycle. Sabbagh and Barnard (1984) found that when women live together their menstrual cycles may synchronise. It isn't clear why, but it may be linked to pheromones (chemicals that can affect the behaviour or physiology of others).

3) Ultradian rhythms — have cycles that occur more than once every 24 hours. For example, the sleep cycle has several repeating stages of light and deep sleep. Research using EEGs to monitor brain activity during sleep has shown that a regular sleep pattern is really important. Disrupting these cycles can have very serious consequences (see next page).

Biological Rhythms are **Regulated** by **Internal** and **External Influences**

The timing of biological rhythms is determined by factors both **inside** and **outside** our bodies.

Endogenous pacemakers

1) Some aspects of our biological rhythms are set by **genetically determined** biological structures and mechanisms **within the body**.

2) The **suprachiasmatic nucleus** (SCN), part of the **hypothalamus**, seems to act as an **internal clock** to keep the body on an approximate 24-hour sleep-waking cycle.

3) It is sensitive to light and regulates the **pineal gland**, which secretes **melatonin** — a hormone which seems to induce sleep. When there is **less** light, more melatonin is produced. When there is **more** light, secretion is reduced and waking occurs.

4) **Menaker et al (1978)** lesioned this structure in hamsters — their sleep-waking cycle was **disrupted**.

Exogenous zeitgebers

1) These are influences outside of the body that act like a **prompt**, which may trigger a **biological rhythm**.

2) **Light** is the most important zeitgeber. **Siffre (1975)** spent six months in a cave. He had **no clocks** and **no natural light** as zeitgebers. His sleep-waking cycle **extended** from a 24-hour to a 25-30 hour cycle. It therefore seems that natural light is needed to fine-tune our normal 24-hour cycle.

Endogenous and Exogenous Factors **Interact**

Endogenous and exogenous factors **interact** to regulate the timing of our biological rhythms.

1) In some cases, endogenous factors may **completely determine** a cycle. **Pengelly and Fisher (1957)** found that squirrels will hibernate even when kept in laboratory conditions very different from their natural environment.

2) However, many animals can **react more flexibly**, especially humans who are able to adapt to their surroundings. We can make ourselves stay awake and **change the environment** to suit our needs, e.g. by using artificial light.

3) **Cultural factors** are also important. For example, Eskimos often live in permanent daylight or permanent night-time but can maintain **regular daily sleep cycles** — so the cycle can't just be determined by levels of light acting on the pineal gland.

4) **Individual differences** can also affect the rhythms. **Aschoff and Wever (1976)** found that in a group of people isolated from daylight, some maintained their **regular** sleep-wake cycles. Other members of the group displayed their own very **extreme** idiosyncrasies, e.g. 29 hours awake followed by 21 hours asleep. This also shows that factors must interact to control or influence biological rhythms.

Biological Rhythms

Disrupting Biological Rhythms can have Negative Consequences

When endogenous pacemakers become out of line with exogenous zeitgebers, it can **disrupt** the sleep-wake cycle.

1) In the natural environment, zeitgebers normally **change slowly**, e.g. light levels during the year change gradually.

2) However, in modern society, zeitgebers can change quickly. This can have **negative effects** on our ability to function — slowing **reaction times**, impairing **problem-solving skills**, and limiting our **ability to concentrate**.

Jet lag

1) Jet planes allow fast travel to different time zones. Leaving the UK at 9am means that you'd get to New York at about 4pm UK time. New York is 5 hours behind the UK, so the local time would be about 11am.

2) Consequently you'll feel sleepy at an earlier (local) time. If you then went to sleep you would wake-up earlier and be out of sync with local timing. It appears easiest to adapt by forcing yourself to stay awake.

3) It can take about a week to fully synchronise to a new time zone. Wegman et al (1986) found that travelling east to west (phase delay) seems easier to adapt to than travelling west to east (phase advance).

4) Schwartz et al (1995) found that baseball teams from the east coast of the USA got better results travelling to play in the west than teams based in the west did when travelling to play in the east.

Shift work

Modern work patterns mean some people work shifts throughout the 24-hour period, disrupting their sleep cycle.

Czeisler et al (1982) studied workers at a factory whose shift patterns appeared to cause sleep and health problems. The researchers recommended 21-day shifts (allowing more time for workers to adapt), and changing shifts forward in time (phase delay). After implementing the changes productivity and job satisfaction increased.

As described on p.91, psychological research such as this can have a positive impact on the economy.

Research on Biological Rhythms has Limitations

1) Findings from animal studies can't accurately be **generalised** to humans — humans have greater **adaptability**.

2) Studies that have deprived humans of natural light have still allowed **artificial light**, which may give many of the **benefits** of natural light — this reduces the **validity** of these studies.

3) Things like **individual differences** need further study. Some people are more alert early in the day, and others later on, and the speed with which we **adapt to disruptions** can vary. It's difficult to determine whether a person's lifestyle is a **cause or effect** of their biological rhythms.

4) If we fully understand what causes the problems linked to jet lag and shift work, we can **minimise** or **avoid them**, reducing accidents in work environments. There are different ways to deal with these problems, e.g. taking time to **naturally adjust**, or using **drugs** to reduce the effects of sleep deprivation.

Warm-Up Questions

Q1 What is an infradian rhythm?
Q2 Give an example of an exogenous zeitgeber.

Exam Questions

Q1 Distinguish between circadian and ultradian rhythms. [2 marks]

Q2 Outline the effect of endogenous pacemakers and exogenous zeitgebers on the sleep-wake cycle. [8 marks]

Q3 Discuss research studies that have examined the role of endogenous pacemakers and exogenous zeitgebers in human biological rhythms. [16 marks]

"I didn't mean to fall asleep Miss — the melatonin made me do it..."

It's scientific fact that if you're a rock star, your biological rhythm immediately changes to 'We Will Rock You' by Queen. Actually, that's not scientific at all. Nor is it fact. When you've had a decent crack at all the questions on this page, think about what your rock rhythm would be... Are you ready? It's 'We Will Rock You', by Queen. Fact.

The Scientific Process

The scientific process is all about how we develop and test scientific ideas. It's what scientists do all day, every day. Well, except at coffee time. Never come between scientists and their coffee.

Science is about Establishing Truths

1) Scientific research should be **objective** — independent of **beliefs** or **opinions**.

2) So, the methods used should be **empirical** — based on **data**, not just theory. The best way to make sure of this is to carry out an **experiment** that collects **quantitative data** and has strictly **controlled variables**.

3) This means that you should be able to **replicate** the research, and also to establish **cause** and **effect**.

Science Answers Real-life Questions and Tests Hypotheses

Science tries to explain **how** and **why** things happen — it **tests hypotheses** and **constructs theories** by asking questions. This is the **scientific process**:

1) **Ask** a question — make an **observation** and ask **why or how** it happens.

2) **Suggest** an answer, or part of an answer, by forming a **theory** (a possible explanation of the observations).

3) Make a **prediction** or **hypothesis** — a **specific testable statement**, based on the theory, about what will happen in a test situation.

4) Carry out a **test** — to provide **evidence** that will support the hypothesis (or help to disprove it).

Suggesting explanations is all very well and good, but if there's **no way to test** them then it just ain't science. A theory is **only scientific** if it can be tested.

Science is All About Testing Theories

It starts off with one experiment backing up a prediction and theory. It can then end up with all the scientists in the world **agreeing** with it and you **learning** it. Stirring stuff. This is how the magical process takes place:

1) The results are **published** — scientists need to let others know about their work, so they try to get their results published in **scientific journals**. These are just like normal magazines, only they contain **scientific reports** (called papers) instead of celebrity gossip. All work must undergo **peer review** before it's published.

   • Peer review is a process used to ensure the integrity of published scientific work. Before publication, scientific work is sent to experts in that field (peers) so they can assess the quality of the work.

   • This process helps to keep scientists honest — e.g. you can't 'sex-up' your conclusions if the data doesn't support it, because it won't pass peer review.

   • Peer review helps to validate conclusions — it means published theories, data and conclusions are more trustworthy. But it can't guarantee that the conclusions are 100% right. More rounds of predicting and testing are needed before they can be taken as 'fact'.

   • Sometimes mistakes are made and bad science is published. Peer review isn't perfect, but it's probably the best way for scientists to self-regulate their work, and to ensure reliable scientific work is published.

2) Other scientists read the published theories and results, and try to **repeat them** — this involves repeating the **exact experiments**, and using the theory to make **new predictions** that are tested by **new experiments**.

3) If all the experiments in all the world provide evidence to back it up, the theory is thought of as scientific 'fact'.

4) If **new evidence** comes to light that **conflicts** with the current evidence, the theory is questioned all over again. More rounds of **testing** will be carried out to see which evidence, and so which theory, **prevails**.

Popper (1969) Argued that Theories Should be Falsifiable

If you're doing AS Level, you don't need to know about falsifiability.

1) **Popper (1969)** argued that theories are **abstract**, so it's impossible to **prove them right** through **empirical research**.

2) Instead, he claimed that a theory is **scientific** if it's **falsifiable** — if it can be proved **wrong**. So, every **test** of a theory should be an attempt to **falsify** it.

3) This sounds a bit weird, but if you think about a **non-scientific** psychological theory then you can see how it fits. For example, Freud's psychodynamic explanation of gender development (page 162) is **non-falsifiable** — you can't prove it wrong because it's based on the unconscious mind.

The Scientific Process

Theories Get **Tested** Over and Over and Over and Over and...

Our currently accepted theories have survived this '**trial by evidence**'. They've been tested **over and over and over** and each time the results have backed them up. **BUT**, and this is a big but (teehee), they never become totally undisputable fact. Scientific **breakthroughs or advances** could provide new ways to question and test a theory, which could lead to **changes and challenges** to it. Then the testing starts all over again...

Science Uses **Paradigms** | *If you're doing* <u>AS Level</u>, *you don't need to know about paradigms.*

1) A **paradigm** is a set of principles, methods and techniques which define a scientific discipline.

2) **Kuhn (1970)** believed that for something to be a science, it needs to have a paradigm. This has resulted in **two different opinions** as to whether psychology is truly a science.

3) Some believe that psychology **has a paradigm**. It was initially **behaviourism**, but then it underwent a change to cognitive psychology. This change in principles and practices is known as a **paradigm shift**.

4) Others argue that psychology might be made up of **mini-paradigms**, and so psychology is in a state of **pre-science** (it hasn't quite become a widely recognised science yet).

Psychological Research Can Impact the **Economy**

Despite the ongoing debate as to whether psychology is a true science, psychology has a big impact on the world. Psychologists conduct research into a wide range of areas. Their findings can have implications for the **economy**.

E.g. People with untreated mental health disorders may need more time off work

- People suffering from conditions like depression or obsessive-compulsive disorder which aren't being treated may need to take more days off work than those who are receiving treatment.

- Treatments for mental health disorders come about as a result of psychological research (e.g. cognitive-behaviour therapy, antidepressants, etc.), and can help people continue a normal lifestyle, such as going to work. Less time off work is better for the economy.

E.g. Research into sleep behaviour can help shift workers

- Modern work patterns mean some people work shifts throughout the 24-hour period, disrupting their **sleep cycle**.

- **Czeisler et al (1982)** studied workers at a factory whose shift patterns appeared to cause sleep and health problems. The researchers recommended **rotating shifts** every **21 days** (allowing more time for workers to adapt), and changing shifts forward in time (phase delay).

- The employees had previously worked a backwards rotation — working during the nights for the first week, late afternoons in the second week and only mornings during the third week (phase advance). They would then restart the pattern again in the fourth week.

- After implementing the changes, **productivity** and **job satisfaction** increased.

- **More productive** workers lead to a **better** economy.

Warm-Up Questions | *If you're doing* <u>AS Level</u>, *you don't need to answer Warm-Up Question 2.*

Q1 Briefly outline the scientific process.

Q2 Describe the meaning of a 'paradigm' and 'paradigm shift' in reference to psychology.

PRACTICE QUESTIONS

Exam Questions

Q1 Outline why research should undergo a peer review before it is published. [1 mark]

Q2 Briefly discuss the implications of psychological research for the economy. [6 marks]

Happy people make a happy place to work...

Or is it the other way around? A happy place to work makes happy people? Either way, a happy and productive workforce is much more likely to influence the economy in a positive way. So if psychological research can figure out how to make people super-happy all of the time, we'll be rolling in it before you can say 'spaghetti bolognese'...

Research Methods

This is everything you could ever want to know (and probably a bit more too...) about how psychologists go about testing their theories. Have a look at pages 108-110 for more on the ethical issues surrounding different research methods.

There are Several Types of **Experiment**

An **experiment** is a way of conducting research in a **controlled** way.
There are several types:

1) **Laboratory** Experiments

The aim of laboratory experiments is to **control** all relevant variables except for **one key variable**, which is altered to see what the effect is. The variable that you alter is called the **independent variable** (see page 97). Laboratory experiments are conducted in an **artificial setting**, e.g. Milgram's study (see page 7).

Strengths

Control — the effects of confounding variables (those that have an effect in addition to the variable of interest — see page 97) are minimised.

Replication — strict controls mean you can run the study again to check the findings.

Causal relationships — ideally it's possible to establish whether one variable actually causes change in another.

Limitations

Artificial — experiments might not measure real-life behaviour (i.e. they may lack ecological validity).

Demand characteristics — participants may respond according to what they think is being investigated, which can bias the results.

Ethics — deception is often used, making informed consent difficult.

2) **Field** Experiments

Laboratory and field experiments are 'true experiments' because variables can be controlled and manipulated.

Field experiments are conducted **outside** the laboratory.
Behaviour is measured in a **natural environment** like a school, the street or on a train.
A **key variable** is still altered so that its effect can be measured.

Strengths

Causal relationships — you can still establish causal relationships by manipulating the key variable and measuring its effect, although it's very difficult to do in a field experiment.

Ecological validity — field experiments are less artificial than those done in a laboratory, so they relate to real life better.

Demand characteristics (participants trying to guess what the researcher expects from them and performing differently because of it) — these can be avoided if participants don't know they're in a study.

Pierre was quite a pro at carrying out field experiments.

Limitations

Less control — confounding variables may be more likely in a natural environment.

Ethics — participants who didn't agree to take part might experience distress and often can't be debriefed. Observation must respect privacy.

Research Methods

3) **Natural** Experiments

This is where the researcher looks at how an **independent variable**, which **isn't manipulated** by the researchers, affects a **dependent variable**. The independent variable isn't manipulated because it's an **event** which occurs **naturally**. An **example** is research into the **effect** of a single-sex school and a mixed-sex school on **behaviour**. Participants are usually allocated to conditions **randomly**.

Strengths

Ethical — it's possible to study variables that it would be unethical to manipulate, e.g. you can compare a community that has TV with a community that doesn't to see which is more aggressive.

Demand characteristics — participants might not know they're in a study, so their behaviour is likely to be more natural.

Ecological validity — they tend to be less artificial than laboratory experiments.

Limitations

Causal relationships — because you don't manipulate the independent variable, and because other variables could be having an effect, it's hard to establish causal relationships.

Ethics — deception is often used, making informed consent difficult. Also, confidentiality may be compromised if the community is identifiable.

4) **Quasi** Experiments

In a **quasi experiment**, the researcher **isn't** able to use **random allocation** to put participants in different conditions. This is usually because the **independent variable** is a particular **feature** of the participants, such as **gender** or the existence of a **mental disorder**.

Strengths

Control — quasi experiments are often carried out under controlled conditions.

Ecological validity — the research is often less artificial than laboratory studies, so you're more likely to be able to generalise the results to real life.

Limitations

Participant allocation — you can't randomly allocate participants to each condition, and so confounding variables (e.g. what area the participants live in) may affect results. Let's face it — you've got no control over these variables, so it's ridiculously hard to say what's caused by what.

Causal relationships — it can be hard to establish cause and effect because the independent variable isn't being directly manipulated.

Warm-Up Questions

Q1 What are the main strengths of laboratory experiments?
Q2 Outline one limitation of field experiments.
Q3 What is a quasi experiment?

Exam Questions

Q1 Outline one limitation of a laboratory experiment. [2 marks]

Q2 Outline one strength of a field experiment. [2 marks]

Q3 Outline two limitations of natural experiments. [4 marks]

It's only natural to feel a bit quasi at this point in time...

This is one hefty section on research methods, so it's understandable that you may feel a bit daunted by it all. But fear not — all will be fine. I promise. Once you've mastered these pages on experimental methods, you can move on to observational, self-report and correlation methods. You'll be experimenting on people in no time*...

*as long as it's done ethically, please.

Research Methods

And yes, there are more...

Observational Techniques Involve Observing — NOT Interfering

Naturalistic observation involves observing subjects in their natural environment. Researchers take great care not to interfere in any way with the subjects they're studying.

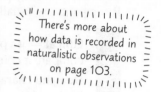

There's more about how data is recorded in naturalistic observations on page 103.

Strengths

Ecological validity — the participants' behaviour is natural and there are no demand characteristics, as the participant is unaware of being observed.

Theory development — these studies can be a useful way of developing ideas about behaviour that could be tested in more controlled conditions later.

Limitations

Extraneous variables — you can't control variables that may affect behaviour.

Observer bias — the observers' expectations may affect what they focus on and record. This means the reliability of the results may be a problem — another observer may have come up with very different results.

Ethics — you should only conduct observations where people might expect to be observed by strangers. This limits the situations where you can do a naturalistic observation. Debriefing is difficult. Observation must respect privacy. Getting informed consent can be tricky.

Another type of observation is **controlled observation**. This is where the situation is carried out in conditions set up by the researcher. Although the variables are **more controlled**, these studies have **lower** ecological validity and participants may behave **differently** if they know they're being observed.

Correlational Research Looks for Relationships Between Variables

Correlational research looks for a **relationship** between **two variables**. As these variables **aren't manipulated** as in an experiment, it's not possible to state that **just** these two variables rise and fall together, or that one variable is **causing** the change in the other — the pattern may be the result of a third **unknown variable** or be just a **coincidence**.

Strengths

Causal relationships — these can be ruled out if no correlation exists.

Ethics — you can study variables that it would be unethical to manipulate, e.g. is there a relationship between the number of cigarettes smoked and incidences of ill health?

Limitations

Causal relationships — these cannot be assumed from a correlation, which may be caused by a third, unknown variable.

Ethics — misinterpretation can be an issue. Sometimes the media (and researchers) infer causality from a correlation.

Self-Report Techniques Involve Questionnaires and Interviews

1) Questionnaires Can be Written, Face-to-Face, on the Phone or Via the Internet

Strengths   **Practical** — you can collect a large amount of information quickly and relatively cheaply.

Limitations

Bad questions — leading questions (questions that suggest answers) or unclear questions can be a problem.

Biased samples — some people are more likely to respond, making a sample unrepresentative.

Self-report — people often wish to present themselves in a good light (social desirability bias — see p. 106). What they say and what they actually think could be different, making any results unreliable.

Ethics — confidentiality can be a problem, especially around sensitive issues.

Research Methods

2) Interviews are More Like a Conversation than a Face-to-Face Questionnaire

Structured interviews follow a fixed set of questions that are the same for all participants.
Unstructured interviews may have discussion topics, but are less constrained about how the conversation goes.

Strengths

Rich data — you can get detailed information, as there are fewer constraints than with a questionnaire. Unstructured interviews provide richer information than structured interviews.

Pilot study — interviews are a useful way to get information before a study.

Limitations

Self-report — the results can be unreliable and affected by social desirability bias (see questionnaires).

Impractical — conducting interviews can be time-consuming and requires skilled researchers.

Data analysis — analysing the data can be hard, particularly for unstructured interviews, because there could be a huge amount of qualitative data, which can be tricky to analyse (see page 112).

Ethics — confidentiality can be a problem, especially around sensitive issues.

Case Studies are Intensive Descriptions of a Single Individual or Case

Case studies allow researchers to analyse unusual cases in a lot of detail, e.g. Milner et al's study of **HM** (page 17).

Strengths

Rich data — researchers have the opportunity to study rare phenomena in a lot of detail.

Unique cases — can challenge existing ideas and theories, and suggest ideas for future research.

Limitations

Causal relationships — cause-and-effect of a relationship cannot be established.

Generalisation — only studying a single case makes generalising the results extremely difficult.

Ethics — informed consent can be difficult to obtain in some cases.

Content Analysis Involves Assessing Behaviours, Words or Concepts

If you're doing AS, you don't need to know about content analysis.

Content analysis is a research method used to analyse secondary data (see page 113) and data you've already collected (e.g. through unstructured interviews). It involves splitting the data into assigned categories (page 112).

Strengths

Inexpensive — it is usually an easy and inexpensive method to use.

Ethics — there may be fewer ethical issues as participants aren't directly involved.

E.g. content analysis could be used to investigate the number of times sex-role stereotypes are used in TV adverts.

Limitations

Data analysis — analysing the data can often be time-consuming.

Subjectivity — interpretation and categorising the data can be subjective.

Warm-Up Questions

If you're doing AS Level, you don't need to answer Warm-Up Question 3.

Q1 What does correlational research look for?
Q2 Describe two strengths of case studies.
Q3 What is content analysis?

Exam Questions

Q1 Outline one limitation of collecting data using naturalistic observation. [1 mark]

Q2 Which of the following do not involve self-report techniques?
A structured interviews   B observations   C unstructured interviews   D questionnaires   [1 mark]

Reality TV — naturalistic observation at its finest...?

When you're carrying out an observation, you want to see behaviour that's as natural as possible. You don't want folk to put on an act just because they're aware that they're being watched — makes you wonder how real reality TV is...

Aims and Hypotheses

When research is conducted, the idea is to carry out an objective test of something, i.e. to obtain a scientific measurement of how people behave — not just someone's opinion. Well that's what I reckon...

Research Aims are Important

An **aim** is a statement of a study's purpose — for example, Asch's aim might have been: 'To study majority influence in an unambiguous task'. (See page 3 for the details of Asch's study.)

Research should state its aim **beforehand** so that it's **clear** what the study intends to investigate.

Hypotheses are Theories Tested by Research

Although the **aim** states the **purpose** of a study, it isn't usually **precise** enough to **test**.
What is needed are clear statements of what's actually being tested — the **hypotheses**.
A hypothesis is worded in a way that states a **prediction** of what will be shown by the research.

1) **NULL HYPOTHESIS**

   The **null hypothesis** is what you're going to **assume is true** during the study. Any data you collect will either back this assumption up, or it won't. If the data **doesn't support** your null hypothesis, you **reject** it and go with your **alternative hypothesis** instead.

   Very often, the null hypothesis is a prediction that there will be **no relationship** between the key variables in a study (and any correlation is due to **chance**), or that there will be **no difference** between the scores from the various conditions of an experiment. (An example might be that there will be no significant difference in exam grades between students who use a revision guide and students who don't.)

   (Note: It's quite usual to have something you **don't actually believe** as your null hypothesis. You assume it **is** true for the duration of the study, then if your results lead you to reject this null hypothesis, you've **proved** it **wasn't true** after all.)

2) **ALTERNATIVE HYPOTHESIS**

   If the data forces you to **reject** your null hypothesis, then you accept your **alternative hypothesis** instead.

   So if your null hypothesis was that two variables **aren't** linked, then your alternative hypothesis would be that they **are** linked. Or you can be more specific, and be a bit more precise about **how** they are linked, using **directional** hypotheses (see below).

3) **DIRECTIONAL HYPOTHESIS**

   A hypothesis might predict a difference between the exam results obtained by two groups of students — a group that uses a revision guide and another group that doesn't.

   If the hypothesis states which group will do better, it is making a **directional prediction**.

   For example, you might say that students who use a revision guide will get **significantly higher** exam grades than students who don't — this is a directional hypothesis.

   Directional hypotheses are often used when **previous research findings** suggest which way the results will go.

4) **NON-DIRECTIONAL HYPOTHESIS**

   A **non-directional hypothesis** would predict a difference, but wouldn't say which group would do better.

   For example, you might just say that there will be a **significant difference** in exam grades between students who use a revision guide and students who don't — this is a **non-directional** hypothesis, since you're not saying which group will do better.

   Non-directional hypotheses can be used when there is **little previous research** in the area under investigation, or when previous research findings are **mixed** and **inconclusive**.

Aims and Hypotheses

Some **Variables** are **Manipulated** by the Researcher — Others Aren't

A **variable** is a quantity whose **value** can **change** — for example, the time taken to do a task, someone's anxiety level, or an exam result. In an experiment, there are various different kinds of variable.

The **Independent Variable** is **Directly** Manipulated

1) An **independent variable (IV)** is a variable **directly manipulated** by the researcher.

2) In the example on the previous page about students, exams and revision guides, there are two variables. One is 'whether or not a revision guide is used' (so this variable has only two possible values: yes and no). The other is the 'exam grade' (and this could have lots of possible values: e.g. A*, A, B, C, D, E, U).

3) In this case, the **independent variable** is 'whether or not a revision guide is used' — since this is **directly** under the control of the researcher.

The **Dependent Variable** is Only Affected **Indirectly**

1) The **dependent variable (DV)** is the variable that you think will be **affected** by changes in the independent variable. (So the DV is **dependent on** the **IV**.)

2) In the exam grades example, the dependent variable is the 'exam grade'. The exam grade is dependent on whether a revision guide was used (or at least, that's what's being **investigated**).

Ideally in a study the *only* thing that would influence the **DV** (the thing you're measuring) would be the **IV** (the thing you're manipulating). Usually though, there are other things that will have an effect.

An **extraneous variable** is any variable (other than the **IV**) that **could** affect what you're trying to measure. If these things **are** actually **influencing** the DV then they're called **confounding variables**.

Operationalisation is **Showing** How the Variables Will Be **Measured**

1) Variables must be **operationalised**. This means describing the **process** by which the variable is **measured**.

2) Some things are easy to operationalise (e.g. **height** might be operationalised as 'the distance in centimetres from the bottom of an object to the top'). Other things are difficult to operationalise (e.g. a mother's love for her newborn baby).

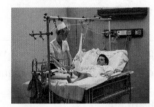

3) **Operationalisation** allows others to see exactly how you're going to define and measure your variables. It also has 18 letters, which is the same as soporiferousnesses, or yaaaaaaawwwwwwwwwn.

"Don't worry, sir — once we get your variable operationalised you'll be right as rain."

Warm-Up Questions

Q1 When would you reject the null hypothesis?

Q2 What is the difference between a directional and a non-directional hypothesis?

Q3 What is an independent variable?

Exam Question

Q1 Eva is interested in whether taking fish oil supplements every day for a month can improve memory performance.

a) Identify the independent variable in Eva's study. [1 mark]

b) What would be an appropriate hypothesis for her study? [3 marks]

Aim to learn this page — I hypothesise you'll need it...

Remember, you assume the null hypothesis is true unless your data suggests otherwise — if it does then you quickly switch allegiance to the alternative hypothesis instead. And remember, the IV is deliberately manipulated by the researcher. This might lead to an effect on the DV, but it's often a kind of indirect, knock-on effect. That's enough now.

Experimental Design

Once you've got a theory, this is how you'd actually go about researching it...

The **Experimental Design** Must Make the Hypothesis **Testable**

> **Research example** — does the presence of an audience help or hinder people doing the 'wiggly wire' task (moving a loop along a wire without touching it and setting off the buzzer)?
>
> Based on previous research, we expect people to do this better without anyone watching them.

1) The **IV** (the variable being manipulated) is the presence or absence of an audience.

2) The **DV** (the variable being measured) is 'how well' the participants do on the task — but it must be testable. You need a **precisely defined** (or **operationalised**) DV, which should be **quantitative** wherever possible. An operationalised DV for this experiment might be 'the time taken to move the loop from one end of the wire to the other without setting off the buzzer'.

There are Three **Experimental Designs** that are Used Loads

1) An **independent groups design** means there are **different participants** in each group. Here, for example, one group does the task **with** an audience and another group does it **alone**.

   This avoids the problem that if all the participants did the test in both conditions, any improvement in performance might be due to them having two goes at the task (which would be a confounding variable).

Advantages	**Disadvantages**
No **order effects** — no one gets better through practice (**learning effect**) or gets worse through being bored or tired (**fatigue effect**).	**Participant variables** — differences between the **people** in each group might affect the results (e.g. the 'without audience' group may just have people who are better at the task — so we can't safely compare groups). **Number of participants** — **twice as many** participants are needed to get the same amount of data, compared to having everyone do both conditions.

2) A **repeated measures design** is where, e.g., all participants do the task both **with** an audience and then **without**. You can compare the performances in each condition knowing the differences weren't due to participant variables.

Advantages	**Disadvantages**
Participant variables — now the same people do the test in both conditions, so any differences between individuals shouldn't affect the results. **Number of participants** — **fewer** participants are needed to get the same amount of data.	**Order effects** — if all participants did the 'with audience' condition first, any improvements in the second condition could be due to **practice**, not the audience's absence. (But see **counterbalancing** on the next page.)

3) A **matched pairs design** means there are different participants in each condition, but they're **matched** on important variables (like age, sex and personality). For example, the participants are paired on a relevant characteristic, such as age, and then the two members of the pair are **randomly assigned** to **either** the 'audience' or 'no audience' condition to ensure that **each condition** has a **similar age range**.

Advantages	**Disadvantages**
No **order effects** — there are **different people** in each condition. **Participant variables** — important differences are minimised through **matching**.	**Number of participants** — need twice as many people compared to repeated measures. **Practicalities** — **time-consuming** and difficult to find participants who **match**.

Some studies use **control groups**. These groups have not experienced any of the manipulations of the **IV** that an experimental group might have. This allows the researcher to make a direct comparison between them.

Experimental Design

Research Should Be Highly **Controlled**

1) Research needs to be highly **controlled** to avoid the effects of **extraneous variables** (see page 97).

2) Extraneous variables can be **controlled** in a study so that they're **kept constant** for all participants. For example, everyone could do the task in the same place so distractions are similar.

3) Extraneous variables can also be **eliminated altogether**. For example, everyone could do the task somewhere with no noise distractions — shhhh...

4) There are lots of other ways that research can be controlled to eliminate extraneous variables:

Counterbalancing (mixing up the order of the tasks) can solve **order effects** in **repeated measures** designs.

Half the participants do the task **with** an audience **first** and **then without**. The others do the conditions the **other way round**. Any order effects would then be equal across conditions.

Random allocation (e.g. by drawing names out of a hat) means everyone has an **equal chance** of doing **either** condition.

An **independent measures** study with, for example, more men in one group than the other could have a confounding variable (see page 97). Any difference in performance may be due to **sex** rather than the real IV. Random allocation should ensure groups are **not biased** on key variables.

Standardised instructions should ensure the **experimenters** act in a similar way with all participants.

Everything should be **as similar as possible** for all the participants, including each participant's **experience** in such studies.

Randomisation is when the **material** is presented to the participants in a **random order**.

It avoids the possibility of **order effects**. For example, in a **repeated measures** memory experiment, participants may be asked to learn a list of words in two different conditions. In each condition, the words on their lists would be in a **random** order.

It's Sometimes Good to Run a Small **Pilot Study** First

1) No piece of research is perfect. To help foresee any problems, a small-scale **pilot study** can be run first. This should establish whether the **design** works, whether **participants** understand the wording in **instructions**, or whether something important has been **missed out**.

2) They also give researchers practice at following the procedures. Problems can be tackled before running the **main study**, which could save wasting **time** and **money**.

3) Pilot studies allow the **validity** and **reliability** of the test to be assessed in advance (page 100), which then gives the opportunity for improvements to be made.

A pilot study. The jokes don't get much better than this. Sorry.

Warm-Up Questions

Q1 Give one disadvantage of an independent groups design.

Q2 Give one design that overcomes the disadvantage you identified in Q1.

Q3 What are the main benefits of running a pilot study?

PRACTICE QUESTIONS

Exam Question

Q1 Design an independent measures study to investigate the relationship between sleep and memory. [12 marks]

Random matches, no... repeated randomisation, no... oh pants... zzzzzzzzz...

There are lots of details here, but they're all really important. If you're not really careful when you design a piece of research, the results you get might not be worth the paper you end up writing them down on. And that'd be no good.

Reliability and Validity

*If you're doing **AS Level** you **don't** need to **learn** all of the information on these **two pages**. But (as I'm sure you've realised by now) 'reliability' and 'validity' are two words that crop up a lot in Psychology, so these pages might still be worth a read to give you a better understanding of what the words actually mean. A-Level folks, you need to learn it all properly, soz.*

Reliable Tests Give Consistent Results

Reliability refers to how **consistent** or **dependable** a test is. A reliable test carried out in the **same circumstances**, on the **same participants** should always give the **same results**. There are different types of reliability:

1) Internal Reliability

- **Different parts** of the test should give **consistent results**.
- For example, if an IQ test contains sections of supposedly equal difficulty, participants should achieve similar scores on all sections.

> The internal reliability of a test can be assessed using the **split-half method**. This splits the test into two halves, e.g. odd and even numbered questions, and the results from each half should produce a **high positive correlation**.

2) External Reliability

- **External reliability** — the test should produce **consistent results** regardless of **when** it's used.
- For example, if you took the same IQ test on two different days you should achieve the same score.

> The external reliability of a test can be assessed using the **test-retest method**. This involves **repeating** the test using the **same participants**. A reliable test should produce a **high positive correlation** between the two scores. A problem with this is that the participants may have changed in some way since the first test, e.g. they may have learnt more. To avoid this, external reliability can be checked using the **equivalent forms test**. This compares participants' scores on two different, but equivalent (equally hard), versions of the test.

3) Inter-observer Reliability

- The test should give **consistent results** regardless of **who** administers it.
- For example, if two researchers observe behaviour and categorise infants as showing signs of a strong attachment or a weak attachment, they should both record the same score.

> This can be assessed by **correlating** the scores that **each researcher** produces for **each participant**. A **high positive correlation** should be found.

Valid Tests Give Accurate Results

Validity refers to how well a test measures what it **claims to**. For example, an IQ test with only **maths questions** would not be a valid measure of **general intelligence**. There are different types of validity:

1) **Face validity** — the extent to which the test looks, to the participants, like it will measure what it is supposed to be measuring.
2) **Concurrent validity** — the extent to which the test produces the same results as another established measure, e.g. two different IQ tests should produce the same measure of IQ. Inferential tests can be used to determine whether both measures are highly correlated, and therefore valid (see page 123).
3) **Ecological validity** — the extent to which the results of the test reflect real-life.
4) **Temporal validity** — the extent to which the test provides results that can be generalised across time.

Reliability and Validity

Validity Can Be Assessed in Different Ways

- A quick (but not very thorough) way of assessing validity is to simply **look** at the test and make a judgement on whether it **appears** to measure what it claims to. For example, an IQ test that just consisted of maths questions could be identified as having low validity by this method.
- **Comparing** the results of the test with the results of an **existing measure** (that's already accepted as valid) can help to determine the validity of the test.
- The results of the test can be used to **predict** results of **future tests**. If the **initial** results **correlate** with the **later** results it suggests that the test has some validity and can continue to be used.

Reliability and Validity Can Both be Improved

There are several ways that the **reliability** and **validity** of tests can be **improved**:

Standardising research

Standardising research involves creating **specific procedures** which are followed every time the test is carried out. This ensures that all the researchers will test all the participants in **exactly the same way**, e.g. in the same sequence, at the same time of day, in the same environment, and with all participants receiving exactly the same instructions. This reduces the possibility of extraneous variables affecting the research. Therefore it will help to improve **external reliability** and **inter-observer reliability**.

Like most children, Idris spent all morning standardising his favourite procedure and was feeling pretty smug about the end result.

Operationalising variables

1) **Operationalising variables** involves **clearly defining** all of the research **variables**.
2) For example, in a study of whether watching aggressive TV influences aggressive behaviour, the terms '**aggressive TV**' and '**aggressive behaviour**' need to be defined.
3) 'Aggressive TV' could include cartoons or human actors. One of these might influence human behaviour and the other might not — this needs to be taken into account when planning, carrying out and drawing conclusions from the investigation.
4) Similarly, 'aggressive behaviour' could refer to physical and verbal aggression, or just physical aggression.
5) Clarifying this from the start improves the **reliability** and **validity** of the test.

Warm-Up Questions
If you're doing <u>AS Level</u>, you don't need to answer any of these Practice Questions.

Q1 Explain the difference between internal reliability and external reliability.

Q2 How does the split-half method test for internal reliability?

Q3 Why does standardisation help to improve the reliability and validity of research?

Exam Questions

Q1 Briefly explain how validity could be assessed in psychological research. [4 marks]

Q2 Briefly outline how reliability could be improved in psychological research. [4 marks]

Reliable tests? Who cares. Reliable results are what you need right now.

So, it turns out that 'reliable' and 'valid' are more than just terms to bandy around and throw into answers with some sort of vague idea that they're good things for studies to be. They've got specific meanings you need to know. These examiners are so demanding — it's like they've got nothing better to do than sit around thinking up stuff for you to learn.

Observations, Questionnaires and Interviews

These pages will tell you everything you could ever wish to know about observations, questionnaires and interviews. Bit of a jam-packed few pages, eh? Best get reading...

Researchers Can use Participant or Non-Participant Observation

1) **Participant observation** is when the researcher **participates** in the activity under study.

   Advantages: — The researcher develops a relationship with the group under study, so they can gain a greater understanding of the group's behaviour.

   Disadvantages: — The researcher loses objectivity by becoming part of the group.
   — The participants may act differently if they know a researcher is amongst them.

2) **Non-participant observation** is when the researcher observes the activity without getting involved in it.

   Advantages: — The researcher can remain objective throughout the study.

   Disadvantages: — The researcher loses a sense of the group dynamics by staying separate from the group.

   Sometimes researchers undertake structured observations.
   This is where the behaviour categories that are going to be used are defined in advance. There's more on this on the next page.

   Advantages: — It's easier to gather relevant data because you already know what you're looking for.

   Disadvantages: — Interesting behaviours could go unrecorded because they haven't been pre-defined as important.

Participant and Non-Participant Observations Can be Overt or Covert

Participant and non-participant observations can either be:

Overt Observations

Overt observations are where the researcher's presence is **obvious** to the participants.

   Advantage: — They are much more ethically sound than other methods because the participants are aware of the research.

   Disadvantage: — People might change their behaviour if they know they're being observed.

Covert Observations

Covert observations are where the researcher's presence is **unknown** to the participants.

   Advantage: — The participants are much more likely to behave naturally.

   Disadvantage: — Gaining ethical approval may be difficult.

Arthur brought out his matching tracksuit to carry out his covert observation.

Controlled Observations have Conditions Set Up by the Experimenter

Controlled observations often take place in a laboratory so the researcher can control the conditions. Bandura's **Bobo doll study** (page 59) is an example of this type of observation.

   Advantages: — Because the study is highly controlled, it is possible to replicate it to check that the results are reliable.
   — A controlled environment means that extraneous variables can be controlled, so it becomes possible for cause and effect to be established.

   Disadvantages: — They will have lower ecological validity than naturalistic observations.
   — Participants may alter their behaviour if they know they're being observed.

Observations, Questionnaires and Interviews

Naturalistic Observation Involves Making Design Decisions

Naturalistic observations take place in a natural environment, rather than a lab. They can be structured in advance to make sure no behaviours are missed.

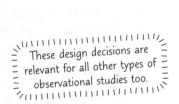
These design decisions are relevant for all other types of observational studies too.

Recording Data

If you want **qualitative data** you could just make **written notes**. But **video** or **audio recording** means that you have a more accurate permanent record.

Categorising Behaviour

You must **define** the behaviours you aim to observe. For example, if you were going to observe children in a school playground to see how many behave aggressively, you'd have to decide what counts as aggression. This involves giving an operationalised definition (i.e. some specific, observable behaviours).

For example, you might say that *'aggression is any physical act made with the intention to harm another person — such as punching, kicking, etc.'*

But you have to be careful not to miss out anything important otherwise your definition may not be valid, e.g. aggression can also be verbal.

Rating Behaviour

The behaviours that you're interested in may be things that are a matter of **degree**, so you might need to use a rating scale to classify behaviour.

You could put each participant's behaviour into one of several **categories**, e.g. *not aggressive*, *mildly aggressive* or *very aggressive*.

Or you could use a **coding system** where each participant is given a **number** (e.g. between 1 and 10) to represent how aggressive they are, where a **higher score** indicates **more aggression**.

However, you still have to **define** what kinds of behaviour are included for each number on the scale (e.g. 5 = *pushing* and 10 = *kicking or punching more than once*). Behaviour rated in this way provides **quantitative data** (data in the form of **numbers**).

Sampling Behaviour

You have to decide how often and for how long you're going to observe the participants.

Event sampling — this is when you only record particular events that you're interested in (e.g. aggression shown by the children) and ignore other behaviours.

> Advantage — Researchers know exactly what behaviours they're looking for.
> Disadvantage — Potentially interesting behaviours could be ignored.

Time-interval sampling — if the behaviours occur over a long time period you might choose to observe for only set time intervals, e.g. the first 10 minutes of every hour. The time intervals could be chosen randomly.

> Advantage — Very convenient for the researchers to carry out.
> Disadvantage — If interesting behaviours occur outside the sample intervals they won't be recorded.

Inter-Observer Reliability

Even after you've **defined** the behaviours you're interested in, you have to make sure that the observers are actually putting each participant in the **right category** or giving the **right rating**.

This might involve **comparing** the data from two or more observers to make sure they're giving the **same** scores (i.e. that they are 'reliable').

Observations, Questionnaires and Interviews

Questionnaires Need to be Designed Carefully

There are various things you need to consider when designing a questionnaire for a survey.

1) **Type of data** — whether you want **qualitative data** and/or **quantitative data** will affect whether you ask **open** and/or **closed questions**.

   a) **Open questions** are questions such as *What kinds of music do you like?*
   The participant can reply in **any way**, and in as much detail as they want. This gives detailed, qualitative information, although it may be **hard to analyse**, as the participants could give very different answers.

   b) **Closed questions** limit the answers that can be given, e.g. *Which do you like: Pop, Rock or neither?*
   They give **quantitative** data that is relatively **easy to analyse** — e.g. you can say exactly **how many** people liked each type of music. However, less detail is obtained about each participant.

2) **Ambiguity** — you have to avoid questions and answer options which are **not** clearly **defined**, e.g. *Do you listen to music frequently?* What is meant here by 'frequently' — once a day, once a week?

3) **Double-barrelled questions** — it's best not to use these, since a person may wish to answer **differently** to each part. For example, *Do you agree that modern music is not as good as the music of the 1960s and that there should be more guitar-based music in the charts?*

4) **Leading questions** — these are questions that **lead** the participant towards a particular answer. E.g. *How old was the boy in the distance?* They might have seen an older person, but by saying '*boy*' you're leading them to describe the person as young. You're also leading them to think that the person was male, but they might not have been sure. (It's really important to avoid leading questions in **eyewitness testimony** — see p.22-25.)

5) **Complexity** — whenever possible, **clear English** should be used, avoiding **jargon**.
   However, if specialist terms are included, they should be clearly defined.
   (So the question *Do you prefer music written in unusual time signatures?* probably isn't ideal for most people.)

All of the Above Goes for Interviews As Well

But you also have to consider the following:

1) **How structured** the interview will be:
   Interviews can be very **informal** with **few set questions**, and new questions being asked **depending on** the participant's **previous answers**. This gives detailed qualitative data, which may be difficult to analyse. Alternatively, they may be more **structured**, with set questions and **closed answers**, giving **less detail** but being **easier to analyse**.

2) Using a **question checklist** — if the interview is structured, a checklist ensures that no questions are left out and questions aren't asked twice.

3) The behaviour or appearance of the **interviewer** — this could **influence** how the participants react.

Warm-Up Questions

Q1 What is 'non-participant observation'?

Q2 Give two advantages of using controlled observation.

Q3 Why is it important to define behavioural categories in naturalistic observations?

Q4 Outline three considerations involved in designing questionnaires.

Exam Questions

Q1 Outline how event sampling can be used as part of an observational research method. [2 marks]

Q2 Briefly outline **two** issues that a researcher must consider when conducting an interview. [4 marks]

I've always wanted to be an undercover cop...

Covert and participant observations sound like fun. It'd be a bit like being in one of those exciting crime TV programmes, where a policeman dresses up as a 'normal' person, gets involved in a high-speed car chase and saves the day by catching the criminal in his tracks. What I'd give to lead an exciting life. Oh, wait. I have Psychology. Yay.

Selecting and Using Participants

It'd be great if you could study everyone in the world. It might take ages, but you're bound to find something interesting eventually. Most psychologists can't be bothered to do this though, so they just pick a selection of people to study...

Selecting a **Sample** of Participants Should be Done **Carefully**

1) The part of a **population** that you're interested in studying is called the **target group** — e.g. all the people in a particular city, or all people of a certain age or background.

2) Usually you can't include everyone in the target group in a study, so you choose a certain **sample** of **participants**.

3) This sample should be **representative** (i.e. it should reflect the variety of characteristics that are found in the target group) so that the results can be generalised to the whole target group.

4) A sample that is unrepresentative is **biased** and **can't** reliably be **generalised** to the whole target group.

There are five main ways of selecting a sample:

Random Sampling

This is when **every** member of the target group has an **equal chance** of being selected for the sample. This could be done either **manually** or by a **computer**. Manually, each person could be assigned a number. Each number could be put in a hat, and then numbers selected at random from it. Using a computer, everyone in the target group could be given a number, then the computer could randomly pick numbers to select participants. Sounds like being in a catalogue store. Order number 103 to the collection point...

Advantages: Random sampling is 'fair'. Everyone has an equal chance of being selected and the sample is **likely** to be representative.

Disadvantages: This method doesn't **guarantee** a representative sample — there's still a chance that some subgroups in the target group may not be selected (e.g. people from a minority cultural group). Also, if the target group is large it may not be practical (or possible) to give everyone a number that might be picked. So in practice, completely random samples are rarely used.

Opportunity Sampling

This is when the researcher samples whoever is **available and willing** to be studied. Since many researchers work in universities, they often use opportunity samples made up of students.

Advantages: This is a **quick** and **practical** way of getting a sample.

Disadvantages: The sample is **unlikely** to be **representative** of the target group or population as a whole. This means that we can't confidently **generalise** the findings of the research. However, because it's **quick** and **easy**, opportunity sampling is **often used**.

Volunteer Sampling

This is when people actively **volunteer** to be in a study by responding to a request for participants advertised by the researcher, e.g. in a newspaper or on a noticeboard.
The researcher may then select only those who are **suitable** for the study.
(This method was used by Milgram — see page 7.)

Advantages: If an advert is placed prominently (e.g. in a national newspaper) a **large number** of people may respond, giving more participants to study. This may allow more **in-depth analysis** and **more accurate** statistical results.

Disadvantages: Even though a large number of people may respond, these will only include people who saw or heard about the advertisement — no one else would have a chance of being selected. Also, people who volunteer may be more **cooperative** than others, so the sample is **unlikely** to be **representative** of the target population.

Selecting and Using Participants

Systematic Sampling

This is where every *n*th name from a **sampling frame** (a record of all the names in a population) is taken, e.g. every 3rd name from a register, or every 50th name from a phone book. This is useful if there is a sampling frame available.

Advantages: This is a **simple** and **effective** way of generating a sample with a random element. It also means that the population is more likely to be **evenly sampled** than by using opportunity or volunteer samples.

Disadvantages: Subgroups might be **missed**. It will not be **representative** if the pattern used for the **samples** coincides with a pattern in the **population**.

Annie was promised systematic sampling was simple. Even her granny could do it.

Stratified Sampling

This is where all of the **important subgroups** in the population (e.g. different age or ethnic groups) are identified and a proportionate number of each is randomly obtained. For example, in a class of **20** students, **ten** are 16 years old, **eight** are 17 years old and **two** are 18 years old. If you take a stratified sample of 10 students, the number of 16-, 17- and 18-year-olds in the sample will need to be **50%** of the full class. So you'll need **five** 16-year-olds, **four** 17-year-olds and **one** 18-year-old in your stratified sample.

Advantages: This can produce a fairly **representative** sample. It can also be used with random and systematic sampling.

Disadvantages: It can take a lot of **time** and **money** to do it, and some subgroups may be **missed**. It can often be **difficult** to identify traits and characteristics (such as people's ages or backgrounds) effectively enough to stratify the sample properly.

No method can guarantee a representative sample, but you should have confidence that your sample is (quite) representative if you want to generalise your results to the entire target group.

Participants Sometimes **Act Differently** When They're Being **Observed**

Human participants will usually be aware that they are being **studied**. This may mean they don't show their **true response**, and so their data may not be **valid** or **reliable**. Some of these effects are explained below...

1 **THE HAWTHORNE EFFECT:** If people are **interested** in something and in the attention they are getting (e.g. from researchers), then they show a more **positive** response, try **harder** at tasks, and so on.

This means their results for tests are often **artificially high** (because they're trying harder than normal), which could make a researcher's conclusions **invalid**.

The opposite effect may occur if the participants are **uninterested** in the task.

2 **DEMAND CHARACTERISTICS:** There are aspects of a study which allow the participants to form an idea about its **purpose**. If they think they know what kind of response the researcher is **expecting** from them, they may show that response to '**please**' the researcher (or they may **deliberately** do the **opposite**). Either way, the conclusions drawn from the study would be **invalid**.

3 **SOCIAL DESIRABILITY BIAS:** People usually try to show themselves in the **best possible light**. So in a survey, they may **not** be completely **truthful**, but give answers that are more **socially acceptable** instead (e.g. people may say they give more money to charity than they really do). This would make the results **less valid**.

Selecting and Using Participants

The **Researchers** Can **Affect** the Outcomes in **Undesirable Ways**

The **reliability** and **validity** of results may also be influenced by the researcher, since he or she has **expectations** about what will happen. This can produce the following effects:

1   RESEARCHER (or EXPERIMENTER) BIAS: The researchers' **expectations** can influence how they **design** their study and how they **behave** towards the participants. Also, their expectations may influence **how** they take **measurements** and **analyse** their data, resulting in errors that can lead, for example, to accepting a hypothesis that was actually false. Their expectations may also lead them to only ask questions about what **they** are **interested** in, and they may **focus** on the aspects of the participant's answers which **fit** their **expectations**.

2   INVESTIGATOR EFFECTS: These can be anything that the researcher does which can affect how the participant **behaves**. If a researcher's expectations influence how they behave towards their participants, the participants might respond to **demand characteristics**. Also, a researcher's **expectations** could result in them asking **leading questions**. Finally, the participant may react to the **behaviour** or **appearance** of an investigator and answer differently.

Warm-Up Questions

Q1 What is random sampling?
Q2 Give a disadvantage of opportunity sampling.
Q3 Give an advantage of volunteer sampling.
Q4 What is a systematic sample?
Q5 Give a disadvantage of stratified sampling.
Q6 What are demand characteristics?
Q7 Give an example of experimenter bias.

Exam Questions

Q1   Describe one advantage of using a systematic sample.   [2 marks]

Q2   Read the item below and then answer the questions that follow.

> A psychologist was investigating the relationship between the number of sick-days taken by Year 12 students over one academic year and their final exam results.
>
> A sample of 50 Year 12 students was taken from one school. Their absences over the whole year, as recorded in the daily register, were correlated with the results of their final exam taken at the end of Year 12.

a)   Describe how the psychologist could have used random sampling to select the participants.   [2 marks]

b)   Outline one disadvantage of using random sampling to select participants.   [2 marks]

c)   Describe another sampling technique which could have made the sample more representative than random sampling.   [3 marks]

Q3   Outline the effects of demand characteristics on scientific research.   [2 marks]

Q4   Outline how investigator effects might influence the outcome of a psychological study.   [2 marks]

Volunteers needed for study into pain and embarrassment... (and stupidity)

Bear in mind that loads of the studies here were done in universities. Students are pretty easy to get your hands on in universities, so they make up most of the samples. Trouble is, students are quite different to the rest of the population (lots of beans on toast, sleeping through the day, you know the type) so the samples could be pretty unrepresentative...

Ethical Issues in Psychological Research

Remember Milgram's obedience research? The one that made participants think they were giving lethal electric shocks to others. It was a bit... "unethical", some might say. If you're not sure what that means, worry not, just read on...

Ethics are an **Important Issue** in Psychology

Psychological research and practice should aim to improve our **self-understanding**, be **beneficial** to people and try to **improve the quality of life** for individuals. As professionals, psychologists are expected to do their work in an **ethical manner**.

The British Psychological Society (BPS) Produces **Ethical Guidelines**

The **British Psychological Society** (BPS) has developed ethical guidelines for psychologists to follow when they're designing studies, so that participants are protected. They are **formal principles** for what is considered to be acceptable or unacceptable, and include advice on **deception**, **consent** and **psychological harm**.

1	**Informed Consent**	• BPS guidelines state that participants should always give **informed consent**. • They should be told the aims and nature of the study before agreeing to it. • They should also know that they have the **right to withdraw** at any time.

1) **BUT** if the participant is under 16 years of age they can't **legally** give consent (although a parent can).

2) In **naturalistic observation** studies, consent is not obtained. In this case the research is acceptable provided that it is done in a **public location** where people would expect to be observed by others.

3) Even when informed consent is supposedly obtained, issues may be raised. **Menges (1973)** reviewed about 1000 American studies and found that **97%** had not given people all the information about the research.

2	**Deception**	• If participants have been deceived then they cannot have given **informed consent**. • However, sometimes researchers must **withhold information** about the study because the participants wouldn't behave **naturally** if they knew what the aim was.

1) The BPS guidelines state that deception is only acceptable if there is strong **scientific justification** for the research and there's **no alternative procedure** available to obtain the data.

2) Researchers can also ask **independent people** if they would object to the study. If they wouldn't, it may be done with naïve participants (although they **may not agree** with others' opinions about the study).

3) Participants could just be given **general** details — although if too little is said they may feel **deceived** (but if participants know too much then they may not behave naturally).

4) The **severity** of deception differs, e.g. research on memory may involve **unexpected** memory tests (that participants weren't informed about). This is **less objectionable** than the deception involved in Milgram's study.

3	**Protection from harm**	• The BPS guidelines say that the risk of harm to participants should be **no greater** than they would face in their normal lives. It's hard to **accurately assess** this.

1) Research procedures can involve physical and psychological discomfort, e.g. **Glass and Singer (1972)** exposed participants to noise to make them stressed, and participants in **Milgram's** research suffered extreme distress.

2) Some people face **risks** in their work (e.g. soldiers), but that doesn't mean they can be exposed to risks in research.

3) Researchers don't always **know in advance** what might be distressing for participants.

Ethical Issues in Psychological Research

4 Debriefing	• Debriefing is supposed to return participants to the state they were in **before the research**.
	• It's especially important if **deception** has been used.

1) Researchers must fully explain what the research involved and what the results might show.
2) Participants are given the **right to withdraw their data**.

5 Confidentiality	• None of the participants in a psychological study should be **identifiable** from any reports that are produced.

1) Data collected during research must be **confidential** — researchers can't use people's **names** in reports.
2) Participants must be **warned** if their data is not going to be completely anonymous.
3) However, some groups or people might be **easily identifiable** from their **characteristics** — more so if the report says where and when the study was carried out, etc.

Researchers Have to Deal with **Ethical Issues in Their Studies**

Deception

Sometimes it's difficult to conduct meaningful research without a bit of **deception**. If participants know exactly what's being studied then their behaviour might change, and the data you get would be useless.

Psychologists don't usually tell participants every last detail, but they do try to minimise deception. That way participants aren't likely to be upset when they find out the true nature of the study.

Milgram's experiment (page 7) is an example of a study that would probably not be considered ethical today. He deceived participants about the true purpose of the study and many of them showed signs of **stress** when taking part.

Consent

Gaining consent is central to conducting research ethically. But telling participants they're being observed could **change** the way they **behave**.

Milgram's participants couldn't give informed consent until after they were debriefed. If they'd known about the nature of the study, it wouldn't have worked.

Animal Rights are Also an **Ethical Issue**

Research with non-human animals has caused heated debate.

1) In **support**, people argue that animal research has provided **valuable information** for psychological and medical research. Some **experimental designs** couldn't have been conducted on humans — e.g. Harlow's study on attachment, where young monkeys were separated from their mothers and reared alone (page 28).
2) Some **disagree** with the idea of conducting research with non-human animals. They may argue that it's **ethically wrong** to inflict harm and suffering on animals, and obviously animals can't give consent to take part.
3) Some argue that it's cruel to experiment on animals that have a **similar intelligence** to humans, because they might suffer the same problems we would. It'd be OK to experiment on animals that are far less developed than us, but there is no point because they'll be **too different** from us to give results that apply to humans.

Ethical Issues in Psychological Research

Ethical Guidelines **Don't Solve** All the Problems

1) There may be researchers who don't follow the guidelines properly. Naughty.

2) If a psychologist conducts research in an unacceptable way, they can't be banned from research (unlike a doctor who can be 'struck off' for misconduct). But they'd probably be kicked out of their university and the BPS.

3) Even when guidelines are followed, it can be difficult to assess things like psychological harm, or to fully justify the use of deception.

4) Deciding whether the ends (benefits from the study) justify the means (how it was done and at what cost) is not straightforward either. This creates another dilemma for psychologists.

The lasting harm to Milgram's participants was beginning to show.

Warm-Up Questions

Q1 What are 'ethical guidelines' and why are they needed in psychology?

Q2 Why is it sometimes impossible to obtain informed consent from participants?

Q3 If you have used deception, what should you do immediately after the study?

Q4 For the issue of psychological harm, what level of risk is said to be acceptable in research?

Q5 What is the purpose of debriefing?

Q6 Why might people disagree with the idea of conducting non-human animal research?

PRACTICE QUESTIONS

Exam Questions

Q1 Read the item below, then answer the question that follows.

> A psychologist aims to investigate the relationship between anxiety and response time. The psychologist will ask participants to either watch a calm or frightening movie clip, then respond to a series of cognitive tasks.

Outline why the participants would need debriefing after this study.

[2 marks]

Q2 Read the item below, then answer the question that follows.

> A researcher wants to study the effect of sleep deprivation on memory. He intends to divide participants into two groups and ask them to learn a list of 15 words. The first group will then be deprived of sleep for 24 hours, whilst the second group will maintain a normal level of rest.
>
> Both groups will then be asked to recall the list of words.

Outline at least **two** ethical principles that will need to be considered for this psychological research, as developed by the British Psychological Society.

[6 marks]

Don't let someone debrief you unless you love them very much...

Psychological experiments create many ethical dilemmas. Take Milgram's study — there's no doubting that the results reveal interesting things about how people interact. But do these results justify the possible psychological damage done to the participants? There's no right or wrong answer, but the BPS guidelines are there to address this issue exactly.

Data Analysis

*Data analysis might sound vaguely maths-like — but relax, it isn't too tricky really. If you're doing **AS Level**, you need to learn about Data Analysis but you **don't** need to know about **thematic analysis** or **content analysis** (p.112).*

Data from **Observations** Should be Analysed **Carefully**

1) If you've got **quantitative** data (i.e. numbers), you can use **statistics** to show, for example, the most common behaviours. Quantitative data can be obtained by **categorising** and **rating** behaviour — see page 112.

2) **Qualitative** data might consist of a video or audio **recording**, or written **notes** on what the observers witnessed. Analysis of qualitative data is **less straightforward**, but it can still be done.

3) Whatever kind of data you've got, there are some important issues to bear in mind:

> a) There must be **adequate data sampling** (see page 103) to ensure that a **representative** sample of participants' behaviour has been seen.
>
> b) **Language** must be used **accurately** — the words used to describe behaviour should be **accurate** and **appropriate** (and must have valid **operationalised definitions** — see page 97). For example, it might not be appropriate to describe a child's behaviour as 'aggressive' if he or she is play-fighting.
>
> c) Researcher **bias** must be **avoided** — e.g. it's not okay to make notes **only** on events that **support** the researcher's theories, or to have a **biased interpretation** of what is observed.

The Same Goes for Data Obtained from **Interviews**

1) When **closed** questions are used as part of an interview's structure, **quantitative** data can be produced (e.g. the **number** of participants who replied 'Yes' to a particular question). **Statistics** can then be used (see pages 114-116 and 123-133) to further analyse the data.

2) When **open** questions are used, more **detailed**, **qualitative** data is obtained.

3) Again, whatever you've got, there are certain things you'll need to remember:

> a) **Context** — the **situation** in which a participant says something, and the way they are **behaving** at the time, may be important. It may help the researcher understand **why** something is said, and give clues about the **honesty** of a statement.
>
> b) The researcher should clearly distinguish **what** is said by the participant from **how** they interpret it.
>
> c) **Selection** of data — a lot of **qualitative** data may be produced by an interview, which may be difficult for the researcher to **summarise** in a report. The researcher must **avoid bias** in selecting what to include (e.g. only including statements that support their ideas). The interviewees may be consulted when deciding **what** to include and **how** to present it.
>
> d) The interviewer should be aware of how *their* feelings about the interviewee could lead to **biased interpretations** of what they say, or how it is later reported.

Bertha was disappointed to learn that she'd been reduced to a number.

And Likewise for Data from **Questionnaires**

1) Like observations and interviews, **questionnaires** can give you both **quantitative** and **qualitative** data, and so most of the points above are relevant to surveys as well.

2) Again, it's especially important to distinguish the **interpretations** of the **researcher** from the **statements** of the **participant**, and to be **unbiased** in selecting what to include in any report on the research.

3) However, the analysis of **written** answers may be especially difficult because the participant is not present to **clarify** any **ambiguities**, plus you don't know the **context** for their answers (e.g. what mood they were in, and so on).

Data Analysis

Qualitative Data Can Be Tricky to Analyse

1) Once **quantitative data** is collected, it can be **easily** and **objectively** analysed.

2) However, **qualitative data** (such as an interview transcript) is sometimes seen as 'of **limited use**' because it's difficult to analyse **objectively**.

Thematic analysis is a form of qualitative analysis — it involves subjective decisions

Thematic analysis is one of the most frequently used forms of qualitative analysis. It involves making **summaries** of data and identifying **key themes** and **categories**.

- Firstly, the researcher becomes **familiar with the data**. Then they start to **look** for different themes, **review** the themes, **define** and **name** the themes and then **write** a report.

- However, different researchers may read different things into the themes — it can be **subjective**.

- Such analysis may give the basis for **hypotheses**, e.g. about what may be found in other sources / other things the participant may say — the hypothesis formation is therefore **grounded in the data** (but could still be subjective).

Strengths

1) Qualitative analysis preserves the **detail** in the data.

2) Creating hypotheses during the analysis allows for new **insights** to be developed.

3) Some **objectivity** can be established by using **triangulation** — other sources of data are used to check conclusions (e.g. previous interviews). With more sources researchers can cross-check their interpretations.

Criticisms

1) How do you decide **which categories to use** and whether a statement fits a particular category?

2) How do you decide what to **leave out** of the summary, or which quotations to use?

These are **subjective** decisions and researchers may be **biased**, possibly showing statements or events **out of context**.

Content Analysis is a Way to Quantify Qualitative Data

1) Because of the **detail** (and hence the **insight**) that **qualitative** data can give, some researchers prefer to **avoid** 'reducing' it to **numbers**.

2) Instead they analyse the data into **categories** or '**typologies**' (e.g. sarcastic remarks, statements about feelings, etc.), **quotations**, **summaries**, and so on.

3) This is called **content analysis** and the method is outlined below.

4) **Hypotheses** may be developed during this analysis so that they are 'grounded in the data'.

- A representative sample of qualitative data is first collected — e.g. from an interview, printed material (newspapers, etc.) or other media (such as TV programmes).

- Coding units are identified to analyse the data. A coding unit could be, for example, an act of violence, or the use of gender stereotypes (though both of these must be given valid operationalised definitions first — e.g. a definition of an 'act of violence').

- The qualitative data is then analysed to see how often each coding unit occurs (or how much is said about it, etc.).

- Statistical analysis can then be carried out (see pages 114-116 and 123-133).

Strengths

- A **clear summary** of the patterns in the data may be established.

- Once a coding system has been set up, **replication** is easy, improving reliability.

Limitations

- Often an individual's judgement is used to define coding units, so they can be **subjective**.

- Reducing the data to particular coding units **removes detail**, and the true meaning of things may be lost when taken out of context.

Data Analysis

There are **Advantages** and **Disadvantages** of **Quantifying Data**

Advantages of Quantifying Data

1) It becomes **easier** to see **patterns** in the data, and easier to **summarise** and **present** it (see pages 120-122).
2) **Statistical analysis** can be carried out.

Disadvantages of Quantifying Data

1) Care is needed to avoid bias in defining coding units (see p.112), or deciding which behaviours fit particular units.
2) Qualitative data has more detail (context, etc.), which is lost when it's converted into numbers.

Psychologists Gather **Primary** and **Secondary Data**

Researchers gather **primary** and **secondary data** when they collect results.

- **Primary data** — information collected during a researcher's direct observations of participants, e.g. test results, answers to questionnaires, observation notes.

- **Secondary data** — information collected from other studies. This data can be used to check the validity of studies, or used to provide evidence to support or discredit a new theory.

Summarising Lots of Studies is Called a **Meta-Analysis**

Both **quantitative** data and **qualitative** data can be analysed using a **meta-analysis**. This is where you analyse the results from loads of different studies and come up with some **general conclusions**.

They're a good way of **bringing together data** (which is a general aim of the scientific process), and by doing this they reduce the problem of **sample size**. However, one problem is that there are often loads of **conflicting results** out there, which obviously makes doing a meta-analysis a bit tricky...

Warm-Up Questions

Q1 What is quantitative data?

Q2 In what ways could a researcher be biased when analysing data from observations?

Q3 What type of questions will lead to detailed, qualitative data?

Q4 What is the difference between primary and secondary data?

Q5 What is a meta-analysis?

Exam Questions   If you're doing AS Level, you don't need to do Exam Question 3.

Q1 Collecting data on which of the following would produce qualitative data?

    A shoe size   **B** age   **C** opinions on car park charges   **D** time spent online each day   [1 mark]

Q2 Outline the main differences between qualitative and quantitative data-collection techniques.   [4 marks]

Q3 Outline and evaluate how content analysis can be used to analyse qualitative data.   [4 marks]

You must keep an open mind — but just don't let all the facts escape...

It's fairly obvious-ish, I guess, that qualitative data needs to be analysed with an open mind — it's not OK to fit the facts to your theory... you have to fit your theory to the facts. The same goes for analysing quantitative data — it's not just a case of 'doing some maths' — you have to be sure you're not being biased in your interpretations.

Descriptive Statistics

Run for your lives... panic. This really looks like maths... Well, actually, it's not too bad. So calm down.

Descriptive Statistics — Just Say What You See...

1) **Descriptive statistics** simply describe the **patterns** found in a set of data.

2) Descriptive statistics uses the fancy term '**central tendency**' to describe an **average**. For example, the central tendency (average) for the height of a group of 18-year-old boys might be about 1.70 metres.

3) Measures of **dispersion** describe **how spread out** the data is.
For example, the difference in height between the shortest 18-year-old boy and the tallest might be 35 cm.

There are 3 Measures of **Central Tendency** (aka Average) You Need to Know

The Mean — This is the 'Normal Average'

You calculate the **mean** by **adding** all of the scores in a data set and then **dividing** by the number of scores.

$$\text{Mean} = \bar{X} = \frac{\sum X}{N}, \text{ where } \sum X \text{ is the sum of all the scores (and there are } N \text{ of them).}$$

EXAMPLE:

If you've got scores of 2, 5, 6, 7 and 10, then...

$\sum X = 30$ (since all the scores add up to 30),

and $N = 5$ (since there are 5 of them)...

...so the **mean** is $\bar{X} = \dfrac{30}{5} = 6$

Remember to change N to the number of values in the data set.

EXAMPLE:

If you've got scores of 34, 45, 2, 37, 11, 53 and 19, then...

$\sum X = 201$ (since all the scores add up to 201),

and $N = 7$ (since there are 7 of them)...

...so the **mean** is $\bar{X} = \dfrac{201}{7} = 28.71$

Σ (pronounced 'sigma') just means you add things up.

ADVANTAGES:

a) It uses **all** the scores in a data set.

b) It's used in **further calculations** and so it's handy to work it out.

DISADVANTAGES:

a) It can be **skewed** (distorted) by extremely **high** or **low** scores. This can make it **unrepresentative** of most of the scores, and so it may be **misleading**. In these cases, it's best not to use the mean. For example, the scores 10, 40, 25, 20 and 650 have a mean of 149, which is not representative of the central tendency of the data set.

b) It can sometimes give an **unrealistically precise** value (e.g. the average family has 2.4 children — but what does 0.4 of a child mean...?).

The Mode — The Score that Occurs **Most Often**

EXAMPLE:

The mode (or the modal score) of 2, 5, 2, 9, 6, 11 and 2 is **2**.

If there are two scores which are most common then the data set is 'bimodal'. If there are three or more scores which are most common then the data set is 'multimodal'.

ADVANTAGES:

a) It shows the **most common** or 'important' score.

b) It's always a result from the actual **data set**, so it can be a more **useful** or **realistic** statistic, e.g. the modal average family has 2 children, not 2.4.

DISADVANTAGES:

a) It's not very useful if there are **several** modal values, or if the modal value is only **slightly** more common than other scores.

b) It has **little further use** in data analysis.

Descriptive Statistics

The Median — The Middle Score When the Data is Put in Order

EXAMPLE:

The **median** of the scores 4, 5, 10, 12 and 14 is **10**.

In the above example there was **one score** in the **middle**, as there was an odd number of scores.
If there is an even number of scores, there will be **two** middle scores.
Add them together and then **divide by 2** to get the median:

EXAMPLE:

The **median** of the scores 2, 6, 27, 45, 52 and 63 is **36**.
In this example there are two middle scores (27 and 45).
So you do: 27 + 45 = 72, 72 ÷ 2 = **36**

Don't forget to arrange the scores in numerical order first.

ADVANTAGES:

a) It's relatively **quick** and **easy** to calculate.

b) It's **not** affected by extremely high or low scores, so it can be used on 'skewed' sets of data to give a '**representative**' average score.

DISADVANTAGES:

a) Not **all** the scores are used to work out the median.

b) It has **little further use** in data analysis.

Measures of Dispersion Tell You How Spread Out the Data Is

Range — Highest Score Minus the Lowest Score

EXAMPLE:

The **range** of the scores 6, 10, 35 and 50 is 50 – 6 = **44**.

ADVANTAGE:

It's **quick** and **easy** to calculate.

DISADVANTAGE:

It completely ignores the **central** values of a data set, so it can be misleading if there are very **high** or **low** scores.

1) The **interquartile range (IQR)** can be calculated to help **avoid** this disadvantage.

2) First the **median** is identified (this is sometimes called **Q2**).

3) If there's an **odd** number of values then you take the middle number as the median.
   If there's an **even** number of values then you take the 2 middle numbers, add them together and divide them by 2 to find the median.

4) The **median** of the **lower half** of the data is called the **lower quartile** (or **Q1**).
   The **median** of the **upper half** of the data is called the **upper quartile** (or **Q3**).

5) The **IQR = Q3 – Q1**.

EXAMPLE:

Look at the data set: 3, 3, **4**, 5, 6, **8**, 10, 13, **14**, 16, 19.

There are 11 values, so median (Q2) = 6th value = **8**.

Then Q1 = **4**, Q3 = **14**, and so IQR = 14 – 4 = **10**.

Tom had conquered the range.
In more ways than one.

Descriptive Statistics

Standard Deviation — Measures, on Average, How Much Scores Deviate from the Mean

$$s = \sqrt{\frac{\sum (X - \bar{X})^2}{N}}, \text{ where } s = \text{standard deviation}$$

Remember — $\bar{X}$ is the mean.

EXAMPLE:

If you've got scores of 5, 9, 10, 11 and 15, then...

Start by working out the mean: $(5 + 9 + 10 + 11 + 15) \div 5 = 50 \div 5 = 10$.

Now put the numbers into the formula to find the standard deviation:

$$s = \sqrt{\frac{(5-10)^2 + (9-10)^2 + (10-10)^2 + (11-10)^2 + (15-10)^2}{5}} = \mathbf{3.22} \text{ (3 s.f.)}$$

A high standard deviation shows more variability in a set of data.

This answer just means that the scores in the data set are, on average, 3.22 away from the mean.

ADVANTAGES:

a) **All** scores in the set are taken into account, so it's **more accurate** than the range.

b) It can also be used in further analysis.

DISADVANTAGE:

It's **not** as quick or easy to calculate as the range.

Warm-Up Questions

Q1 Explain how to calculate the mean.

Q2 What is the difference between the mean and the mode?

Q3 How is the range calculated?

Q4 What is meant by 'standard deviation'?

PRACTICE QUESTIONS

Exam Questions

Q1 Work out the mean, median and mode for the following data set: 2, 2, 4, 6, 8, 9, 10.   [3 marks]

Q2 Which of the following is a measure of dispersion?
  A standard deviation   **B** mean   **C** median   **D** mode   [1 mark]

Q3 Read the item below and then answer the questions that follow.

> Liya was investigating the effect of caffeine on typing speed. Her results are shown in Table 1.
>
> **Table 1: Time taken by 10 participants to type five sentences.**
>
> | | Time to type five sentences (seconds) | | | | | | | | | |
> |---|---|---|---|---|---|---|---|---|---|---|
> | **Before Caffeine** | 20 | 18 | 15 | 12 | 11 | 9 | 15 | 15 | 14 | 12 |
> | **After Caffeine** | 30 | 24 | 12 | 10 | 15 | 12 | 28 | 30 | 20 | 12 |

a) Calculate the range of the scores after the participants had taken caffeine.   [1 mark]

b) Calculate the mean for the participants' scores before caffeine.   [2 marks]

Did you know, 99.99% of statistics are made up...

These statistics are used to describe a collection of scores in a data set (how big the scores are, how spread out they are, and so on), so they're called... wait for it... descriptive statistics. Don't be put off by the weirdy maths notation either — a bar on top of a letter (e.g. $\bar{x}$) means you work out the mean. And a sigma (Σ) means you add things up.

Correlations and Distributions

You know what they say — correlation is as correlation does.
Remember that as you read this page... then you won't go far wrong.

Correlation Measures How Closely **Two Variables** are **Related**

1) **Correlation** is a measure of the relationship between **two variables**, e.g. it can tell you how closely exam grades are related to the amount of revision that someone's done.

2) In a **correlational study** data is collected for some kind of **correlational analysis**.

The **Correlation Coefficient** is a Number Between **−1** and **+1**

1) To find the correlation between two variables, you first have to collect some **data**.

   For example, you could ask every student in a class how many hours of study they did each week, and note their average test result.

Student	Hours of study	Average test score — %
A	4	58
B	1	23
C	7	67
D	15	89

One statistical test that calculates a correlation coefficient is the Spearman's rho test. You can read all about it on page 126.

2) You can then work out a **correlation coefficient**. This is a number between −1 and +1, and shows:

   a) **How closely** the variables are linked. This is shown by the size of the number — if it's close to +1 or −1, then they are very closely related, while a smaller number means the relationship is less strong (or maybe not there at all if it's close to 0).

   b) The type of correlation — a positive correlation coefficient (i.e. between 0 and +1) means that the variables rise and fall together, while a negative correlation coefficient (i.e. between −1 and 0) means that as one variable rises, the other falls. (See below for more info.)

Correlation is Easy to See on **Scattergrams**

1) **Positive correlation** — this means that as one variable rises, so does the other (and likewise, if one falls, so does the other).

   Example: hours of study and average test score.

   The correlation coefficient is roughly **0.75** (close to +1).

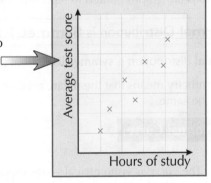

2) **Negative correlation** — this means that as one variable rises, the other one falls (and vice versa).

   Example: hours of TV watched each week and average test score.

   The correlation coefficient is roughly **−0.75** (close to −1).

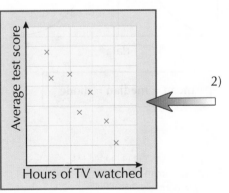

3) **Zero correlation** — if the correlation coefficient is 0 (or close to 0), then the two variables aren't linked.

   Example: students' heights and average test score.

   The correlation coefficient is roughly **0.01** (close to 0).

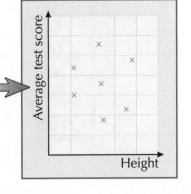

Correlations and Distributions

Correlational Research has some Advantages...

1) Because correlational research doesn't involve **controlling** any variables, you can do it when (for **practical** or **ethical** reasons) you couldn't do a **controlled experiment**. Handy.

2) For example, an experiment into the effects of smoking on humans probably wouldn't be done for ethical reasons, but a correlation between smoking and cancer could be established from hospital records.

3) Correlational analysis can give ideas for **future** research (e.g. biological research on the effects of smoking).

4) Correlation can even be used to test for **reliability** and **validity** (e.g. by testing the results of the same test taken twice by the same people — a good **reliable** test will show a **high correlation**).

...but some Limitations

1) Correlational analysis **can't** establish 'cause and effect' relationships — it can only show that there's a **statistical link** between variables. Variables can be closely correlated without changes in one causing changes in the other — a **third variable** could be involved. Only a **controlled experiment** can show cause-and-effect relationships.

2) Care must be taken when **interpreting** correlation coefficients — high correlation coefficients could be down to **chance**. To decide whether a coefficient is **significant**, you have to use a proper **significance test** (see p.123).

For example, the number of births in a town was found to be positively correlated to the number of storks that nested in that town — but that didn't mean that more storks caused the increase.

(It was because more people in the town led to more births, and also to more houses with chimneys to nest on.)

Normal and Skewed Distributions Look Very Different

Distributions are graphs plotted to represent the **average** and **spread** of some **characteristic** of the population.

A Normal Distribution is Symmetrical

A **normal** distribution is **symmetrical** about the **mean**.

This symmetry means that the **mean**, **median** and **mode** are all the **same**.

The Normal Curve

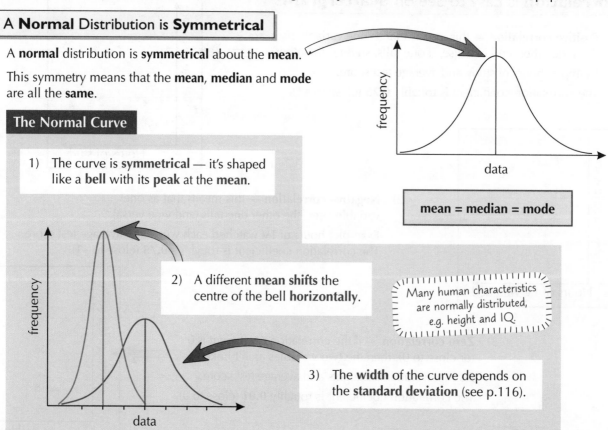

1) The curve is **symmetrical** — it's shaped like a **bell** with its **peak** at the **mean**.

mean = median = mode

2) A different **mean** shifts the centre of the bell **horizontally**.

Many human characteristics are normally distributed, e.g. height and IQ.

3) The **width** of the curve depends on the **standard deviation** (see p.116).

Correlations and Distributions

A **Skewed** Distribution can be **Positive** or **Negative**

When there are **scores** that **cluster** together at either end of the data, it results in a **skewed distribution**.

Positive Skew

If data is **positively skewed**, there is a cluster of scores at the **lower** end of the data set.

The curve has a tail on the **right** side of the peak — it is said to be **skewed to the right**.

The mode is **less than** the median, which is **less than** the mean.

Examples are **reaction times**, the number of **children** in a family, and **income**.

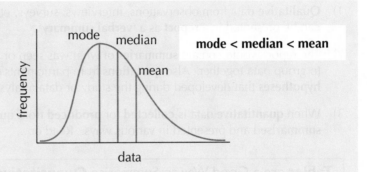

mode < median < mean

Negative Skew

For a **negative** skew, there are **more** scores at the **higher** end of the data set.

The tail is on the **left** side of the peak — it is **skewed to the left**.

The mode is **more than** the median, which is **more than** the mean.

Negative skew is less common but an example is **age at retirement**.

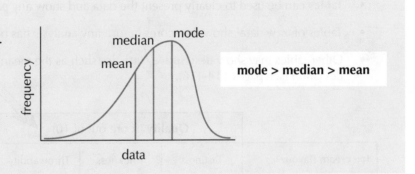

mode > median > mean

Warm-Up Questions

Q1 Explain what is meant by correlation.

Q2 What is a correlation coefficient?

Q3 What two things are shown by a correlation coefficient?

Q4 Explain the difference between a negative correlation and no correlation.

Q5 What does a normal distribution curve look like?

Q6 Is the mean greater or less than the mode in a positively skewed distribution?

PRACTICE QUESTIONS

Exam Questions

Q1 A study has found a negative correlation between tiredness and reaction time.
Explain what this means. [1 mark]

Q2 Outline why psychologists cannot use correlational research to draw conclusions such as
"eating an apple every day increases life expectancy". [2 marks]

Q3 Read the item below and then answer the question that follows.

> 50 participants were asked to complete a personality questionnaire to see how introverted they were.
> The mean score for the group was 4.5, the modal score was 8 and the median score was 6.

What type of distribution would these results show? [1 mark]

Stats sucks...

Look at the graphs showing the large positive and large negative correlations — all the points lie close-ish to a straight line, which slopes either upwards (positive correlation) or downwards (negative correlation). And don't forget about distributions too. Normal curves are symmetrical and skewed curves have tails. Not real tails obviously. That'd be odd.

Summarising the Data

It's not very scientific or anything, but the only bit about statistics I don't find mind-numbingly boring is the bit where you get to make all the lovely numbers look pretty... Ignore me — stats has turned my brain to mush.

Data Can be Presented in Various Ways

1) **Qualitative** data from observations, interviews, surveys, etc. (see pages 94-95 and 102-104) can be presented in a **report** as a '**verbal summary**'.

2) The report would contain **summaries** of what was seen or said, possibly using **categories** to group data together. Also **quotations** from participants can be used, and any **research hypotheses** that developed during the study or data analysis may be discussed.

3) When **quantitative** data is **collected** (or **produced** from **qualitative** data) it can be **summarised** and presented in various ways. Read on...

Tables are a Good Way to Summarise Quantitative Data

- Tables can be used to clearly present the data and show any patterns in the scores.

- Tables of '**raw data**' show the scores before any analysis has been done on them.

- Other tables may show descriptive statistics such as the mean, range and standard deviation (see pages 114-116).

Ice cream flavour	Quality (score out of 10)		
	Tastiness	Thickness	Throwability
Chocolate	5	7	6
Toffee	8	6	7
Strawberry	6	5	4
Earwax	6	9	8

Table to Show the Qualities of Different Flavour Ice Cream

Harold and Madge could spot a good table a mile off.

Examiners sometimes like to make you do some **maths** with the numbers in **tables** and **graphs**.

EXAMPLE:

What **percentage** of the participants who obeyed were boys?

	Boys	Girls
Number of participants who obeyed	36	24
Number of participants who didn't obey	52	64

To find the percentage, divide the number of boys who obeyed by the total number of participants who obeyed, then multiply by 100.

Find the total number of participants who obeyed: 36 + 24 = 60

Mr Boggis's data was summarised nicely on his table.

Percentage of boys among those who obeyed: (36 ÷ 60) × 100 = **60%**

Summarising the Data

Nearly done — just a little bit more...

Line Graphs are Good for Showing More Than One Set of Data

Line graphs are for use with **continuous data**. The **independent variable** is plotted along the **x-axis** and the **dependent variable** is plotted up the **y-axis**.

They show the plotted data points, which are then **joined up** with **straight lines**.

It can be useful to combine **two or more** line graphs on the same set of axes — then it's easy to **make comparisons** between groups.

If you need to plot a line graph, you'll get marks for labelling the axes (including the units), accurate plotting, and including a title.

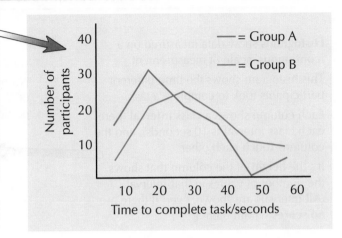

Bar Charts Can be Used for Non-continuous Data

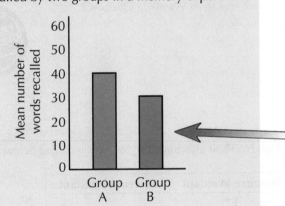

Bar chart showing the mean number of words recalled by two groups in a memory experiment.

Bar charts are usually used to present **'non-continuous data'** (like when a variable falls into **categories** rather than being measured on a numbered scale).

This bar chart shows the mean number of words recalled by different groups in a memory experiment.

Note that the columns in bar charts **don't touch** each other. Also, it's preferable to always show the **full vertical scale**, or **clearly indicate** when it isn't all shown (otherwise it can be **misleading**).

Scattergrams Can Tell You if Two Variables are Related

Scattergrams are used when you've got **two different variables** — you plot one variable along the bottom of the graph, and the second one up the side. Scattergrams are good for showing whether there's a **correlation** (see p.117).

EXAMPLE:

Gill is investigating the relationship between height and scores on a depression index.

Height (cm)	Depression Score
150	20
164	32
100	10
130	18
140	30

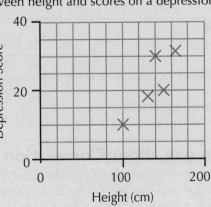

- Choose a suitable scale for each axis.

- Carefully plot the data points — but don't join them up.

- Instead, you can draw a line of best fit to show a trend — draw a line which passes through or as near to as many of the points as possible.

Summarising the Data

*... okay — I lied... one more and then you're done. Unless you're studying **AS Level** — then you **don't** need to know about **histograms** so you can head straight to the Practice Questions.*

Histograms are for When You Have Continuous Data

Histograms show data measured on a 'continuous' scale of measurement.

This histogram shows the time different participants took to complete a task.

Each column shows a class interval (here, each class interval is 10 seconds), and the columns touch each other.

It's the height of the column that shows the number of values in that interval. (All intervals are shown, even if there are no scores within them.)

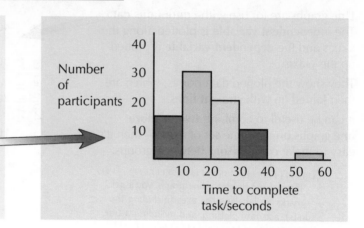

Histograms are for when you have continuous data. This includes things like height, temperature and time — things that fall on a continuous scale. Non-continuous data includes things like exam grades, types of ice cream and names of football teams — things that fall into distinct categories.

Warm-Up Questions
If you're doing AS Level, you don't need to do Warm-Up Question 3.

Q1 What kind of information is typically shown in tables?

Q2 What kind of data is shown on bar charts?

Q3 What does each column in a histogram represent?

Exam Questions

Q1 A sample of children were observed in an observational study. Their attachment styles were recorded below.

	Secure	Insecure-avoidant	Insecure-resistant
Number of children	56	17	7

Calculate the percentage of the children from the sample who had a secure attachment. [2 marks]

Q2 Draw a bar chart showing the percentage obedience for boys and girls from the table on page 120. [6 marks]

Q3 Look at the table below, then answer the questions that follow.

Participant	1	2	3	4	5	6	7	8	9	10
Percentage Mark on Psychology Exam	70	50	20	85	90	60	30	24	10	75
Average Number of Minutes Exercise per Day	30	20	5	50	75	60	10	15	5	40

a) Draw a scattergram to display the data shown in the table above. [3 marks]

b) Draw a line of best fit through your data points. [1 mark]

Is it too late to make a gag about Correlation Street...

Hmm, I think I've missed the boat with that one. But if you like it, maybe turn back a page and imagine I put it there instead. How we laughed. Now wipe away the tears of joy and let's think about the fun of summarising data. Here's one — what did the table say to the bar chart... Oh who am I kidding — let's just be thankful it's almost over...

Inferential Statistics

*If you're doing **AS Level** you don't need to know as much about inferential statistics as those doing A-Level. However, you do need to know about one statistical test (the **sign test**, see **p.129**) — so it'd be helpful for you to understand why statistical tests are used (this page) and what critical value and critical value tables are (p.124-125).*

Inferential Statistics are about Ruling Out Chance

1) You can never be 100% certain that results aren't all down to chance. So instead of 'proving' a hypothesis, you have to be content with finding out whether it's **likely** to be true. This is called **statistical significance**.

2) If your results are statistically significant, it means that you can **read something into them** — they're unlikely to be just down to chance.

3) If your results are **not statistically significant**, it means they could have happened by chance rather than being the effect of changes in your independent variable, so you can't really read anything into them.

Use Statistical Tests to Find Out if Your Results Mean Anything

OK, it's not easy, this bit — so stop texting people and concentrate...

1
- The first thing you do is write out your **null hypothesis** — this is the prediction you want to **test**.
- In a statistical test, you assume that your null hypothesis is **true** for the time being, and that any hint of a significant difference between your groups (or correlation between your variables) is actually just a **fluke**.

2
- Next you choose a **significance level** — this is a '**level of proof**' that you're looking for before you read anything into your results.
- The smaller the significance level, the stronger the evidence you're looking for that your results aren't just down to chance.
- A significance level is a **probability**, and so is a number between 0 and 1. (Probabilities near 1 mean things are very **likely**, and probabilities near 0 mean things are very **unlikely**.)
- Significance levels are always **very small** — usually 0.05 (5%) or less. (Because a significance level is very **small**, events with probabilities smaller than the significance level are very **unlikely** to happen.)

3
- You then turn all your experimental results into a single test statistic.
- Then you can find out what the probability is that this test statistic, and therefore your results, were the result of a fluke (making your null hypothesis true after all).

4
- If the probability of your results being a fluke is **less than** the significance level (e.g. 5%), then it's pretty safe to say that your null hypothesis **wasn't actually true**. You can therefore assume that the **difference** you've noticed between your groups was down to the change you made in your **independent variable**.
- This is what stats-folk mean when they talk about 'rejecting the null hypothesis'. (If you reject your null hypothesis, you assume your **alternative hypothesis** is true instead.)

5
- If you reject your null hypothesis, you can proudly shout out that your results are **statistically significant**.

6
- If you don't reject the null hypothesis, it means that your results could have occurred by chance, rather than because your null hypothesis was wrong.
- If this happens, you've proved nothing — not rejecting the null hypothesis doesn't mean it must be true.

7
- Using a significance level of **0.05** (5%) is okay for most tests.
- If the probability of your results being down to chance is **less than** or **equal to** this ($p \leq 0.05$), then it's **pretty good evidence** that the null hypothesis **wasn't true** after all. So the researchers can be at least **95% confident** in their conclusion.
- If you use a significance level of **0.01** (1%), then you're looking for **really strong evidence** that the null hypothesis is untrue before you're going to reject it. The researchers can be at least **99% confident**.

Inferential Statistics

There are Two Types of Potential Error

It's possible to make errors when you're deciding whether or not to reject the null hypothesis.

A **Type I error** is when you **reject** the null hypothesis when it was **actually true**.

The significance level gives you the **probability** of this happening. E.g. a $p = 0.05$ level means the probability that the null hypothesis is actually true is **5%**.

This is why significance levels are **small**.

A very small significance level (e.g. 0.01 or 1%) is used when you need to be very confident in your results, like when testing new theories.

A **Type II error** is when you **don't reject** the null hypothesis when it was **actually false**.

This can happen if your significance level is **too small** (e.g. if you want very strong evidence of the need to reject a null hypothesis and so use a 0.01 significance level).

So if you don't reject your null hypothesis, even if your alternative hypothesis was significant at $p = 0.05$, then there's a **95% chance** you'll have made a **Type II** error.

Choosing significance levels is a **compromise** — if the level you choose is **too big** you risk making a Type I error. If the significance level you choose is **too small**, you could make a Type II error.

Statistical Test Results are Compared with Critical Values

1) Remember that you can never be 100% sure that a hypothesis is correct — it's always possible that results are just due to **chance**.

2) Significance levels are assigned to establish the **probability** of the result being due to chance, and if this is acceptably low (e.g. 5%), then you can reject the **null hypothesis**.

3) **Inferential statistical tests** help to decide whether or not to reject the null hypothesis. However, there are many **different tests** and it is crucial that you use the **correct one** for your data. We'll get to the specific tests over the next few pages.

4) You use inferential tests to calculate what's called an **observed value** (the value you get when you carry out the test on your results). The observed value is then **compared** against a **critical value**, which is provided for each test in a **critical value table**. This indicates whether or not the results are significant.

5) In some tests, if the observed value is **more than or equal to** the critical value, the results are considered to **be significant**. In others, the observed value must be **equal to or less than** the critical value to **show significance**.

You Need to Know How to Use Critical Values Tables

Example: A psychologist investigating eating behaviour uses Spearman's rho correlation coefficient to analyse his data set. His null hypothesis is that there will be no correlation between mood and calorie consumption. His alternative hypothesis is that there will be a correlation between mood and calorie consumption. He tested 20 participants and produced an observed value of 0.518.

To test the significance of his results, the psychologist must **compare** his observed value against the critical values for Spearman's rho correlation coefficient.

If you're doing AS Level, you don't need to know how to determine when a one- or two-tailed test would be used.

1) Firstly he must decide if it's a one-tailed or a two-tailed test.

A **one-tailed test** is used when the researcher has predicted an association and has also stated which way the results will go (i.e. a directional hypothesis, such as 'the lower the mood, the higher the calorie consumption').

A **two-tailed test** is used when the researcher has predicted an association, but hasn't stated which way the results will go (i.e. a non-directional hypothesis). The hypothesis in this correlation is non-directional, so it's a two-tailed test.

Inferential Statistics

2) The observed value is then looked up in a critical value table.

Some of the critical values for a Spearman's rho correlation coefficient are shown here. As the test is two-tailed, the researcher needs to look at the row of significance levels for two-tailed tests.

3) Read off the table.

If the psychologist wants to see if his results are significant at the $p = 0.05$ level, he should use the column highlighted in purple.

N = the number of values in the data set. As there were 20 participants in this study, the critical value at the $p = 0.05$ level = 0.447.

4) Make a conclusion about significance.

For the data to be significant, the observed value from the Spearman's rho calculation must be greater than or equal to the relevant critical value.

The observed value in this experiment is 0.518, which is greater than 0.447. This means that the psychologist's results are significant at the $p = 0.05$ level. Consequently, the researcher can reject his null hypothesis, and accept his alternative hypothesis.

	Level of significance for two-tailed test			
	0.10	0.05	0.02	0.01
	Level of significance for one-tailed test			
N	0.05	0.025	0.01	0.005
15	0.443	0.521	0.604	0.654
16	0.429	0.503	0.582	0.635
17	0.414	0.485	0.566	0.615
18	0.401	0.472	0.550	0.600
19	0.391	0.460	0.535	0.584
20	0.380	0.447	0.520	0.570
21	0.370	0.435	0.508	0.556
22	0.361	0.425	0.496	0.544

Critical values of Spearman's rho correlation coefficient.

Several Things Determine Which Inferential Test Should be Used

Inferential statistics allow you to make an educated guess about whether or not a hypothesis is correct. Deciding which inferential test you use for your data is determined by the following factors:

Experimental Design

Research may have either **related measures** (if a repeated measures or matched participants design was used), or **unrelated measures** (if an independent measures design was used).

Research Aims

Some inferential statistics test whether there is a **significant difference** between two (or more) groups of scores:

- For example, 'did the participants in group A have significantly higher average scores than those in group B?'.
- This is what happens in an **experiment**. The IV is manipulated to see if it produces **changes** in the DV that are significantly different from the **control condition** (or other experimental conditions).

Some inferential statistics test to see if there is a **significant association** between two (or more) variables:

- For example, whether they occur together more than would be expected by chance.
- This is what we look for in **correlation studies** — to see if two variables are positively or negatively associated, more than would be expected by chance factors alone. If they are, a **significant** correlation has been shown.

Level of Measurement / Type of Data

Studies can collect different types of data, which affects how it can be analysed.

- **Nominal data** — This is the most basic level of measurement — a **frequency count** for completely **distinct categories**. For example, in a study where a confederate pretends to need help, you could assign each passer-by to either an 'altruistic' category (if they helped) or a 'non-altruistic' category (if they did nothing).
- **Ordinal data** — All of the measurements relate to the **same variable**, and measurements can be placed in ascending or descending **rank order**, e.g. on a **rating scale** for aggression where 1 = 'not aggressive' and 10 = 'extremely aggressive'. But you can't say a person with a score of 10 is twice as aggressive as a person with a score of 5, just which one was **more** or **less** aggressive.
- **Interval data** — Measurements are taken on a scale where **each unit is the same size**, e.g. length in centimetres. Interval data places participants along an objective, scientific scale. You then know exactly how far apart the scores are. E.g. in a race, participant 'F' was quickest, in 15.8 seconds and participant 'B' was second, in 16.5 seconds. Technically, an **absolute zero point** is needed to make judgements about whether one score is twice that of another. When we have this (e.g. 0 seconds, 0 centimetres, etc.) then we call it a **ratio scale**.

Spearman's Rho and Pearson's *r*

If the thought of maths in general, and statistics in particular, makes you want to run for the hills, then take a ticket and get in line. But don't worry — you only need to know when each test is used and how to interpret the results — you don't have to calculate the observed values (except for the sign test (see page 129)... there's always one).

Spearman's Rho is a **Correlation Coefficient**

Spearman's rho can also be used on interval or ratio data if they're not normally distributed.

1) Spearman's rho correlation coefficient is an observed value used to see if there's a significant association between two variables that have at least **ordinal** data.

2) To work out (and then test the significance of) **Spearman's rho** correlation coefficient, you need values for two different variables (e.g. hours of sleep and test scores for 10 students).

Example: A psychologist is investigating the relationship between sleep and cognitive function. His hypothesis is that students who get **more** hours of sleep the night before a test will score **higher** in the test. Students' hours of sleep the night before a test and their test scores are shown below.

Spearman's rho can be used to establish concurrent validity (page 100).

Student	Hours sleep	Test score (%)
A	3	12
B	6	71
C	9	83
D	4	46
E	5	38
F	13	94
G	10	100
H	1	15
I	8	32
J	12	87

Spearman was no ordinary rower...

3) Using the Spearman's rho calculation, the psychologist calculates an observed value of **0.867** (3 s.f.).

4) The observed value is very close to +1, showing that there is a **strong positive correlation** between hours of sleep and test score.

5) The result of the calculation is then compared with a critical value.

6) For the data to be significant, the observed value must be **greater than or equal to** the relevant critical value in the table.

Positive correlation means the variables rise and fall together. A negative correlation would mean that as one variable increases, the other decreases.

7) As the hypothesis is directional, a one-tailed test is used.

	Level of significance for two-tailed test			
	0.10	*0.05*	*0.02*	*0.01*
	Level of significance for one-tailed test			
N	*0.05*	*0.025*	*0.01*	*0.005*
7	0.714	0.786	0.893	0.929
8	0.643	0.738	0.833	0.881
9	0.600	0.700	0.783	0.833
10	0.564	0.648	0.745	0.794
11	0.536	0.618	0.709	0.755
12	0.503	0.587	0.671	0.727

In this example, you read the values off the N = 10 row, as there are 10 participants.

8) From the table it can be seen that the critical value for *p* = 0.05 is **0.564**. The observed value (0.867) is **greater than** this, therefore the results are **significant** at the *p* = 0.05 level.

9) The psychologist **can reject** the null hypothesis.

Spearman's Rho and Pearson's *r*

Pearson's *r* is also a **Correlation Coefficient**

Pearson's *r* can also be used to establish concurrent validity (page 100).

1) A Pearson's *r* test investigates the association between two variables.
   Both variables must have **interval** or **ratio** data and be **normally distributed** (see page 118).

2) The correlation between the two variables will fall between –1 and +1. This value is called *r*.

3) The closer *r* is to –1 or +1, the stronger the relationship.

4) If *r* is **positive**, the relationship between the two variables is positive (one **goes up** as the other **goes up**).
   If *r* is **negative**, the relationship between the two variables is negative (one **goes down** as the other **goes up**).
   Makes sense if you think about it...

Example: A psychologist was investigating the hypothesis that there is a **relationship** between weight and serotonin levels. **Five** participants had their weight recorded and had a blood test to determine their serotonin level, measured in nanograms per millilitre. Their results are shown in the table.

Student	Weight (kg)	Serotonin Level (ng/mL)
A	61	160
B	58	245
C	55	282
D	64	172
E	60	161

5) Using the Pearson's *r* test, the observed value is **–0.854** (3 s.f.). You can ignore the minus sign though (it just shows it's a negative correlation), so it's **0.854**.

6) For Pearson's *r*, the observed value must be **greater than or equal to** the critical value to be significant.

7) Before you look up the critical value, you'll need to calculate the **degrees of freedom (*df*)**. For Pearson's *r*, this is $N - 2$. So in this case, it is 3 (since $5 - 2 = 3$).

8) The hypothesis is **non-directional**, which means it's a two-tailed test. So the critical value for $p = 0.05$ is **0.878**.

9) The observed value (0.854) is **less than** this, so the results are **not significant** at the $p = 0.05$ level.

10) The psychologist **cannot reject** the null hypothesis.

	Level of significance for two-tailed test			
	0.10	*0.05*	*0.01*	*0.001*
Level of significance for one-tailed test				
df = N – 2	*0.05*	*0.025*	*0.005*	*0.0005*
2	0.900	0.950	0.990	0.999
3	0.805	0.878	0.959	0.991
4	0.729	0.811	0.917	0.974
5	0.669	0.754	0.875	0.951

Warm-Up Questions

Q1 A psychologist conducts a Spearman's rho test and calculates an observed value of 0.4. She used 12 participants and had a two-tailed hypothesis. Use the table on page 126 to determine if her data is significant at the $p = 0.05$ level.

Q2 What type of data can a Pearson's *r* test be used for?

Exam Question

Q1 A psychologist investigated the relationship between TV watching and weight. These are the results.

Participant	1	2	3	4	5	6
TV watching per day (mins)	180	124	80	52	12	16
Weight (kg)	64	70	68	62	55	54

a) Name an appropriate statistical test that could be used to analyse the results in the table. [1 mark]

b) Given that the correlation coefficient is 0.716 (3 s.f.), determine if the results are significant at the $p = 0.05$ level. [2 marks]

You'll be given the critical values tables in the exam, so you don't need to learn them. Phew.

Rho, rho, rho your boat, gently down the stream...

Don't get freaked out by these pages of tables of critical values. You don't have to memorise them— just make sure you feel comfortable being able to use them to work out whether your data is significant or not...

Wilcoxon and The Sign Test

*Drum roll please... I now proudly introduce the Wilcoxon Test. *Rapturous applause, whoops and cheers*. If you're doing **AS Level**, you **don't** need to know about the **Wilcoxon Test** so you can skip straight to the sign test (next page).*

The **Wilcoxon** Test is a Test of Difference for **Related** Data

The Wilcoxon test is a test of difference for related data. It is used when:

- A **hypothesis** states that there'll be a **difference** between two sets of data.
- The data is **ordinal**.
- The experiment is a **repeated measures** or **matched pairs** design.

See page 125 if you don't know what ordinal data is.

> **Example:** A psychologist is investigating **two methods** of memorising words. Her hypothesis is that Method 1 will be **more effective** than Method 2. Her **null hypothesis** is that there will be **no difference** between the two methods.
>
> Each participant will do two memory tests — one for each method, in a **repeated measures** design. The results are shown below.

Participant no.	1	2	3	4	5	6	7	8
No. words recalled — **Method 1**	6	5	10	6	8	5	9	8
Method 2	7	7	8	8	7	6	9	9

1) The Wilcoxon test involves working out the **difference** between participants' scores across **both conditions**. If one condition gives considerably different results to the other, the data will be **significant**.

2) The Wilcoxon test is used to calculate an observed value of **8.5** for the results above.

3) Compare this observed value with the critical value from the critical values table for this test.

4) The observed value must be **less than or equal to** the **critical value** to be significant.

5) In this case N is **7**. For a Wilcoxon test, N is calculated by only including participants who **did show** a difference between the two conditions.

Participant 7 scored 9 using both methods. This is why their score isn't included when calculating N.

	Level of significance for two-tailed test			
	0.10	**0.05**	**0.02**	**0.01**
	Level of significance for one-tailed test			
N	**0.05**	**0.025**	**0.01**	**0.005**
5	0			
6	2	0		
7	3	2	0	
8	5	3	1	0
9	8	5	3	1
10	10	8	5	3
11	13	10	7	5
12	17	13	9	7
13	21	17	12	9

6) As the psychologist's hypothesis is directional, a **one-tailed test** is used.

7) From the table you can see that the critical value for $p = 0.05$ is **3**.

8) The observed value (8.5) is **more than** this, therefore the results are **not significant** at the $p = 0.05$ level.

9) The psychologist **cannot reject** her null hypothesis.

Toby laughed in the face of rejection. He quite liked bins.

Wilcoxon and The Sign Test

You Can Use the **Sign Test** When You've Got **Nominal** Data

One of the easiest statistical tests to use is the **sign test**. It compares scores in data from **repeated measures** or **matched pairs** designs by turning the **change** in scores into **nominal** data. You could be asked to **calculate** the observed value here — so make sure you learn the method.

Example hypothesis:	Participants' scores on a depression index before drug treatment will be significantly different to their scores after treatment.

Participant no.	1	2	3	4	5	6	7	8
Before Treatment	12	5	6	8	10	12	15	9
After Treatment	5	6	4	2	3	2	16	9

Depression Index (1-20)

1) The **difference** between each participant's two scores is calculated:

Participant no.	1	2	3	4	5	6	7	8
Difference	7	1	2	6	7	10	1	0
Sign (+/−)	−	+	−	−	−	−	+	

Always subtract in the same direction, noting if the result is a positive or negative value. Any differences of zero are removed from the results.

2) Add up the number of positive signs and negative signs. The **smallest** one is the **observed value**.

3) There are **5 negative** signs and **2 positive** signs. So the observed value is **2**.

4) The observed value must be **less than or equal to** the **critical value** to be significant.

5) Since the hypothesis is non-directional, a **two-tailed test** is used. Here, N is the number of participants not including zeros (7).

6) In this case, the **critical value** is 0. Since the observed value is **greater than** 0, the results are **not significant**.

	Level of significance for two-tailed test			
	0.10	**0.05**	**0.02**	**0.01**
	Level of significance for one-tailed test			
N	**0.05**	**0.025**	**0.01**	**0.005**
5	0	—	—	—
6	0	0	—	—
7	0	0	0	—
8	1	0	0	0
9	1	1	0	0
10	1	1	0	0
11	2	1	1	0

Warm-Up Questions

If you're doing <u>AS Level</u>, you don't need to do Warm-Up Question 1.

Q1 What type of data can a Wilcoxon test be used on?

Q2 What types of research design can a sign test be used on?

Q3 Describe the steps of the sign test.

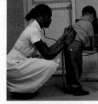

Sandra wanted to work out the observed value but had totally forgotten where the heart was.

Exam Question

Q1 Read the item below, then answer the question that follows.

Bella investigated students' stress levels on a scale of 1-10 before and after their Psychology exam (1 = low stress, 10 = high stress). She hypothesised that they would be significantly more stressed before the exam than after the exam. Her results are shown in the table:

Participant	1	2	3	4	5	6	7	8	9	10
Stress level before exam	8	7	9	10	5	6	8	9	9	10
Stress level after exam	4	3	5	8	8	7	9	8	5	4

Use the sign test to determine if Bella's results support her hypothesis. [4 marks]

No U-turns permitted ahead...

Oh wait — wrong sort of sign test. Although they won't tell you how to drive, the Wilcoxon and sign tests are mighty useful. Just remember — the Wilcoxon is for ordinal data and the sign test uses nominal data.

t-Tests and the Mann-Whitney Test

Spearman's, Pearson's, Wilcoxon... not only are the stats confusing, but the names aren't that easy to remember either. They certainly like their fancy names. Here we have the t-tests and the Mann-Whitney test. Hoorah.

The **Related *t*-Test** is Used in **Repeated Measures** Designs

It's also called a dependent t-test.

The **related *t*-test** is a test of difference (or similarity) for **repeated measures** or **matched pairs** designs. It's used when you have **interval** or **ratio** data which is normally distributed. A trusty example will make it clearer:

> **Example:** A psychologist investigated the hypothesis that the weight of participants will be significantly **lower** after following a new diet plan, than their weight before. In a **repeated measures design**, participants' weight was recorded before and after the trial diet.

Participant	Weight before diet (kg)	Weight after diet (kg)
A	94	71
B	82	63
C	96	68
D	85	76

1) Running a related *t*-test on this data gives an observed value of **4.903** (3 d.p.).

2) The **degrees of freedom (*df*)** are calculated by doing $N - 1$. So here, $df = 4 - 1 = $ **3**.

3) The observed value in a related *t*-test must be **greater than or equal to** the **critical value** to be significant.

4) As the psychologist's hypothesis is directional, a **one-tailed test** is used.

5) From the table you can see that the critical value for $p = 0.05$ is **2.353**.

6) The observed value for *t* (4.903) is **greater than** this, therefore the results **are significant** at the $p = 0.05$ level. The psychologist **can reject** the null hypothesis.

	Level of significance for two-tailed test			
	0.10	**0.05**	**0.02**	**0.01**
	Level of significance for one-tailed test			
***df* = N – 1**	**0.05**	**0.025**	**0.01**	**0.005**
1	6.314	12.706	31.821	63.657
2	2.920	4.303	6.965	9.925
3	2.353	3.182	4.541	5.841
4	2.132	2.776	3.747	4.604
5	2.015	2.571	3.365	4.032

From Statistical Tables for Biological, Agricultural & Medical Research by R A Fisher & F Yates, 6th edition © 1974. Reprinted by permission of Pearson Business.

The **Unrelated *t*-Test** is Used in **Independent Measures** Designs

It shouldn't come as a great surprise that the unrelated *t*-test is similar to the related *t*-test. The main difference is that in the **unrelated *t*-test**, there should be **two separate groups** of participants (i.e. unpaired).

> **Example hypothesis:** There will be a significant **difference** between male and female Psychology test scores.

It's also called an independent t-test.

1) An unrelated *t*-test on this data gives an observed value of **0.719** (3 d.p.).

2) To calculate the degrees of freedom, add up the number of participants in both groups and subtract 2. So here, it'll be $4 + 4 - 2 = $ **6**.

3) Look up your value of *t* in a **critical values table**.

4) The observed value must be **greater than or equal to** the critical value for the results to be significant.

5) The hypothesis is non-directional, so it is a **two-tailed** test.

6) The table shows the critical value is 2.447 for $p = 0.05$.

7) The observed value of *t* (0.719) is **less than** this, so the results are **not significant**.

8) This means the null hypothesis **cannot** be rejected.

Female Test Score (%)	Male Test Score (%)
84	78
70	90
80	65
92	73

	Level of significance for two-tailed test			
	0.10	**0.05**	**0.02**	**0.01**
	Level of significance for one-tailed test			
df	**0.05**	**0.025**	**0.01**	**0.005**
4	2.132	2.776	3.747	4.604
5	2.015	2.571	3.365	4.032
6	1.943	2.447	3.143	3.707

From Statistical Tables for Biological, Agricultural & Medical Research by R A Fisher & F Yates, 6th edition © 1974. Reprinted by permission of Pearson Business.

t-Tests and the Mann-Whitney Test

The **Mann-Whitney Test** is Used with **Ordinal Data**

The **Mann-Whitney Test** is a test of difference (or of similarity) for data from an **independent measures** design. It focuses on **ranks** and is used when you have **ordinal** data. Take a look at the following example:

Example: Two groups took part in a study investigating whether drinking one **vitamin drink** daily for 4 weeks improved **verbal memory** test performance compared to a group who had no vitamin drinks.

Number of words recalled	Vitamin group	19	13	9	12	21	15	14
	No vitamin group	7	5	10	8	6	11	18

1) Using the Mann-Whitney test, an observed value, U, is calculated. Here, $U = \textbf{7}$.

2) This table shows the critical values for U for a one-tailed test at $p = 0.01$.

3) In the Mann-Whitney test, the observed U value must be **less than or equal to** the critical value to be **significant**.

4) As N_1 and N_2 are both **7**, the critical value is 6.

5) As $U = 7$ here, it can be concluded that there's **no significant difference** between the two groups.

6) This means the **null** hypothesis **cannot** be rejected.

		N_1				
		5	**6**	**7**	**8**	**9**
N_2	**5**	1	2	3	4	5
	6	2	3	4	6	7
	7	3	4	6	7	9
	8	4	6	7	9	11
	9	5	7	9	11	14

Republished with permission of McGraw-Hill Education from Fundamentals of Behavioural Statistics by R Runyon & A Haber (3rd Edn) © 1976 permission conveyed through Copyright Clearance Center Inc.

Warm-Up Questions

Q1 When can a related *t*-test be used?

Q2 What type of data is a Mann-Whitney test used on?

PRACTICE QUESTIONS

Exam Questions

Q1 Donel is investigating a new drug to lower blood cortisol level. He divides participants into two groups and both groups partake in the same stressful event. The first group have been taking a placebo drug for one month, whilst the second group have been taking the new drug for one month. Their cortisol levels are then recorded after the event.

Name an appropriate statistical test that Donel could use to analyse his findings. Explain your answer. [4 marks]

Q2 Read the item below, then answer the questions that follow.

> Two separate groups of participants took part in a study to investigate the influence of music on stress levels.
>
> The researcher's hypothesis stated that the addition of music would make an event more stressful.
>
> Both groups took a simulated driving test and were then asked to rate their stress levels.
>
> **Group A** completed the driving test whilst listening to loud music.
> **Group B** did not listen to music during the driving test.
>
> The results are given in the table:
>
> | Stress Level (1 = Low, 10 = High) | **Group A** | 8 | 7 | 8 | 8 | 9 | 10 | 2 | 4 | 6 |
> |---|---|---|---|---|---|---|---|---|---|---|
> | | **Group B** | 2 | 4 | 1 | 5 | 3 | 8 | 2 | 1 | 7 |

a) Write a hypothesis for the experiment described above. [2 marks]

b) Given that the observed $U = 14.5$, determine whether the results are significant at the $p = 0.05$ level. [2 marks]

Oh man... Whitney didn't see the sign on page 129...

I don't blame you for groaning at not only this massive amount of statistics, but also these increasingly bad jokes. But... keep your spirits up and your brain switched on, and you'll be flying through these pages in no time at all.

Chi-Squared and Choosing the Right Test

As the sun starts to set, the owls awaken and the bats begin to flutter, we come to the end of the tale of inferential statistics. It has been a momentous journey, full of ups and downs. But, to finish... here's one more good 'un.

The **Chi-Squared Test** is Used with **Nominal Data** and **Independent Samples**

There's no better way of explaining this than showing you an example. So, hey presto...

> **Example:** A student is interested in seeing whether finding reality TV programmes **entertaining** is related to being either **male** or **female**. His results are shown in the table below.

The **Chi-Squared test** tests the **null hypothesis**. In this example, the null hypothesis would be that there's **no association** between finding reality TV entertaining and being male or female — this is shown by the **expected frequencies**. Under the null hypothesis, the expected frequencies show that **equal amounts** of men and women find reality TV entertaining, and equal amounts do not.

	Men	Women	Totals
Finds reality TV entertaining (expected frequency)	19 (27)	35 (27)	54
Does not find reality TV entertaining (expected frequency)	41 (33)	25 (33)	66
Totals	60	60	120

Danai was stunned that the "chai test" involved more than just "add boiling water and brew for 4 minutes".

The expected frequencies are worked out using the following formula:

$$E = \frac{\text{row total} \times \text{column total}}{\text{overall total}}$$

The **Expected** and **Observed** Frequencies are **Compared**

> In a Chi-Squared test, the **expected frequencies** tell you what the outcome would be if the **null hypothesis** was **true**. They indicate that there would be **no difference** between groups. The **observed frequencies** are the **actual results**.
>
> So, if there is a **big difference** between the expected and the observed frequencies, it is more likely that the results **will be significant** — they won't match what would happen if the null hypothesis was true.

1) This example has an observed value, χ^2, of **8.62**.

2) You can use a critical value table to see if this is significant.

3) In a Chi-Squared test, **degrees of freedom (df)** = (No. of rows − 1) × (No. of columns − 1). In this example $df = (2 − 1) \times (2 − 1) = 1$

df	\multicolumn{5}{c}{Level of significance for two-tailed test}
df	*0.20*	*0.10*	*0.05*	*0.02*	*0.01*
1	1.64	2.71	3.84	5.41	6.64
2	3.22	4.60	5.99	7.82	9.21
3	4.64	6.25	7.82	9.84	11.34
4	5.99	7.78	9.49	11.67	13.28
5	7.29	9.24	11.07	13.39	15.09
6	8.56	10.64	12.59	15.03	16.81

From Statistical Tables for Biological, Agricultural & Medical Research by R A Fisher & F Yates, 6th edition © 1974. Reprinted by permission of Pearson Business.

The table was critical in the formation of Hank and Yasmine's holiday romance.

4) For the Chi-Squared result to be significant, χ^2 needs to be **greater than or equal to** the critical value.

5) In this example, the results are significant as the critical value at $p = 0.05$ is 3.84, which is **less than** 8.62.

6) This means that the **null** hypothesis is **rejected**.

Chi-Squared and Choosing the Right Test

It's Really Important to **Choose** the **Right Test** for the Job

When deciding which inferential statistics test to use, you need to think about several **factors**. These include things like the **research aims**, the **level of measurement** or **types of data**, and the **experimental design** that is being used in the study.

Repeated and **independent measures** designs test to see if there is a **significant difference** between two or more groups of scores. **Correlation studies** test to see if there is a **significant relationship** between two variables.

This table can help you to decide which test you need to use in different situations.

	Nominal	Ordinal	Interval/Ratio
Repeated Measures or Matched Pairs Design	sign test	Wilcoxon	related *t*-test
Independent Measures Design	Chi-Squared test	Mann-Whitney	unrelated *t*-test
Correlation	Chi-Squared test	Spearman's rho	Pearson's r

The tests which require interval or ratio data (the related and unrelated t-tests and Pearson's r) are called parametric tests. To use them, the data must be normally distributed.

Make Sure You **Check** if your **Hypothesis** Has a **Direction**

- When looking up critical values it's important to remember to look back to the hypothesis.

- You need to know whether it's **directional** or **non-directional**, so that you can tell whether your test is **one-tailed** or **two-tailed**.

Remember, a directional hypothesis states which way the results will go, whereas a non-directional hypothesis doesn't.

- It's also important to remember to check whether your **observed value** needs to be **greater than** or **less than** the critical value for the test you are doing — it differs for each statistical test.

Warm-Up Questions

Q1 When would a researcher use a Chi-Squared test?

Q2 What do expected frequencies show?

Q3 Which inferential test would you use in a repeated measures design which gathered nominal data?

Q4 Name three different inferential tests which can be used with ordinal data.

PRACTICE QUESTIONS

Exam Questions

Q1 Read the item below, then answer the question that follows.

> Ian is interested in whether there is an association between being an only child and having a pet.

Name a suitable inferential test for this study and explain your answer. [4 marks]

Q2 Complete the sentence below.

Ashley is investigating the correlation between the time it takes someone to swim 100 m and their height.
To determine the significance of his results, he should use a:

A sign test   **B** Chi-Squared test   **C** Spearman's rho test   **D** Pearson's *r* test   [1 mark]

Just to throw another spanner in the works, you say "kai", not "chi"...

... but this isn't an inferential statistical test speaking exam (and thank goodness for that, by the way), so that's useless info. What will help, though, is knowing the factors which affect which statistical test you should choose. Luckily for you, there's a nifty little table above. Think of it as an early birthday present.

Reporting on Psychological Investigations

Once the research study has been done you'd think that'd be the end of it and the poor overworked psychologist could have a break. But no — the study has to be written up, and it has to be done in a certain way. Some people are so picky.

Reports on Psychological Studies Have a Specific Structure

Title — The first thing a report needs is a **title**. It should say what the study's **about** and include the **independent variable (IV)** and the **dependent variable (DV)**. For example, 'An Investigation into the Effect of Hunger on Reaction Times'.

Abstract — The abstract's a **concise summary** of the report (often no more than 120 words), telling the reader about the research and findings without them having to read the **whole report**. It should include brief descriptions of the **aims** and **hypotheses** of the study, the **method**, and a summary of the **results**. The abstract should also contain interpretations of the findings and any significant **flaws** in the study. A lot to fit into a small space...

Introduction — The introduction is a general **overview** of the **area** being studied, including **existing theories**. It should also discuss a few **studies closely related** to the current study.

Aim and Hypotheses — The aim is a sentence stating the **purpose** of the study. For example, 'To investigate whether reaction times are affected by hunger levels'. The hypothesis is what's actually going to be **tested**, and should include the **independent variable** and the **dependent variable**. For example, 'Hunger will have no significant effect on reaction times'.

Method — The method describes **how** the research was **carried out**. Someone should be able to **replicate** the study by following the method, so it needs to be **detailed**. It should include information on:

The **design of the investigation**, for example:
- The **research method** used, e.g. field experiment, interview.
- The **research design**, e.g. repeated measures, and any potential problems with the design.
- How **extraneous variables** were **controlled**, e.g. counterbalancing, randomisation.
- How **materials**, e.g. **word-lists**, **questions**, etc. were chosen.
- How **ethical issues** were dealt with.

The **procedure used**:
- This should be a blow-by-blow account of **what happened** each time a participant took part.
- It should start with **how** the researcher and the investigation were **introduced** to the participant and how **informed consent** was obtained.
- It needs to include what was **said** to the participants (the standardised instructions), how the study was **carried out** and how the participants were **debriefed**.
- The method should also contain details of how the **data** was **recorded**.

The **use of participants**, for example:
- The **number** of participants used.
- The **demographics** of the participants, e.g. age, employment, gender, etc.
- The **sampling method** used (see pages 105-106).
- How participants were **allocated** to **conditions**.

The **resources used**, for example:
- The **materials** used, e.g. questionnaires, pictures, word lists, etc.
- Any **apparatus** used — it's often useful to include diagrams or photographs of these.

Reporting on Psychological Investigations

Results   The results of the study can be reported as **descriptive** or **inferential** statistics. Descriptive statistics include **tables**, **graphs** and **charts** (see p.120-122). Inferential statistics (see p. 123-133) involve doing **statistical tests** on the data. The results section needs to include explanations of **why** certain tests were chosen, e.g. because the study was looking for a correlation. They should also include the **results** of the test — the observed value, the critical value and level of significance.

Discussion   The discussion covers a range of things including:

- **An explanation of the findings** — **summarising** the results and **relating** them to the **aim** and **hypothesis**. It should be stated whether or not the null hypothesis is rejected. Any **unexpected** findings should also be addressed and explained here.
- **The implications of the study** — for example, whether the study relates to **real-life situations**, e.g. interviews, exams, etc.
- **The limitations and modifications of the study** — any **problems** or **limitations** need to be explained, along with modifications that could **improve** the study.
- **The relationship to background research** — the results need to be related to the **background research** covered in the introduction. The data should be compared to other data and comments made on whether or not the findings of the study support the findings of other studies.
- **Suggestions for further research** — some ideas for further research should be included.

References   The references section contains a list of all the books, articles and websites that have been used for **information** during the study. It allows the reader to see where the information on the **research** and **theories** mentioned in the report (e.g. in the introduction) came from. References should be presented in **alphabetical order** of first author's surname.

Appendices   Any **materials** used, e.g. questionnaires or diagrams, can be put in the appendix. **Raw data** and **statistical test calculations** also go here.

When Ellie said she needed help with her appendix, a hospital trip wasn't what she had in mind.

General Tips   The report should be written in the **third person**, e.g. 'the participants were asked to recall numbers' rather than 'I asked the participants to recall numbers'. The language used should be **formal**, e.g. 'the participants in the study were an opportunity sample', rather than 'the participants were basically anyone we could get hold of.'

Warm-Up Questions

Q1 What should be included in an abstract?

Q2 In which section of a report would you find an overview of the research area?

Q3 List six things that should be included in a method.

Q4 Name two types of statistics that could be included in the results section of a report.

Q5 In which section should materials such as questionnaires be included?

PRACTICE QUESTIONS

You've achieved your aim and reached the end of the section — result...

If you're the kind of person that has their own special celebratory dance for moments of crowning glory or achievement, I suggest you perform it now — because this is the end of the section. If you've made it this far and learned everything in between then you are now (unofficially) an unstoppable psychological research machine. And very smart, too.

Gender Bias

It's easy for psychologists to make statements that can disguise any differences between men and women. Or, they might say there are differences when there aren't any. So, watch out for sneaky gender bias.

There are **Different Types** of **Gender Bias**

Gender bias is a preference towards one gender. It can either **exaggerate** or **minimise** differences between males and females. There are different types of **gender bias** that may crop up in psychological theories and research.

Alpha Bias

1) Alpha bias is where differences between males and females are **exaggerated**.
2) This type of bias can be used to **undervalue** one of the sexes.
3) The differences are sometimes attributed to differences in **biology** — for example, differences in **genetics** or **hormones**.

My friend is always being mean about my little car, but he's just got Alpha Romeo bias.

Beta Bias

1) Beta bias is where differences between males and females are **ignored** or **minimised**.
2) This can happen when studies just include participants of **one gender** but then the conclusions are applied to the **whole population**.

Research can also be **androcentric** (male-centred) or **estrocentric** (female-centred).

Androcentrism

1) This is where **males** are viewed as being at the centre of culture.
2) In psychological terms, male behaviour is seen as the **norm**. This can mean that theories made in relation to males are also **applied to women**, or it can mean that **any differences** that women display are seen as **exceptions** to the rule.

Estrocentrism

1) This is where **female** behaviour is seen as the **norm**.
2) This is a much **rarer** phenomenon than androcentrism.

Some **Research Designs** Can Make Gender Bias **More Likely**

Research designs are really important, because the **research methods** that psychologists use can cause the results and conclusions to be **gender biased**. Different research designs can **unintentionally** cause either **alpha bias** or **beta bias**.

1) When a **research question** is first proposed and an **aim** is formed (see page 96), psychologists need to be careful that they're not unconsciously including any gender **stereotypes**. For example, studies on aggression often use male stereotypes to provide a measure of what it means to be aggressive.

2) **Participants** for research should be selected in a non-biased way. Many early studies in psychology only used **male university students**, and this could have had the effect of producing **beta biased** theories. They would have been based on results from males, but **generalised** to the **whole population**.

3) Researchers can sometimes unconsciously treat male and female participants **differently** during a study. To avoid this, they should make sure that male and female participants are spoken to in the **same manner**. If participants are treated differently, the researchers will be introducing **extraneous variables** (see page 97) that may produce a false **gender difference** in the results that **isn't actually there**.

4) Researchers should be aware that **gender stereotypes** can affect their **expectations** about the outcomes of research. These expectations can affect the **results** that they record, or the way that they **interpret** their results. For example, in an **observational study** (see pages 102-103) comparing men and women, researchers should be careful not to just record behaviours that fit in with their ideas about how men and women **should** behave. They also shouldn't be led to **interpret** their results to show a gender difference that **isn't actually there**.

Gender Bias

Not All Studies are **Published**

1) Gender bias can be created as a result of **publication bias**.

2) It has been reported that studies that produced **positive findings** are more likely to be published than studies that don't find any differences. In terms of gender research, this would mean that studies showing a **difference** between males and females would be **more likely** to appear in **scientific journals** than ones with no gender differences.

3) This can **exaggerate differences** between males and females, and so produce an **alpha bias**.

Theories Can Show **Gender Bias** Too

There are plenty of **theories** out there that show gender bias...

Freud's theories

- **Freud's** theories usually described **male behaviour** as the **norm**, explaining female behaviour as anything which differed from the norm. For example, Freud proposed that when girls find out that they don't have a penis, they suffer from what he termed '**penis envy**' (page 162).

Asch's theory

- Asch's research into **conformity** (see page 3) was **androcentric** — he used a **male-only** sample, meaning that his results couldn't be generalised to women.

Bem's theory

- **Bem's (1974)** theory of **psychological androgyny** (page 156) is a **beta biased** theory. Her theory centres on the idea that the most psychologically healthy men and women can **choose** which **personality traits** they want to have, regardless of whether they're typically masculine or feminine qualities.
- In other words, she classed the various masculine and feminine traits as all being on a **level playing field**. This is why the theory is **beta biased**. It ignores the fact that different traits are **valued** differently in **society** — for example, a lot of masculine traits are valued highly.

Warm-Up Questions

Q1 What is alpha bias?
Q2 What is beta bias?
Q3 What is meant by androcentrism?
Q4 Explain one way that research design can create a gender biased experiment.
Q5 Why might Freud's theories be considered androcentric?

Exam Question

Q1 Read the item below, and then answer the questions that follow.

> A researcher is designing an experiment to study conformity amongst university students.
> He intends to use a sample of 50 male students from his university and record whether they are affected by minority influence in a shape-naming task.

Outline why the researcher's study could be considered to be androcentric. [2 marks]

You just can't win...

Studies that appear to be 'gender neutral' could actually be showing beta bias. There might simply be no difference between the two genders, or it might be the case that the difference is being ignored or minimised due to the design of the research. It's a right old mine field out there. Don't take everything as gospel — remember to question everything.

Cultural Bias

The list of stuff to think about when you're evaluating an experiment goes on and on... and on and on. There's yet another thing to add on now — cultural differences. And these can throw up all kinds of issues.

Psychologists Have Often Ignored Cultural Differences

Culture refers to the set of **customs**, **social roles**, **behavioural norms** and **moral values** that are **shared** by a group of people. As psychology developed in **western** countries, researchers would typically study people who were **available** — people from their own cultural background. Historically, there hasn't been much research to **compare** people of **different** cultures. There are various possible **reasons** for this:

1) Researchers **assumed** that people from **western** cultures are essentially the **same** as people in **other** cultures. So, whatever was found about people from one culture was **applied** to all other people.

2) It may have been assumed that **non-western** cultures were more '**primitive**' and less **worthy** of study.

3) Researchers who wanted to do **cross-cultural** research couldn't because they lacked **time** and **resources**.

Research Methods Can Cause Cultural Bias

Cultural bias can be the result of a researcher's **assumptions** and **research aims**.
Berry (1969) identified **two** main **approaches** to research which could lead to cultural bias:

> 'Universality' means using one set of rules or theories to explain everything.

Etic research

- **Etic research** is research from a specific culture which is then applied to other cultures to find **universal laws**, giving the studies **universality**.

- It's possible that there are lots of these. All humans have basically the **same physiology** and many behaviours are found in **all cultures**, e.g. language, attachment formation, aggression.

- However, because studies have to take **samples** of the population, it's **difficult** to **generalise** the findings to **all** cultures. If researchers do this, they could be guilty of **bias** in the form of an **imposed etic**.

Emic research

- **Emic research** is research based on a specific culture that's used to understand that culture from within. It isn't generalised to other cultures. Instead it studies **variations** in behaviour **between** groups of people. This avoids the problem of cultural bias through an imposed etic (i.e. making universal laws).

- However, bias may still occur by **exaggerating** differences **between** different cultural groups, and neglecting to look at the differences **within** the cultural groups.

- This is what happens in claims like 'people from country X are more generous than people from country Y'. Even if evidence showed that, on average, country X residents are more generous, it's still likely that many of them aren't, and that many people from country Y are. So it's important not to neglect the **variety** found **within** groups — individual differences.

The issue of **sub-culture bias** is also important — etic or emic bias for sub-groups **within** larger groups. For example, research on relationships might **focus** on studying **heterosexuals**, and so **neglect homosexual** relationships (**emic bias**). The findings might then be **generalised** to homosexual relationships, despite not having studied them (**etic bias**).

Ethnocentrism is a Type of Cultural Bias

Ethnocentrism is where our own culture is taken as the **norm** that we judge other cultures against. Ethnocentric research is **centred** around the one culture it's **based** in — so because most psychological studies have studied people from **western** cultures, a lot of them are **ethnocentric**. For example:

- Asch's (1951) research into conformity involved seeing whether people would change their answer to an **easy** question (judging the length of a line) to conform with the people around them (page 3). This study was ethnocentric because it only studied Americans. It showed etic bias because Asch generalised the results to members of groups that hadn't actually been studied.

- Further research found variations in levels of conformity depending on the culture being studied.

Milgram's (1963) study of obedience (page 7) challenged the view that the German soldiers who had carried out the Holocaust must be inherently evil. Milgram found that people could commit evil acts because of the situation they were in, rather than because of their character. However, he used American participants in his study, and didn't take cultural differences between Germany and the USA into account, making this an imposed etic.

Cultural Bias

Cultural Bias Has Social Implications

Culturally biased **studies** will produce culturally biased **theories**. This has important **implications** for society because psychologists might be making claims that aren't actually true. It's especially problematic when biased views influence **psychological practice**, e.g. understanding and treating **abnormality**.

1) **Cochrane and Sashidharan (1995)** found that people of African-Caribbean origin in the UK were up to **seven** times more likely than white patients to be diagnosed with **schizophrenia**. The rate of schizophrenia in the Caribbean is **no higher** than in the UK, so it seems that African-Caribbeans **don't** have a **genetic predisposition** towards it.

2) **Littlewood and Lipsedge (1989)** found that African-Caribbean patients were often prescribed **stronger** doses of **medication** than white patients, even though their **symptoms** were the **same**. This suggests that their symptoms are **interpreted** as being more **severe** than they actually are.

3) These findings could be the result of **culture biased assumptions** influencing how people's behaviours are **interpreted**. It seems that all patients may be judged against **norms** for the **white population**, even if they're originally from a different culture.

There are Problems With Doing Cross-Cultural Research

Cross-cultural research can help to reduce cultural bias, but the results aren't always **valid**.

1) Even with a **translator** it can be **difficult** to **interpret** what participants say and do — some beliefs and customs may be difficult for people from other cultures to understand. This means that findings can be **misinterpreted** and research can be **ethnocentric** because the researchers judge behaviour against their own **cultural norms**.

2) **Cross-cultural replications** of studies are difficult to do. **Smith and Bond (1988)** argued that perfect cross-cultural replications are impossible because **procedures** will have different **meanings** to people in different **cultures**. This means that studies can lack **validity** — they might not be testing what they aim to test.

There Are Ways to Reduce Cultural Bias in Research

Cultural bias usually **isn't intentional**, so it can be difficult to prevent. However, there are ways to **reduce** it:

1) Research should recognise **cultural relativism**. This is accepting that there are no universal standards for behaviour, and that any research done must take into account the culture it takes place in.

2) Samples should be **representative** of the groups you want to generalise the results to — they should include all relevant sub-groups.

3) **Berry (1969)** recommended conducting research in **meaningful contexts** and using **local researchers** who are part of the culture being studied. This **avoids** the problems of an **imposed etic**.

Warm-Up Questions

Q1 What is the difference between etic and emic research?
Q2 What is ethnocentrism?
Q3 How did Asch's (1951) research show etic bias?
Q4 Explain one of the difficulties encountered in cross-cultural research.
Q5 What is cultural relativism?
Q6 Outline one thing which could be done to reduce cultural bias in psychological research.

Exam Question

Q1 Outline the impact of cultural bias on psychological research. [6 marks]

Cultural bias — too much theatre and art, not enough revision...

So to do a super-duper psychological study you need to make sure that your research is neither etic nor emic, that it doesn't show sub-culture bias and it isn't ethnocentric. No problem. Assuming that you know what those words mean.

Free Will and Determinism

Hey, guess what — you don't actually have to look at these pages at all. But you can choose to look at them of your own free will... But it's probably best if you do look at them, even if you don't really want to. Flippin' exams.

There's **Debate** About **Whether** People have **Free Will**

Psychology aims to explain **why** people **behave** in certain ways. The **free will versus determinism** debate centres around whether people can **choose** how to behave, or whether what they do is **influenced** by **other forces**.

Free will

People are able to **choose** how to behave — their behaviour **isn't** a response to **external** or **biological** factors, and **isn't** influenced by **past behaviour**.

Comments on free will

- People can **explain** behaviours in terms of **decisions** and **intentions**.
- However, **free will** is **subjective** — someone might **think** they're **choosing** how to behave, but actually be **influenced** by **other forces**.
- Some people with **psychological** disorders **don't** appear to have **free will**, e.g. people with **OCD** feel that they **can't control** their thoughts and actions.

Determinism

All of the physical events in the universe (including human behaviour) occur in **cause and effect relationships**. So, our thoughts, beliefs and behaviours are determined by **past events** and **causes**. This is a **scientific** view that implies that complete knowledge of a cause and effect relationship will mean you can **predict** future behaviour in the same situation.

Yes, Colette had in fact chosen to wear her hair like this of her own free will.

Comments on determinism

- The determinist approach is very **scientific**. Other scientific subjects (e.g. physics) have shown that events in the **physical universe** operate according to **cause and effect** relationships that follow certain laws.
- However, determinism is **unfalsifiable** — it can't be proved wrong, because it assumes that events **can** be the **result** of **forces** that **haven't** been **discovered** yet.

Different **Psychological Approaches** Fall on **Different Sides** of the **Debate**

- Most psychological approaches are **determinist** to a certain extent, because they look for **patterns** and **causes** of behaviour. If the answer was always just that behaviour was down to free will, psychologists wouldn't have much to study. Many approaches do **acknowledge** the existence of **free will** though.

- As opposed to **hard determinism**, which completely rules out the idea of free will, **soft determinism** is the viewpoint that we choose our behaviour, but the choices that we make are a result of our own personality traits and intentions. Most **psychological approaches** hold this view, just to different **degrees**:

1) **Psychodynamic** — **Freud** argued that behaviour is **determined** by **unconscious forces**. This is known as **psychic determinism**. For example, if you forget to go to a dentist's appointment, you might consciously think it was an accident. But Freud would claim it was actually determined by **unconscious influences**, e.g. you didn't really want to go. However, he also acknowledged that behaviours have many causes, including **conscious intentions**, e.g. a person can **choose** to have psychoanalysis.

2) **Biological** — Behaviours are **determined** by biological influences, e.g. genetics and brain structure. For example, **schizophrenia** has been linked to genes and brain structure abnormalities. The idea that this is the **sole cause** of behaviour is known as **biological determinism**.

3) **Cognitive** — Behaviour is the result of both **free will** and **determinism**. The approach looks for **patterns** in how the brain **processes** external information, and what **behaviours** this leads to. However, it acknowledges that people use cognitive processes like **language** to **reason** and make **decisions**.

4) **Behaviourist** — **Skinner** claimed that behaviour is **determined** by the **environment** and is the result of **punishment** and **reinforcement**. This is known as **environmental determinism**. Everyone has a different **history of reinforcement**, so knowing this about someone would allow you to **predict** their behaviour. If the environmental **conditioning** changes then their **behaviour** will also change.

5) **Humanistic** — This approach falls on the **free will** side of the debate. Humanistic psychologists believe that individuals are **in control** of their behaviour and are trying to achieve **personal growth**.

Holism and Reductionism

Reductionism is About Explaining Complex Things in Simple Terms

Reductionism

Reductionism is the **scientific** view that it should be possible to explain **complex** things by **reducing** them to their most **simple** structures or processes. In psychology this means explaining **behaviour** by boiling theories down to some **basic principles** — e.g. **aggression** is caused by **conditioning**. Testing this in an experiment means that it's possible to establish **cause and effect**. However, experiments are often **unrealistically simplified** and **ignore** other **influences**, so they may not be testing real behaviour.

Holism

Holism is the argument that human behaviour is more **complex** than the processes that other sciences study, e.g. chemical reactions. This means it should be viewed as the **product** of **different influences**, which all **interact**. Trying to **separate** these influences by just studying one of them means that complex behaviour can be **misunderstood**, so a holistic approach avoids this problem. However, it's **difficult** to **test** integrated theories because you can't **isolate** the **variables** — this means it's **hard** to establish **cause and effect**.

Rose (1976) Talked About Levels of Explanation in Psychology

Rose (1976) put forward a range of explanations used in psychology, from the most **reductionist** (and therefore the **most scientific**), to the most **holistic** (and therefore the **least scientific**).

the molecular level (physics) → the cellular level (biochemistry) → parts of individuals (biology) → the behaviour of individuals (psychology) → the behaviour of groups (sociology)

These are known as **levels of explanation** — how reductionist or holistic an explanation of something is.

Different Psychological Approaches Fall on Different Sides of the Debate

1) **Psychodynamic** — by considering unconscious forces and childhood experiences, the psychodynamic approach is a relatively **holistic** approach. For instance, Freud emphasised that personality is the result of **interaction** between different **components**, such as the id and the ego, which is a more **holistic** view.

2) **Biological** — all behaviours can be explained as the product of biological influences like **genetics**, **brain structure** and **brain chemistry**. This is **biological reductionism**. It aims to establish **cause and effect**, but it **focuses less** on other influences on behaviour, e.g. behavioural or social.

3) **Cognitive** — the brain's cognitive processes are compared to the working of a computer — **machine reductionism**. There is input, various stages of processing, and then an output. This is reductionist because it doesn't explain why humans function **differently** to computers, e.g. they can forget.

4) **Behaviourist** — all human behaviour (except biological reflexes and instincts) is shaped by the environment through the processes of classical and operant conditioning. This is known as **environmental (stimulus-response) reductionism**. Other possible influences (e.g. genetic, social) are focused on less.

5) **Humanistic** — the approach is **holistic** as it studies the individual in context and tries to understand their subjective experiences. It uses **self-report** techniques, rather than breaking down behaviour into its component parts. Humanistic psychologists **disagree** with reducing behaviour to cause and effect reactions.

Warm-Up Questions

Q1 Outline the argument for the existence of free will.

Q2 Explain the difference between reductionism and holism.

Q3 Is the behaviourist approach reductionist? Explain your answer.

PRACTICE QUESTIONS

Exam Questions

Q1 Outline the difference between hard determinism and soft determinism. [2 marks]

Q2 Outline **two** types of reductionism. [4 marks]

Keep things as simple as possible — yep, that's my idea of a good theory...

There's lots of new terminology on these pages, so don't go rushing past it — stick around until you know your free will from your holism. You can then impress the examiners by flashing your new-found vocabulary around.

The Nature-Nurture Debate

This has got to be one of the biggest debates of all time — are you the product of your genes or your environment? Well, unfortunately the conclusion is a bit less exciting than you might expect — it's probably just a bit of both.

The **Nature-Nurture Debate** Has a **Long History**

Firstly, let's just get the definitions of **nature** and **nurture** absolutely clear:

> • **Nature (genotype)** — **innate** characteristics determined by **physiological** and **genetic** factors.
> • **Nurture** — the influence of the **environment** and **learning** experiences.

1) Philosophers have debated for centuries about **how far** human behaviour is the product of **innate characteristics**, and how far it's the product of the **environment**.

2) For example, in the 18th century there was debate between **nativists** and **empiricists**. **Nativists** like **Jean Rousseau** argued that all human characteristics were in-born. **Empiricists** like **John Locke** claimed that everyone is a '**blank slate**' when they're born, so the **environment** 'writes' unique characteristics onto us.

3) Nowadays, almost all psychologists accept that **nature** and **nurture** must **interact**, because personality and behaviour seem to be influenced by **both**. This is known as the **interactionist** approach.

> • Rats raised in **bare**, dark cages have been compared to rats that grew up in **stimulating** environments.
> • It's found that the rats raised in the unstimulating environments do **less** well in problem-solving tasks and **learn** much more **slowly** than the other rats.
> • This suggests that **environment** can affect **innate genetic potential**.

4) The debate now focuses on the **relative contribution** of **inherited traits** and the **role of the environment** in accounting for behaviour.

It's **Hard** to **Separate Nature** and **Nurture**

The **interactionist approach** states that nature and nurture **interact** to form a person's character.

1) Gottesman (1963) suggested that people have a reaction range. This means everyone has a certain genetic potential for things like intelligence and height — the genotype.

2) The environment determines how much this potential is fulfilled (how people turn out) — the phenotype.

3) For example, someone with a high genetic potential for intelligence, who didn't go to school, may have the same IQ as someone with low genetic potential for intelligence, who received a good education.

1) The diathesis-stress model suggests that people have genetic predispositions for disorders like schizophrenia.

2) A person with a higher diathesis (vulnerability) is more likely to develop the trait, but whether they do depends on the amount of stress they experience (i.e. the environment).

1) One influence can sometimes override another. For example, phenylketonuria (PKU), is a genetic metabolic disorder that can cause brain damage.

2) But if the person doesn't eat particular proteins, then the disorder won't get worse. This shows how environment can override a genetic disposition.

Determining how far nature or nurture control characteristics can be complicated by **genotype-environment correlations** — correlations between a person's genes and their environment. **Plomin et al (1977)** identified **three types** of genotype-environment correlations:

1) **Passive** — people with similar **genes** (e.g. members of the same family) are likely to experience similar **environments**. For example, two siblings may be aggressive because they have both **inherited** aggressive tendencies from their parents, or because their parents' predisposition towards aggression means that they provide a hostile home **environment**.

2) **Reactive** — **genetically determined** characteristics may **shape** a person's **experiences**. For example, people **react** more **positively** towards **attractive** people, so the kind of environment a person experiences depends partly on their **inherited** characteristics.

3) **Active** — people with particular **inherited** tendencies might **seek out** certain **environments**, which will then **shape** their behaviour just as their genetic background does. **Bandura (1986)** called this **reciprocal determinism** — environment determines behaviour and behaviour determines environment.

The Nature-Nurture Debate

Nature-Nurture **Influences** Can be **Studied** Using **Different Methods**

Family studies

- If family members share a trait more frequently than unrelated people do, then this could imply a genetic influence for that behaviour. For example, Solyom et al (1974) showed that phobias can run in families.

- However, similarities between family members may actually be the result of their shared environment — relatives might learn the behaviour from each other through observational learning.

Adoption studies

- These compare an adopted child with its biological and adoptive parents. If the child has more similarity with its adoptive parents then this would imply that nurture is important, because they share the same environment.

- Similarity with the biological parents suggests that nature is more important. Plomin et al (1988) showed a stronger correlation of IQ within biological families than adopted families.

Twin studies

- Identical (MZ) twins share 100% of their genes. Non-identical (DZ) twins share about 50% of their genes. So if MZ twins are more likely to share a characteristic than DZ twins, it implies a genetic influence. This is shown by concordance rates — concordance means how likely it is that both people in a pair will have a certain characteristic, given that one of them does. For example, Holland et al (1988) found a 56% MZ concordance for anorexia (i.e. in MZ twins, if one twin had anorexia, then 56% of the time both twins did), compared to 5% DZ concordance. Which suggests that genes influence the development of anorexia.

- However, if a trait was completely genetic then MZ concordance would be 100%, so their behaviour must also be influenced by environment. For example, people might treat MZ twins more similarly than DZ twins. As such, it's more useful (but also more difficult) to do research on twins who haven't been brought up together.

Different **Psychological Approaches** Fall on **Different Sides** of the **Debate**

1) **Psychodynamic** — Freud argued that personalities are the result of an **interaction** of nature and nurture. He emphasised the importance of **inborn instincts** and drives (represented in the id). However, he also said that **experiences** can result in **fixations** in the stages of **development**.

2) **Biological** — emphasises **genetically** determined brain structures and processes. **Evolutionary** psychology states that many behaviours, e.g. aggression, are genetically influenced because they have **survival value**. However, the **environment** influences brain **development**, so learning can **override** genetic predispositions.

3) **Cognitive** — studies **genetically** determined mental processes, but accepts that the **environment** influences their **development** and **functioning**. **Piaget's** theory of **cognitive development** argues that **environmental** stimulation is needed for the **genetically** determined process of development to **unfold**.

4) **Behaviourist** — all behaviours are **learnt** through **conditioning**, apart from inborn **reflexes** and **instincts** (e.g. blinking). This approach falls most heavily on the **nurture** side of the debate.

5) **Humanistic** — behaviour is part of a **natural** need to reach your **full potential** (to self-actualise — see p.72). However, whether you reach it depends on your experiences in the world, and so the humanistic approach falls more towards the **nurture** side of the debate.

Warm-Up Questions

Q1 What is the interactionist approach to the nature-nurture debate?

Q2 Outline two ways of studying the relative influence of nature or nurture.

Q3 Outline two approaches to psychology that focus more on nurture than nature.

PRACTICE QUESTIONS

Exam Question

Q1 Briefly outline the nature-nurture debate in psychology. [2 marks]

I hope it's not nurture — this isn't a very stimulating environment...

Nature or nurture — this debate is as old as they get. Luckily, you only have to worry about it for your exams. So, I recommend you learn this stuff really well, walk into that exam room, add your thought to this endless debate in a knowledgeable and memorable way, then walk back out again and leave the experts to continue arguing about it.

Idiographic and Nomothetic Approaches

Some topics in psychology lend themselves to an idiographic approach, and others are more suited to a nomothetic approach. I can tell you're wondering what that's all about, so you're in luck — here's a page especially for you.

The **Idiographic** and **Nomothetic** Approaches Have Different **Aims**

The Nomothetic Approach

1) In psychology, the nomothetic approach applies **general laws** and **theories** to explain behaviour across a **whole population**.

2) Nomothetic research uses **research methods** such as **laboratory experiments** and **correlational research**, which involve **groups** of participants to draw **general conclusions**.

3) It usually uses **quantitative methods** (see page 111) to draw conclusions.

Nomothetic studies try to use large samples to get lots of data.

Sometimes a nomothetic approach uses idiographic methods, or vice versa.

The Idiographic Approach

1) The idiographic approach focuses on the **individual** in detail.

2) It looks at what makes each person different, and **avoids** making general laws and theories.

3) Idiographic research uses **research methods** such as **case studies**, **interviews** and **observations**, that focus on the individual.

4) It usually uses **qualitative methods** to analyse its findings.

Idiographic and Nomothetic Approaches Have **Strengths** and **Weaknesses**

Evaluation of the Nomothetic Approach

1) The **research methods** frequently used in the nomothetic approach mean that it's a pretty **controlled**, **objective** and **scientific** approach. The **theories** it produces can then be **scientifically tested**.

2) However, these research methods can lack **ecological validity**, and so can't **reliably** be **generalised** to real life.

3) In creating general laws, **individual differences** are ignored. So, it's less useful for explaining behaviour that **doesn't fit in** with the norms of the general laws.

Evaluation of the Idiographic Approach

1) The idiographic approach focuses on the **individual**, so it can give a more **complete** explanation of behaviour than the nomothetic explanation.

2) However, this often means that **fewer people** are studied (but in more detail), so it's tricky to **generalise** findings to larger populations. It can also be seen as a **less scientific** approach than the nomothetic approach.

3) On the other hand, **detailed studies** of individual cases can help to **develop nomothetic laws** by providing extra information. For example, theories of memory have often come about from laboratory studies **combined** with more detailed case studies of people who have suffered from brain damage (e.g. HM — see page 17).

Different **Psychological Approaches** Fall on **Different Sides**

1) **Psychodynamic** — can be seen as having **both** nomothetic and idiographic components. For example, Freud's theory of **psychosexual development** (see page 70) assumed that the same stages could explain everyone's development, showing a **nomothetic approach**. However, his approach was also partially **idiographic** because it involved investigating how an individual experiences the world through the use of case studies.

2) **Biological** — aims to find the cause of behaviour in **biological structures** and **processes**. It assumes these are the same across the population, so it's a **nomothetic approach**.

3) **Cognitive** — assumes the same **mental processes** apply across the population, and so falls more towards being a **nomothetic approach**.

4) **Behaviourist** — psychologists from the behaviourist approach apply **cause and effect laws** to explain behaviour in general, which is thought to be a result of classical and operant **conditioning**. So it is a **nomothetic approach**.

5) **Humanistic** — this approach is heavily focused on **individuals** and their drive for self-actualisation (see page 72). It's therefore completely on the **idiographic** side of the debate.

Socially Sensitive Research

Some Research Raises Sensitive Social Issues

1) As well as the ethical guidelines that psychologists have to stick to when they plan research (see pages 108-109), there are also **ethical implications** when it comes to what the **research findings** might tell us.

2) Findings from psychological research may highlight **social issues** that create negative effects or reactions in society.

3) They might lead to certain groups of people being **stigmatised**, or even to **laws** being passed that put some people at a disadvantage.

4) This sort of research is known as **socially sensitive research**. It can be defined as research that may have **implications** for the **individuals** in the research, or for **groups in society**, such as the participants' families, or particular cultural groups.

Research into genetic influences raises many issues

1) Research into whether there are genetic influences on criminal behaviour could have important consequences. For example, genetics could be used as a defence against being convicted for a crime, or could be used to stigmatise people who have the relevant genes even if they haven't shown any antisocial behaviour.

2) Also, there's the possibility of compulsory genetic testing to identify people with a particular gene.

3) Such screening could also identify genes linked to psychological disorders such as schizophrenia.

4) Although this may potentially help people it could also lead to anxiety and social stigma, especially as people may have a genetic vulnerability for a disorder but not actually develop it.

Using a factor like race as an independent variable is a very sensitive issue

1) Some studies using IQ tests have shown possible racial differences in intelligence.

2) The issue is whether this is an appropriate topic for research because of social tensions that the results and conclusions may produce.

3) Such research is often discredited because of methodological problems with the IQ tests that were used. For instance, they may have been biased towards some social-cultural groups. An example of this is an IQ test developed by Yerkes (1917). Many of the questions in the test required cultural knowledge of the US, therefore lower scores were due to a lack of culturalisation, rather than low intelligence.

5) There's an argument that socially sensitive research **shouldn't** be carried out for ethical reasons. However, other people argue that researchers have to carry out this type of research because it could help society **as a whole**. E.g. research showing that the father can be the primary caregiver (p. 27) has had a positive effect on the economy.

Warm-Up Questions

Q1 What's the difference between idiographic and nomothetic approaches?

Q2 Which side of the idiographic/nomothetic debate does the biological approach to psychology sit on? Explain why.

Q3 How might research into genetic influences raise socially sensitive issues?

Exam Questions

Q1 Which approach aims to find general laws to explain behaviour?
A idiographic   B holism   C nomothetic   D free will   [1 mark]

Q2 a) Briefly outline what is meant by an idiographic approach to psychology.   [2 marks]

   b) Explain one limitation of an idiographic approach to psychological investigation.   [2 marks]

Q3 Describe one example of research that could be considered socially sensitive.
   Give reasons for your answer.   [4 marks]

They're an argumentative bunch, those psychologists...

There are debates going on all over the place in psychological research — nature-nurture, holistic-reductionist, idiographic-nomothetic... you name it, it's being argued about. More importantly for you — make sure you're prepared for the exam, and can discuss these debates in the context of the various psychological topics you know all about.

Evolutionary Explanations for Partner Choice

If you've ever wondered why we find certain characteristics attractive in people, evolutionary psychology has some explanations. If you've never wondered this, evolutionary psychology still has some explanations.

Evolutionary Psychology Says Our Preferences are Evolved Adaptations

1) **Evolutionary psychologists** believe that the **psychological processes** that people use to choose a partner come from **evolution**.

These processes may not be conscious.

2) The idea is that these processes came about because, in the past, when humans lived as **hunter-gatherers**, having them made people well **adapted** to the environment. (There's more about the mechanics of this below.)

3) A key part of this explanation is the theory that **attractive traits** are **reliable indicators** that a partner is a good bet for passing on our genes. For example, **Singh** found that **waist to hip ratio** was related to **attractiveness** in women, and argued that this is because it's a reliable indicator of a woman's ability to **reproduce**:

> Singh (1993) got male participants aged 18-22 to rank drawings of female figures with a waist to hip ratio (WHR) of 0.7 to 1.0 (i.e. waist size 70% to 100% of hip size) in terms of attractiveness and ability to have children. The drawings with a waist to hip ratio 0.7 were rated the most attractive and the most able to have children.
>
> Singh (2002) argued that low WHR is a reliable indicator of health and ability to reproduce in women. He cited evidence that females have higher WHR before puberty and after menopause (i.e. low WHR correlates with fertility), and that high WHR in women has been shown to correlate with health issues like diabetes.

Attractive Characteristics Evolve Through Sexual Selection

1) **Natural selection** is the process where characteristics that make an individual more **likely to reproduce** and pass on their **genes** become more prevalent in a population.

2) Darwin's theory of natural selection, which is generally accepted, says that this is how **evolution** happens.

3) One of the processes of natural selection is **sexual selection**:

- Within a species there are certain **characteristics** that make an individual more able to **find a partner** (e.g. being physically attractive) and **reproduce** (i.e. fertility).

- These characteristics give an individual a **reproductive advantage**, therefore they become **more prevalent** because they're more likely to be **passed on** to future generations. This is known as **sexual selection**.

- There are **two types** of sexual selection:

> **Intra-sexual selection** takes place when males compete (often aggressively) and the winner is rewarded with the female. The female is **passive** in this process — she doesn't choose her own mate.

> **Inter-sexual selection** takes place when males compete for the **attention** of a female. The female plays an **active** role, choosing her mate.

In some species females compete for males, but this is quite rare.

There Can Be Conflict Between Natural Selection and Sexual Selection

1) As well as traits that give a reproductive advantage, natural selection also happens with traits that give a **survival advantage** — traits that make it more likely an individual will **survive** long enough to reproduce (e.g. health).

2) Sometimes the traits that are **attractive** to a mate make an individual **less likely** to survive, so sexual selection can **conflict** with natural selection more generally. For example, female peacocks find the **long, brightly coloured tails** of male peacocks attractive, but very brightly coloured tails are more noticeable to **predators**.

3) One theory from **evolutionary psychology** explaining why this happens is the **handicap principle**:

> **The Handicap Principle**
>
> Zahavi (1975) argued that displaying a noticeable handicap to survival (e.g. a large colourful tail) actually indicates survival strength. Zahavi called this the handicap principle.
>
> If an individual has managed to survive (and their ancestors survived long enough to reproduce) despite having the unhelpful characteristic, then they must have superior genes.

4) The handicap principle can be applied to humans too. For example, **masculine facial features** (e.g. a strong jaw) result from high levels of **testosterone**. Testosterone causes the immune system to be **less responsive**, so having these features indicates a **cost** to the individual. This cost means masculine facial features can be seen as an **honest indicator** of 'quality' genes — they're only displayed by individuals who can **afford** the handicap.

Evolutionary Explanations for Partner Choice

Evolution Could Explain Gender Differences in Partner Preferences

Buss (1989) did a **cross-cultural** study which looked for **gender differences** in partner preferences.

Buss (1989) — Gender differences in mate selection

Method: **Questionnaires** were used to collect data from over 10 000 men and women from 37 different cultural groups. The questionnaires covered **demographic information** such as age, gender and marital status. They also asked about preferences for variables such as marriage, age differences and characteristics in a mate (e.g. intelligence, sociability and financial prospects).

Results: **Women** valued variables associated with **gaining resources** (e.g. money, safe environment) more highly than men. **Men** valued variables associated with **reproductive capacity** (e.g. youth) more highly than women.

Conclusion: Women have had limited access to the **resources** needed to provide for themselves and their offspring. So, they've evolved (through sexual selection) to select mates who can **provide** these resources. The factor limiting men's reproductive success has been access to **fertile women**, and so they have evolved to be attracted to women with a high likelihood of **reproducing**.

Evaluation: There were **similar findings** across a range of **different cultures**. However, it **wasn't** a truly **representative** study as it was hard to include rural and less educated populations. Cross-cultural research is important as it suggests universality, providing strong evidence for an **evolutionary explanation** of gender differences in sexual selection.

Buss and Schmitt (1993) went on to develop a more detailed **evolutionary explanation** for partner preferences.

Sexual Strategies Theory

Buss and Schmitt (1993) came up with the **sexual strategies theory**. The theory argues that men and women apply various different **strategies** for choosing partners, depending on the situation. These strategies have evolved to help them meet the different requirements they have of **long-term** and **short-term** partners. For example, women try to assess the quality of a short-term partner's **genes**, whereas men are mostly concerned with a short-term partner's **availability** and **fertility**.

Strengths

1) The idea that men and women have different strategies for choosing a partner is supported by **Buss (1989)**.

2) The argument that men use strategies which lead them to choose **fertile women** as partners is also supported by Singh's findings on **waist to hip ratio** (see previous page).

Weaknesses

1) There were more **similarities** than differences between men and women's responses in Buss's (1989) study. Neither resources nor youth were rated as important by men or women — **other factors** like intelligence and mutual attraction were rated as **most important** by both genders. Overall there was a much greater difference **between cultures** than between genders. This doesn't rule out evolutionary explanations for partner preference, but it may suggest that other (e.g. social) factors play a part too.

2) Evolutionary explanations of partner choice don't take into account **social determinants** of behaviour. For example, in lots of societies women still don't have the same opportunity to provide for themselves as men do. This may have **more influence** on the differences in partner preference than evolutionary factors.

3) Lots of the evidence for evolutionary explanations of partner preference comes from studies on **other animals**, and this evidence can't be reliably **generalised** to human partner preferences.

Attitudes have changed quite a lot since Buss's (1989) study. The results might be quite different if the study was carried out today.

Warm-Up Questions

Q1 What are intra-sexual and inter-sexual selection?

Q2 Outline the evolutionary explanation for partner preferences.

Exam Question

Q1 Discuss how sexual selection is related to human reproductive behaviour. [16 marks]

Research into sexual selection — sounds like a very dodgy excuse to me...

Evolutionary psychology is a tricky one — it's hard to prove that psychological processes like attraction have evolved, so there's lots of debate about how accurate these ideas are. Learn this lot so you'll have plenty to say about it though.

Attraction

There's been lots of research into what people are attracted to when they're starting a romantic relationship, and there are plenty of different theories. The main ones you need to know about are filter theory and the matching hypothesis.

Various Factors Affect **Attraction** in Romantic Relationships

Physical Attractiveness

1) One of the most obvious factors affecting whether a relationship will begin is whether or not people find each other **physically attractive**. Attraction isn't always about **physical features**, but there are various features which have been found to match up with attractiveness. For example:

> **Cunningham (1986)** asked 75 male undergraduate students to rate photos of 50 females for **attractiveness**. He found several features that **correlated positively** with attractiveness — large eyes, small noses, small chins, prominent cheekbones and narrow cheeks.

Generally, a low waist to hip ratio is also considered attractive in women (see p.146).

2) Generally, men are **more likely** than women to report appearance as **important** in attraction (as shown by Buss, see previous page), but both **women and men** consider appearance important for a **short-term partner**.

> **Li and Kenrick (2006)** asked participants to choose between different characteristics they would like in a partner for a **casual relationship**. Both men and women chose **physical attractiveness** as the most important.

Self-disclosure

There's a bit more about this on page 152.

1) **Self-disclosure** is sharing information about yourself, including your views and feelings.
2) **Collins and Miller's (1994)** meta-analysis showed that people tend to **like somebody more** if that person has self-disclosed to them. They also found that self-disclosing to somebody tends to **increase liking** for that person.

Filter Theory Says **Different Criteria** are Important at **Different Stages**

Kerckhoff and Davis (1962) explain the development of relationships using **filter theory**.
The theory proposes that there are a series of 'filters' that operate at **different stages** of forming a relationship:

1) Social demographic filter	Initially we form a '**field of availables**' — these are potential people to form a relationship with. This first filter is based on **social** and **demographic** factors such as **age**, **religion**, **living near each other**, and so on.
2) Similarity in attitudes filter	We narrow the set of available people down to a smaller '**field of desirables**' — these are people who a relationship is more likely to **progress** with. This filter is based on sharing **similar attitudes**, **values** and **interests**.
3) Complementarity filter	In the longer term, relationships will progress if both partners are fulfilling each others **needs** (i.e. both partners provide what the other needs). So this filter is based on two people being a good **complement** to each other.

This theoretical model came from **Kerckhoff and Davis's (1962)** study into long-term relationships.

> Kerckhoff and Davis (1962) surveyed female **university students** and their male partners, who were **considering marriage**. The survey asked about their personalities, attitudes and their relationship. **7 months later** they conducted a follow-up survey to see if the couple's relationship had progressed towards a **permanent partnership**.
>
> They found that couples who had been together for **less than 18 months** were more likely to have progressed towards a permanent partnership if they had **similar values**. However, among couples who had been together for **more than 18 months**, it was couples who had **complementary needs** (i.e. each partner met the needs of the other) who were more likely to have progressed towards a permanent partnership.

Evidence For

Winch (1958) surveyed 25 couples who had been married for less than 2 years. He found a significantly **stronger correlation** in spouses between **complementary needs** (e.g. needing to nurture others and needing to be nurtured) than between similar needs.

Evidence Against

Levinger et al (1970) replicated Kerckhoff and Davis's study across other universities, but their results didn't support the theory. They found **no significant difference** over time in the correlation between relationship progress and **either** sharing values or having complementary needs.

Attraction

The **Matching Hypothesis** Says People Want an **Equally Attractive Partner**

Walster et al (1966) developed the **matching hypothesis**, which states that people tend to choose partners who are **as attractive** as themselves. Walster et al's (1966) **computer dance study** aimed to test this hypothesis.

Walster et al (1966) — Computer dance study

Method: A 'Computer Dance' was advertised in a handbook given out to new **university students**, and tickets were sold to **376 men** and **376 women**. The people selling the tickets secretly rated each student for **attractiveness**. The students weren't told they were participating in a study. Instead, they were told that a **computer** would match them with a date for the dance who **shared their interests**. In fact, the participants were paired **randomly** with somebody of the opposite sex, although no men were paired with taller women. During the dance the participants filled in a **questionnaire** about their date. Participants were contacted **four to six months later** to find out if they'd tried to go on any **further dates** with their dance date.

Results: Participants paired with a **similarly attractive** partner were **not significantly more liked** by their date than those paired with a partner with an attractiveness rating **different** to theirs. Instead, participants who were rated as **more attractive** were more **liked** by their date. More **attractive** participants were also **more frequently** asked out on further dates than less attractive participants, whereas there was **no correlation** between **similarity** in attractiveness in a pair and the **number of times** participants were asked out again.

Conclusion: The matching hypothesis was **not supported** — the results showed that people **prefer attractive partners**, regardless of their own attractiveness.

Evaluation: The computer dance was quite different from **usual dating** — the participants didn't **choose** one another, and neither of them had to **ask** each the other on a date. This means that the study has low ecological validity — the results can't really be applied to dating in real life. The way the attractiveness of the participants was judged may mean the results are not that **reliable** — the raters had to judge attractiveness very quickly. The participants were **dressed up** at the dance, and they had **several hours** to judge each other's attractiveness, so their perception might not have matched the rating.

Strengths

1) **Murstein (1972)** asked 99 real couples and 98 fake couples to rate themselves on attractiveness. An independent judge was also asked to rate the couples. For those in a **real relationship** there was a **strong positive correlation** between the attractiveness of the two partners.

2) **White (1980)** studied 123 couples. He found that couples who were only **dating** at the start of the study were more likely to have progressed to a **serious relationship** 9 months later if both partners were **similarly attractive**.

Weaknesses

1) The results of Walster et al's (1966) computer dance study **didn't support** the matching hypothesis.

2) The hypothesis says that matching affects who we choose to **start a relationship** with, but the evidence supporting the theory comes from relationships that have **already started**.

Warm-Up Questions

Q1 Which features did Cunningham (1986) find correlated with female attractiveness?

Q2 What were the results of Kerckhoff and Davis's (1962) study?

Q3 What is the matching hypothesis?

Exam Questions

Q1 Which of these options is **not** a filter described in the filter theory of relationships?

    A Complementarity   **B** Desirability   **C** Social demography   **D** Similarity in attitudes [1 mark]

Q2 Discuss factors affecting attraction in romantic relationships. [16 marks]

Computers matching people up for dates? Whatever next...

Who can ever really hope to understand what attracts one person to another? It's a beautiful mystery... Unfortunately, you can't really write that in your exam, so you'll have to make sure you know all about filter theory and the matching hypothesis. As ever, they've both got strengths and weaknesses, so make sure you know those too.

Theories of Romantic Relationships

These pages are gold — you're not just learning psychology, you're getting free relationship advice. Well, not free, unless you stole this book. Either way, there's a whole load of theories about how relationships work for you to get stuck into.

Social Exchange Theory Says People Minimise Costs and Maximise Benefits

1) **Social exchange theory** (Thibaut and Kelley, 1959) suggests that people try to **maximise rewards** (e.g. attention, self-esteem, happiness) from a relationship and **minimise costs** (e.g. time, effort, emotional support).

2) If the relationship is to continue, then the rewards must not be **outweighed** by the costs — we should end up in **profit**. So, relationships are formed using a sort of 'cost-benefit' analysis.

3) But if we are striving to **get more** and **give less**, this may result in an **unequal relationship**.

A problem with this theory is that it's difficult to define what rewards and costs might be as these will differ between people.

Equity Theory Says People Want Balance

1) **Equity theory** suggests that people expect relationships to be **fair and equal**.

2) They want to receive rewards from relationships that are **in balance** with the rewards they provide for the other person.

3) If a relationship is unequal or unfair then it produces **discomfort and distress** in both partners, even if you're the one getting more and giving less.

4) The disadvantaged person may try to **make things fairer** if it seems possible.

Jo had found that sharing her catch with Tom was key to keeping their relationship in balance.

Hatfield et al's research into contentment in marriages **supports** equity theory:

Hatfield et al (1979) asked newlyweds to assess what they and their partner **contributed** to the relationship and their level of **contentment** with the marriage:

- The least satisfied were those who were **under-benefited** (unhappy about giving the most).
- The next least satisfied were those who were **over-benefited** (perhaps they felt guilty about giving the least).
- Equal relationships were the **most satisfactory**.

But there may be **sex differences** in how we feel about unequal relationships. **Argyle (1988)** found that:

- Over-benefited **men** were almost as satisfied as those in equitable marriages.
- Over-benefited **women**, however, were much **less satisfied** than women in equal relationships.

The Investment Model Gives Three Factors that Create Commitment

Rusbult (1980) came up with the **investment model of commitment**.

The investment model says that the **stability** of a relationship over time (i.e. whether it lasts) is determined by how **committed** the individuals are to the relationship, and that commitment **varies** depending on:

1) Satisfaction — how well the relationship fulfils the person's needs.

2) Comparison with alternatives — to what extent the person thinks their needs could be better fulfilled in another relationship, or by not being in a relationship.

3) Investment — how much the person feels they've put in to the relationship (emotionally, in terms of time, etc.).

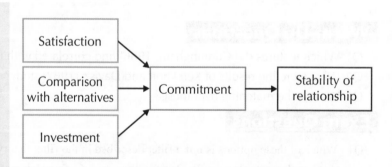

Le and Agnew (2003) did a **meta-analysis** of 52 studies involving 11 582 participants and found a significant correlation between **commitment** to a relationship and **satisfaction**, **quality of alternatives** and **investment**. Commitment level was also found to be a **significant predictor** of whether participants **stayed** in their relationship.

However, some psychologists have argued that these theories are too simplistic in trying to describe how relationships are formed — relationships are actually quite complex. The theories also don't consider cultural and gender factors, which may cause people to treat relationships in different ways.

Theories of Romantic Relationships

Duck's **Phase Model** says that **Relationships End** in **Stages**

Duck (1988) developed a **four-phase model** of the ending of an intimate relationship.

1. **Intra-psychic phase** — inside the head of **one person**. One partner becomes **dissatisfied** with the relationship.

2. **Dyadic phase** — between **two people**. The other partner is told about the dissatisfaction.

3. **Social phase** — beyond the couple. The break-up is **made public** to friends and family. **Implications** are discussed (e.g. care of children). The relationship **can still be saved** here (e.g. intervention of family, external marital support).

4. **Grave-dressing phase** — finishing the relationship completely. The ex-partners organise their lives **post-relationship**. They tell their own version of the break-up and of their current relationship with their ex.

Natasha could never seem to find the right moment to move the break-up to the dyadic phase...

One phase in Duck's model clearly leads onto the next as a **threshold point** is reached. For example, the **intra-psychic** phase becomes the **dyadic** phase when the dissatisfied partner **tells their partner** they're unhappy with the relationship. However, Duck's model doesn't take **individual differences** into account and **research evidence** suggests it doesn't show how **complex** the breakdown of a relationship can be.

Rusbult and Zembrodt (1983) said some people in a relationship breakdown **actively lead** the process (to resolve the problems, or to speed up the ending). Others are **passive** — they believe things will resolve themselves.

Akert (1992) said people who do the breaking up are less likely to be upset or to show physical symptoms (e.g. loss of appetite and sleep) — not surprising really.

Duck's phase model is **descriptive** — it doesn't explain **why** relationships might break down. It also doesn't take **cultural differences** in relationships into account.

Warm-Up Questions

Q1 Briefly outline social exchange theory.

Q2 What relationship did Hatfield et al (1979) find between equity and contentment in marriage?

Q3 What are the factors that determine commitment in Rusbult's investment model?

Q4 Describe the grave-dressing phase in Duck's phase model.

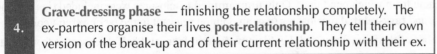

Exam Question

Q1 Read the item below and answer the questions that follow.

> Kalyan and Kate are having trouble with their relationship. Kalyan has recently told Kate that he is unhappy because they don't spend enough time together. They are discussing between themselves what they can do to resolve the problem.

a) Which of Duck's phases of relationship breakdown are Kalyan and Kate at? [1 mark]

b) Evaluate Duck's phase model. [4 marks]

People might try and tell you that a relationship is the best kind of ship...

... but that's clearly a lie. The best kind of ship is probably like that one out of Pirates of the Caribbean. It had cannons. And pirates. But I doubt psychologists are cut out for the high seas. Duck might cope, I suppose. Now, make sure you can describe the main theories concerning the maintenance and breakdown of relationships — then we can quack on...

Virtual Relationships

Online relationships are a bit different from face-to-face ones — people are often fairly anonymous online (they don't necessarily have to use their real name, for example), and they can hide aspects of themselves if they want to...

Self-Disclosure **Increases** When People Communicate **Through Computers**

Altman and Taylor's **social penetration theory (1973)** says that intimacy and closeness develop in relationships through a gradual process of **self-disclosure** — sharing information about yourself (see page 148).

Joinson (2001) found that self-disclosure happens **more** when people communicate via **computer** than face to face.

Joinson (2001) — Self-disclosure in computer communication

Method: Undergraduate students were recruited to participate in a **laboratory study**. Participants were paired (mostly in single sex pairs), and asked to discuss an abstract dilemma which stimulated conversation. Transcripts of the participants' discussions were rated on their levels of **self-disclosure**. Raters weren't told which transcripts came from which condition. Only **unprompted** disclosures were included (i.e. not answers to direct questions), and **task-related** disclosures (e.g. an opinion relevant to the task) weren't counted.

Experiment 1 — Half of the pairs discussed the dilemma **face to face**, and half discussed it from separate rooms using a **computer chat program**.

Experiment 2 — All of the pairs used the chat program, but half of them also had a **video connection**, so could see each another.

Results: In experiment 1, participants in the **computer** condition showed significantly **more self-disclosure** than the face-to-face participants. In experiment 2, pairs who could see one another over **video** had significantly **lower levels** of self-disclosure than pairs without video.

Conclusion: People **disclose more** about themselves when communicating via **computer** than they do face to face, and using **video** reduces the level of self-disclosure in computer communication.

Evaluation: This was a **laboratory experiment**, so the variables were **controlled** and the study can be **replicated**. However, the participants were almost all paired in **same sex** pairs, so the results can't be **generalised** to communication between people who aren't the same sex. In the first experiment, although the raters **weren't** told which transcripts came from which condition, it's likely they could tell which conversations were held face to face and which happened through computer chat. So their ratings may have been **biased**.

Self-awareness Might Affect **Computer Communication**

1) **Self-awareness** means paying attention to yourself, i.e. being **aware** of your thoughts, feelings and behaviour.

   Public self-awareness — this is being aware of how you **appear to others**.

   Private self-awareness — this is '**looking inwards**', i.e. being aware of what's going on inside your head.

2) **Joinson's (2001) study** also included a third experiment where the participants discussed the dilemma through computers in conditions which were designed to induce either **high** or **low** public and private **self-awareness**.

3) Joinson found that the condition designed to create **high private self-awareness** and **low public self-awareness** resulted in significantly **higher** levels of self-disclosure than the other conditions.

4) Chatting via computer usually involves **anonymity** and focussing on your thoughts and feelings to express them in **writing**. Joinson suggested that this is likely to create **low public** and **high private** self-awareness, which may explain why this type of communication results in **more self-disclosure**.

Gating Can **Prevent** Relationships from **Forming**

1) **Gating** is a process that limits how much we **self-disclose** — obstacles known as '**gates**' prevent people from sharing information, which means they can't develop **intimacy** and build a **relationship**.

2) Factors that can act as gates, such as **appearance**, **shyness** or **social skills**, are apparent when you meet somebody **face to face**.

3) However, they aren't obvious in **virtual communication**. People often communicate just through typed messages online, so their appearance, body language and so on are hidden.

4) The **absence of gating** in virtual relationships means **self-disclosure** is higher.

Virtual Relationships

The **Absence of Gating** Means **Virtual Relationships** are **Stronger**

Hill et al (1976) studied dating couples who had met **face to face**. They found that **55%** of the couples were still together after 2 years. **McKenna et al (2002)** found that couples who met **online** were **more likely** to stay together.

	McKenna et al (2002) — Relationship formation on the internet
Method:	**Surveys** were sent to randomly selected members of online **special interest forums**, e.g. forums about cats (rather than forums intended for personal ads). The survey asked about how people interacted **offline**, whether they **shared more** with others online, and how **close** the relationships they formed online were.
	Participants were then sent a **follow-up** survey two years later which asked similar questions to see how the feelings and relationships that they had reported in the earlier survey had **changed**.
Results:	People who shared aspects of themselves online which they **didn't** share with others offline reported developing **internet** relationships **more quickly** than 'real-life' relationships. Over **half** of the participants had met an internet friend **face to face**, on average meeting each internet friend **8 times**.
	After **two years**, of the respondents who had started a **romantic relationship** online, **71%** were still in the relationship.
Conclusion:	People can form close, lasting relationships **online**, and these relationships typically form more **quickly**, and are more **stable** and **long lasting** than offline relationships. McKenna proposed that online relationships have a **stable base**, because they begin based on **mutual interests** and **self-disclosure** rather than **outward appearances**. The **absence of gating** allows strong relationships to form quickly.
Evaluation:	The study used a **self-report survey** which may have involved a **biased sample** (see p.105) or produced **social desirability bias** (see p.106). However, this study looked at real-life interaction, so it has high **ecological validity**.

McKenna et al's research (2002) also included a **laboratory experiment**:

1) Pairs of the opposite sex met once either online or in person, and then a second time in person. The researchers showed that after both meetings, people liked each other significantly more if they had first met online.

2) For participants who only met face to face, their quality of conversation and the level of intimacy they reached didn't affect how much they liked each other. This suggests that liking was based on factors other than what was said, e.g. appearance.

3) However, liking and conversation quality were strongly correlated for participants who had first met online.

4) This supports the conclusion from the surveys that the absence of gating online contributes to the stability of online relationships.

Gating was playing havoc with Betty's relationship.

Warm-Up Questions

Q1 What role does self-disclosure play in forming relationships?

Q2 Describe Joinson's study into self-disclosure.

Q3 What is gating?

Q4 What did McKenna et al (2002) find about the stability of online relationships?

Exam Questions

Q1 Explain how the absence of gating may affect virtual relationships. [4 marks]

Q2 Outline and evaluate research into virtual relationships. [16 marks]

I told my GF I <3 her, she replied lots of love. I think that's what LOL means...

Lots of this is fairly common sense — people tend to share more online, which makes it easier to form relationships. Relationships are also more likely to get going online because you're less likely to trip up at the first hurdle if it's only your sparkling personality you need to worry about. Not that you need to worry about it, obviously.

Parasocial Relationships

"When I grow up, I wanna be famous" trill countless starry-eyed children. Mass media (like TV) is relatively new, so we've only just begun to look for ways to explain our relationships with celebrities. But there are already a few different theories...

Audiences Can Develop **Parasocial Relationships** With **Celebrities**

1) The relationships that audiences develop with celebrities are very **different** from the relationships formed within **normal social networks**.

2) They are **one-sided**, with one person knowing lots and the other usually knowing nothing about the other party.

3) The term used to describe this type of relationship is **parasocial**.

4) The study of **parasocial relationships** between audiences and celebrities has become a branch of **social relationship research** in its own right.

5) As well as audiences developing relationships with celebrities, many people are **attracted** to the **concept of celebrity** and want to be one themselves.

Their relationship was distinctly one sided but that didn't discourage Molly.

McCutcheon et al Identified **Three Levels** of **Parasocial Relationships**

McCutcheon (2002) created a **Celebrity Attitude Scale (CAS)** based on the findings of a set of questionnaires which asked participants to score 23 items describing different aspects of **celebrity worship**.

Using this scale McCutcheon et al (2002) later identified three **increasingly intensive** stages of celebrity worship, known as the **three levels of parasocial relationships** — they range from being a **harmless fan**, to being a **stalker**:

THREE LEVELS OF PARASOCIAL RELATIONSHIPS

1) **Entertainment-Social** — where the relationship with the celebrity exists as a **source of fun**, shared with others in a social group.

2) **Intense-Personal** — **obsessive thoughts** begin to arise in relation to the celebrity (e.g. "Justin Timberlake is my soul mate").

3) **Borderline-Pathological** — obsessive thoughts begin to give rise to **fully-fledged fantasies** (e.g. "Justin Timberlake is my boyfriend") and **behaviours** (e.g. sending love letters to Justin Timberlake). It is at this stage that **stalking** may begin, which involves a level of pursuit that is intimidating.

Parasocial Relationships Can Be Explained by **Attachment Theory**

1) **Theories of attachment** stem from research by **Bowlby** (see page 30), who suggested that people form close attachments with their **caregivers**. These bonds influence how they attach and relate to other people in adulthood.

2) In terms of **celebrities**, attachment theory suggests that children who **didn't** form close attachments with their caregivers may later develop **insecure attachments** as adults. They are then **more likely** to be attracted to celebrities. In one-sided relationships, there is little opportunity for **rejection**.

Evidence for:

The results of **Roberts' (2007)** study **support** the idea that there's a link between childhood attachments and parasocial relationships. Roberts asked 200 students (100 males and 100 females) similar questions to McCutcheon et al (2002), and found a **positive correlation** between **insecurely attached** individuals and frequently **contacting celebrities**.

Evidence against:

McCutcheon et al (2006) asked over 250 university students to complete questionnaires which examined their **personality types** and their **views on celebrities**. They found **no relationship** between having an insecure attachment and forming parasocial relationships.

Parasocial Relationships

The **Absorption Addiction Model** Also Explains **Parasocial Relationships**

1) The **absorption addiction model** was created by **McCutcheon et al (2002)**.

2) The model says that people form parasocial relationships when they have a weak sense of **identity** — an individual finds their own life **deficient**, so they follow a celebrity as a source of **fulfilment**.

3) McCutcheon et al outlined **two stages** of the model — **absorption** and **addiction**.

> **Absorption**   An individual becomes absorbed in following a celebrity — the relationship is a form of **escapism**.

> **Addiction:**   In some cases the parasocial relationship becomes addictive, and the individual becomes more and more obsessed with the celebrity. This can lead to extreme behaviour, like stalking. This usually happens as a result of poor mental health, or some sort of crisis.

4) The **absorption addiction model** is closely linked to the **three levels of parasocial relationships** — the first level (entertainment-social) occurs in the **absorption** stage. If the parasocial relationship becomes **addictive** an individual may move to the second (intense-personal), and sometimes third level (borderline-pathological).

Strengths

1) **Maltby et al (2001)** found evidence that there is a **connection** between **parasocial relationships** and **mental health**. Participants who engaged in parasocial relationships were found to be functioning **less well** psychologically than those who didn't. They also found a **positive correlation** between levels of **anxiety** and **depression** and frequency of more extreme parasocial relationships, which matches the model's predictions.

2) The model explains why **most people** who form parasocial relationships do so at the **entertainment-social** level, and why only a **small minority** develop relationships at the **intense-personal** or **borderline-pathological** level.

Weaknesses

1) This model has been criticised for ignoring the **positive aspects** of being a fan (like being part of a social group), and for **stigmatising** people who form parasocial relationships by linking their behaviour to poor mental health.

2) The studies which are used to support the absorption addiction model don't show that poor psychological functioning **causes** people to form parasocial relationships — they just show that the two things **correlate**.

3) Studies supporting this model have tended to be done in western countries, so the theory is **ethnocentric** (see p.138), and can't be **generalised** to other cultures.

Warm-Up Questions

Q1 What is meant by a parasocial relationship?

Q2 What are the three levels of parasocial relationships?

Q3 Outline one study that supports the attachment theory explanation of parasocial relationships.

Exam Questions

Q1	Outline the attachment theory explanation for the formation of parasocial relationships.	[2 marks]
Q2	Outline and evaluate the absorption addiction model of parasocial relationships.	[6 marks]

Celeb worship is harmless. My fiancé Justin Timberlake totally agrees...

So attachment theory says people form parasocial relationships because they're safe — you can't be rejected if the person you're forming a relationship with hasn't got a clue who you are. The absorption addiction model argues it's all about escapism, which sounds harmless enough, but being a fan can get out of hand if it becomes an addiction.

Sex and Gender

Gender is the way someone acts and identifies themselves — the behaviours that make a person masculine or feminine. Your gender isn't the same thing as your sex, but there are stereotypical sex-roles associated with men and women...

Sex-Role Stereotypes Are Narrow Views of How Men and Women Behave

1) Your **sex** is whether you are biologically male or female.

2) Your **gender** is the way you act and identify yourself — it's determined by the behavioural characteristics that make a person **masculine** or **feminine**.

3) People who have a **balanced combination** of masculine and feminine characteristics are **androgynous**.

4) **Sex-roles** are the particular behaviours **expected** of men and women — they vary over time and between cultures.

5) **Sex-role stereotypes** are ideas about sex-roles that are **widely held** but tend to be **narrow, inflexible,** and **over generalised**. For example: 'Women should care for children while men bring in the money.'

A study by **Seavey et al (1975)** demonstrated adults showing sex-role stereotypes. Participants were asked to interact with a 3-month-old after the child was introduced as either a girl, a boy or just 'a baby' (i.e. no information about sex given). They found that **participants' behaviour** towards the child **differed** depending on what **information** they were given. For example, **sex-stereotyped toys** were used — i.e. most adults chose a doll to play with when they were told the child was a girl.

People Who Don't Fit Sex-Role Stereotypes Show Androgyny

1) **Bem (1974)** developed a self-report questionnaire known as the **Bem Sex Role Inventory (BSRI)** by asking 50 male and 50 female students to rate **personality traits** (e.g. shyness) as being either masculine or feminine.

2) The most highly rated masculine, feminine and neutral words were then used to form a **questionnaire**, which aimed to measure the mix of **stereotypically** masculine and feminine traits present in an individual.

3) Individuals **rate themselves** for these traits on a scale of 1 to 7. Those who score highly for **both** masculine and feminine traits are said to be **psychologically androgynous**.

4) Bem suggests that androgyny is **advantageous** in society as it means people have the traits needed to cope with a **range of situations**. Those who score highly on only one scale have a more limited range of skills.

5) Several studies suggest that **environmental factors** are the cause of psychological androgyny. For example:

Weisner and Wilson-Mitchell (1990) compared children raised in families that put an **emphasis** on traditional gender roles with children raised in families that actively **downplayed** traditional gender roles.

They found that androgyny was **higher** in children who had been encouraged to **ignore** traditional gender roles.

6) Other researchers have argued that androgyny is more likely to be a **lifestyle choice**. As Bem suggested, psychologically androgynous people have the **advantage** of being able to use the best masculine traits as well as the best feminine traits.

7) However, the BSRI is considered to be a **reductionist** theory, as it reduces femininity and masculinity to a single score. It is also based on **outdated** views, i.e. traits that were desirable in the 1970s.

Warm-Up Questions

Q1 What are sex-role stereotypes?

Q2 Why did Bem consider psychological androgyny to be advantageous?

Q3 What were Weisner and Wilson-Mitchell's (1990) findings on psychological androgyny?

Exam Questions

Q1 Explain what is meant by 'gender'. [2 marks]

Q2 Explain how the Bem Sex Role Inventory is carried out. [3 marks]

Stereotypes are a pain in the neck, but they're hard to get rid of...

There are quite a few fixed ideas about what men and women are like generally (sex-role stereotypes). These aren't usually very accurate though — women often have 'masculine' traits and vice versa. This is what the Bem Sex Role Inventory tests — if somebody is measured as having lots of both sorts of trait they're psychologically androgynous.

Atypical Gender Development

Some people have a male body but feel female, or vice versa — their gender and sex don't match.

People with **Gender Dysphoria** Feel Their **Sex** and **Gender Don't Match**

1) Some people feel that their **biological sex** doesn't match their **psychological gender** — they feel that they're in the wrong body. For example, somebody born male may feel they're female **mentally** and want to be **treated** as a girl.

2) **Gender dysphoria** occurs when this causes the person **distress**, such as **anxiety**, and they want to **change their sex**.

3) Gender dysphoria (GD) can begin in **early childhood**.

4) GD is **different** from cross-dressing (wearing clothes of the other gender). People with GD may cross-dress, but lots of people who cross-dress just enjoy it — they **don't** want to change their sex. Some people with GD live **full-time** as the sex other than their birth sex, and this may involve having surgery to change their physical sex.

Gender Dysphoria May have a **Biological Explanation**...

1) One explanation for **gender dysphoria** is that the **brain functioning** of these individuals is more typical of the **other sex** (i.e. not their biological sex).

2) Some researchers believe that male and female brains develop **differently** because they're exposed to different levels of **sex hormones** (e.g. testosterone) in the womb. There's more about this on page 158.

3) An individual might develop brain function typical of the other sex if they have **unusual hormone levels** during brain development. For example if a girl's **testosterone** levels are higher than usual.

Strengths	Weaknesses
1) **Kruijver et al (2000)** found that the number of **neurones** in a region of the brain called the **BSTc** in male-to-female transsexuals was **similar** to the number in women (typically half as many as in men).	1) **Chung et al (2002)** found sex differences in the BSTc didn't appear until **adulthood**, so they may be a **result** of gender developing, not the **cause**.
2) **Hare et al (2009)** found that **male-to-female transsexuals** were more likely than non-transsexual men to have a particular version of an **androgen receptor gene**. (Androgens are male sex hormones.)	2) Most girls with **CAH** (see page 159), who produce more testosterone than usual, **don't** develop gender dysphoria.
	3) Other factors may also have an effect on gender development, such as **social influences**.

The transsexual people in these studies were mostly people living as the gender other than their birth sex. Some of them had changed their physical sex.

... or a **Social Explanation**

1) **Social learning theory** (see pages 58-59) has also been used to explain **gender dysphoria**. If a child imitates a **role model** of the other sex, or has behaviour associated with the other sex **reinforced** (e.g. through praise), then they may develop a gender that **doesn't match** their sex.

2) **Rekers and Lovaas (1974)** argued, in a case study of a boy who behaved in a stereotypically feminine way, that gender dysphoria could be resolved by **reinforcing 'gender appropriate' behaviours** (i.e. changing gender to match sex).

3) Many psychologists don't agree with this idea, and argue that it **stigmatises** people with an atypical gender identity.

4) **Rekers (1977)** linked his suggestion that individuals' gender identity should be changed to match society's expectations to the (now discredited) idea that **homosexuality** was a disorder that could be 'cured'.

Warm-up Questions

Q1 What is gender dysphoria?

Q2 Outline the findings of Kruijver et al's (2000) study.

PRACTICE QUESTIONS

Rekers has been criticised for basing his ideas on religious beliefs rather than scientific support.

Exam Question

Q1 Outline and evaluate biological and social explanations for gender dysphoria. [16 marks]

So it might be nature or nurture, or both. Shocker...

There's been lots of disagreement about gender dysphoria because there isn't one single clear explanation. So make sure you can outline the biological and the social explanations for gender dysphoria, and are able to evaluate them both.

Biological Influences on Gender

Biological factors influence gender. No surprises there — the title gives that one away. You need to know what these factors are and how they influence gender. Luckily, these two pages are here to help you out. I'm too kind to you.

Biological Psychology Says Gender Differences Result From Sex Differences

1) Biological psychology argues that psychological or behavioural differences between males and females can be explained by differences in **brain development** and **brain activity** between males and females.

2) These biological differences between males and females are caused by **sex chromosomes**, which determine the sex which a foetus develops in the womb, and by **sex hormones** which are secreted by the body.

Males and Females Have Different Sex Chromosomes

1) Women and men both have 22 pairs of matched chromosomes in each cell. The 23rd pair are either **XX** or **XY** — they're the two chromosomes that decide whether you turn out **female** or **male** (known as sex chromosomes).

2) **Females** have a **pair of X** chromosomes — XX. So all ova contain an X chromosome.

3) **Males** have **one X** chromosome and **one Y** chromosome — XY. This means sperm may contain either an X chromosome or a Y chromosome. It's the **Y chromosome** that leads to **male development**.

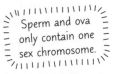
Sperm and ova only contain one sex chromosome.

4) If an ovum is fertilised by a Y carrying sperm, the offspring will be **XY** (**male**). If an ovum is fertilised by an X carrying sperm the offspring will be **XX** (**female**). Which sperm fertilises the ova is determined by chance.

Testosterone Production Caused by the Y Chromosome Affects Brain Development

1) Early on, the reproductive organs of a foetus are the same in males and females.

2) There's a gene on the Y chromosome which causes male genitalia to develop and testosterone to be produced. Without this gene, female genitalia develop and this testosterone isn't produced.

3) The testosterone produced early on in the development of a male foetus also affects brain development — there are some structural differences between female and male brains. This may explain gender.

Testosterone levels day-to-day may also affect brain function (see next page).

4) But differences in male and female brain structure may not affect brain function — some researchers think the combined effect of hormonal differences and structural differences is similar brain function in both sexes.

5) Hyde (2005) reviewed 46 meta-analyses and found there was either a very small or no difference between the sexes in almost all measures, supporting the idea that men and women are very similar psychologically.

Whether or not testosterone is produced is generally considered the **main** way that chromosomes affect gender, but it might not be the only way. Laboratory studies on **animals** have found that some sex differences in early brain development aren't explained by hormone levels during this time, and so they may be **directly caused by genes**.

Chromosomal Variations Have Psychological Effects

Some humans are born with **variations** in the standard sex chromosome pattern — **atypical sex chromosome patterns**.

Studies of people with such variations have shown there are psychological effects of having **different sex chromosomes**. Some of these effects are on aspects of brain function which may have **gender differences** (e.g. spatial ability). This might indicate that gender differences are caused by differing sex chromosomes.

Klinefelter's Syndrome

1) In **Klinefelter's syndrome** males are born with **XXY sex chromosomes** — they have an **extra X chromosome**.

2) Males with this syndrome are **sterile** and tend to be **less muscular** and have **less facial and body hair**.

3) They can have problems using **language** to express themselves and may have trouble with **social interaction**.

Turner's Syndrome

1) In **Turner's syndrome** females are born with only **one complete X sex chromosome** — all or part of their second **X chromosome** is **missing**.

2) Females with this syndrome tend to be **shorter than average** and their ovaries usually don't function, so they're **sterile** and don't go through **puberty** in the usual way.

3) Girls with Turner's syndrome often do less well at **maths**, and have poorer **spatial ability**.

Biological Influences on Gender

Hormones Can Affect Gender

1) Hormones affect the way that the body and brain **develop**, as well as how they **function** day-to-day.

2) The major male and female specific hormones are **androgens** and **oestrogens**.

3) Both types of hormone are present in males and females, but in very **different amounts**.

4) **Men** produce more **testosterone** (the main androgen) each day than females, and **females** produce more **oestrogens** than males.

5) However, some humans produce **smaller** or **larger** quantities of these hormones than normal.

> For example, sometimes people produce much more **testosterone** than is usual
> — this happens with a particular form of a syndrome called **CAH**.
>
> - This form of CAH can cause **early sexual development** in **males**,
>   but doesn't have much of an effect otherwise.
> - The **behaviour** of **girls** with this type of CAH tends to be **masculinised** —
>   they have a preference for playing with boys' toys and enjoy 'tomboyish' activities.
> - **Physically**, girls tend to look more **masculine**. Their **growth** is fast and **puberty** can happen early.
> - In CAH, girls are exposed to high levels of testosterone while they're in the
>   womb, which can cause **physical abnormalities** such as **ambiguous genitalia**.
>   This can make it difficult to tell whether someone is **male** or **female** at birth.

6) Case studies of conditions like this **support** the idea that the effect of **testosterone** on the **brain** is responsible for **gender differences in behaviour**.

7) The role of **oestrogen** has also been studied — particularly in how it can affect and influence female behaviour.

> Oestrogen can lead to **premenstrual tension (PMT)** in some women. This can leave women
> feeling **emotional**, **irritable** and **aggressive**. Whilst many women manage their experience of PMT,
> **Easteal (1991)** believed that PMT could be the reason behind crime in some females.

A Stronger Effect of Oxytocin on Women May Explain Gender Differences

1) **Oxytocin** is a hormone that's been associated with **bonding** and **attachment**, and with **social recognition**:

> **Rimmele et al (2009)** found that **increased** oxytocin levels **improved** male participant's ability to recognise
> if they had **seen a face before**, but it **didn't** improve their recognition of **non-social** images (e.g. objects).

2) Oxytocin is produced by females and males. However, **oestrogens** in the bloodstream **increase the effect** of oxytocin on the brain. So oxytocin may have more impact on the **female brain** than the male brain.

3) It's been argued that this may explain **gender differences** in sociability and **gender roles**, e.g. in parenting.

Warm-Up Questions

Q1 Which chromosome leads to development of male features?

Q2 Describe some of the effects of Klinefelter's syndrome.

Q3 What is the sex chromosome pattern of people with Turner's syndrome?

Q4 Why might oxytocin have a greater effect on women than on men?

Exam Questions

Q1 What is the sex chromosome pattern of individuals with Klinefelter's syndrome?

    A XYY   **B** XY   **C** XX   **D** XXY   **E** X   [1 mark]

Q2 Discuss the role of hormones in sex and gender development.   [16 marks]

So, your gender is influenced by biology — never saw that one coming...

Ah, hormones. They're always popping up as reasons for this, that or the other. Maybe they're why you're feeling so restless and miserable now. No... wait... that would be the revision. Anyway, biological influences on gender — get learning.

Cognitive Explanations of Gender

The basic idea here is that as children mature they gradually develop an understanding of gender, and which gender they are. The theories you need to know (Kohlberg's theory and gender schema theory) are based on Piaget's ideas about how children's thinking develops, so you might want to have a read up on Piaget (p.166-167) before you get stuck in.

Cognitive Developmental Theory Says Ideas about Gender Change With Age

1) **Cognitive developmental theory** was first proposed by Piaget.
   It suggests that children's thoughts and views on the world **change** as they develop.

2) Piaget proposed that children pass through several **stages of development** as they mature
   — at each stage their thinking develops and they gain more **complex cognitive abilities**.

3) **Cognitive explanations of gender** use Piaget's theory to explain how a child's ideas about
   gender **change with age** — they propose that children **develop** their idea of gender over
   time, as their **cognitive abilities** and **understanding** of the world improve.

Kohlberg (1966) Developed a Theory of Gender Constancy

Kohlberg's (1966) theory of **gender constancy** is part of his wider cognitive developmental theory.
It identifies **three stages** of gender development:

> Gender identity — the child becomes aware that they're **male** or **female**, and also begins to categorise
> other people as male and female. Before this stage they're not really aware of gender. During this stage
> children judge gender on **superficial characteristics**, so they think their (or other people's) gender might
> change (e.g. by wearing opposite sex clothes). This stage usually occurs **between the ages of 2 and 3**.

> **Gender stability** — the child realises that their gender will remain **fixed** over **time**
> (e.g. boys will become men). However, they may think that gender can **change**
> in **different situations** (e.g. when doing an 'opposite-sex activity').
> This stage usually occurs **between the ages of 4 and 6**.

> **Gender constancy** — the child becomes aware that gender remains
> fixed in **different situations** (e.g. cross-dressing doesn't change gender).
> At this point the child internalises their gender, because they realise
> it's **permanent**. They begin to develop their **gender role** by looking
> to role models of their gender. This usually occurs around **age 7**.

They'd all agreed that staying in the tree was their best chance of avoiding developing gender roles...

Strengths

1) Thompson (1975) found that **3-year-olds** were much **more likely** than **2-year-olds** to know their own **gender**.

2) Slaby and Frey (1975) used interviews to try and determine if children aged 2 to 5½ had developed gender
   identity, gender stability and gender constancy. Their results were consistent with Kohlberg's theory —
   almost all of the children had only reached each stage if they'd also reached the previous stages.

3) Slaby and Frey also found that when watching a video of a man and a woman, children in the later stages
   of gender development paid more attention to the person of their gender than children in the earlier stages.
   This supports Kohlberg's idea that gender roles become important once a child develops gender constancy.

4) Munroe et al's (1984) study found the same stages in children from different cultures, which suggests the
   stages are universally generalisable and therefore, seem to have some biological basis.

Weaknesses

1) Kohlberg's theory has been criticised for ignoring the effects of social influences and conditioning.

2) The theory describes what happens, but doesn't explain why.

3) Slaby and Frey's (1975) study found that some children had developed gender constancy before age six
   — earlier than Kohlberg suggested. So the ages Kohlberg gave for each stage may be overestimates.

4) Slaby and Frey also found that boys were more likely to pay greater attention to people of their own
   gender than girls were. This effect isn't explained by Kohlberg's theory.

Cognitive Explanations of Gender

Martin and Halverson (1981) Developed the Gender Schema Theory

1) Martin and Halverson's gender schema theory **combines** cognitive developmental theory and social learning theory to suggest how **gender stereotyping** helps children learn what is and what isn't appropriate for their gender.

2) It proposes that, by the age of **three**, children have developed a **basic gender identity**. They also have a **gender schema** which contains the child's ideas about **gender appropriate behaviour**.

3) Through **observation**, children continue to learn gender appropriate behaviours and **add** them to their schema.

4) A child's gender schema is based on the concept of an **in-group** and an **out-group**:

> - Activities, objects and behaviours associated with their **own sex** are seen as **in-group**. Those associated with the **opposite sex** are **out-group**.
> - So, for example, a boy might **label objects** such as cars and trousers as in-group and objects like dolls and skirts as out-group.
> - Through reference to their **in-group/out-group schema**, children will show a **bias** towards **in-group** behaviours.

5) Having a gender schema can help children to manage all the information that they're exposed to. They can focus on **processing** information related to their **in-group** and **filter out** information related to their **out-group**.

6) However, there are also **disadvantages** — reinforcing stereotypical gender roles can discourage children from showing interest in things related to their out-group. This can limit their opportunities and lead to **discrimination**.

7) As children get older they are capable of **more complex cognition** and understand that their gender doesn't limit them rigidly to in-group objects and behaviours.

Evidence For

1) **Bradbard et al (1986)** found that children were more likely to play with (and remember) unfamiliar toys if they were described as being for their **own gender** rather than for the other. So children do show a bias towards **in-group** activities in their gender schema.

2) **Martin and Halverson (1983)** found evidence that children are more likely to take in information if it fits with their **gender schema**. They showed children drawings of males and females either doing an **activity** stereotypical of **their gender** (e.g. a boy sawing wood), or stereotypical of **the other gender**. Children were more likely to **correctly remember** images where the person's gender **matched** the stereotype for the activity.

Evidence Against

1) **Campbell et al (2002)** found that a child's **awareness** of their own gender and of gender stereotypes had **no effect** on how much they engaged in **gender stereotypical behaviour**. This suggests that having a **gender schema** isn't the **main factor** in developing gender.

2) **Alexander et al (2009)** simultaneously showed a **doll** and a **toy truck** to infants aged **3 to 8 months** old. Boys looked at the truck more than girls did, and girls looked at the doll more than boys did. They seemed to show a preference for **gender stereotypical** toys well **before** the age when Martin and Halverson propose gender identity develops.

Warm-Up Questions

Q1 Briefly describe the cognitive approach to explaining gender development.

Q2 Explain what is meant by gender constancy in Kohlberg's (1966) theory.

Exam Questions

Q1 Which of the following is **not** a stage in Kohlberg's theory of gender development?
A Gender stability   B Gender identity   C Gender constancy   D Gender role   [1 mark]

Q2 Describe and evaluate gender schema theory. [16 marks]

In-group, out-group, shake-it-all-about group...

Nothing too scary, just make sure you know all the stages of Kohlberg's theory, and can explain gender schema theory. This stuff's got some interesting implications though. For example, if children only really take in information that fits with their gender schema, then trying to stop people from being restricted by gender stereotypes is likely to be pretty tricky...

Psychodynamic Explanation of Gender

Freud came up with some real corkers... His ideas about gender development might sound a bit off the wall, but you still need to learn them. Luckily that shouldn't be too tricky — there's some pretty memorable terminology in this lot...

Freud Said Gender Develops Through Identification and Internalisation

1) The **psychodynamic explanation** of gender is based on **Freud's ideas** about psychosexual development.

2) Freud thought there were five stages of **psychosexual development** — oral, anal, phallic, latent and genital (see page 70).

The psychodynamic approach is covered on pages 68-71 — it'll help if you're clear on those pages before you tackle this stuff.

3) Freud's **psychoanalytic theory of gender development** says that children develop their gender between age 3 and 5, during the **phallic stage** of development.

4) According to Freud, the child becomes aware of the **difference** between male and female in the phallic stage — in particular they realise male and female **genitalia** is different, and initially think that females have been **castrated**.

5) This leads to **unconscious** desires and anxiety, which children eventually resolve by **identifying** with the parent of their own sex, and then **internalising** that parent — taking on their behaviour and attitudes as their own.

6) Freud called this period of **conflicting** unconscious desires the **Oedipus complex**, which he mostly applied to boys.

7) Later, **Carl Jung** expanded on this by describing the **Electra complex**, which is a similar process for girls.

Boys Go Through the Oedipus Complex

It's pronounced 'ee-duh-puss'.

1) During the **phallic stage**, boys experience conflicting unconscious desires, known as the **Oedipus complex**:

> Boys start to **romantically desire their mother**. They then begin to feel **aggressive** and **jealous** towards their **father** because he's getting in the way of them fulfilling this desire.
>
> They know that their father is more powerful than them, and begin to experience **castration anxiety** — they fear their father because they think he will castrate them if he finds out about their feelings towards their mother.

2) They deal with this by starting to **identify** with their father, and then **internalise** him (incorporate him into their own personality) as their **superego** — this is when the superego develops.

3) This means that they develop a **male gender identity**.

4) Once they've developed their gender they deal with their desire for their mother by **displacing** it onto other women.

This theory has been criticised for suggesting that 'normal' gender development involves becoming heterosexual.

Girls Go Through the Electra Complex

1) While boys go through the Oedipus complex, girls have the **Electra complex**:

> Girls experience penis envy — they realise they have no penis, and wish that they had one (because they feel powerless). They start to desire their father, because he has one.
>
> They feel hostile towards their mother, because they blame her for their castration, but also fear losing their mother's love because of their feelings for their father.

2) Eventually, they repress these feelings and start to **identify** with their mother. They then **internalise** her as their **superego**.

3) This means they develop a **female gender identity**.

4) Through developing their gender they **repress** their desire for a penis, and **substitute** it with desire for a **baby**.

Freud's theories aren't always met with acceptance.

Freud didn't agree with calling this process the Electra complex, though it's the accepted term now. He thought the Oedipus complex applied to girls too, but that they switched their desire from mother to father because of penis envy.

Psychodynamic Explanation of Gender

Freud **Supported** His Theory with His **Case Study** of **Little Hans**

1) **Freud (1909)** did a **case study** of a boy (Little Hans) who was afraid of horses (see page 70). Freud's study was based around his correspondence with the boy's **father**, who reported to Freud **conversations** he'd had with Hans.

2) According to his father, Hans developed an interest in his own **penis** (which he called his 'widdler') when he was around **three years old**, and asked whether his **mother** had one.

Hans isn't his real name. (Probably for the best...)

3) Hans also reportedly **dreamt** that he was married to his mother.

4) When Hans was **three-and-a-half** his mother told him off for touching himself and threatened to **cut off** his penis.

5) Freud thought that Hans had **displaced** fear of his father onto horses, and argued that Hans was especially afraid of white horses with blinkers and black mouths because they **resembled his father** (who had glasses and a moustache).

6) Freud argued that the Little Hans case was evidence for his theory of psychosexual development, because Hans exhibited fear of his father that came from **castration anxiety**, and was part of the **Oedipus complex**.

Freud's **Psychoanalytic Theory** of **Gender Development** Has Been **Criticised**

1) This explanation of gender is based on Freud's **subjective interpretation** of behaviour — the theory can't be **scientifically tested**, so it's difficult to support (or refute) it with research. It could be argued that Freud deliberately came up with interpretations of case studies that **agreed** with his theories, rather than considering other ideas.

2) Freud argued that **everyone** experiences the Oedipus complex. However, the case studies he based his theory on generally involved people who were having **psychological problems**, so it's unclear if it's possible to **generalise** his ideas to the whole population.

3) The idea that girls experience penis envy might have had more relevance in the **early 1900s** when Freud came up with his theory than it does now — back then, being a woman generally meant you had very **little power**, but in most western societies this isn't really the case anymore.

4) Freud's theory implies that children need to be brought up by a mother and father who are in a **heterosexual** relationship together to develop a 'normal' gender identity, but this isn't supported by studies involving children in **non-traditional families**:

> **Kirkpatrick et al (1981)** looked at the gender development of 40 children aged 5 to 12. Half of the children had **heterosexual mothers** and half had **lesbian mothers**. They found **no identifiable differences** between the gender development of the two groups.

Warm-Up Questions

Q1 Between what ages did Freud think that children develop their gender?

Q2 Briefly explain castration anxiety.

Q3 Describe Freud's case study of Little Hans.

Q4 What did Kirkpatrick et al (1981) find about gender development in non-traditional families?

Exam Questions

Q1 Which **one** of the options below is best described by the following sentence:
The girl incorporates the mother into their personality.

   A Electra complex   **B** Identification   **C** Internalisation   **D** Repression   [1 mark]

Q2 Describe and evaluate the psychodynamic explanation of gender development.   [16 marks]

You laugh, but horses do have a nasty bite on them...

Make sure you can explain the Oedipus complex and the Electra complex, especially how identification and internalisation are involved in resolving them — examiners love it when you use proper terms. It's easy to think this stuff is nonsense, but you need to know it. On the upside, you'll be pleased to hear that 'Hans' grew up to have a successful career in opera...

Social Explanations of Gender

Like most things in psychology, gender is influenced by social factors. These factors include the way that family and friends behave, the media you're exposed to, and the culture you grow up in. Read on...

Social Learning Theory May Explain Gender Development

⁞ There's more about ⁞ social learning ⁞ theory on p. 58-59. ⁞

1) **Social learning theory** suggests that we learn by **observing** and **copying** the behaviour of people around us. We particularly imitate the behaviour of people we **identify** with.

2) This learning can be **passive** (when the behaviour is simply watched and copied) or it can be **active** (when the behaviour is reinforced by rewards, or discouraged by punishments).

3) Social learning theory can explain how **gender typical behaviours** are learnt — there are two aspects to this.

4) One aspect is that children identify with and imitate models of their **own gender**. So males copy the behaviour of **other males** and females copy the behaviour of **other females**. For example, girls may imitate the behaviour of their **mothers** — the behaviour becomes part of their idea of the female **gender role**.

5) The other aspect is learning through **reinforcement** — children may experience positive reinforcement (e.g. praise) or negative reinforcement (e.g. less disapproval) for behaviour that's considered **gender appropriate**. This will lead them to adopt **gender typical** behaviour.

6) There is evidence that parents and peers **react differently** to children depending on their gender, which may **reinforce gender typical behaviour**:

Parents

- Rubin et al (1974) found that fathers used words like 'soft' and '**beautiful**' to describe newborn **daughters** and '**strong**' and '**firm**' to describe **sons**.
- Culp et al (1983) found that women treated babies differently according to how they were dressed — **talking** more to those dressed as **girls** and **smiling** more at those dressed as **boys**.
- Hron-Stewart's (1988) study found that adults were **quicker** to comfort a crying baby **girl** than a crying baby boy, expecting boys to be hardier and braver. Also, mothers were more likely to help a **daughter** complete a task than a son.

Peers

- Maccoby and Jacklin (1987) found that children as young as three prefer same-sex playmates. Maccoby (1990) found that when children organise their own activities they tend to segregate themselves according to their gender.
- Lamb and Roopnarine's (1979) study of nursery behaviours found that children encouraged gender appropriate behaviour and criticised gender inappropriate behaviour.

But This Explanation has Weaknesses

1) Smith and Daglish (1977) found no correlation between how stereotyped parents' views of gender appropriate behaviour were and how much their 1-2 year old children showed gender typical behaviour.

2) Social learning theory doesn't explain where stereotypical gender roles came from in the first place.

The Media May Influence Gender Roles

1) **TV**, **films**, **magazines** and **computer games** usually show **gender stereotypical behaviour**.

2) Several studies have shown that the behaviour displayed in these media can influence **gender roles**. For example, **Williams (1986)** showed that the **more TV** a child watches the **more stereotypical** their views on gender are:

Williams (1986) carried out a two year **natural experiment** (see page 93) in Canada. She looked at the **effect of TV being introduced** to a town (she called it Notel), and compared it to a nearby town that already had TV (Multitel). She found that at the start of the experiment, gender stereotyping was much greater in Multitel than Notel. Williams found that **gender stereotypes** of Notel children **increased** and became more like those of Multitel children after the introduction of TV.

Since the Williams' study was a natural experiment, it had **high ecological validity**. It has also been supported by other studies into the role of media on gender roles. For example, **Leary's (1982)** correlational study suggested that the more TV a child watched, the more likely they were to have stereotypes about different gender roles.

Social Explanations of Gender

There's Been **Cross-Cultural Research** Into **Gender Roles**

1) **Cross-cultural research** has been carried out to identify how gender roles differ between cultures.

2) Cross-cultural research can also help us to understand the **causes** of gender roles — if roles are **similar** in different cultures it suggests a **biological** explanation. However, if they **vary** between cultures a **social** explanation of gender roles is more likely.

- **Whiting and Edwards (1988)** observed the behaviour of children in the USA, Mexico, Japan, India, the Philippines and Kenya.
- They found that gender behaviour was very **similar to Western stereotypes** and that there were clear differences between **male** and **female** behaviour.
- For example, girls were more **caring** than boys, and boys were more **aggressive** than girls.
- In societies where children were expected to work to contribute towards the family, there were further gender differences. Girls were more likely to look after **younger siblings** and do **domestic work**, whilst boys were more likely to look after **animals** and were less likely to work within the home.
- These findings suggest that **similar** gender roles are found **across cultures**, suggesting that there's a **biological** explanation, supporting the **nature** side of the nature-nurture debate.

3) Other research suggests a social explanation. For example, **Margaret Mead (1935)** carried out a thorough study of gender roles in different cultures. She looked at **three** different tribes in Papua New Guinea and showed that each tribe had a different role for men and women. Not only were the gender roles of each tribe **different** to the Western world, they were also different to **each other**. Her study clearly shows that gender roles do appear to be influenced by our culture and environment, and aren't controlled by our **biology**.

4) However, cross-cultural research is difficult to conduct without involving some form of **ethnocentric bias** (p. 138).

Responsibility for **Childcare** May Determine **Gender Roles**

1) Katz and Konner (1981) looked at **80 different cultures** — they found that in **90%** of them **women** had the main responsibility for child rearing.

2) This **gender division** has implications for men and women in terms of **occupation**, **finance** and **mobility**.

3) D'Andrade (1966) looked at information from **224 societies** to investigate what **types of tasks** and jobs were performed by males and females. He found that:

- **Men** were more likely to **travel further** from the home, and be involved in **weapon making** and **hunting**.
- **Women** were more likely to **make** and **repair clothes**, **prepare** and **cook food**, and **make objects** for **home**.

4) Segal (1983) suggested that the differences in **activities** associated with gender roles are related to the differences in **involvement in childcare**.

Warm-Up Questions

Q1 What did Rubin et al (1974) discover about the way fathers describe their newborn children?

Q2 What did Maccoby and Jacklin (1987) find from their study on the type of playmates children prefer?

Q3 How can cross-cultural research help us to understand the causes of gender roles?

Q4 Outline the activities associated with males and females in the D'Andrade (1966) study.

Exam Questions

Q1 Outline how social learning theory can explain gender development. [6 marks]

Q2 Outline the influence of the media on gender roles. [4 marks]

Q3 Describe and discuss the influence of culture on gender roles. [16 marks]

A whole town with no TV. In Canada. In 1986. Mad.

It seems everyone's plotting to force us into gender roles and turn us into stereotypes — parents, friends, and the media. There's no getting away from it. I say we fight back. We could start off by getting rid of TVs. We'll just chuck 'em out — it's proven to work and then we'll be free. Except there's still parents, and friends. Hmmm... I'll keep thinking...

Piaget's Theory of Cognitive Development

This bright and shiny new section is all about thinking, and how your thinking develops as you get older. As you might be learning to expect by now, there are a lot of different theories about this. And I bet you want to know all about them. Well, as luck would have it, these pages are all about these theories. It's almost like they were designed just for you...

Piaget Proposed That Cognition Progresses in Stages

Cognition just means thinking.

Piaget said that we're all born with the **basics** to allow **cognitive progression** — reflexes and senses. He reckoned that more **complex** abilities become possible as children move through **stages of intellectual development** as they get older:

Sensorimotor stage (0–2 years)	The child's knowledge is limited to what their **senses** tell them when they're exploring their surroundings. This exploration brings about an understanding of the concept of **object permanence** (if you put a towel over a toy, the toy is still there).
Preoperational stage (2–7 years)	The child has some language now, but makes **logic mistakes** — e.g. cats have four legs, so everything with four legs must be a cat. They typically can't do the **three mountains task** (see below) or **conservation tasks** (see next page). Children at this stage show **egocentrism**, **irreversibility** and **centration** (see below).
Concrete operational stage (7–11 years)	The child's use of logic improves and they can do **conservation tasks**. They no longer show **egocentrism**, **irreversibility** and **centration** but can't yet use **abstract reasoning** (reasoning in their head). They also understand **class inclusion** (knowing that objects can belong to two or more categories at once — for example, that a Labrador belongs to the category 'dog' and the category 'animal').
Formal operational stage (11+ years)	The child is much more advanced now, and can use **abstract reasoning** in **problem solving**. They can also use **hypotheses** and **theoretical principles**, and deal with **hypothetical situations**.

1) Piaget used the idea of **schemas** a lot in his work. A schema contains all the information you **know** about an object, action or concept — e.g. the schema of a human face has two eyes, a mouth and a nose, and the schema of riding a bike contains all the movements you'd need to make.

2) Schemas help you to **organise** and **interpret** information — new experiences are either **assimilated** or **accommodated** (see page 62).

3) Assimilation and accommodation are part of a process that Piaget called **equilibration** — he believed that this process **drives** cognitive development.

4) Piaget reckoned that through equilibration, children try to find a **balance** between assimilation and accommodation. Where possible, new information is assimilated, but when it doesn't fit, accommodation is used to change or alter their existing schemas.

Piaget Used the Three Mountains Task (1956) as Evidence for His Theory

1) Piaget and Inhelder (1956) built a **3-D model** of **three mountains** (well, Piaget was from Switzerland).

2) The mountains had different **landmarks** on them — e.g. one had a cross on it, and another had a house.

3) They put a small doll on one of the mountains and then showed children photos of the mountains taken from **various angles**. The children were asked to pick the photo that matched what the **doll** could see.

4) They found that children at Piaget's **preoperational stage** (2–7 years old) picked the photo taken from their **own perspective**, rather than the one taken from the **doll's perspective**.

5) Piaget and Inhelder concluded that children at this stage were unable to put themselves in the doll's shoes.

Piaget used this and other experiments as evidence that children at his preoperational stage have the following qualities:

1) Egocentrism — they can only view the world from their own viewpoint. They're not sensitive to the fact that others may have different views or thoughts (as demonstrated by the three mountains task).

2) Irreversibility — they don't understand that you can undo an action (e.g. that you can reform a sausage-shaped piece of clay into its original ball shape).

3) Centration — they focus on small aspects of a task, not the task as a whole.

Piaget's Theory of Cognitive Development

Piaget Showed How **Other Skills** Develop in **Later Stages**

Understanding of conservation

1) **Conservation** is the understanding that a **set quantity** stays the **same**, even if it **looks** different. For example, if liquid is poured from a short, fat glass into a tall, thin glass, the amount of liquid is still the same. Another example is counters in a row — two rows of five counters both have the same number of counters, even if the counters in one row are spaced out so that it looks longer.

2) Children at the **concrete operational stage** can **correctly identify** that the amount of liquid or the number of counters stays the same even after they've been rearranged. But children at the **preoperational stage** will say that the spaced out row contains **more** counters or the tall glass **more** liquid.

3) However, **McGarrigle and Donaldson (1974)** found that if a puppet (Naughty Teddy) 'accidentally' knocked the counters so that the row looked longer, even younger children at the **preoperational stage** said that the number of counters was the **same**. This suggests that they **did** understand conservation.

Understanding of class inclusion

1) **Piaget and Szeminksa (1941)** wanted to investigate children's understanding of class inclusion. They gave children **20 wooden beads** (18 brown and 2 white), then asked the children **three questions** — 'Are all the beads wooden?', 'Are there more brown beads or more white beads?' and 'Are there more brown beads or more wooden beads?'.

2) Children at the **concrete operational stage** (over seven years old) were more likely to answer the third question correctly than children younger than seven. They could distinguish between the **whole class** (wooden beads) and the **subclass** (brown beads) showing they can understand class inclusion.

3) Some psychologists argue that the third question in Piaget and Szeminksa's study is quite confusing. However, a study by **McGarrigle et al (1978)** used a more accessible version of the task involving cows **standing up** or **'sleeping'** (lying down). They found similar results to Piaget and Szeminksa.

There's Evidence **For** and **Against** Piaget's Stages of Cognitive Development

1) There's **cross-cultural similarity** in the stages — studies have suggested that children of all backgrounds progress through the stages in the same way, which provides **support** for Piaget's theory.

2) Piaget **underestimated abilities** at each age — for example, the experiment with Naughty Teddy showed that preoperational children **can** understand the concept of conservation.

3) He said that **practice** and **teaching wouldn't** speed up progression through the stages, but this isn't true — it's been found that teaching **can** help to move children on through the stages.

4) Piaget's **methodology** was also questionable. His use of **observations** and clinical **interviews** were open to **subjective** interpretation.

5) Piaget didn't think that **language** was important in cognitive development. He thought you needed **cognitive development first** in order to allow language to develop. But other theorists, such as **Vygotsky**, have taken a different view on this, as you'll find out on the next page...

Warm-Up Questions

Q1 Name Piaget's four main stages of cognitive development.

Q2 Did McGarrigle and Donaldson's (1974) experiment provide evidence for or against Piaget's theory? Why?

Exam Questions

Q1 Emma's mother pours the same amount of juice into two glasses of different sizes. Emma thinks that the taller, thinner of the two glasses contains more juice. Which concept does Emma not understand?

    A conservation   **B** object permanence   **C** egocentrism   **D** class inclusion   [1 mark]

Q2 Describe and evaluate Piaget's theory of cognitive development.   [16 marks]

Naughty Teddy! You've wrecked my theory...

Piaget's stages were an attempt to explain how children's understanding of the world changes as they develop, and the stages do help to show this. The trouble with any stage theory is that they tend to overestimate any differences between stages, and underestimate differences between individuals within the same stage. Oh well, nothing's perfect I suppose...

Vygotsky's Theory of Cognitive Development

Another highly interesting theory on cognitive development coming up — over to you, Vygotsky.

Vygotsky Reckoned Culture Plays a Big Part in Cognitive Development

1) **Vygotsky** said there were two types of mental function — **elementary** and **higher**. Elementary functions can be thought of as **innate reflexes**, **sensory abilities** and certain types of **memory**. Higher functions include more complex tasks like **language comprehension** and **decision-making**.

2) **Social** and **cultural factors** play a necessary part in moving from one type of functioning to the other — it's the influence of **others** around you that drives cognitive development. Because of this, Vygotsky's theory is known as a **social interactionist theory**.

3) One of Vygotsky's ideas was the **zone of proximal development**. This is the difference between the problem solving a child can do on their **own** and the problem solving they can do with a **more able peer** or **adult**.

4) If your teacher has an idea of what your **potential** is, they can help you reach it by pushing and guiding. So it's **interaction** with the teacher that's important (unlike Piaget's idea that progression happens on its own).

5) Instruction is **social** and driven by the teacher using **language** and **cultural** influences. The intention is to help the child to be **self-regulated** and responsible for their own learning.

Language is Also Important in Cognitive Development

Vygotsky suggests that **language** is a **driving influence** on cognitive development:

1) Children first learn language as a means to **communicate** with caregivers. It's also a tool that allows adults to communicate **social** and **cultural information** to children.

2) As the child grows older they use language not only to communicate but also to **guide** their **behaviour** — they use **self-talk** (talking out loud) to **regulate** and **direct** themselves.

3) This self-talk eventually becomes **internalised** and becomes silent **inner speech**. At this point the child has developed two very different forms of language — **inner speech** and **external oral speech**.

4) **Oral speech** is used socially for **communication**, whilst **inner speech** is a **cognitive tool** that allows individuals to **direct** and **monitor** their **thoughts** and **behaviour**.

5) If someone finds a task difficult they may re-employ **self-talk** to exert greater **control** over their thoughts.

Vygotsky Also Came Up With Stages of Development

Vygotsky's stages **aren't as rigidly defined** as Piaget's — they're broader areas of development (without specified ages) giving an idea of the stages children go through as their thinking matures (**concept formation**).
He came up with these 4 stages after studying how children of various ages went about solving a problem:

1) **Vague syncretic** — **trial and error** methods are used, with **no understanding** of the underlying concepts.
2) **Complex** — use of **strategies** begins but they're **not** used successfully.
3) **Potential concept** — successful strategies are used but only **one at a time**.
4) **Mature concept** — **lots** of strategies used at the same time. Thinking becomes **mature** and **developed**.

Vygotsky's Theory Has Some Support

Vygotsky carried out **very few studies** whilst coming up with his theory. However, other people have carried out studies that have provided evidence that **supports** Vygotsky's theory:

1) **Gardner and Gardner (1969)** found that, with **instruction**, animals can reach **higher levels** of functioning. For example, they taught a chimp, Washoe, sign language and she passed down her knowledge to her adoptive son. This is evidence for the role of **culture** and **language** in learning.

2) **Chi et al (1989)** showed that pretending to **talk to the author** as you read (self-explanation) can help increase understanding. This is evidence for the use of speech in thought.

3) **Berk (1994)** found that children who used **more self-talk** when solving maths problems did better over the following year. This is evidence for the use of **self-talk** in problem-solving.

Vygotsky's Theory of Cognitive Development

Vygotsky's Theory Emphasises Social Interaction

Vygotsky's theory is a **teacher-guided approach** and suggests that **interactions** with others are important in learning. In other words, **other people** are needed to stimulate cognitive development. For example, **scaffolding** is an important concept developed from Vygotsky's theory where other people assist a child's cognitive development:

- Scaffolding is when a teacher, another adult or a more cognitively advanced child acts as an expert to guide the child.
- They do this by making suggestions or doing demonstrations to provide a framework by which the child learns to do a task.
- At first the child might need lots of help, but as they learn less help is needed, and they can carry on learning independently.
- For scaffolding to work it needs to take place within the child's zone of proximal development (see previous page).

Prof. Telfer's trainee teachers suddenly realised he didn't know what he was talking about.

Wood et al (1976) — The effectiveness of scaffolding

Method: **Thirty** children aged 3–5 were given the task of building a model and were **observed**. A **tutor** gave help to each child according to how well they were doing — the help was either in the form of showing or telling.

Results: Scaffolding allowed the children to complete a task they **wouldn't** have been able to do alone. The **effectiveness** of the scaffolding was influenced by various factors, e.g. how the tutor **simplified** the task, and how they helped them **identify important steps**. **Showing** was used most when helping **younger** children, whilst **telling** was used more with the **older** children. Also, the **older** the child was the **less** scaffolding was needed for them to complete the task.

Conclusion: Scaffolding **can** be helpful but consideration needs to be given to **maximise** its effectiveness.

Evaluation: This study had fairly **good ecological validity**, but there was less control over variables, **reducing reliability**.

Vygotsky's Theory Has Some Weaknesses

Although Vygotsky's theory can be **successfully applied to education**, it has some limitations:

1) Some psychologists think that the theory over-emphasises social and cultural factors in intelligence and **ignores biological factors**.

2) Vygotsky didn't give any suggestions of the **cognitive processes** that might underlie development.

On a positive note, improved teaching methods due to influence from psychological theories can help to better educate children. It's these children who will be entering the workforce next, so better education leads to a more productive workforce and therefore a better economy.

Warm-Up Questions

Q1 What is the zone of proximal development?

Q2 According to Vygotsky, what is inner speech used for?

Q3 Outline two pieces of evidence that support Vygotsky's theory of cognitive development.

PRACTICE QUESTIONS

Exam Questions

Q1 Briefly outline how a teacher could use scaffolding to help the cognitive development of his pupils. [2 marks]

Q2 Explain one limitation of Vygotsky's theory of cognitive development. [2 marks]

It'll take me a week just to learn how to spell ~~Vgyot Vyogt~~ Vygotsky...

I wonder how many different spellings of Vygotsky's name crop up on exam papers... Quite a few, I imagine. If you're like me and struggle to remember how to spell your own name, it's worth taking the time to learn it now. Vygotsky, that is — not your name. If you really can't spell that by now I doubt you'll ever be able to. Sorry to be the one to tell you.

Early Infant Abilities

When one psychologist has come up with a theory, others like to come along and point out why it's not right. Baillargeon came along and pointed out why she thought some of Piaget's ideas needed a bit of a tweak. Read on...

Baillargeon Looked At Object Expectations

> Remember, object permanence means understanding that just because you can no longer see something, it doesn't mean that it's not there.

1) Piaget put forward in his theory of cognitive development that infants develop **object permanence** during the sensorimotor stage. He thought that this was at around **8 to 12 months**.

2) Baillargeon **disagreed** with this — she believed that what Piaget was classing as a lack of object permanence was actually just a **lack of motor ability** to be able to carry out searches for the objects in the studies.

3) From her own studies, she believed that infants develop object permanence at a much **younger** age than Piaget had originally said.

4) Baillargeon suggested that infants are born with very basic expectations about objects. These **innate** abilities would then develop as infants **interact** with the world and learn to more accurately **predict** the outcome of events.

5) Piaget and Baillargeon's theories disagree on how much understanding a child is born with. Baillargeon is a **nativist** — she believes that infants are born with some understanding. Piaget was an **interactionist** — he believed that infants are born with the cognitive ability to understand the world, but that all their understanding is learnt through experience.

Baillargeon Carried Out Violation of Expectation Research

1) Baillargeon's studies were designed differently to Piaget's — rather than requiring the infants to physically search for a hidden object, Baillargeon compared the time that infants spent **looking** at events that were either impossible or possible.

2) Baillargeon's studies became known as **violation of expectation (VOE)** research. Here's the idea:

- VOE research is based on the idea that infants will look at **new** things for **longer** than they'll look at things they've encountered before. Infants become **habituated** to (they respond less to) situations they've seen before.

- In VOE research, the infant is presented with a **new stimulus**. This is shown to them until they look away — looking away shows that they have been habituated to the stimulus and no longer consider it to be new.

- The infants are then shown **two new stimuli**. They're both **similar** to the stimulus that they have just been habituated to. However, one of these stimuli is a **possible event** (something that could physically happen), and one is an **impossible event** (one that seems like it couldn't physically happen in the real world).

- If the infants have object permanence, they'll look at the **impossible event** for **significantly longer**.

One Study Used an Impossible Drawbridge...

Baillargeon found evidence that infants as young as **five months** understood object permanence.

	Baillargeon et al (1985) — The impossible drawbridge study
Method:	**Five-month-old** infants were habituated to a drawbridge that moved through 180°. They were then shown two new stimuli where a box was placed in the path of the drawbridge. In the **possible** event, the drawbridge came to a stop when it came into contact with the box. In the **impossible** event, the drawbridge looked like it passed through the box.
Results:	The infants looked for **significantly longer** at the **impossible event**.
Conclusion:	The infants looked longer at the impossible event because they were surprised. They were aware that the box was behind the drawbridge and knew that the drawbridge **shouldn't** be able to pass through it. The five-month-old infants had **object permanence**.

Early Infant Abilities

... and Another Used a **Truck** and a **Ramp**

Baillargeon (1987) — Another impossible event study

Method: **Three-month-old** infants were habituated to a truck rolling down a ramp and then passing behind a screen. The infants then watched the screen being removed, and a box being placed either **beside** the track or **on** the track (where it would **block** the truck from passing). The screen was then put back. In both the possible and impossible events, the truck passed behind the screen and appeared at the other side.

Results: Infants looked for **significantly longer** at the **impossible event**.

Conclusion: Infants knew that the box was still behind the screen even though they couldn't see it, and knew that it should have blocked the truck from passing by. Three-month-old infants show evidence of **object permanence**.

Baillargeon's Research Has **Strengths** and **Weaknesses**

Baillargeon's research has provided a lot of **evidence** that very young infants do have knowledge of the physical world — they understand that objects are still there even if they can't be seen. Her studies were **laboratory experiments**, which meant that variables could be **controlled** and the effect of **extraneous variables** reduced. Some other psychologists have used Baillargeon's **VOE methods** in their studies and have produced **supporting results**.

However, some psychologists have **criticised** her work:

1) Some psychologists have suggested that the infants in the studies weren't responding to the fact that the situation was impossible, and that they were just noticing a **difference** from the stimulus they'd been habituated to. These psychologists have suggested that Baillargeon has drawn a conclusion **beyond** what the data showed.

2) The infants are unable to **communicate** their thoughts and so the data relies on how the researchers **interpret** the infants' behaviour. It might be that 'looking time' doesn't indicate surprise, and therefore object permanence, at all.

3) **Rivera et al (1999)** carried out VOE research but found that there was **no difference** in the amount of time that infants looked at a possible versus an impossible event. Other psychologists have also **failed** to **replicate** Baillargeon's findings.

Warm-Up Questions

Q1 When did Piaget think that infants develop object permanence?

Q2 Does Baillargeon hold a nativist or interactionist view of early infant abilities?

Q3 What was Baillargeon's research involving possible and impossible scenarios known as?

Q4 What is meant by habituation?

Q5 Give one criticism of Baillargeon's research.

Exam Questions

Q1 Briefly outline Baillargeon's explanation of early infant abilities. [4 marks]

Q2 Discuss the use of violation of expectation research. [16 marks]

Expecting a cuppa at the end of each page...?

Well, you're going to get your expectations violated. Sorry. There's an extra charge for that service. Anyway, the examiners have some expectations themselves. They're expecting you to have learnt this stuff, so there's only one thing for it. Give it another read, and check that you've got all the facts straight. If you haven't, head to the top again.

Development of Social Cognition

Social cognition involves understanding about yourself and others, and being able to see things from other people's perspective. So, for example, I know that I'm awesome and that you're probably not having much fun right now...

A **Sense of Self** Develops During Childhood

Having a **sense of self** includes things like:

- being able to **distinguish** between self and others, and referring to each with **appropriate language**
- having knowledge of our **experiences**, **abilities**, **motivations**, etc.
- having ideas about **body image**

Important stages during development include:

1) **Existential self** — from about three months old we learn to **distinguish** self from non-self, and find out that we exist separately from other things. The development of **object permanence** (see page 166) may help this.

2) **Categorical self** — from about two years old we start to use language to **describe ourselves**, using culturally defined categories, e.g. age, male/female, tall/short, etc. We are also described by **other people** in this way, which can influence our idea of ourself. For example, describing a child as 'clever' or 'naughty' could influence their **self-esteem**.

3) **Identity crisis** — Erikson (1968) claimed that during **adolescence**, when going through body changes and starting to make plans for the future, we may **try out** different roles until we find our true identity.

Having a sense of self also involves being able to see yourself as **others** see you.
This requires some understanding of the minds of others, and being able to see things from **their perspective**.

Theory of Mind (ToM) is About Understanding Other People's Minds

Humans have a unique ability to **cooperate** and carry out **complex interactions**. It's thought this is possible because we have a **theory of mind**. This involves **understanding that we and others have minds** with knowledge, feelings, beliefs, motivations, intentions, etc. We can **explain** and **predict** other people's behaviour by making inferences about their mental states. This includes the knowledge that others may have **false beliefs** about the world.

Problems with ToM have been linked to the **social** and **communication difficulties** associated with **autism**.

> Autism is a developmental disorder. People with autism often have trouble interacting and communicating with others.

Baron-Cohen et al (1985) — The Sally-Anne study

Method:	Three groups were studied — children with autism with an average age of 12 years, children with Down's Syndrome with an average age of 11 years, and 'normal' children with an average age of 4 years. The experiment used two dolls — Sally had a basket, Anne a box. Children were asked to name the dolls (the **naming question**). Then Sally was seen to hide a marble in her basket and leave the room. Anne took the marble and put it in her box. Sally returned and the child was asked, 'Where will Sally look for her marble?' (**belief question**). The correct response is to point to the basket, where Sally believes the marble to be. They were also asked, 'Where is the marble really?' (**reality question**) and 'Where was the marble in the beginning?' (**memory question**). Each child was tested again with the marble in a different place.
Results:	**All** of the children got the **naming**, **reality** and **memory** questions correct. In the **belief** question, the children with Down's Syndrome scored **86%**, the 'normal' children **85%**, but the children with autism scored **20%**.
Conclusion:	The findings suggest that children with autism have an **under-developed theory of mind**, sometimes called **mind-blindness**. They seem unable to predict or understand the beliefs of others.
Evaluation:	Dolls were used in the study so it lacked **ecological validity**. Also, children with autism may in fact have a more highly developed theory of mind and understand that dolls don't have beliefs. Repeating the study by acting out the scenes with **humans** might show an increase in ability on the tasks. However, **Leslie and Frith (1988)** did a similar study with real people and not dolls and found the same pattern of results.

According to evidence, most children develop ToM at around **four** years old. However, the kind of questions asked in Baron-Cohen et al's false belief task may be difficult for younger children to understand. It seems that **three-year-old** children can pass some versions of the test, so ToM may actually develop **earlier**.

There's also disagreement about the **development** of ToM. It may have an **innate** basis, but **nurture** and **experience** are also likely to be important in its development.

Development of Social Cognition

Understanding Others Involves **Perspective-taking**

One aspect of having a ToM is understanding that other people's **perspectives** can differ from your own. Children gradually become more skilful in their **perspective-taking ability**. **Selman (1980)** studied children's perspective-taking ability by analysing their responses to stories presenting dilemmas. For example:

> Selman told children a story about a girl who could rescue a friend's cat by climbing a tree. However, she'd promised her father that she wouldn't climb trees. Selman asked the children if she should be punished if she did climb the tree.

Like all children, Molly had perfected the "who, me?" look. She knew Daddy wouldn't mind about the tree.

From the children's answers, Selman identified **five** levels of **perspective-taking**:

1) **Undifferentiated and Egocentric** — up to about six years of age, children can separate **self** and **other**, but in a physical sense only. They don't perceive any psychological differences, seeing the other person in the same way they see an object.

2) **Differentiated and Subjective** — from five to nine, children understand that other people have **different perspectives** because they have access to **different information** (i.e. know different things). However, only their own perspective is seen as important and they can't take the perspective of the other person.

3) **Second-Person and Reciprocal** — between seven and twelve, children can put themselves in someone else's shoes and view a situation from **another's perspective**. They also realise that other people can do the same.

4) **Third-Person and Mutual** — between ten and fifteen years old, children develop the ability to take the perspective of a **third impartial person** who's viewing an interaction between other people.

5) **In-Depth and Societal-Symbolic** — from about fourteen, children understand that **third-party perspectives** can be influenced by factors such as **social or cultural values**. They can see a situation from a variety of different perspectives, e.g. moral, legal, etc.

As children go through these stages they become better able to understand that other people have different perspectives, and can use information to put themselves in other people's shoes.

Selman's ideas about perspective-taking can have **practical applications** in **education**. For example, using **multi-cultural** materials and having **class discussions** can expose children to different perspectives. This may help to promote their perspective-taking ability.

Warm-Up Questions

Q1 Explain what is meant by 'existential self', 'categorical self' and 'identity crisis'.

Q2 How does Baron-Cohen et al's false belief task show whether or not a child has a theory of mind?

Q3 How did Selman study perspective-taking ability?

Q4 Give one way that Selman's theory can be applied to education.

Exam Questions

Q1   Describe and evaluate research that supports theory of mind as an explanation for autism.   [8 marks]

Q2   Outline Selman's theory on the development of social cognition.   [6 marks]

Actually, I took the marble while your back was turned and swallowed it...

One of my friends at school definitely went through that identity crisis thing. He started out as an emo kid, suddenly went really sporty and obsessed with football, and then for a term he seemed to think he was a rapper. He also spent nearly a whole year dressing like a cowboy. I think he's settled down now though — last I heard he was an accountant.

The Mirror Neuron System

Here comes the science bit — all about the biological basis for social cognition. I knew you'd be thrilled. Enjoy.

Social Cognition Has a Biological Basis

1) **Neurons** in the cerebral cortex are organised into **four** main areas: the **frontal**, **temporal**, **parietal** and **occipital** lobes.

2) Different processes, such as **visual perception**, involve one or more of these lobes. Some areas of the brain seem to have very specialised roles in **cognition**.

3) It seems likely that many of our sophisticated **social** abilities, such as **theory of mind** (see page 172), also involve complex brain mechanisms — these may have **evolved** as our brains and intelligence grew. Abilities like this could have been stimulated by our complex **social living**.

4) Attempts have been made to **connect** findings from neuroscience and social psychology and combine them into more complete theories — this is known as **social neuroscience**.

Mirror Neurons Respond to the Actions of Others

Mirror neurons are brain cells that are involved in **performing** an action, such as holding a cup. However, they're **also** active when you **observe** someone else doing the same action. So, whether you're actually holding a cup, or only observing someone else holding a cup, particular mirror neurons will be **active**.

Di Pellegrino et al (1992) — Recording neuron activity

Method:	**Electrodes** were inserted into individual neurons in the **premotor cortex** of macaque monkeys. When the monkeys reached for food, the **activity** in the neurons was recorded.
Results:	The neurons were **active** when the monkeys reached for food, but also, unexpectedly, active when they observed **someone else** reach for food.
Conclusion:	This was the **first** study to provide evidence for the existence of **mirror neurons**. Although the function of mirror neurons is not yet clear, they may help in understanding observed behaviour.
Evaluation:	The experiment was **not** designed to study mirror neurons, so the information gathered about them was **limited**. Also, it involved inserting electrodes into animals' brains, which raises **ethical issues**.

It's hard to record the activity of individual neurons in the brains of **humans**. So, studies have been done using brain scanning techniques such as **functional Magnetic Resonance Imaging** (fMRI, see page 86), which analyse **brain activity** during particular kinds of behaviours. For example, Iacoboni et al (1999) found that there are areas of the **frontal** and **parietal cortex** that are active when people carry out and observe actions.

Mirror Neurons May Be Important for Social Cognition

Neurons that are active both when **you** do something and when you see **other people** do the same thing may help you **understand** the behaviour of others.

Fogassi et al (2005) — Mirror neurons and intentions

Method:	The activity of **41 mirror neurons** in 2 macaque monkeys were recorded as they observed a person pick up an apple as if to eat it, or pick up the apple and place it in a cup.
Results:	**Different** groups of neurons responded to the two outcomes (eat or place). Also, some neurons fired **after** the apple was picked up but **before** the second action (eat or place) was carried out.
Conclusion:	Different patterns of response link with different **behavioural objectives** and some neurons seem to predict the **intention** of actions. So, mirror neurons may help to **understand** and **predict** the behaviour of others.
Evaluation:	Animals may behave differently under lab conditions, meaning the experiment has **low ecological validity**. Also, the experiment was carried out on monkeys so it's difficult to **generalise** the results to humans — neurons in humans may not respond in the same way.

Experiments with **humans** using **fMRI** show that brain areas that are active when we feel particular emotions (e.g. happiness or pain) are also active when we see others feel the same emotion. This supports suggestions that mirror neurons may be involved in **empathy**.

The Mirror Neuron System

There's a Lot of **Debate** About the **Role** of Mirror Neurons

1) The **function** and **importance** of mirror neurons is not yet fully understood. For example, they may be involved in **imitation** — but macaque monkeys (which have mirror neurons) have a **limited ability** for imitation learning.

2) A connection between mirror neurons and **theory of mind (ToM)** has also been debated. However, mirror neurons are found in monkeys that **don't** seem to have ToM in the same way that humans do. Also, **fMRI research** shows that ToM tests activate brain regions that **aren't** generally thought to be part of the mirror neuron system. It may be that mirror neurons can be involved in **learning by imitation**, but that the development of ToM involves **more** than this.

3) More needs to be learnt about the **development** of mirror neurons. **Falck-Ytter (2006)** reckoned that mirror neurons start to develop during the **first year** of life. However, **Meltzoff and Moore (1977)** found that human infants can imitate facial expressions **soon after birth**. This could either suggest that mirror neurons have an **innate** basis, or else that imitation **doesn't** necessarily involve mirror neurons.

Social Neuroscience Has Raised **Important Issues**

Jake and Milo still couldn't understand human social cognition. But at least they had each other.

1) **Social neuroscience** is **inter-disciplinary** — it involves both **biological** and **social** concepts and theories. These different types of theories may **mutually inform** each other — biological research can help understand social processes better, and vice versa. This means we can understand behaviour at different levels of explanation.

2) This approach may bring important **insights** into human **social cognition** (e.g. the basis of **empathy**). Also, some conditions associated with developmental problems (e.g. **autism**) might be better understood.

3) Animal experiments involve invasive methods, e.g. inserting electrodes into the brain — this raises **ethical issues**.

Warm-Up Questions

Q1 What are mirror neurons?

Q2 How have mirror neurons been studied in animals and in humans?

Q3 Who first identified mirror neurons?

Q4 Outline a piece of evidence supporting the idea that mirror neurons may be involved in empathy.

Q5 Why is social neuroscience a particularly valuable new field of research?

Q6 What ethical issues could be associated with mirror neuron research?

PRACTICE QUESTIONS

Exam Question

Q1 Outline and evaluate research on the role of the mirror neuron system. [16 marks]

OK, he's picking up the cup — ready neurons... aim... and fire...

This is an interesting little topic to end the section with — it's fairly new stuff and nobody knows quite what's going on yet. There are new ideas springing up and being shot down all over the place. And to think, if a monkey hadn't happened to look over and see someone picking up some food, these pages might never have existed.

Diagnosing Schizophrenia

*A lot of people think that schizophrenia involves having multiple personalities, but it **really really doesn't**, so don't make this mistake in the exam or else you'll look like a right banana. And nobody wants to look like a right banana.*

Schizophrenia Disrupts the Mind's Ability to Function

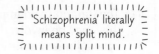
'Schizophrenia' literally means 'split mind'.

1) **Schizophrenia** is a **thought process disorder**. It's characterised by **disruption** to a person's **perceptions**, **emotions** and **beliefs**.

2) The onset of schizophrenia can be **acute** (a **sudden** onset, where behaviour changes within a few days), or **chronic** (a **gradual** deterioration in mental health that develops slowly over time).

3) **Males** and **females** are **equally** affected. In **males**, schizophrenia usually develops in their **late teens** or **early 20s**, while **females** tend to develop it 4 or 5 years **later**. Overall, **0.5%** of the population is affected.

4) It's thought that schizophrenia **isn't** a **single disorder** but that there are various **subtypes** — however, there still **isn't** an agreed **definition**.

Schizophrenia has Lots of Different Clinical Characteristics

People with schizophrenia can experience a **range** of possible **symptoms**:

1. Perceptual symptoms

- **Auditory hallucinations** — **hearing** things that **aren't there**. People often hear **voices** saying **abusive** things.
- Auditory hallucinations are the **most common** type of hallucination in schizophrenia, but there are **other types** of hallucination too. Sometimes people **see**, **feel**, **smell** or **taste** things that aren't there.

2. Social symptoms

- **Social withdrawal** — not **taking part** in or **enjoying** social situations.
- People might be **aloof** or **avoid eye contact**.

3. Cognitive symptoms

- **Delusions** — **believing** things that **aren't true**. People can have **delusions** of **grandeur** (where they believe they're more **important** than they are, e.g. that they're the king) or of **paranoia** and **persecution** (where they believe people are out to **get them**). Some people with schizophrenia also experience **delusions** of **control** — they believe that their **behaviour** is being **controlled** by **somebody else**. For example, **thought insertion** is when someone feels that thoughts are being put into their head. **Thought withdrawal** is when they believe that someone is **removing** their thoughts. They might also believe that **people** can **read** their thoughts — this is **thought broadcasting**.
- **Language impairments** — **irrelevant** and **incoherent** speech. People often show signs of **cognitive distractibility**, where they **can't maintain** a **train of thought**. They might also **repeat sounds others say** (**echolalia**), speak **nonsense** or **gibberish** (**word salad**), speak in **nonsensical rhymes** (**clang associations**), experience **speech poverty** (give **very brief** replies in conversation and show **no extra**, spontaneous speech) and **invent words** (**neologisms**).

4. Affective / emotional symptoms

- **Avolition** — a **lack** of **drive**, **motivation** or **interest** in achieving **goals**.
- **Lack** of **interest** in **hygiene** and **personal care**.
- **Lack of emotion** — **not reacting** to typically emotional situations. This is also called **emotional blunting**.
- **Inappropriate emotions** — **reacting** in an **inappropriate** way, e.g. laughing at bad news.

5. Behavioural symptoms

- **Stereotyped behaviours** — continuously **repeating** actions, which are often **strange** and **don't** have a **purpose**.
- **Psychomotor disturbance** — **not** having **control** of your **muscles**. People may experience **catatonia**, where they sit in an **awkward position** for a **long time**. In this state people will sometimes **stay** in whatever position they're **put** in (so if you lift their arm over their head it'll stay like that **until** you move it **back**). **Catatonic stupor** involves lying **rigidly** and **not moving** for **long periods** of **time**. People are **conscious** during these episodes and can **remember** what was going on **around** them, although they **don't** seem **aware** of it at the **time**.

Diagnosing Schizophrenia

Schizophrenia has **Positive** and **Negative** Symptoms

The symptoms experienced by people with schizophrenia can be split into **two** types — **positive** and **negative** symptoms. Positive and negative symptoms **don't mean** they're 'good' or 'bad' symptoms. They refer to whether experiences and behaviours are **extra** (positive) or **lacking** (negative).

Positive Symptoms

This is where people experience something, feel that something is happening to them, or display certain behaviours — they are extra experiences and behaviours that are not normally there.

They include:
- hallucinations
- delusions
- jumbled speech
- disorganised behaviour

Negative Symptoms

This is where people **don't** display 'normal' behaviours — these symptoms are a **lack** of experiences or behaviours which **are** normally there.

They include:
- **speech poverty**
- **lack of emotion**
- **avolition (becoming disinterested)**
- **lack of ability to function normally**

Positive symptoms are also known as Type 1 symptoms, and negative symptoms are also known as Type 2 symptoms.

The **DSM** Classifies Mental Disorders

1) The **DSM** is the American Psychiatric Association's Diagnostic and Statistical Manual of Mental Disorders (see page 42 to read more about it).

2) It contains a list of **mental health disorders**, outlining the symptoms themselves and how long these symptoms should be present for, to result in a **diagnosis**.

3) It aims to give diagnosis of mental disorders **reliability** and **validity**:

Reliability

Reliability is how far the classification system produces the **same diagnosis** for a particular set of symptoms. In order for a classification system to be reliable the **same diagnosis** should be made **each time** it's used. This means that **different clinicians** should reach the **same diagnosis**.

Validity

Validity is whether the classification system is actually measuring what it aims to measure.

- Descriptive validity — how similar individuals diagnosed with the disorder are.

- Aetiological validity — how similar the cause of the disorder is for each sufferer.

- Predictive validity — how useful the diagnostic categories are for predicting the right treatment.

4) For a person to be diagnosed as having schizophrenia, the DSM states that they must show **at least two** of:

- delusions
- hallucinations
- disorganised speech
- disorganised or catatonic behaviour
- any negative symptoms

At least one of their symptoms must be from the first three of these (delusions, hallucinations or disorganised speech).

Their symptoms have to have been present for **at least six months**, with at least **one month** of active symptoms.

Diagnosing Schizophrenia

There can be **Problems** with the **Reliability** and **Validity** of **Diagnoses**

Problems with reliability

1) Schizophrenia diagnosis may be affected by cultural bias. For example, Harrison et al (1984) showed that there was an over-diagnosis of schizophrenia in West Indian psychiatric patients in Bristol. No research has found any cause for this, so it suggests that the symptoms of ethnic minority patients have been misinterpreted. This questions the reliability of the diagnosis of schizophrenia — it suggests that patients can display the same symptoms but receive different diagnoses because of their ethnic background.

2) Cultural bias has also been shown to stem from the medical staff themselves. Copeland et al (1971) found that 69% of American psychiatrists in the study diagnosed a particular patient (shown in a video) as having schizophrenia compared with only 2% of British psychiatrists asked to diagnose the same patient.

3) Reliably diagnosing schizophrenia can also be difficult due to gender bias. Loring and Powell (1988) conducted a study where 290 psychiatrists were asked to diagnose the same two patients. When they were told the patient was male, 56% diagnosed the patient as having schizophrenia. If they were told the patient was female, this dropped to around 20%, despite symptoms being identical. This gender bias wasn't as clear if the psychiatrists were female. So, gender bias comes not only from the gender of the patient, but also from the gender of the practitioner.

Problems with validity

1) Rosenhan (1973) conducted a study where people with no mental health problem got themselves admitted into a psychiatric unit by saying they heard voices — they became pseudopatients. Once they'd been admitted they behaved 'normally'. However, their behaviour was still seen as a symptom of their disorder by the staff in the unit. For example, one pseudopatient who wrote in a diary was recorded as displaying 'writing behaviour'. This questions the validity of the diagnosis of mental disorders — once people are labelled as having a disorder, all of their behaviour can be interpreted as being caused by the disorder.

2) Symptom overlap can also cause problems with the validity of diagnosis. Lots of the most common symptoms in schizophrenia are also found in other disorders. For example, avolition is also a symptom of depression. This makes it hard to determine which disorder the patient may have.

Comorbidity Can be a Problem Too...

- **Comorbidity** can also be an issue in making a **reliable** and **valid** diagnosis of schizophrenia.
- Comorbidity means having **two or more** conditions at the same time. For example, patients with **schizophrenia** may also have **depression**. Having **more than one** condition makes it really **difficult** for healthcare professionals to diagnose schizophrenia as a **distinct** mental illness.
- It could be that some of their symptoms belong to one known disorder, but that the others belong to an **untreated** mental disorder which **hasn't** been **recognised** yet.

Warm-Up Questions

Q1 When does schizophrenia most often develop in males and females?

Q2 What are delusions?

Q3 What is meant by avolition?

Q4 What is the difference between positive and negative symptoms of schizophrenia?

Exam Question

Q1 Describe how schizophrenia is diagnosed, and evaluate the issues surrounding its diagnosis. [16 marks]

Word salad — like crunchy alphabet spaghetti...

Like so many things in psychology, schizophrenia is incredibly hard to define. People can show a variety of symptoms, which can be classified in different ways. Learning this is a bit of a pain now, but at least it means you should have loads to say in the exam, and you can't really ask for more than that. Well, apart from a holiday in the Caribbean...

Explanations of Schizophrenia

Different people have different ideas about what causes schizophrenia. This was mostly a sneaky little ploy dreamt up by psychologists and examiners to make your revision harder. OK, that's not strictly true, but it does feel like it sometimes.

Schizophrenia Could be Caused by Biological Factors

> Concordance rates show the chance that both people in a pair have a disorder, given one of them does.

Genetic Factors

Being **genetically related** to someone with schizophrenia can significantly **increase** a person's **chances** of developing it. **Family** and **twin** studies have looked at **concordance rates**:

Gottesman (1991) reviewed about 40 twin studies and found that with **identical (MZ) twins** there was about a **48%** concordance rate (i.e. there is a **48% chance** that one MZ twin will have schizophrenia if the other does). With **non-identical (DZ) twins** the concordance rate was about **17%**. This is significant because, if it's assumed that MZ and DZ twins share the same amount of environmental influences, it means the reason for increased concordance is the **genetic difference** — MZ twins share **100%** of their genes, compared to DZ who share **50%**.

Evidence for...

1) **Shields (1962)** found **MZ twins** raised in **different families** still showed around **50%** concordance.

2) **Adoption studies** found that if children are **adopted** because one or both of their **biological parents** has schizophrenia, the **chance** of them developing it stays the **same**. It suggests that **genetics** are more significant than the **environment**.

Evidence against...

1) No study has found a **100%** concordance rate between MZ twins, so schizophrenia **can't** just be caused by **genes**. **Shared environment** may cause higher concordance rates in **family** studies because children **imitate** 'schizophrenic' **behaviours**.

2) This means **other factors** need to be considered, e.g. biochemical or psychological factors.

Biochemical Factors

Post-mortems and **PET scans** have shown that people with schizophrenia have abnormally high levels of the neurotransmitter **dopamine**. These findings led to the development of the **dopamine hypothesis**, which states that **synapses** that use **dopamine** as a **neurotransmitter** are **overactive** in the brains of people with schizophrenia.

Evidence for...

1) **Antipsychotic** drugs **reduce** the **symptoms** of schizophrenia by **blocking** dopamine receptors. This suggests that it's the **overactive** dopamine receptors **causing** the symptoms.

2) Drugs like **amphetamines**, which **increase dopamine function**, can sometimes cause **schizophrenia-like** symptoms in people without schizophrenia.

Evidence against...

1) **Antipsychotic** drugs only work on the **positive symptoms** of schizophrenia, e.g. hallucinations. This means increased dopamine function **doesn't** explain **negative symptoms** like social withdrawal.

2) The **link** with dopamine is **correlational**, so it doesn't show **cause and effect**. It may be that increased dopamine function is a **symptom** of schizophrenia, rather than a cause of it.

Neurological Factors

> A neural correlate is something within the brain that can be linked to a behaviour or condition. The dopamine hypothesis is also an example of a neural correlate.

Neural correlates, such as **abnormal brain structure**, could explain schizophrenia.

Evidence for...

1) **Johnstone et al (1976)** compared the **size of the ventricles** (hollow areas) in the brains of people with schizophrenia with the brains of those without schizophrenia. They found that the people with schizophrenia had **enlarged ventricles**, which suggests that **schizophrenia is linked** to a **reduction** in the **temporal** and **frontal lobe** volume.

2) **Buchsbaum's (1990) MRI scans** on the brains of people with schizophrenia found **abnormalities** in the **prefrontal cortex**.

Evidence against...

1) **People without schizophrenia** can also have **enlarged ventricles**, showing the relationship isn't that simple.

2) These findings are **correlational**, so they don't show **cause and effect**. It may be that abnormal brain structure is a **symptom** of schizophrenia, rather than a cause of it.

Explanations of Schizophrenia

Evolutionary Explanation

- Some **evolutionary** explanations of schizophrenia suggests that there must have been an **advantage** to having schizophrenia for it to remain in the population.
- One evolutionary idea is that people diagnosed with schizophrenia today share **similar characteristics** to **shamans** of the past.
- They were likely to lead people to **split off** from a group when it got too big, starting new cultures.

Evidence for...	There is such a strong genetic link to schizophrenia, that there must be some form of evolutionary explanation.

Evidence against...	There is little evidence and the theory is difficult to prove.

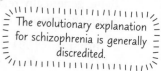
The evolutionary explanation for schizophrenia is generally discredited.

Schizophrenia Could be Caused by Psychological Factors

Family Dysfunction

- Psychologists have suggested that conditions in **dysfunctional families** could cause schizophrenia.
- One idea is that a **cold** and **dominant** 'schizophrenogenic' mother could **create conflict**, causing **schizophrenia**.
- Another idea is Bateson's (1956) **Double Bind Theory**, which suggested that **faulty communication** in families could lead to **contradictory messages** for children and cause schizophrenia.
- **Expressed emotion (EE)** environments contain high levels of **hostility** and **criticism** towards the person with schizophrenia. EE has been found in dysfunctional families and **correlates** with **relapse** in people with schizophrenia. For example, **Vaughn and Leff (1976)** found that people with schizophrenia were **more likely** to **relapse** once discharged from hospital in environments of **high EE**.

Evidence for... Other research investigating the role of the family on schizophrenia **supports** the theory of family dysfunction. For example, **Lidz et al (1958)** investigated families and proposed that **dysfunctions** such as emotionally distant parents and unequal marriages could have an impact on the children in the family, ultimately leading to schizophrenia.

Evidence against... The theory **ignores** the **biological evidence** for schizophrenia and puts the **blame** on the **family** and **parents**. Most of the studies into the effects of family dysfunction were also retrospective — the families were only studied **after** the disorder had developed, and so it could have been the condition itself that had disrupted family life.

Research into family dysfunction as a cause of schizophrenia has been criticised for having poor methodology, so it's generally discredited as a theory.

Cognitive Explanations

- **Cognitive** psychologists argue that schizophrenia is caused by **dysfunctional thought processing**.
- This leads to **delusions**, **thought interference**, **language impairment** and **memory problems**.

Evidence for...
1) **Neufeld (1978)** compared the cognitive processes of people with schizophrenia with a **control** group. Participants with schizophrenia took **longer** to **encode stimuli** and showed **short-term memory problems**. This suggests their ability to process information was impaired.
2) **Meyer-Lindenberg et al (2002)** found that people with schizophrenia did worse in a **memory** and **reasoning** task, showing **reduced activity** in the area of the brain associated with this.

Evidence against...
1) **Biochemical** research suggests that **cognitive** problems are **caused by increased dopamine function**, rather than faulty information processing. So the faulty information processing may be a **result** of increased dopamine levels, meaning it's a **symptom**, not a **cause** of schizophrenia.
2) Cognitive explanations don't exclusively **explain** the cause of schizophrenia — they might need to be linked to **biological explanations**.

Explanations of Schizophrenia

Socio-cultural Factors

The **social causation hypothesis** states that people with **low social status** are more likely to suffer from schizophrenia than people with higher social status. It's thought that factors like **poverty** and **discrimination** cause **high stress levels**, and that this can cause schizophrenia.

Evidence for...	Harrison et al (2001) found that people who were born in deprived areas were more likely to develop schizophrenia. This suggests that factors like poverty, unemployment and crowding have an impact on schizophrenia.
Evidence against...	These results are correlational, so they don't show cause and effect. The social drift hypothesis suggests that there are more people with schizophrenia in deprived areas because having schizophrenia gives them a lower social status, e.g. because they might be unemployed.

The **Diathesis-Stress Model** Combines **Biological** and **Psychological** Factors

1) The **biological approach** to schizophrenia has been **criticised** for being a **reductionist** theory.

2) It attempts to explain schizophrenia by reducing it down into the **simplest**, **smallest components** possible, such as **genetics**, **neurotransmitters** and **parts of the brain**.

3) An **interactionist approach** does the **opposite** — it assumes that processes interact with each other to cause behaviour.

4) For instance, to explain schizophrenia, an interactionist approach looks at a **combination** of **biological** and **psychological** factors:

Interactionism is a holistic approach — you can read more about holistic approaches on page 141.

The **diathesis-stress model** proposes that people who are biologically vulnerable to developing a mental disorder may be more likely to develop it if they are subjected to certain social or environmental stressors.

Lots of research has been conducted in this area. The fact that concordance rates in twin studies (see page 143) aren't 100% indicates that there does seem to be some genetic link, but that other factors must play a role as well.

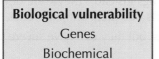

Biological vulnerability
Genes
Biochemical

+

Environmental stressor
E.g. Job worries
Family Problems
Money worries

→ **Schizophrenia**

Warm-Up Questions

PRACTICE QUESTIONS

Q1 Outline the role that dopamine might have in causing schizophrenia.

Q2 Outline how family dysfunction could explain schizophrenia.

Q3 Give an example of an environmental stressor that could cause schizophrenia according to the diathesis-stress model.

Exam Questions

Q1 Read the item below then answer the question that follows.

> Rosie has just had a PET scan. It showed that she has enlarged ventricles, which has reduced the volume of her temporal lobe. Doctors have also identified abnormalities in her prefrontal cortex.

Use the biological approach to explain why Rosie may be experiencing symptoms of schizophrenia. [2 marks]

Q2 Briefly outline how the diathesis-stress model explains schizophrenia. [4 marks]

Q3 Discuss psychological explanations for schizophrenia. [16 marks]

Explain schizophrenia? I can barely even spell it...

So there isn't just one definite idea about what causes schizophrenia — surprise surprise. At least these pages are useful though. When you're evaluating one explanation of schizophrenia, you can use all the other explanations as evidence against it — so you could use the evidence for genetic factors as evidence against cognitive explanations. Or whatever.

Treating Schizophrenia

There are a number of different treatments for schizophrenia, and most people benefit from having a combination of a few of them. Lots to learn here. First up, antipsychotics...

Schizophrenia Can be Treated Using Biological Therapy

Therapy using drugs is also called chemotherapy.

1) The **biological** approach to treating schizophrenia involves **drug therapy**.

2) Treatment is based on the **dopamine hypothesis** (p.179) — the theory that schizophrenia is linked to increased dopamine activity in the brain. **Antipsychotic drugs (neuroleptics)** work by **blocking dopamine receptors**.

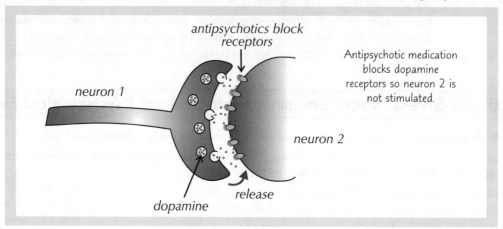

antipsychotics block receptors

neuron 1

neuron 2

Antipsychotic medication blocks dopamine receptors so neuron 2 is not stimulated.

dopamine

release

3) There are two types of antipsychotics — **typical** and **atypical**.

4) **Typical antipsychotics** were developed in the 1950s. Although they are still used to treat schizophrenia today, they are less widely used due to their side effects. This is because they mainly appear to treat only the **positive symptoms** and their side effects can be **severe**. These side effects include **dry mouth**, **blurred vision**, **dizziness**, **muscle spasms** or **cramps** and **tremors**.

5) Whilst **typical** antipsychotics act upon **dopamine** receptors, **atypical** antipsychotics act on both **serotonin** and **dopamine** receptors.

6) Nowadays, people are most often prescribed **atypical antipsychotic drugs** instead. They were developed in the **1950s** and introduced in the **1970s** as a result of the adverse **side effects** of typical antipsychotics.

7) **Atypical antipsychotics** can treat both **positive** and **negative symptoms**, but they can have severe side effects too.

Advantages

- Drug therapy is more effective at reducing **positive symptoms**, e.g. hallucinations.
- It's **successful** for a large number of patients with schizophrenia, meaning that more people can live in the **community** rather than being institutionalised.
- It's the most **widely-used** and **effective** form of treatment for schizophrenia. Almost all other treatments are used **alongside** drug therapy.

When you're evaluating a treatment for schizophrenia, you can use the advantages of another treatment as a disadvantage of the one you're evaluating.

Disadvantages

- Drug therapy **isn't** very effective for treating **negative symptoms** like social withdrawal.
- There are **ethical issues** surrounding the use of drug therapy. Some people argue that drug treatment is a **'chemical straitjacket'** — it **doesn't** really **help** the patient, it just **controls** their **behaviour** to make it more socially acceptable and easier to manage.
- Most people will experience some **short-term side effects** when taking antipsychotic drugs, e.g. drowsiness, blurred vision, dry mouth, constipation and weight gain.
- **Long-term side effects** include increased risk of **diabetes** and **tardive dyskinesia** (involuntary repetitive movements that continue even after they've stopped taking the medication).
- **Clinical trials** have shown that as many as **two-thirds** of people stop taking antipsychotic drugs because of the side-effects. However, **newer** antipsychotic drugs seem to have **fewer long-term side effects** than the **older** ones.
- It treats the **symptoms** of schizophrenia but **not** the **cause**. Symptoms often **come back** if people stop taking antipsychotic drugs. This leads to the **'revolving door phenomenon'**, where patients are constantly being discharged and re-admitted to hospital.

Treating Schizophrenia

Schizophrenia Can be Treated Using Psychological Therapies

Cognitive Behaviour Therapy

1) Cognitive behaviour therapy (CBT) is based on the assumption that patients can be helped by **identifying** and **changing** their 'faulty cognitions'.

2) One of the main **techniques** of CBT is based on Ellis's **ABC model**. Cognitive restructuring can occur by patients identifying their **activating event** (A), **exploring** their **beliefs** (B) and **recognising** the **consequences** (C).

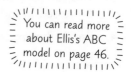

You can read more about Ellis's ABC model on page 46.

3) People with schizophrenia are encouraged to **reality-test** their **hallucinations** and **delusions**, e.g. to question and try to accept and ignore the voices they hear. This is with the aim of **reducing** their levels of **distress**.

4) They are pushed to **challenge** their **beliefs** and to **question** where the voices may have **originated** from.

5) Patients are encouraged to use strategies such as **positive self-talk** to help themselves.

6) They do **role-play exercises** and **homework** to test out their 'faulty thinking' and are helped to see the **consequences** of thinking differently.

7) Through this they can gradually realise where the 'faults' in their **thought patterns** are, and can begin to **change** them.

Chadwick et al (1996) — A study of CBT

Method:	Chadwick et al (1996) reported the case of Nigel, a man with schizophrenia who believed he had the **ability to predict** what people were about to say. Nigel himself asked to prove his 'power' to Chadwick's team and so they showed him over 50 video tapes of different scenarios, paused at certain intervals. Nigel was asked to predict what was going to happen next.
Results:	Nigel **didn't** get one prediction **correct**.
Conclusion:	Nigel concluded, through this **reality testing** form of CBT, that he didn't in fact hold any 'special power'.
Evaluation:	Although this is a case study, and therefore can't be generalised to a wider population, it does show that CBT **can be successful** in certain situations.

Advantages

- **Sensky et al (2000)** found that CBT was **effective** in treating patients with schizophrenia who **hadn't responded** to **drug treatment**. It was helpful with **positive and negative** symptoms, and patients **continued** to **improve** 9 months after treatment had ended.
- CBT puts patients **in charge** of their own treatment by teaching them **self-help strategies**. This means there are **fewer ethical issues** than with other therapies (e.g. drug therapy).

Disadvantages

- CBT only treats the **symptoms** of schizophrenia — it **doesn't address** the **cause** of the disorder.
- It's difficult to **measure** the effectiveness of CBT because it relies on **self-report** from the patient, and the **therapist's opinions**. This makes it **less objective**.
- Patients can become **dependent** on their therapist.
- The patient has to have a level of **self-awareness** and to voluntarily **participate**. This can be difficult when a patient has symptoms such as a **lack of awareness** or an **inability to engage** with others.
- CBT can be a very **time-intensive** treatment and so **drop out** rates can be high when people have severe symptoms.
- The style of CBT doesn't work for everyone — **individual differences** mean some people don't respond well to being **confronted**.

Treating Schizophrenia

Family Therapy

1) Family therapy, or **family intervention**, has developed over the past 40 years. It is based on the idea that **family dysfunction** can lead to an **increased risk** of relapse in people with schizophrenia (see page 180).

2) The **aim** of family therapy is to **reduce conflict** and **high emotion** amongst family members.

3) This can happen by **helping** the family **form alliances**, **reduce** the **burden of care**, **limit** outbursts of **anger** expressed by individual family members and **encourage** people to set **realistic goals**.

4) Family therapy is often used alongside **other treatments**, mainly **drug** treatments.

Advantages
- Family therapy has experienced some success. Pilling et al (2002) found family therapy reduced the rate of readmission in some patients with schizophrenia.
- It is particularly useful in patients who lack insight into their own condition or who can't coherently explain their thoughts.

Disadvantages
- Getting informed consent from all members of the family can be difficult. There are also issues surrounding confidentiality which need to be addressed.
- Families need to be engaged and open to changing behaviour — not every family will be.

Token Economies Can be Used to **Manage** Schizophrenia

1) **Behavioural** treatments for schizophrenia are based on **operant conditioning** — learning through **reinforcement**.

2) **Token economies** can help encourage people in **psychiatric institutions** to perform **socially desirable behaviours**, e.g. getting dressed and making their beds. Patients are given **tokens** which reinforce these behaviours — they can then **exchange** these for something they want, like sweets or cigarettes.

Ayllon and Azrin (1968) — Token economy in a psychiatric ward

Method: 45 female patients with schizophrenia received tokens for 'good' behaviours (e.g. making their beds). These could later be exchanged for **rewards**. Tokens were taken away for bizarre behaviour. Naturalistic observation was used to assess the effectiveness of this procedure in changing behaviour in the hospital ward.

Results: The women, who had been institutionalised for an average of 16 years and displayed bouts of screaming, incontinence, aggression and low social skills (e.g. eating by shoving their faces into the food), showed a massive **improvement** through the incentive of receiving privileges.

Conclusion: Token economies can exert control over behaviour to give patients back a sense of dignity.

Evaluation: The participants were all women, so the results **can't be generalised** to the real world.

Advantages
- Token economy programmes can produce significant improvements in self care and desirable behaviour, even with chronic institutionalised people with schizophrenia.
- This means they work best within institutions — people who stay in institutions often lose the motivation to care for themselves, something token economies directly address.
- For example, Paul and Lentz (1977) compared the use of a token economy system with standard hospitalisation. They found that the people with schizophrenia whose disorder was managed using token economies showed the greatest improvement in behaviour.

Disadvantages
- Token economies don't have high ecological validity — they don't transfer into the real world. Once people are away from institutions they often don't continue showing desirable behaviour, because there's nothing to reinforce it.
- The patients' behaviour might be superficial — they might only produce desirable behaviour if they're going to receive a token.
- There are ethical issues surrounding the use of behavioural therapy. It could be argued that it doesn't really help the patient, it just makes their behaviour more acceptable to other people. Depriving patients of rewards may be seen as infringing on their human rights. However, it may be justified if the outcome is that the patients get back their independence.

Treating Schizophrenia

An **Interactionist Approach** Can Be Used To **Treat** Schizophrenia

1) The **interactionist approach** uses a combination of approaches to explain behaviour (see page 142). It is also called the **biopsychosocial approach**.

2) Because it is a **holistic** approach, it emphasises that the treatment should be holistic too. So treatment should involve **biological**, **cognitive** and **behavioural** therapies.

3) Medication only seems to treat the **symptoms** and not the **cause** of schizophrenia. Also, lots of patients don't take it regularly due to **forgetting**, or **stop** taking it altogether due to the **unpleasant side effects**. Therefore, the interactionist approach suggests that **other treatments** should be used alongside medication.

Advantages
- Since not **one treatment** seems to work exclusively to treat or manage schizophrenia, it makes sense to use a **variety** of treatments.
- Using psychological therapies alongside drug therapies not only allows the patient to **manage** their **behavioural symptoms**, but also provides them with the **skills** to tackle their condition and challenge any 'faulty cognitions'.

Disadvantages
- It is **difficult** to know which treatment is **working**.
- People with **severe symptoms** of schizophrenia are more likely to need **higher** levels of medication. These patients often have a **lower** willingness to try new things, or **learn** new social skills.
- Therefore, the **treatments** need to be **appropriate** and **flexible** to the needs of the patient at the time.
- It can get very **complicated** and **time consuming** — patients may be required to take **medication**, undergo **family therapy** and **cognitive therapy**, and also have forms of **social support**.

Warm-Up Questions

Q1 Outline some disadvantages of drug therapy in the treatment of schizophrenia.

Q2 Outline one advantage of CBT in the treatment of schizophrenia.

Q3 Describe how Chadwick et al (1996) investigated the use of CBT in patients with schizophrenia.

Q4 How can token economies benefit patients with schizophrenia?

Q5 Give one disadvantage of the interactionist approach to treating schizophrenia.

PRACTICE QUESTIONS

Exam Questions

Q1 Outline one difference between typical and atypical antipsychotics in the treatment of schizophrenia. [2 marks]

Q2 Read the item below and then answer the question that follows.

> Jung is 16. He has a younger brother and lives with his Mum and Dad. Jung has just been diagnosed with schizophrenia. His doctor strongly believes his condition has developed as a direct result of the continuous conflict between Jung and his mother. Jung's family are now undergoing family therapy to help Jung manage his condition.

Outline the use of family therapy as a treatment for Jung's schizophrenia. [4 marks]

Q3 Outline how token economies can be used in the management of schizophrenia. [4 marks]

Q4 Discuss why the interactionist approach could be considered important in treating schizophrenia. [16 marks]

Chemical straitjackets — might be a bit itchy...

Well, at least after reading about all the things that can go wrong with your brain it's nice to know there are treatments. Not as nice as walks in the rain or a cuddle or pink wafers, no, but quite nice all the same. I'd love a cuddle right about now. If you're in a similar predicament then take a moment to hold this book close to you and have a little snuggle.

Explanations for Food Preferences

Would you rather have a large cream cake, or the mouldy left-over sprouts found at the back of the fridge? I know which I'd go for... but psychologists claim there are reasons we might prefer certain foods. Read on to find out more.

There Are **Evolutionary** Reasons For **Food Preferences**

People need food to **survive** and throughout history it's been a driving force for **evolution**. This can help explain why so many people would rather have a chocolate eclair than a slice of grapefruit.

Why we like sweet stuff...

- **Harris (1987)** found that **newborn babies** have a preference for sweet things and dislike bitter things.
- These preferences and dislikes are **universal**, suggesting a **genetic** (therefore evolutionary) explanation.
- Early mammals were **frugivores** (ate mainly fruit). Sweet food now triggers the release of the pleasure-inducing brain chemical **dopamine**, which acts as a reinforcer.
- Most **poisons** have a strong bitter taste — so our dislike of this type of taste could be a **survival reflex**.

Why we prefer food that's bad for us...

- **Burnham and Phelan (2000)** suggest that a preference for **fatty foods** would have helped our ancestors survive in times of **food scarcity** — these foods are full of energy-giving **calories**.
- Even though food is no longer scarce, we're still programmed to stuff ourselves with burgers and cakes when they're available, in order to **build up fat reserves** in case there's ever a shortage. Again, **dopamine** may act as a reinforcing reward.

Why we like our meat spicy...

- **Sherman and Hash (2001)** analysed almost 7000 recipes from 36 countries and found that **meat** dishes contained far more **spices** than **vegetable** dishes. They hypothesised that this was because spices have **antimicrobial** properties — meat is more vulnerable to being infested with bacteria and fungi than vegetables are.
- This may also explain why people in **hot climates** tend to eat **more** spicy food — microbes grow faster in warmer conditions.

For the ultimate dopamine hit Jessie liked to take her sugar neat.

Why we're careful about what foods we eat...

- **Taste aversion** happens when we **associate** the taste of a food that has made us ill with the feeling of illness. This is thought to have an evolutionary basis, as it prevents us from eating foods that make us unwell.
- Food **neophobia** is where we're reluctant to eat foods that we've not encountered before — we're more likely to eat food we know is safe. **Birch et al (1987)** found that preferences for food **increased** as familiarity with the food increased.

Social Influences Can Also Explain **Food Preferences**...

- Social learning theory (p.58) involves **observation**, **imitation**, **identification** and **vicarious reinforcement**. These processes can all result in the development of food preferences and eating behaviours in people.
- **Brown and Ogden's (2004)** study provided support for the social learning theory of eating behaviour. They found that the snacking habits of children were **significantly correlated** to the snacking habits of their parents. This seems to provide evidence for **observation**, **identification** and **imitation**.
- Role models don't just have to be parents. **Lowe et al (2004)** found that when children watched videos featuring characters who enjoyed eating fruit and vegetables, they were more likely to eat healthily after watching the video than before.
- The **media** can also influence food preferences. **Hastings et al (2003)** concluded that food advertising directly affected which types of food children selected in a supermarket.

Explanations for Food Preferences

... and So Can **Cultural Influences**

In the UK today we tend to assume that you have to be **skinny** to be **beautiful**.
But that's actually quite a **recent** idea.

1) Throughout human history, being **voluptuous** (curvy) was considered an attractive trait in a potential partner — it signalled **health** and access to **plentiful resources** in times of scarcity. People were proud to gorge themselves on food and drink because it signalled their **wealth** and **status**.

2) However, in the last 40 years the '**supermodel**' and '**size zero**' figure has become popular in Western culture. Highly profitable diet, exercise and surgery industries have sprung up as a result of this popularity.

3) In many other places big is **still** seen as best though — for example, in many **African** cultures plump females are regarded as wiser and more fertile, in **Asian** cultures weight is often still linked to affluence and success, and **Pacific Islanders** (Hawaiians/Samoans) equate large physical size in both genders with beauty and status.

Food is also an important part of many **religions**:

> 1) Some **fast** to show devotion (e.g. **Muslim** Ramadan).
>
> 2) Some **feast** to celebrate important events (e.g. **Christian** Christmas).
>
> 3) Some **forbid** certain foods (e.g. **Judaism** — pork isn't eaten).
>
> 4) Some incorporate food in **rituals** (e.g. **Catholicism** — communion wafers).

Different cultures attach different **meanings** to foods, and eating forms a major part of many **celebrations** and **ceremonies** worldwide. Imagine birthdays without cake, or Christmas without sprouts...

Warm-Up Questions

Q1 Why do evolutionary psychologists argue that humans have a preference for spices?

Q2 What is meant by taste aversion?

Q3 Outline how food preferences could be influenced by a role model.

Q4 Explain why a fuller figure has traditionally been considered attractive in many cultures.

Q5 Explain how religion might influence food preferences.

Exam Questions

Q1 Complete the sentence below.
Neophobia is a reluctance to eat:
A salty foods   **B** sweet foods   **C** unknown foods   **D** spicy foods   [1 mark]

Q2 Read the item below then answer the question that follows.

> Gretal's favourite actress is the new advertising face of a healthy eating campaign, 'Fruit Matters'. 'Fruit Matters' encourages people to eat three pieces of fruit each day. Before Gretal saw the campaign, she ate one piece of fruit a day. Now she has started eating three pieces of fruit each day.

Describe how Gretal's food preferences may have occurred as a result of social influence. [4 marks]

Q3 Briefly outline the role of cultural influences on eating behaviour. [4 marks]

Q4 Discuss evolutionary explanations for food preferences. [16 marks]

Knobbly ones, hairy ones, disconnected ones. Knees can be scary...

Oh wait... neophobia is something else. Either way... it kinda makes sense when you think about it. If you're presented with a dodgy snack that appeared from goodness-knows-where, would you really eat it? Well — even if you would, I think you'd be downright bonkers (as would evolutionary psychologists). So leave it be and learn these pages.

Controlling Eating

Interestingly enough, there are biological reasons for why you feel hungry or full at different times. And here they are...

Neural Mechanisms Control Eating and Satiation

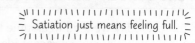
Satiation just means feeling full.

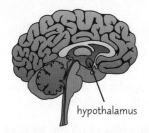
hypothalamus

1) The **hypothalamus** is a gland in the brain responsible for **homeostasis** (keeping conditions in the body constant).
2) It helps to **regulate** things like temperature, circadian rhythms and intake of food and drink.
3) The **ventromedial hypothalamus (VMH)** and the **lateral hypothalamus (LH)** are parts of the hypothalamus that are thought to be involved in **food regulation**.

Ventromedial just means the bit at the bottom in the middle, and lateral means the side parts.

The Ventromedial Hypothalamus (VMH) is involved in Satiety

1) Satiety is the **unconscious physiological process** that **stops** you eating.
2) The **VMH** provides the signal to stop eating when it picks up **hormonal messages**. For example, when food is being digested the level of the hormone CCK in the bloodstream is high. This stimulates receptors in the VMH.
3) Experimental **electrical stimulation** of the VMH has been shown to **reduce food intake**.
4) Malfunctions in the VMH may cause **obesity**. This was demonstrated by Baylis et al (1996).

The VMH is also called the ventromedial nucleus.

Baylis et al (1996) — VMH lesioning in rats

Method:	Two **symmetrical lesions** (injuries) were made in the VMH of eight male and five female rats. Their body weight was later compared with **age-matched controls**.
Results:	The rats with lesions in their VMH had become **obese**, while the control rats had not.
Conclusion:	Lesions in the VMH cause **hyperphagia** (overeating) and obesity, so the VMH must play a role in satiation.
Evaluation:	This was a very **small sample** using only one breed of rat, so the findings can't be generalised. Also, **other tissues** surrounding the VMH might have been damaged when the lesions were created, so it might not necessarily be just the VMH that is involved.

The Lateral Hypothalamus (LH) is involved in Hunger

1) When the body's blood sugar level drops, homeostatic responses kick in to help restore the **equilibrium**.
2) **Receptors** in the LH detect the drop in blood sugar. This then causes neurons to fire that create the sensation of hunger.
3) The person is driven to eat, and blood glucose levels increase. Receptors then send a hormonal message to the **VMH** to give the sensation of fullness (see above).

The LH is also called the lateral nucleus.

Damage to the LH can reduce food intake. For example, chemical lesions are known to produce **aphagia** (failure to eat). However, as with VMH studies, there may be **methodological problems** muddying the water.

Winn et al (1990) — LH lesioning in rats

Method:	The toxin **NMDA** was used to make **lesions** in the LH of rats. A small dose (lesions in **LH only**) and a large dose (lesions spread to **adjacent areas**) condition was used, and there was also a **control group**.
Results:	Rats that had the small dose of NMDA showed **no changes** in their eating behaviour after a brief recovery period. However, rats that had the large dose showed **long-term deficits** in their eating behaviour.
Conclusion:	Damage to the **hypothalamus** impairs feeding responses, but the LH may **not** have as much of an effect as previously thought.
Evaluation:	This research is useful as it shows that the localisation of brain function is **more complex** than originally thought. However, this was an **exploratory study** to test whether NMDA was an effective toxin for use on the hypothalamus and wasn't originally intended to investigate hunger. Therefore, all the relevant variables may not have been controlled, reducing the **reliability** of the results.

Controlling Eating

Hormones Tell You When You're Hungry or Full

Ghrelin tells your brain when you're hungry

- **Ghrelin** is a **hormone** that's released into the bloodstream from the stomach and small intestine.
- When **food is eaten**, the stomach **stops** releasing ghrelin.
- Ghrelin level then **rises over time**, until the next meal.
- The **more** ghrelin is released, the **hungrier** you are.

Anna and Matteo bonded over the croissants and their shared release of ghrelin.

	Cummings et al (2004) — The role of ghrelin in eating behaviour
Method:	**Six** male participants were asked to record their hunger level every **30 minutes** after they were given lunch. Their **ghrelin level** was monitored every five minutes using blood samples. The participants chose when to eat dinner, and were told to request their dinner when they felt **hungry enough**.
Results:	Immediately after they had eaten lunch, ghrelin levels **fell** in all of the participants. It was at the lowest level about 70 minutes after they'd eaten, then began to rise again until the participants ate dinner. There was a **positive correlation** in most of the participants between **hunger level** and the **amount of ghrelin** in their blood (the hungrier they were the higher their ghrelin level).
Conclusion:	Ghrelin does seem to **signal** appetite and hunger in humans.
Evaluation:	This experiment used a **small sample size** and only used **male participants** so the results can't be generalised to a wider population. Although the results only provide a **correlation** rather than a cause and effect relationship, they do support other findings linking ghrelin to eating behaviour.

Leptin tells your brain when you should stop eating

- Leptin works in a **different** way to ghrelin.
- It is a hormone made by fat cells that tells the brain when the body is **full**.
- When a certain amount of **fat** is stored in your body, **leptin** is released to tell you to stop eating.
- Lots of studies into the role of leptin in **obesity** have involved mice. **Halaas et al (1995)** looked at mice who were missing the gene that makes leptin.
- They concluded that these mice **didn't** have any **satiety signals** telling them to stop eating and so they were **obese**.
- Halaas et al found that when they were given **injections** of leptin, they appeared to be able to **control** their eating and their **weight** returned to a **normal** level.
- Lots of studies into leptin have been carried out on **animals**, which means these findings **can't** reliably be **generalised** to humans. However, some research has been carried out on **humans**. E.g. **Montague et al (1997)** found that two obese cousins both had **faulty** leptin production genes. There's more about this on p.193.

Warm-Up Questions

Q1 Name the two parts of the hypothalamus involved in controlling eating behaviour.

Q2 What did Winn et al conclude in their 1990 study?

Q3 Outline the results found by Cummings et al (2004) in their investigation into ghrelin.

Q4 Describe the role of leptin in eating behaviour.

PRACTICE QUESTIONS

Exam Questions

Q1 Complete the following sentence.
The release of ghrelin signals:

   A satiety   **B** hunger   **C** high fat stores   **D** excess leptin   [1 mark]

Q2 Discuss the neural mechanisms involved in the control of eating behaviour.   [16 marks]

Grumbling stomach in the middle of an exam? We've all been there...

But it's just your ghrelin talking. It can be a bit awkward right in the middle of somewhere really quiet — like in a library, or during the middle of your Psychology lesson. But, next time it happens, explain to people that it's just your hormones. Then demand lots of chocolate to stop it grumbling. It always works. Beautiful...

Anorexia Nervosa

Lots of people are worried about their weight, but for some this preoccupation leads to really serious health problems. Eating disorders, like anorexia nervosa, are more common than you might think.

Anorexia Nervosa Leads to Significant Weight Loss

Anorexia nervosa is one of the most common eating disorders in the UK. The NHS claim that about **1 in 250 females** and **1 in 2000 males** will suffer from anorexia nervosa at some point in their lives. It usually occurs between 16-17 years old. It involves a dramatic reduction in the amount of food eaten, leading to significant **weight loss**.

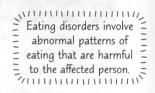
Eating disorders involve abnormal patterns of eating that are harmful to the affected person.

The **DSM** (the main diagnostic manual for mental disorders) describes **three** main characteristics of anorexia:

Restriction of energy intake — when a person consistently consumes **fewer** calories than they require, it results in a significantly **low** body weight.

See page 42 for more about the DSM.

Intense fear of gaining weight — people with anorexia nervosa are very **fearful** of gaining weight or getting fat even though they're seriously **underweight**. As a result, they often carry out behaviours to **avoid** gaining weight, such as extreme dieting or excessive exercise.

Body-image distortion — people with anorexia nervosa have **distorted self-perception**. They believe they're **overweight** even when very **thin**, **judge** themselves based largely on their weight, and don't accept the **seriousness** of their low weight.

There Are Biological Explanations For Anorexia Nervosa

Genetic Explanations Have Been Suggested

	Holland et al (1988) — Concordance rates in twins
Method:	**Concordance rates** were studied in 45 pairs of twins. At least one twin of each pair had been diagnosed as having anorexia nervosa — the study examined how often the other twin also suffered from the disorder.
Results:	The concordance rate was **56%** for **identical** (MZ) twins and only **5%** for **non-identical** (DZ) twins.
Conclusion:	Anorexia has a **genetic basis**.
Evaluation:	Identical twins share 100% of their genetic material, so **other factors** must also be involved in causing anorexia nervosa as the concordance rate was only **56%**. The higher concordance in MZ twins could be due to **environmental** rather than genetic factors, as looking the same may lead to more shared experiences.

Neural Causes Have Also Been Investigated

1) Researchers have suggested that anorexia nervosa may be due to **damage to the hypothalamus**, specifically the **lateral hypothalamus** (an area of the brain involved in controlling hunger — see page 188). **Lesion studies** show that damage to this area can produce **aphagia** (a failure to eat) in animals, and recent research suggests that people with anorexia have **reduced blood flow** to this area. But it hasn't yet been proven whether this is a **cause** or an **effect** of the disorder.

Take a look at page 67 to read about the strengths and limitations of biological explanations.

2) People with anorexia often also have **abnormally high levels** of the neurotransmitter **serotonin** and this causes abnormally high levels of **anxiety**. Serotonin production is stimulated by biological components (amino acids) in **food**, so starvation may actually make people with anorexia feel better. But again, it's not clear whether these serotonin levels are a **cause** or an **effect** of the disorder.

Anorexia Nervosa

There Are Also **Psychological Explanations** For Anorexia Nervosa

1) Family Systems Theory

> Family systems theory is the idea that disorders (e.g. anorexia nervosa) are a product of, and can be treated through, the whole family and not just the individual.

1) Some studies have found that the parents of people with anorexia are often **high achievers**, have **high expectations** and may be **controlling**.

2) **Minuchin et al (1978)** explored the influence of the **family** on the development of anorexia nervosa within children. They applied a '**family systems**' approach to anorexia nervosa.

3) Their theory states that families of people with anorexia nervosa show:

- **Enmeshment** — families have a very **strong emotional connection**, with no real **role boundaries**. This means individual members don't have their own **clear identities**.

- **Overprotectiveness** — the child feels they cannot become an **autonomous** (independent) individual because of the enmeshment, and because the family is **overcontrolling** and **overprotective**.

- **Rigidity** — the family upholds very **strict** beliefs, especially in showing **loyalty** towards one another.

4) Minuchin et al (1978) explain that families might **appear** to be **functional**, but they are often over-protective, rigid and **cannot** manage **conflict**.

Strength of the family systems theory

Kramer (1983) conducted a study investigating the family characteristics of people with **eating disorders** compared to a **control group**. Their findings showed that those with eating disorders did have **higher levels** of **family dysfunction** than people with normal eating behaviour.

Limitations of the family systems theory

1) The family systems theory could be seen to **blame** the family for the eating disorder. **Changing** the way a family **functions** could be **harmful** to the patient's health and wellbeing.

2) Cases of anorexia nervosa can start when a young person has **left home**, or even in **adulthood**. But the family systems theory only explains the development of anorexia nervosa in young people still at home.

2) Social Learning Theory

1) Social learning theory states that the environment influences behaviour through **modelling**, **observation**, **imitation** and **reinforcement** (see page 58).

2) In Western societies, culturally-defined beauty comes partly from being **slim** (page 187).

3) People often **imitate** those they admire. For example, young girls frequently look up to celebrity **role models**.

4) These role models may **control** their appearance, or appear to be **successful** by being slim.

5) Other role models may include **family members** and **peers**, all of whom may appear to be **successful** if they are slim.

6) This may lead to the girls **observing** and **imitating** the role model's behaviour. **Vicarious reinforcement** comes from seeing their role model being **praised** for their figure and attracting attention. They then **adjust** their own behaviour to try to **achieve** the same **rewards**.

7) Family and friends can **reinforce** the behaviour, by initially complimenting the person on their thinner figure. However, the girl may then continue to **lose more weight**, leading to the development of anorexia nervosa.

Anorexia Nervosa

Research into the role of the media in anorexia nervosa can be used to support social learning theory.

	Keel and Klump (2003) — The role of media influences
Method:	A review of studies looking at anorexia nervosa and the **role of media** influences was conducted. The review looked at studies conducted all over the world to get an idea of how **culture** might affect the results.
Results:	Anorexia nervosa was found in **all** countries, but the **more** Westernised the influences were in a country, the **higher** the rates of anorexia nervosa.
Conclusion:	Western media may have a role in determining anorexia nervosa prevalence rates, but because it's present in all countries, there must be **other** factors too.

Strength of social learning theory

Social learning theory helps to explain why the number of people diagnosed with eating disorders has increased over the years — the media and advertising are becoming a lot more noticeable within our society.

Limitation of social learning theory

All Western women are subject to the same pressures from the media, but they don't all get eating disorders. So social learning theory can't be the only explanation for anorexia nervosa — other factors must be involved, for example, genetic or neural factors.

3) Cognitive Theory

The **cognitive theory** of anorexia nervosa suggests that those with the disorder have a **distorted perception** of themselves as well as a set of **irrational beliefs** about their appearance and behaviour.

For example, people with anorexia may:

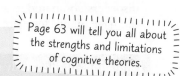
Page 63 will tell you all about the strengths and limitations of cognitive theories.

- Believe that they are fat, even though they are underweight.
- Form thoughts about themselves based entirely on their appearance.
- Hold a set of irrational beliefs about food and dieting behaviours.
- Form thoughts about their sense of self based on how well they can control their eating.

Evidence of this sort of thinking has been found in people with anorexia. For example, **Gardner and Moncrieff (1988)** found that **people with anorexia** were more likely than a control group to state that an **image of themselves** had been **distorted**, whether or not the image had actually been altered.

Warm-Up Questions

Q1 Explain how Holland et al's (1988) study provides evidence for a genetic explanation of anorexia nervosa.

Q2 How does cognitive theory explain the cause of anorexia nervosa?

Exam Question

Q1 Read the item below then answer the question that follows.

> Donna's parents have very high expectations of her, and make sure that she follows a strict study schedule, so that she meets these expectations. Her family have a very strong emotional bond and Donna and her younger sister are often being mistaken for each other, as they're so alike. Last year, Donna was diagnosed with anorexia nervosa.

Describe how Donna's anorexia could be explained by the family systems theory. [6 marks]

Anorexia nervosa isn't as recent a problem as you might think...

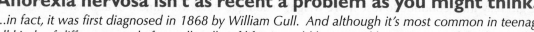
...in fact, it was first diagnosed in 1868 by William Gull. And although it's most common in teenage girls, it can affect all kinds of different people from all walks of life. It could be caused by a mixture of the factors listed on these pages.

Obesity

It might seem odd to consider obesity as an eating disorder — but overeating to the point of being clinically obese certainly counts as an abnormal eating pattern that's harmful to the person affected. And that's why it's in here.

Obesity is When Someone Has an **Abnormally High Body Mass Index**

1) A person is **obese** if they're carrying too much adipose (fatty) tissue. People are generally classed as obese if their **BMI** (body mass index) is **30 kg/m² or higher** (though BMI is also affected by how muscular you are).

2) Obesity is generally caused by a person **taking in more calories** (food) than they **burn off** (by exercise), but there are some genetic conditions and medications that can increase the risk of obesity.

3) It's estimated that by **2050** over half of the people in the UK will be obese.

4) The most effective way to treat obesity is with a **sensible diet and plenty of exercise**. However, increasingly people are turning to quick fixes — 'miracle' pills or surgery such as stomach stapling, gastric band fitting or gastric bypass surgery.

Body mass index is a measurement of height relative to weight. A normal BMI is between 18.5 and 25.

Kai had found a way to exercise and stop himself gorging on triple-decker sandwiches.

Obesity Can Have **Biological Explanations**

There could be a genetic link... Some studies have shown that there is a **genetic** element to obesity.

Stunkard et al (1986) — Adoption studies and obesity

Method:	The weight of 540 **adult adoptees** from Denmark was compared with that of both their **biological and adoptive parents**. The adoptees were split into 4 weight classes — thin, median, overweight and obese.
Results:	There was a **strong relationship** between the weight of the adoptees and their biological parents. There was **no relationship** between the weight of the adoptees and their adoptive parents in any of the classes.
Conclusion:	Genetic influences have an important role in determining adult weight, whereas **environment** seems to have **little effect**.
Evaluation:	This finding is **supported** by other biological versus adoptive relative research, and even by some **twin studies**. However, it's probably too **reductionist** to say that genetics alone are responsible for obesity. Also, the participants were all from Denmark, so the results **can't be generalised** to other cultures.

Montague et al (1997) investigated two obese children and found that they both had a defective '**ob gene**'. This is the gene which produces **leptin** (see page 189). If the body **doesn't have enough** leptin, it won't know when to stop eating, resulting in **obesity**.

Montague et al (1997) — Leptin's role in obesity

Method:	Two severely obese children (male and female cousins) were studied — a large proportion of their total body weight was made up of **adipose (fatty) tissue**.
Results:	A **mutation** on the part of their DNA responsible for controlling their supply of **leptin** was found — they didn't produce enough leptin. Leptin is a protein produced by adipose tissue to signal that **fat reserves** in the body are **full**.
Conclusion:	Their leptin deficiency had caused the children's obesity. They did not have enough of this chemical to **suppress appetite** in the normal way.
Evaluation:	A number of trials in which obese patients were given doses of leptin have had **very little success**, so leptin deficiency may **not** explain obesity in the **population as a whole**.

... or there could be a neural explanation

Obesity is a result of **eating behaviour**, and it might have a neural explanation. Eating behaviour is controlled by the **hypothalamus** (as you'll have read all about on page 188) and animal studies which have involved creating **lesions** in the **VMH** (the 'satiety centre') have led to the development of **obesity** in these cases.

Hetherington and Ranson (1940) found that lesioning the VMH in rats led to **excessive overeating**, leading to **obesity**.

Obesity

Psychological Explanations Might Also Explain Obesity

The Boundary Model

The **boundary model** was developed by **Herman and Polivy (1983)**. Their model proposed that:

- Biological processes drive people's need for food.
- Feeling hungry means that you'll always eat at least the minimum amount of food needed by your body.
- Eating food will bring about a feeling of satiety to stop you eating too much.
- Social, environmental and psychological factors all affect the size of the range between hunger and satiety.

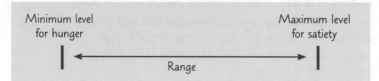

The **boundary model** shows the minimum level of food needed to **eliminate hunger** and the maximum level of food needed to **feel full**. **Biological pressures** usually ensure we eat enough food to **stay within** this range.

Restraint Theory

Restraint theory is the idea that when someone tries to **not** eat, they end up eating more.

The boundary model shows two **biological** boundaries (**hunger** and **satiety**).
Restraint theory proposes that dieters also have a **cognitive** boundary.

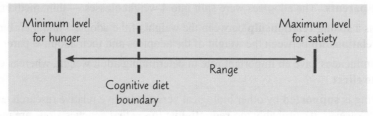

Restraint theory states that:

- A restrained eater, or dieter, will eat until they reach their cognitive diet boundary.
- But — if they cross their cognitive diet boundary, they reach a stage of disinhibition.
- Disinhibition means they 'give up'. At this point, the dieter thinks there isn't any point in trying to restrict anymore, and so they'll eat until they're full, or even beyond.
- Dieters can lose the ability to recognise hunger and satiety cues, and so their range may be bigger.

If dieters regularly eat **over** their **biological boundary**, this could lead to **obesity**.
Herman and Mack (1975) illustrated **restraint theory** in their study of dieters.

Herman and Mack (1975) — Disinhibition in restrained eaters

Method:	In a study with an independent measures design, samples of **dieting** and **non-dieting** students were placed in three '**pre-load**' conditions — drinking either one or two glasses of milkshake or nothing at all. They were then given unlimited supplies of ice cream.
Results:	The non-dieters ate **less** ice cream the more milkshakes they had drunk. The dieters ate **more** ice cream the more milkshakes they had drunk.
Conclusion:	Drinking the milkshake had damaged the dieters' determination — they gave in to total indulgence after failure, showing **disinhibition**. This is known as '**the counter-regulation effect**'.
Evaluation:	These findings **support** what we already know about dieting (the 'diet starts tomorrow' mentality). **Follow-up studies** have found that many people have an 'all-or-nothing' mentality to dieting — if they break the diet they tend to see it as immediate failure and so eat as much as they like.

Obesity

But Restraint Theory **Can't** Explain it All

- Restraint theory proposes that **dieting** and **restricting** food intake can lead to **overeating**.
  But, this doesn't explain why some dieters are **successful**. There's a bit more about this below.
- People with **anorexia nervosa** can also have episodes of **overeating**, but they aren't obese.
- Similarly, people with anorexia nervosa **restrict** their eating. But again, this **doesn't** tend to lead to obesity.

Dieting Doesn't Always Lead to **Weight Loss**

It's not as easy as just going on a diet and watching the weight drop off. Whether a person **succeeds** in losing weight depends on things like motivation, willpower, genetics, lifestyle and medical conditions (e.g. diabetes or thyroid problems). Other factors include:

Support and Encouragement

1) Eating is often a part of **social interaction**, so many experts think dieting should be too.
2) Informing friends and family of weight loss goals should help reduce the **temptations** of food and encourage **positive reinforcement** (and punishment) from others. Lots of dieters also join a weight loss group or diet with a friend or partner to maintain **motivation**.
3) But this approach doesn't work for everyone — some people find constant monitoring by others stressful and use **secretive binge eating** as a defence mechanism.

They were meant to be on a diet, but Mike sensed that his wife's resolve had slipped.

Wing and Jeffrey (1999) recruited participants to a **4 month weight loss program** either **alone**, or **with 3 friends or family members**. Participants recruited with friends and family were instructed to use **social support** to help them during the weight loss program (i.e. to encourage each other). **6 months after the end** of the program **66%** of the participants with **social support** had kept off **all of the weight** they lost, compared to **24%** of participants who were recruited **alone**.

Physiological Changes Due to Dieting

1) Your body has evolved to cope with **chronic food shortages** by lowering your metabolic rate (how fast energy is burned) to protect fat stores in times of **starvation**. Extreme dieting triggers this response.
2) People who go on an extreme diet and then return to normal eating end up with **more excess calories** than before, which are then converted to fat. Also, people often **overeat** after a diet, causing more weight gain.
3) They may then start **another**, even more restrictive diet to undo the weight gain. But this will just reduce their metabolic rate **further**, and so the pattern of **'yo-yo' dieting** continues.

Warm-Up Questions

Q1 Why did Stunkard et al (1986) reject environmental factors as causes of obesity?

Q2 Outline the boundary model.

Q3 What is restraint theory?

Q4 Describe Herman and Mack's (1975) experiment into the disinhibition of restrained eaters.

Exam Questions

Q1	Briefly outline the genetic explanation for obesity.	[2 marks]
Q2	Outline how disinhibition can lead to obesity.	[4 marks]
Q3	Discuss explanations for the success and failure of dieting.	[16 marks]

So it could be my genes stopping me fitting into my jeans...

Hmmm, this section has given me some food for thought and no mistake. Eating can be a complicated business and trying to explain it isn't straightforward either. As usual, a single, simple explanation just won't cut it. Terribly sorry.

Stress as a Bodily Response

I'm sure you all know what stress is. It's having 3 hours left to revise before an exam, or having to visit your girlfriend or boyfriend's parents. We all feel it — but this is Psychology, so it needs a proper scientific explanation.

Stress is a Response to **Stimuli** in the **Environment**

Stress is one of those annoying words with two meanings... How helpful.

1) It can be the environmental **stimulus** that triggers a stress response, e.g. a giant cockroach dancing towards you. In other words, it's the thing that causes you to act stressed.

2) But it can also be the **response** to the stimulus — our reaction, e.g. running for the hills.

However, the white-coated ones have agreed to explain stress as '**the response that occurs when we think we can't cope with the pressures in our environment**'. This is shown in the diagram below:

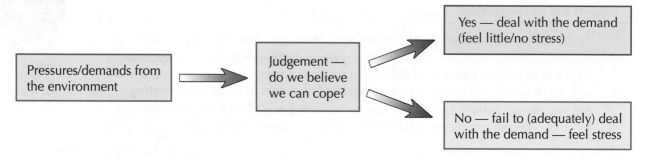

So, stress is the response that occurs when we think the demands being placed on us are greater than our ability to cope. These are our **own judgements** — so we could **over** or **underestimate** the demands, or our ability to cope.

Whether the stress is justified or not doesn't matter — if we **think** we can't cope we get stressed. And when we get stressed something physically changes in us.

The **Hypothalamus** is the Bit of the Brain that **Responds to Stress**

The evaluation of whether something is a **stressor** occurs in the **higher brain centres** — the **cerebral cortex**. When there's an environmental stressor, these higher areas send a signal to the **hypothalamus**.

The hypothalamus has many functions — including controlling the **physiological activities** involved in stress. It triggers **two processes** in the body, depending on whether the stressful event is immediate or not:

The Activation of the **Sympathomedullary Pathway...**

1) When the body experiences immediate stress, the **hypothalamus** triggers activity in the **sympathetic branch** of the **autonomic nervous system** (page 76) and the sympathetic branch becomes more active.

This is the 'fight or flight' response which you can read about in more detail on page 81.

2) **Adrenaline** and **noradrenaline** are then released into the bloodstream from the **adrenal medulla**. The adrenal medulla is the **central** part of the **adrenal gland**, which is near the **kidneys**.

3) This affects the body in many ways, such as decreasing digestion and increasing breathing.

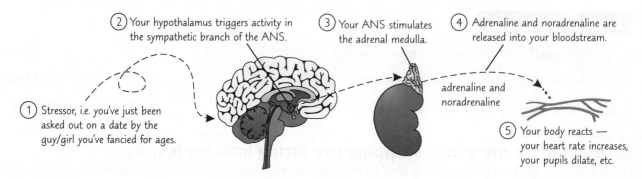

Stress as a Bodily Response

... Followed by the Activation of the **Hypothalamic Pituitary-Adrenal System**

If the stress is **long-term**, then the sympathomedullary response will start to use up the body's **resources**. So, a second system produces a **countershock response** — which supplies the body with more fuel. It's like putting your body on red alert.

1) The hypothalamus also triggers the release of **CRH** (corticotropin-releasing hormone).

2) CRH stimulates the **anterior pituitary gland**.

3) This then releases a hormone called **ACTH** (adrenocorticotropic hormone).

4) ACTH travels through the body and then stimulates the **adrenal cortex**, which is the **outer** part of the **adrenal gland**.

5) The adrenal cortex then releases **cortisol**, which increases blood sugar by converting **protein** to **glucose**, giving the body **energy**.

6) This energy is needed to **replace** what was used up by the body's initial reaction to the stress, e.g. running away.

7) In the long term, high cortisol levels can damage the **immune system**, and have a negative effect on **memory**.

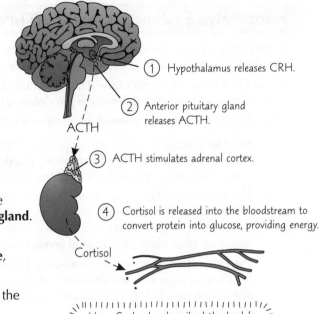

① Hypothalamus releases CRH.

② Anterior pituitary gland releases ACTH.

③ ACTH stimulates adrenal cortex.

④ Cortisol is released into the bloodstream to convert protein into glucose, providing energy.

ACTH

Cortisol

Hans Seyle also described the body's physiological response to stress. You can read about this on the next page.

Changes in the Body Can Be Seen as Having **Survival Value**

1) During our evolution many threats to us would have been from **predators** or other **physical dangers**.

2) To successfully respond to them, we'd have required **energy** to fight or run away — the **'fight or flight'** response.

3) However, in **modern society** stressors are more likely to be **psychological** than physical and are more **long-term**, e.g. the stresses of working at a desk, commuting, noisy neighbours, etc.

4) Therefore the physical stress response is not really needed, and in the long term it may actually be harmful to our bodies — the next two pages explain how.

5) Some stress can be positive and exhilarating — this is known as **eustress**, e.g. a parachute jump might lead to this kind of arousal.

Warm-Up Questions

Q1 What is stress?
Q2 Which part of the brain triggers activity in the sympathomedullary pathway in response to stress?
Q3 What does the adrenal medulla release in response to immediate stress?
Q4 Where is cortisol released from?

Exam Questions

Q1 Outline the role of the sympathomedullary pathway during stress. [6 marks]

Q2 Outline the response of the hypothalamic pituitary-adrenal system to stress. [6 marks]

Well, as bodily responses go, I guess stress isn't so bad...

Stress is a natural reaction in response to anything which threatens you. In the past, it would have been a lion chasing you. Now it's more likely to be a deadline or late train. So next time you see someone getting stressed, try telling them, "relax, it could be worse — at least you're not being chased by a lion" — that'll soon calm them down.

Stress and Physical Illness

The last couple of pages made it blindingly obvious that stress isn't just something in your head — it's a physical response. These pages cover what stress can do to your physical state in the long run.

Hans Selye Explained Stress as a Three-Stage Response

In the 1930s, Hans Selye was researching the effects of hormones when he noticed that rats would become ill (e.g. develop stomach ulcers) even when they were given harmless injections (can't have been that 'harmless').

He concluded that the **stress** of the daily injections **caused the illness** and suggested that all animals and humans react to stressors through a **three-stage physiological response**.

Selye (1936) called this the **general adaptation syndrome (GAS)**.

1) **The Alarm Stage** — when we perceive a stressor, our body's first reaction is to **increase arousal levels** so that we're ready to make any necessary **physical response** (described on page 81). These mean we're able to run away (the 'fight or flight' response) if we're faced with a big-toothed hairy monster.

2) **The Resistance Stage** — if the stressor remains for a long time, our bodies can **adapt** to the situation and we seem to be able to cope in a normal way. For example, if we start a high-pressure job we would initially be unable to cope and go into the alarm stage, but after time we would seem to adapt. However, physiologically, **arousal levels** would still be **higher** than normal to cope with the situation.

3) **The Exhaustion Stage** — after **long-term exposure** to a stressor our bodies will eventually be **unable** to continue to cope with the situation. Alarm signs may return and we may **develop illnesses**, e.g. ulcers, high blood pressure, depression, etc. Selye called these 'diseases of adaptation'.

> **Comment** — the stages Selye identified are **supported** by a lot of scientific research. However, the GAS theory describes a single type of response, and so **neglects** the fact that the body's reaction to stress does vary. E.g. how much adrenaline is released depends on how the stressor is perceived by the person (how frightening it is, etc.). Also, a certain **bacterium** has been found to be involved in the formation of ulcers. It could still be the case, though, that stress **weakens** the immune system, making ulcers more likely.

Long-Term Stress Can Affect the Cardiovascular System

The **cardiovascular system** is just a fancy name for the **heart** and **blood vessels**. A **long-term stress response** may have a direct effect on this system. For instance, increased stress levels can lead to an increase in blood pressure. This in turn can increase the risk of various **cardiovascular disorders**.

For example, high blood pressure can lead to **arteriosclerosis** (hardening of the blood vessels) and **coronary heart disease** (restricted blood flow to the heart). These disorders may lead to potentially fatal conditions, such as **thrombosis** (blood clots), **heart attacks** and **strokes** (decreased blood flow to the brain, which can cause loss of brain function). **Krantz et al (1991)** conducted a study to investigate the effects of stress on the heart:

Krantz et al (1991) — Stress and the heart

Method:	In a **laboratory experiment**, 39 participants did one of three stress-inducing tasks (a maths test, an attention test and public speaking). Their **blood pressure** and the extent to which the vessels around their heart **contracted** (low, medium or high myocardial ischaemia) was measured. Participants were instructed not to take any prescribed heart medication prior to the study.
Results:	Participants with the greatest myocardial ischaemia showed the highest increases in blood pressure. A small number of participants who showed mild or no myocardial ischaemia only had a very moderate increase in blood pressure.
Conclusion:	Stress may have a **direct influence** on aspects of body functioning, making **cardiovascular disorders** more likely.
Evaluation:	Although these effects occurred in stressful situations, it can't be said that stress **caused** them. Also, it wasn't shown whether the effects also occur at other times. They might sometimes happen even if the person feels relaxed — and therefore couldn't just be linked to feeling stressed. Not everybody showed the same reaction, which suggests that **individual differences** between the participants may also have played a role. The **ecological validity** of the study was reduced because it took place under **laboratory conditions** that weren't fully representative of real-life stress. However, the findings of the study are supported by **Williams (2000)** — it was seen that people who got angry easily or reacted more angrily to situations had a higher risk of cardiovascular disorders.

Stress and Physical Illness

Stress Can Also Affect the **Immune System**

The immune system is made of cells (e.g. white blood cells) and chemicals that **seek and destroy bacteria** and **viruses**. When someone experiences stress over a long time (a **long-term, chronic stress response**) their immune system stops functioning properly. This is called **immunosuppression**. Loads of studies have tested whether chronic stress makes us more vulnerable to infection and illness.

Brady et al (1958) — Stress and the development of ulcers

Method:	**Monkeys** were put in pairs and given electric shocks every 20 seconds for 6 hour sessions. One monkey of each pair (the 'executive') could push a lever to postpone each shock. The other could not delay them.
Results:	The 'executive' monkeys were **more likely** to develop illness (ulcers) and later die.
Conclusion:	The illness and death was not due to the shocks but due to the **stress** that the executives felt in trying to avoid them. In the long term, this stress **reduced** the immune system's ability to fight illness.
Evaluation:	The experiment has **ethical** issues — the experiment was very cruel and would not be allowed today. Also, we can't **generalise** results from monkeys to humans. Furthermore, we know that people with **little control** over their own lives (such as those with low-level jobs and the long-term unemployed), can experience **high levels** of stress, which this research cannot explain.

Immunosuppression Happens in **Humans** Too

Research on humans (fortunately much more ethical than the monkey study) has also supported the theory that stress can **reduce** the effectiveness of the immune system. Take the following study, for example:

Kiecolt-Glaser et al (1995) — Stress and wound healing

Method:	In a study with an **independent measures** design, a punch biopsy was used to create a small wound on the arms of 13 women who cared for relatives with Alzheimer's disease (a very stressful responsibility). A **control group** of 13 people also took part.
Results:	Wound healing took an average of 9 days longer for the carers than those in the control group.
Conclusion:	Chronic, long-term stress **impairs** the effectiveness of the immune system to heal wounds.
Evaluation:	**Sweeney (1995)** also found that people caring for relatives with dementia took longer than a control group to heal their wounds. However, for both studies the two groups may have **varied in other ways** apart from the stress of being a carer. The effects on the carers could be due to poor diet, lack of sleep, etc, and not just the stress they experienced. The study only contained a small number of participants — for more reliable results it should be repeated with a larger number.

Warm-Up Questions

Q1 What conclusion did Krantz et al (1991) make from their study into cardiovascular disorders?

Q2 What were the results of the Brady et al (1958) study?

Q3 Who were the experimental group in the Kiecolt-Glaser et al (1995) study?

PRACTICE QUESTIONS

Exam Questions

Q1 Which of following is **not** a stage of the general adaptation syndrome?

    A resistance   **B** stress   **C** alarm   **D** exhaustion   [1 mark]

Q2 Discuss the role of stress in illness.   [16 marks]

No more exams thanks — can't be doing with ulcers...

If you think about it, it kind of stands to reason that being really stressed out all the time will have some effect on your body. It can affect your heart and your immune system, and generally just isn't very good for you. So try not to stress out — it's really not worth it. Take a deep breath, take in the lessons for life on these pages and chill out.

Stress and Life Changes

There are loads of sources of stress — for some unfortunate individuals it's the thought of peanut butter sticking to their teeth, but for normal folk, it's the major life changes which can make things stressful.

Life Changes are a Source of Stress

- Throughout our lives, we all experience **major life events** — like the death of a close relative, getting married or moving house. These events, and the adjustments they cause us to make, can be a major source of stress. When psychologists want to find out what level of stress these events cause, they look at health, because it's likely to be linked to stress.

- **Holmes and Rahe (1967)** developed a measuring scale to investigate the relationship between life changes and stress.

Holmes and Rahe Studied Life Change Stress and Illness

1) Holmes and Rahe assumed that both positive and negative life events involve change, and that change leads to experiencing stress.

2) To test this assumption, they studied approximately **5000** hospital patients' records and noted any major life events that had occurred before the person became ill.

3) It was found that patients were likely to have experienced life changes prior to becoming ill, and that more serious life changes seemed to be more linked to stress and illness.

When José got his car stuck in a ditch, he wasn't best pleased to a get a cold the very next day.

They Ranked Life Events on the Social Readjustment Rating Scale (SRRS)

1) **Holmes and Rahe (1967)** made a list of 43 common life events and asked loads of people to give each one a score to say how stressful it was.

2) They called the numbers that made up each score the **Life Change Units (LCU)**. The higher this number of LCUs, the more stressful it was.

3) Then they **ranked** the events from most stressful to least stressful and called this **self-report scale** the **Social Readjustment Rating Scale (SRRS)**. Examples are shown in the table to the right.

Life Event	Rank	Score (LCU)
Death of a spouse	1	100
Divorce	2	73
Retirement	10	45
Change in School	17	37
Christmas	42	12

Retirement, stressful? Pah, I can't wait...

Further Correlational Research Supported Their Findings

See above for a reminder of what LCU scores are.

Rahe et al (1970) — LCU score and illness

Method:	In a **correlational study**, more than 2500 American Navy seamen were given a form of the SRRS to complete just before they set sail on military duty. They had to indicate all of the events that they had experienced over the previous six months.
Results:	There was a significant correlation between LCU scores and illness. Higher LCU scores were found to be linked to a higher incidence of illness over the next seven months.
Conclusion:	The stress involved in the changes that life events bring is linked to an increased risk of illness.
Evaluation:	The results are **not representative** of the population and can only be **generalised** to American Navy seamen. Also, the results don't explain **individual differences** in response to stress. There are also limitations associated with using correlational research. You can't assume a **causal relationship** between the variables — the correlation might be caused by a third unknown variable. As well as this, there are problems with using the SRRS to rank stressful events (see the next page).

Stress and Life Changes

There are Some **Issues** with the SRRS

1) People can have positive <u>and</u> negative life events

The SRRS doesn't separate **positive and negative life events**. Stress and illness might be more linked to negative life changes. For example, a wedding might be stressful, but positive overall, while the death of a spouse might have a very negative stressful effect.

Long-term, minor sources of stress, such as everyday **hassles** (see page 202), are not considered.

2) Holmes and Rahe's research was biased

Most of the research conducted by Holmes and Rahe involved male participants, meaning it is **gender biased** (p.136). It's also **ethnocentric** (page 138) so it can't be **generalised** to everybody. For example, people who don't celebrate Christmas won't find it stressful.

3) The findings relied on self-report

The questionnaires used within the SRRS rely on **self-report**. So the findings may be **unreliable** as people may not always remember events and things that happened to them accurately.

4) The research is correlational, not experimental

Correlational studies aim to establish if two variables are **related** to each other. They're useful because they allow us to investigate **relationships** between stress and lots of other variables. For example, it's likely that our stress levels are the result of many **interrelated factors**, rather than one single factor. On the other hand...

Experiments aim to establish if a change in one variable **causes a change** in another. They have an advantage if we want to find out exactly what is **causing** stress.

Several of the life changes within the SRRS could be **related** to each other. For example, a big change in **job conditions** or getting **fired** are likely to affect a person's **financial situation**. **Pregnancy** or a change in **personal habits** and **living conditions** may affect **personal health**. This means that life changes could be both the cause **and** effect of stress.

Despite criticisms the SRRS was useful for showing that changes in life may link to stress and illness.

Warm-Up Questions

Q1 What did Holmes and Rahe investigate as a cause of stress?
Q2 What does SRRS stand for?
Q3 Which research method was used in the Rahe et al (1970) study?
Q4 Suggest some life changes that could be related to each other.

Exam Question

Q1 Describe and evaluate the Social Readjustment Ratings Scale. [16 marks]

The sauces of stress — feels like you're always playing ketchup...

As a quick break, make your own SRRS by putting these stressful situations in order: 1) meeting your girl/boyfriend's parents, 2) walking into a job interview and realising your fly's undone, 3) feeling a spider run across your face in bed, 4) getting peanut butter stuck to the roof of your mouth (don't try it if you can help it, trust me), 5) knowing that what you're writing will be read by thousands of cynical A-Level students and you can't think of anything funny to write.

Stress and Daily Hassles

For some people, it's the more niggly things that cause stress. Psychologists call these daily hassles. These are things like having a busy commute everyday, not having enough sleep, having to put up with really noisy neighbours...

Daily Hassles are Everyday Events that are Stressful...

Some psychologists have suggested that stress is related to more **mundane events** than the major life events put forward by Holmes and Rahe. Examples of these daily problems, which they named **hassles**, include:

- Having too many things to do
- Misplacing objects
- Getting stuck in traffic

...But Uplifts Can Reduce Stress

- In addition to investigating the impact of hassles on daily life, psychologists have looked at the effects of uplifts (things that make you feel good) in predicting peoples' stress levels.
- Whilst hassles include the ongoing strains of daily living, uplifts may be things like doing well at school, spending time with your partner or socialising with friends.

Hassles and Uplifts Scales Can be Used to Measure Life Stresses

Hassles and uplifts scales have been developed to assess how the hassles and uplifts people experience affect their stress levels, and therefore their health.

	Kanner et al (1981) — Stress and daily hassles
Method:	**100 adults** completed a questionnaire each month which asked them to choose which **hassles** they had experienced that month from a list of 117. They then had to **rate** each hassle to show how severe it had been for them. They were also asked to complete a 135-item uplifts scale asking about positive experiences they'd had in the last month. Both scales were repeated for 9 months.
Results:	Certain hassles occurred more frequently than others, such as worrying about weight, family health and the rising cost of living. They found that those with high scores were **more likely** to have physical and psychological health problems. They also found that scores on the uplifts scale were negatively related to ill health. Events on the uplifts scale may reduce stress, or protect us from it.
Conclusion:	Daily hassles are **linked** to stress and health, with a stronger correlation than that found with the SRRS (see page 200).
Evaluation:	The weaknesses of **correlational methods** are relevant here — it isn't possible to establish a cause and effect relationship between the variables. Using questionnaires resulted in **quantitative data**, which is useful for making comparisons, but they don't allow participants to explain why certain experiences are stressful to them, so potentially useful data is missed. They rely on **honesty** in order for the results to be valid — participants may not be completely truthful about admitting mundane daily events that they find stressful. They also rely on the participants' **recall** being accurate.

Other studies have also **supported** Kanner et al's findings:

In a study by **Bouteyre et al (2007)**, 223 first year Psychology students at a French university completed a hassles scale and a scale ranking depression. It was found that **41%** of students experienced depressive symptoms and that there was a positive correlation between hassles and depressive symptoms. This suggests that the **hassles** associated with the initial transition period at university could be a **risk factor for depression**.

Learning to punt was just another hassle for Norman when he started University.

Stress and Daily Hassles

DeLongis et al developed a Combined Hassles and Uplifts Scale

DeLongis et al (1988) developed a 53-item combined hassles and uplifts scale (the Hassles and Uplifts Scale). Each item (e.g. 'family') was rated as to how much of a hassle or uplift it was to the person that day.

Participants were then asked to complete a questionnaire measuring major life events alongside the 'Hassles and Uplifts Scale'. The researchers found no relationship between life events and illness — but a relationship between hassles and subsequent next day illness was observed. They concluded that the everyday hassles had a bigger impact on stress levels and health than the less frequent major life changing events.

There are Some Issues with the Hassles and Uplifts Scale

1) The research is correlational, not experimental

Just like the SRRS, the Hassles and Uplifts Scale can't show a cause-and-effect relationship. Also, hassles can influence someone's health, but health can also influence how people perceive daily activities and events — making them seem more stressful when ill than when seen in normal health.

2) Other resources should also be considered

The Hassles and Uplifts Scale doesn't consider the social resources available to each individual (i.e. money, health, work, etc.). Moos and Swindle (1990) have shown that the impact of ongoing and chronic sources of stress, such as an unfulfilling job, can be moderated by various social resources.

3) Everyone is different

Individual differences mean that everyone treats events and situations in a different way. Some people might be able to cope better with daily stresses, but be more affected by major life events. Some people are just naturally better at dealing with stress than others.

Cultural differences can also influence how people see daily hassles and uplifts, meaning the scale is ethnocentric, as it's based on Western views and lifestyles. Social support can affect peoples' perceptions of stress (see page 210).

4) The findings relied on self-report

The Hassles and Uplifts Scale relies on self-report which can make the findings unreliable. People taking part may lie to suggest they are coping better than they really are.

Cynthia didn't need any experiments — she knew exactly what was causing her stress.

Warm-Up Questions

Q1 Give an example of a daily hassle.

Q2 What are uplifts?

Q3 Describe the method used by Kanner et al (1981).

Q4 What conclusion did DeLongis et al (1988) make from their study?

PRACTICE QUESTIONS

Exam Question

Q1 Briefly outline and evaluate one study which used the Hassles and Uplifts Scale.   [4 marks]

My momma always said, life is like a box of daily hassles and uplifts...

...you never know what you're gonna get. You could get stuck in a queue at the self-checkouts where the person in front is paying with a bag of coppers, or you could win a tenner on the lottery. So — try not to get worked up over the little things and focus on the uplifting things. Gee — I feel like a proper motivational psychologist now.

Stress at Work

I could say my job is stressful... writing witty, engaging intro lines for A-Level students across the country. But — I'm sat here, with a steaming mug of tea, listening to the wind outside thinking (rather smugly) that it's not that bad really...

The **Workplace** is a Massive Source of Stress

Unfortunately, most people need to work. Some aspects of the **work they do**, **where they work**, or **who they have to work with**, become a source of stress. This is important because if a person is very stressed at work they may be more likely to get ill. Stress in the workplace comes from **five** key areas.

> *Stress is not only bad for the individual, but also for their employer and the economy, because they will take more days off sick.*

1) **Relationships at work** — relationships with bosses, colleagues and customers may be stressful. E.g. we might feel **undervalued** and that we **lack support**.

2) **Work pressures** — having a large **workload**, perhaps with **strict deadlines**.

3) **The physical environment** — workplaces may be very noisy, overcrowded, or too hot or cold (aren't we fussy...). Work may also involve health risks or unsociable working hours.

4) **Stresses linked to our role** — worrying about **job security** or our **prospects for promotion**. Also, the range of our responsibilities may be unclear, and we may experience conflict, e.g. trying to please our bosses and the people who work for us.

5) **Lack of control** — we may not have much **influence over the type and amount of work** we do, or where and when we do it. There's more about this below.

A **Lack of Control** in the Workplace is Stressful

Feeling that we don't have much influence over the **type of work** we do and our **workload** (how much work we have to do) can lead to stress. This can be seen in **Marmot et al's (1997)** study:

Marmot et al (1997) — Illness in the workplace

Method:	Over **7000** civil service employees working in London were surveyed. Information was obtained about their grade of employment, how much control they felt they had, how much support they felt they had, etc.
Results:	When the medical records of these employees were followed up **5 years later**, those on lower employment grades who felt less control over their work (and less social support) were found to be more likely to have **cardiovascular disorders**. Participants on the lowest grade of employment were four times more likely to die of a heart attack than those on the highest grade.
Conclusion:	Believing that you have little control over your work influences work stress and the development of illness.
Evaluation:	The study only looked at '**white collar**' work (office-type jobs), so the results may not apply to other jobs. **Smoking** was found to be common in those who developed illnesses. So, perhaps those who felt less control at work were more likely to smoke — and the smoking caused the heart problems rather than stress. Other **factors** (e.g. diet and exercise) may be linked to job grade and could be causing illness rather than the perceived lack of control.

Frankenhaeuser (1975) also investigated the link between lack of control and stress in the workplace using urine samples and blood pressure. These are **physiological measures** of stress (see next page).

Frankenhaeuser (1975) — Stress levels in sawmill workers

Method:	Frankenhaeuser studied **2 groups** of workers at a sawmill. One group had the repetitive task of feeding logs into a machine all day. The job was very noisy and the workers were socially isolated. They didn't have much control over their work as the machine dictated how quickly they should feed the logs in. The other group had a different task which gave them more control of their workload, and more social contact. Stress levels were measured by testing **urine samples** and **blood pressure**.
Results:	The workers who had minimal control and social contact had **higher levels** of stress hormones in their urine. They were more likely to suffer from high blood pressure and stomach ulcers.
Conclusion:	A **lack** of control and social contact at work can lead to stress.
Evaluation:	This was a field experiment, so it has high **ecological validity**. The findings are **supported** by Marmot's study. However, it doesn't take individual differences into account — some individuals may just be more prone to stress. The results could have been affected by extraneous variables, such as how much the workers were paid.

Stress at Work

Physiological Measures of Stress Can be Taken

Stress affects the **body** in different ways, and as Frankenhaeuser's study showed on the previous page, **stress levels** can be measured using **physiological tests**.

1) **Heart rate** — A **chest strap** containing a **transmitter** measures **electrical activity** and indicates heart rate. **Increased** heart rate is a sign of **stress**.

2) **Blood pressure** — This is measured by putting an inflatable cuff on the arm which restricts blood flow. As it deflates, the pulse rate in the arm indicates blood pressure levels. **Stress** is associated with **high blood pressure**.

3) **Hormone levels** — **Blood** and **urine** can be tested for stress-related hormones. For example, **increased** levels of **adrenaline** and **cortisol** indicate **higher** levels of **stress**.

Having sweaty hands was not an option for Tim and Neo.

4) **Skin conductance response** — This measures the **electrical resistance** of the skin, which is affected by **moisture level** (sweat). An **increased** skin conductance response is associated with **stress**.

There are Strengths and Weaknesses of Using Physiological Measures

Strengths
- Physiological tests are **objective** — it's not possible to lie, and the results **won't** be **influenced** by the participant or the researcher.
- The test results can indicate appropriate **treatments** for the stress — e.g. if someone has an **increased heart rate**, they can be put on drugs called **betablockers** to slow their heart down.

Weaknesses
- The tests might not be measuring stress. Other behaviours such as **poor diet**, **poor sleeping patterns** and **alcohol consumption** can also cause changes in these measurements. Each of these behaviours can be used as **coping mechanisms** when people are **stressed**. So it could be that **physiological changes** are caused by one of these **stress-related behaviours**.
- Technology isn't always 100% accurate.

Warm-Up Questions

Q1 Give one reason why the workplace might be a source of stress.
Q2 Who were the participants in Marmot et al's (1997) study?
Q3 Name two different physiological measures of stress.

PRACTICE QUESTIONS

Exam Questions

Q1 Outline and evaluate physiological measures of stress. [8 marks]

Q2 Discuss the workplace as a source of stress, including the effects of workload and control. [16 marks]

Hormone-filled urine and sweaty hands — no wonder work is stressful...

Being prepared for your exams will hopefully make you much less stressed. So... you could liken CGP to a giant stress ball. Just give the book a squeeze and all your stresses will disappear. Well, maybe learn the stuff first. Better to be safe than sorry. You can thank me when you've picked up your results and dried off your sweaty palms.

Stress — Individual Differences

By now you hopefully know all about how stress affects the body. But that doesn't mean stress affects everyone in the same way. If you stick two people in a pit and drop spiders on them, it's unlikely they're going to react in exactly the same way. Psychologists call different personal reactions 'individual differences'.

Different **Personalities** Can Lead to Different Stress Levels

Psychologists love sticking people into groups. One theory about personality is that you can split everyone into three groups called '**Type A**', '**Type B**' or '**Type X**'. Type A people are competitive and ambitious. Type Bs are non-competitive, relaxed and easy-going. Type Xs have a balance of Type A and Type B behaviours.

Friedman and Rosenman (1974) tested how these different types of personality affect the likelihood of CHD (coronary heart disease) — one of the most obvious effects of stress.

Friedman and Rosenman (1974) — Type A personality & illness

Method:	Approximately **3000**, 39-59 year old American males were assessed to class their personality characteristics into Type A, Type B or Type X using interviews and observation. At the start of the study **none of them** had CHD (coronary heart disease).
Results:	Eight years later, **257** of them had developed CHD. 70% of these were classed as **Type A** personality. This includes being 'workaholic', extremely competitive, hostile to others, and always in a rush. Participants classed as Type B were less competitive and less impatient. They were found to have half the rate of heart disease of Type A. These results were found even when the extraneous variables of weight and smoking were taken into account.
Conclusion:	Type A personalities seem to be at a **higher risk** of stress-related illnesses, such as CHD.
Evaluation:	Having only three personality types seems a bit **simplistic**. The study doesn't prove that personality characteristics can **cause** stress and illness. It could be the other way round. For example, Type A personality may develop as a **response** to being under stress (from work etc.). Also, the **sample** used in the study was quite limited — middle-aged, male Americans. This means that it may not be possible to **generalise** the results to the rest of the population. In addition, participants may not have been completely **honest** in their interviews so that their characteristics appeared desirable to the researcher (**social desirability bias**).

Later research also identified Type C personalities — mild-mannered, easy-going people who may not react well to stressful situations, and suppress their emotions. These people seem to have a higher risk of cancer.

Kobasa (1979) Identified **Hardiness** as an Important **Individual Difference**

Kobasa described people as being **hardy** or **non-hardy**. There are three main characteristics of hardy personalities:

1) Hardy personalities are very involved in what they do, and show a high level of **commitment**. This means that they work hard at relationships, jobs and other activities in life.

2) They view change in a positive rather than a negative way, seeing it as an opportunity for **challenge**. Hardy personalities enjoy a challenge and see it as an opportunity to develop themselves.

3) They have a strong feeling of **control** over their life and what happens to them. This is known as having an **internal locus of control**.

In comparison, **non-hardy** personalities view any life experiences in a much more **negative** way, and feel that they're **unable to cope** with situations. They feel that **external agencies** have control over what happens to them and that it isn't worth trying to become more powerful. They **give up** easily and don't see any value in trying to change what's happening around them.

It's difficult to **quantify** what's meant by a hardy personality, making it difficult to **measure** and test. We should also avoid making assumptions about **cause and effect** — it could be that some people have hardy personalities because of a lack of stress in their lives, rather than low stress being the result of personality. Levels of hardiness could **fluctuate** and may decrease when the person is experiencing lots of stress, such as after a bereavement.

Stress — Individual Differences

Research has Shown a Relationship Between **Stress** and **Hardiness**

There is evidence suggesting that people with a hardy personality are less likely to suffer from illness as a result of stress. For instance, a study by **Maddi et al (1987)** looked at employees of a US phone company that was reducing its workforce. During the downsize, **two-thirds** of the workforce suffered from stress-related health problems. However, the other **one-third** of the workforce **thrived** during the period. It was found that these people were much more likely to have a **hardy personality**.

Lifton et al (2006) measured the hardiness of **1432 students** at five US universities. Students who displayed **hardy personalities** were significantly **more likely** to successfully **complete** their degrees. A large number of students who dropped out had low hardiness scores.

Stress can also be Related to **Gender**

There are some differences in the way men and women behave, so psychologists (who don't miss a trick) thought that maybe these differences could affect what kinds of things men and women find stressful, and how they cope. They looked at how **biological**, **social** and **cognitive** differences between males and females influence their response to stress.

Biological Explanation — through evolution, men in their role of 'hunter-gatherer' may have developed a stronger 'fight or flight' response than women, who had the role of caring for the kids. In this way, males and females may have developed different physiological responses to stress.

Taylor et al (2000) suggest that women produce a calmer response to stress due to a hormone. Oxytocin is released in response to stress and has been shown to lead to maternal behaviour and social affiliation. Taylor called this the 'tend and befriend' response (instead of the 'fight or flight' response) and thought it might make females more likely to seek social support to help them cope with stress.

Social Explanation — to fulfil their Western stereotypical social role, men are expected to be less open about their feelings than women. This means they're less likely to discuss stressful experiences with others and may use harmful coping methods instead, e.g. smoking and drinking.

Carroll (1992) found that women do generally make more use of social support to deal with stress. However, coronary heart disease has increased in women — but this could just be because a change in social roles means that it's now more acceptable for women to drink and smoke.

Cognitive Explanation — **Vogele et al (1997)** claim that women are better able to control anger and therefore respond more calmly to stressful situations. Men may feel that anger is an acceptable way to respond, and feel stress if they cannot show it. These cognitive differences could be the result of biology or the roles we are taught to follow, or a bit of both.

Warm-Up Questions

Q1 Explain the differences between Type A and Type B personalities.
Q2 Give a criticism of Friedman and Rosenman's (1974) research.
Q3 What are the three characteristics associated with a hardy personality?
Q4 What did Vogele et al (1997) claim about stress?

Exam Questions

Q1 Discuss gender differences in coping with stress. [8 marks]

Q2 Describe and evaluate research into personality types and stress. [16 marks]

We are all individuals, we are all individuals, we are all individuals...

This is an important thing to remember throughout Psychology. People are divided into groups to show how different things affect people — but there are also individual differences, which means that when put in the same situation, people will often react differently. This seems obvious but it's easy to forget if you get wrapped up in all the theories.

Stress Management

Biological methods of stress management help people cope with stress by changing the way their body responds to it. You need to know about drug treatments and biofeedback...

Drug Treatments Work in Two Ways

1) They **slow down** the activity of the **central nervous system** (CNS). Anti-anxiety drugs called **benzodiazepines** (BZs) increase the body's reaction to its own natural anxiety-relieving chemical **GABA** (gamma-aminobutyric acid), which slows down the activity of neurones and makes us feel relaxed.

OR...

2) They **reduce** the activity of the **sympathetic nervous system** (SNS).
The SNS increases heart rate, blood pressure and levels of the hormone **cortisol**. High levels of cortisol can make our immune system **weak** and also cause heart disease. The group of drugs called **beta blockers** reduce all these unpleasant symptoms.

Biofeedback Uses Information About What's Happening in the Body

Biofeedback gives people information about **internal physical processes** that they wouldn't otherwise be aware of, e.g. muscle tension. The idea is to give them more **control** over these internal processes and the ability to **alter** them. There are **four** main steps involved:

1) The person is attached to a machine that monitors and gives feedback on internal physical processes such as heart rate, blood pressure or muscle tension.

2) They are then taught how to control these symptoms of stress through a variety of techniques. These can include muscle relaxation — muscle groups are tensed and relaxed in turn until the whole body is relaxed. This teaches people to notice when their body is becoming tense. Other techniques include actively clearing the mind using meditation, or breathing control exercises.

Trisha didn't need biofeedback — she had stress totally sorted.

3) This feeling of relaxation acts like a reward and encourages the person to repeat this behaviour, so that it becomes a habit. It's a type of behavioural (operant) conditioning.

4) The person learns to use these techniques in real-life situations.

Budzynski et al (1973) investigated the role of biofeedback in stress management:

Budzynski et al (1973) — Biofeedback and tension headaches

Method:	The sample was **18 participants** who volunteered in response to a newspaper advert about headaches. The participants were screened to make sure they only suffered from tension headaches and were then divided into **three groups**. **Group 1** received **relaxation training** twice a week for 8 weeks. Their muscle tension was monitored by an EMG monitor which fed back information by making clicks. They were told that **more clicks** meant **more muscle tension** and **worse headaches**. They were encouraged to **relax** so that the clicks slowed down. **Group 2** received the **same relaxation training**, however they weren't told that the clicks reflected their level of muscle tension and a fake soundtrack of clicks was played to them. **Group 3** were the **control group**. They didn't have any relaxation training. Participants who'd had relaxation training were also told to **practise** the techniques at home.
Results:	At the end of the study and three months afterwards, **Group 1** had the **lowest muscle tension** and **fewer headaches**. They also showed **lower levels** of hysteria, depression and were **less preoccupied** with their health than they were before the study. Participants who'd **practised** the relaxation techniques at home showed **more improvement** than those who hadn't.
Conclusion:	Biofeedback can **reduce stress related illnesses** such as tension headaches.
Evaluation:	The presence of a **control group** and **Group 2** showed that it was the actual feedback that was important, not just the presence of feedback. However, the sample size is small, making **generalisation** difficult. Also, the results can't be generalised to other stress-related symptoms.

Stress Management

Biological Methods of Stress Management Have Strengths and Weaknesses

Both drugs and biofeedback are effective:

Drugs are quick and effective in reducing dangerous symptoms such as high blood pressure. Kahn et al (1986) found that benzodiazepines were superior to a placebo (sugar pill) when they tracked around 250 patients over an 8-week period.

Attanasio et al (1985) found that biofeedback helped teenagers and children with stress-related disorders to gain control over the symptoms of migraine headaches. They also showed an increase in enthusiasm and a more positive attitude.

> Placebos are pills that do nothing at all. They're used to test if any effect happens just because people think they're being treated.

BUT both treat symptoms rather than the underlying causes of stress:

Drugs only help with the symptoms, and only so long as the drugs are taken.

Biofeedback also aims to reduce symptoms, but using relaxation techniques can also give the person a sense of control and have more long-lasting benefits.

Drugs have side effects, biofeedback doesn't:

Drugs can have minor side effects such as dizziness and tiredness, or more serious effects such as blurred vision and changes in sex drive. Withdrawal symptoms when people come off medication, such as increased anxiety, seizures, tremors and headaches, can be distressing. Benzodiazepines can be addictive and people develop dependency on them, so they are generally limited to a maximum of 4 weeks use.

There are no side effects of biofeedback — just relaxation. This method's advantage is that it's voluntary and not invasive.

Drugs are easier to use than biofeedback:

Drugs are relatively easy to prescribe and use.

Biofeedback needs specialist equipment and expert supervision. Some argue that the benefits of biofeedback could be gained from other relaxation techniques, and so this is an unnecessary expense.

Warm-Up Questions

Q1 What is GABA?

Q2 Describe the method Budzynski et al (1973) used in their study on biofeedback and tension headaches.

Q3 Give one problem of using drugs to deal with stress.

Q4 Briefly describe the findings of Kahn et al's (1986) investigation into drug treatments.

Q5 Why is biofeedback a more expensive form of treatment than drugs?

PRACTICE QUESTIONS

Exam Questions

Q1 Describe how drug therapy can help in the management of stress. [4 marks]

Q2 Outline and evaluate the use of biofeedback in enabling people to manage and cope with stress. [16 marks]

Stress management — it's more than squeezing a stress ball...

This ridiculously stressed and hectic lifestyle we choose to live is turning us all into ill people. I can't understand it myself — personally I choose the more Caribbean attitude to time management. I'm quite confident I'll never need to take BZs or try some biofeedback. But then again, I might get into trouble for not finishing this book on time.

Stress Management

The end is in sight — the last two pages on stress. So sit back, relax, and learn how to manage your stress before the exams. And then you can give yourself a brand new book to read and a nice bath to keep you stress-free and happy.

Stress Inoculation Therapy Can be Used to Manage Stress

1) **Cognitive techniques** aim to manage stress by identifying and **altering** the **thought processes** that cause stress.

2) **Meichenbaum (1985)** developed a cognitive stress management approach called **stress inoculation therapy (SIT)**.

3) SIT introduces **minor** levels of stress to individuals, which allows them to **psychologically adjust** and **prepare** for stressful situations.

4) There are **three phases** to SIT:

- **Conceptualisation** — identify fears and concerns with the help of a therapist.
- **Skills acquisition and rehearsal** — train to develop skills like positive thinking and relaxation, in order to improve self-confidence.
- **Application and follow-through** — practise the newly acquired skill in real-life situations, with support and back-up from the therapist.

Alfie's owner made him practise SIT every day.

5) Meichenbaum (1985) found that SIT works both with **short-term stressors** such as preparing for public speaking, and **longer-term stressors** such as medical illness, divorce or work-related stress.

There are **strengths** and **weaknesses** to SIT:

- Because SIT requires people to acknowledge their stress and understand the cause of it, it can result in **longer lasting** coping.
- However, **cognitive methods** don't suit all individuals — they must be determined to stick to the technique.
- Meichenbaum's (1985) research was based on white, middle-class people, and so **can't be generalised** to others.
- The procedures in SIT are **lengthy** and require considerable **insight** and **commitment** of **time** and **effort**.

Social Support Can Play a Big Part in How Stress is Managed

1) From page 199, you know that stress can suppress the immune system.

2) It's been suggested that social support (e.g. from families, friends, help groups) can reduce stress, and so reduce the impact on the immune system.

3) If this is the case, we would expect people with strong social support to be less likely to become ill and more likely to recover from illness than those without a good social support system.

Waxler-Morrison et al's (1991) study can provide **evidence** for this:

Waxler-Morrison et al (1991) — The role of social support

Method:	This was a **natural experiment** investigating the effect of **social support** on **survival chances** of women with breast cancer. Data on social support (e.g. number of supportive friends, extent of contact with friends, size of social network, etc.) was collected from **133 women** with breast cancer using **questionnaires** and **interviews**. The women's **medical records** were followed over 4 years.
Results:	They found that women with **better social support** had **better survival rates**. Types of support that were relevant included being married, having a job, having contact with friends, and getting support from friends.
Conclusion:	**Social support** may be helpful in **reducing stress**, as the women with good social support networks were **more likely** to **survive** breast cancer. This could be because they were less stressed and so their **immune system** was working more efficiently than women without a good support system.
Evaluation:	It's important not to **assume causality** — social support is associated with survival but doesn't necessarily cause it. Further investigation is needed to find the precise relationship between social support and cancer survival. The fact that the study only included women reduces the **reliability** of the conclusions that can be drawn from the results.

Stress Management

There are **Different Types** of Social Support

1) **Instrumental** Support

- Sometimes people need **practical help** — this is called **instrumental support**. It might include going to get someone's **groceries**, doing the **cleaning** or providing **money**, **childcare** or other **resources**.
- Instrumental support **reduces the stress** of those who are **overwhelmed** in terms of worrying about time, money, responsibility, etc.

2) **Emotional** Support

- Giving people a **hug**, a **pat on the back**, or even just listening and **empathising** are all types of **emotional support**.
- These actions make people feel **loved**, and give them **comfort** and **reassurance**.
- Emotional support usually comes from close **friends** and **family** members and **reduces emotional distress**.

3) **Esteem** Support

- When others show esteem support, they provide expressions of encouragement to build up someone's confidence. They might reinforce peoples' strengths and remind them of all the things they are good at.
- For example, life coaches rely on esteem support to make people believe in their own abilities, enhancing their individual self-worth.
- People then feel much more able to cope with stressful situations.

Stress didn't feature highly in Poppy's merry world.

Warm-Up Questions

Q1 What did Meichenbaum (1985) develop?

Q2 Outline some limitations of stress inoculation therapy.

Q3 Name one social factor that increases breast cancer survival chances according to Waxler-Morrison et al (1991).

Q4 What is esteem support?

Exam Questions

Q1 Describe how stress inoculation therapy works. [6 marks]

Q2 Read the item below then answer the questions that follow.

> Rachel and Dominic have recently married. Dominic has just started a new job and Rachel travels a lot through work. They have bought a house and were about to move in when a pipe burst and flooded the kitchen. They now need to redecorate before they can move in, but neither of them has much time to do so.
>
> Luckily, both Rachel and Dominic's parents have loaned them some money and are going to help redecorate.

a) Identify the type of social support that Rachel and Dominic's parents are providing. [1 mark]

b) Discuss the role of social support in coping with stress. [16 marks]

Worth keeping hold of your friends then — you might need 'em one day...

Ahhhh, so the old saying could be true — love really is the best medicine, and having lots of friends could help you survive cancer. That's good to know. Also good to know — the fancily named stress inoculation technique for managing stress. Not quite as heart-warming, but just as necessary seeing as you've got exams coming up soon.

Biological Explanations of Aggression

Aggression is a tendency that humans share with almost all species of animal, as anyone who's tried to give a cat a bath will know. It's a response that can be partially explained by biology. Not sure that'd go down well as an excuse though...

There Are **Genetic Influences** Underlying Aggression

Aggression is behaviour intended to harm — including physical and psychological harm.

1) Species of various animals have been **selectively bred** to produce highly **aggressive** individuals — e.g. Doberman dogs were originally bred by humans to behave aggressively towards intruders so they can be used as guard dogs.

2) This ability to select the most aggressive dogs and breed them together to give **new generations** with the **same** aggressive tendencies suggests that there are specific **genes** that determine levels of aggression.

3) In humans, evidence for a genetic component to aggression comes from **twin studies** and **adoption studies**, where **criminality** is used as a measure of aggression.

Christiansen (1977) — Twin study into aggression

Method:	An analysis of criminality in 3586 pairs of **twins** born between 1881 and 1910 in a region of Denmark was done, in order to find **concordance rates**. Of this sample, **926** individuals were registered by the police for **criminal activity**. **Identical (MZ)** and **non-identical (DZ)** twins were compared for the rate at which **both** twins of the pair were registered.
Results:	**Male MZ twins** showed **35% concordance** for criminality, compared to the **12% concordance** shown between **DZ** twins. **Female MZ** twins showed **21% concordance** compared to **8%** for **DZ** twins.
Conclusion:	Twins of criminals are more likely to **also** be criminals if they share all of their twin's genes (MZ), rather only some of their genes (DZ). So there's a **genetic component** to aggressive behaviour.
Evaluation:	Genetics can't be the only factor, as the concordance rate for MZ twins (who share all of their genetic material) wasn't 100%. By studying **all** the twins born in a specified time frame, this study gives a **representative** rate of concordance. However, as with all twin studies, **environment** might account for the different concordance rates — because they look the same, MZ twins may be treated **more alike**, and have more shared experiences.

The **MAOA Gene** Has Been Linked to **Aggressive Behaviour**

See p.76 and p.79 for more about neurotransmitters.

1) Monoamine oxidase A (**MAOA**) is an **enzyme** involved in processing neurotransmitters, including **serotonin**, in the brain. Serotonin is thought to be involved in **aggression** (see page 214).

2) The **MAOA gene** controls production of MAOA.

3) Some versions of the gene, which result in **lower levels** of MAOA (and therefore lower serotonin activity — i.e. less serotonin being processed in the brain), have been linked to **aggressive behaviour**.

4) The link between this gene and aggression was discovered by researchers studying a **Dutch family**:

Brunner et al (1993) studied an **extended family** in the Netherlands, where several male family members showed patterns of behaviour involving **impulsive aggression**, including violent crime.

They identified a **fault** in the **MAOA gene** of the individuals who showed impulsive aggression, which wasn't present in other male family members. The individuals with this fault were **deficient in MAOA**.

Salem had miaow deficiency.

5) Studies on **mice** have found a similar relationship between MAOA gene variations and aggression.

Cases et al (1995) found that adult male mice who were missing the MAOA-producing gene had specific behaviour patterns, which included heightened aggression.

This is known as a knockout study — animals are bred so that they are missing a specific gene (the gene is knocked-out), and are then studied to observe the effect of the gene.

Biological Explanations of Aggression

The **Genetic Explanation** for **Aggression** Has **Strengths** and **Weaknesses**

Strengths

1) **Twin studies, adoption studies** and **knockout studies** suggest there is a genetic element to aggression.

2) **Caspi et al (2002)** found that men with a 'low MAOA activity' gene were not significantly more likely to engage in anti-social behaviour (including violence). However, there was a significant effect in men who had been maltreated as children. This suggests that genetics interact with environmental factors to influence aggression levels.

Weaknesses

1) The genetic explanation ignores social and environmental factors, which may play a part too.

2) **Walters' (1992)** meta-analysis found only a weak correlation between genetic factors and crime. This effect was weaker for more recent and better designed studies.

The **Limbic System** is an **Area of the Brain** That's Been Linked to **Aggression**

1) Different areas of the **brain**, including the **temporal lobe** and the **limbic system**, have been linked to different forms of aggressive behaviour.

The limbic system is a group of brain structures mostly associated with emotion and memory.

2) One part of the limbic system, the **amygdala**, has been found to have a particularly strong connection to aggression.

3) Animal studies have shown that **electrical stimulation** of different parts of the amygdala can either **cause** or **reduce** aggression. **Lesions** to the amygdala have been found to cause cats to **attack**, but caused dogs to become **more submissive** and **less aggressive** — they needed **more stimulation** to provoke a response.

4) There is some evidence for the role of the amygdala in **human** aggression too. **Charles Whitman**, a sniper who killed 14 innocent people and wounded 31 others, left a note that pleaded for his brain to be examined after death for possible dysfunction. An autopsy showed that he had a **temporal lobe tumour**, pressing on his amygdala.

An **amygdalotomy** is a procedure which involves **disconnecting** the amygdala from the rest of the brain. Studies have shown that, following the procedure, many patients experience a **loss of emotion** and become a lot **less aggressive**.

Mpakopoulou et al (2008) conducted a review looking at studies investigating aggression in patients **before and after** an amygdalotomy. Of the 13 papers they looked at, they found that overall, **aggressive behaviours** in those who'd had an amygdalotomy had **decreased** between 33 and 100% with no impact on the patients' learning or intelligence.

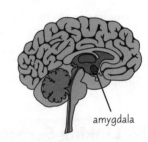

amygdala

Warm-Up Questions

Q1 How can selective breeding support the genetic explanation of aggression?

Q2 What does the MAOA gene do?

Q3 What is a knockout study?

PRACTICE QUESTIONS

Exam Questions

Q1 Outline the role of the limbic system in aggression. [4 marks]

Q2 Discuss the genetic explanation for aggression. [16 marks]

Pardon me for being aggressive — it was not me, it was my amygdala...

Not quite as snappy as the original, but I still have high hopes that it'll catch on. So, plenty to take in here — as well as the amygdala stuff there's genetics. There's lots of evidence that genes play a part in aggression, but it's not as simple as an 'aggression gene' — certain genes may make aggression more likely, but social factors probably play a part too.

Biological Explanations of Aggression

I imagine when you got to the end of those last two pages you were deeply disappointed they'd finished. Luckily, there are two more lovely pages of biological explanations here, just waiting for you to get stuck in. I'm too good to you.

Turnover of **Serotonin** May Affect **Aggression**

Serotonin is important in the limbic system (previous page), so these explanations are linked.

1) **Serotonin** is a neurotransmitter which is thought to **inhibit aggressive behaviour** — **low serotonin** in the brain (or reduced serotonin activity) is thought to be linked to **aggression**.

2) The level of **serotonin activity** in the brain is measured by **turnover** — this is how much serotonin is produced and then **broken down**.

Animal Studies

There's lots of evidence from **animal studies** that **low serotonin turnover** is linked to **increased aggression**.

> **Higley et al (1996)** studied a group of 49 **rhesus monkeys** over 4 years. They determined each individual's **serotonin turnover**. Monkeys with **lower serotonin turnover** were observed to be **more aggressive**. After 4 years, 11 monkeys had died or were missing. All of the monkeys in the **highest serotonin turnover** group **survived**, and the 4 monkeys who had died as a result of **aggressive encounters** were all in the **lowest serotonin group**.

> **Valzelli and Bernasconi (1979)** bred mice with **low serotonin turnover**. They found that, when isolated, these mice were **more aggressive** than mice with normal serotonin turnover.

Diet Manipulation Studies

1) Other studies have used **controlled diets** to attempt to manipulate brain serotonin levels in **healthy participants**.

2) Serotonin is made from an **amino acid** called **tryptophan**. A diet **low** in tryptophan, but **high** in other amino acids, is thought to **reduce brain serotonin** levels.

> **Moeller et al (1996)** found that healthy male subjects showed **increased aggression** 5 or 6 hours after they were given a **tryptophan-free** mixture of amino acids. The researchers proposed that this aggression was likely to have been caused by **decreased serotonin levels** in the participants' brains.

3) Similar research has linked this effect of serotonin on aggression to the **amygdala** (see previous page).

Studies **Linking Serotonin** with **Aggression** Have **Limitations**

There's plenty of evidence that serotonin is **related** to aggression, but scientific support which shows how serotonin **causes** aggression in humans is lacking. There are several weaknesses in the evidence available:

1) Animals studies show a **strong link** between low serotonin turnover and aggression, but this doesn't mean the link is **causal**. Also, findings from animal studies can't be generalised to **humans**.

2) Studies using diet are better **controlled**, and usually involve **healthy participants**. However, they don't **directly** link serotonin to aggression — it's just **thought** that this is why a controlled diet can affect aggression.

3) **Laboratory studies** have low ecological validity. **Natural experiments** (see page 93) have higher ecological validity, and these studies tend to support a **more complicated** relationship between serotonin and aggression. For example, lots of studies have used convictions for **criminal offences** as a measure of aggression:

> **Virkkunen et al (1987)** studied serotonin turnover in 20 arsonists, 20 violent offenders and 10 healthy volunteers. Serotonin turnover was significantly lower in the arsonists than in the other groups. However, serotonin turnover didn't correlate with the severity of the arsonists' offences. Virkkunen et al proposed that this showed a link between serotonin and impulsive behaviour, rather than aggressive behaviour.

4) However, results from studies of **convicted criminals** may not be **generalisable** to the population as a whole.

Biological Explanations of Aggression

Testosterone May Also Be Involved in Aggression

1) Testosterone is an **androgen** (male sex hormone) — it's responsible for the development of **male characteristics**, and may also affect the brain.

2) Men produce much **more** testosterone than women, and men are statistically more likely to engage in **violence** than women. For example, a very **high proportion** of people arrested for violence against another person in the UK are men.

3) It's been argued that this indicates testosterone is related to **aggression**.

4) Studies involving people **convicted of violence** have supported this suggestion.

> Dabbs et al (1987) measured testosterone levels in the saliva of 89 male prison inmates. Those with a higher testosterone concentration were more likely to have been convicted of violent crimes. Almost all of those with the highest levels had been convicted of violent crimes, and almost all of those with the lowest levels had been convicted of non-violent crimes.

Jeff wasn't the aggressive type, but if he ever saw that hairdresser again...

5) However, there's a problem with establishing **cause and effect** — this data is only **correlational**. Another factor could be causing aggressive behaviour, or it could be that being aggressive raises levels of testosterone.

6) **Van Goozen et al (1994)** studied the effects of testosterone **directly**. This avoided having to depend on correlational data, which made it easier to establish cause and effect.

Van Goozen et al (1994) — Aggression in transsexual participants

Method: In a **repeated measures** design, 35 female-to-male and 15 male-to-female transsexuals completed **questionnaires** to assess **proneness to aggression**. They completed the questionnaires before and after receiving hormone treatment to 'change' their sex. Female-to-male transsexuals were given testosterone (an androgen) and male-to-female transsexuals were given anti-androgens. Treatment lasted 3 months.

Results: **Female-to-male** transsexuals reported an **increase** in aggression proneness, whereas **male-to-female** transsexuals reported a **decrease**.

Conclusion: Levels of **testosterone** determine the likelihood of displaying **aggressive behaviours**.

Evaluation: By controlling levels of testosterone **experimentally**, the **direction** of cause and effect between testosterone and aggression can be established. However, **self-report** measures of aggression were used, which are subjective and so may not be valid. The participants may have been conforming to **stereotypes** of their new gender roles by expressing an increase or decrease in aggression.

Warm-Up Questions

Q1 What is serotonin?

Q2 Give an example of a diet manipulation study investigating aggression.

Q3 What is testosterone?

Q4 Give one weakness of evidence from studies of criminals for the role of testosterone in aggression.

Exam Questions

Q1 Briefly outline and evaluate the findings of one study investigating the role of testosterone in aggression. [3 marks]

Q2 Describe and evaluate the role of serotonin in aggression. [16 marks]

All this brain chemistry stuff is enough to make anyone lose their temper...

There are some tricky bits here, but don't let all the jazzy biology words throw you — the key ideas are pretty simple. Serotonin and testosterone are probably both involved in aggression, but it's not totally clear that either of them cause it — lots of the evidence is correlational, and studies often focus on criminals, so the results may not apply to everyone.

Ethological and Evolutionary Explanations

Aggression often (though not always) serves a purpose. That doesn't give you licence to go stomping around throwing things about though — it's not big and it's not clever. Speaking of clever, you'd best get on and learn this stuff...

The **Ethological Explanation** for **Aggression** is Based on **Animal Behaviour**

Ethology is the study of naturally occurring **animal behaviour**, which can include human behaviour. Ethologists usually look at a particular type of behaviour (e.g. aggression) **across species**.

Lorenz proposed a theory of aggression based on **animal behaviour**, which he applied to humans too. He defined aggression as **fighting instinct** directed at members of **your own species**.

Lorenz Believed That Aggression is an **Innate Response**

Aggression as an adaptation is covered more on the next page.

1) Lorenz argued that aggression has evolved as an **adaptive response** — an individual will be more likely to pass on their **genes** if they're able to gain the **upper hand** in competition for food, mates or territory.

2) He described aggression as an **innate tendency** that's triggered by **environmental stimuli**:

- The urge to engage in **aggressive** behaviour builds up **continuously** over time — the **more time** that has passed since the last release of aggression, the more an animal feels **internal pressure** to be aggressive.
- Eventually a **stimulus** (an external event or situation) will **trigger** aggression.
- As the internal pressure to release the aggression **builds up**, the **strength of stimulus** needed to trigger this **decreases**. If the pressure is **very high** then aggression might be triggered **spontaneously**.
- The stimulus triggers an **innate releasing mechanism** — this is a proposed 'innate pathway' in the brain (i.e. a brain network that we're born with), which sets off a **fixed action pattern**.
- A fixed action pattern is an **instinctive behaviour** which is identical **across a species**. For example, babies instinctively grab things they're offered and hold on tightly.

3) Aggression in this form (a fixed action pattern set off by a specific stimulus), has been observed in **red-bellied sticklebacks** (a species of fish).

- During breeding season the male sticklebacks develop bright red bellies. In males, seeing the bright red of another male's belly stimulates an innate releasing mechanism, which triggers specific fighting behaviour (the fixed action pattern) directed towards the rival.
- Tinbergen (1947) found that this response was triggered more by unrealistic models with red undersides (such as diamond shapes with no features) than by real sticklebacks with no red belly.
- This supports the suggestion that the behaviour is instinctive, and set off by a specific trigger.

4) Lorenz also believed that most aggression is **ritualised**, i.e. it's released relatively **harmlessly**.

- A behaviour won't be passed on through genes if it gets an animal **killed** before it produces offspring. If animals were **routinely killed** during everyday power struggles or mating contests, it's likely the species would become **extinct**. So, there are **ritual behaviours** in place to stop confrontations being fatal.
- For example, wolves end a fight by the loser exposing his jugular vein as a sign of **submission**. This puts the winner in prime position to kill their rival, but in fact the winner takes no further action.
- Lorenz claimed that **sport** was an example of harmless ritualised aggression release in **humans**, and argued that sport was an important method for **reducing aggression** in society.

The **Ethological Explanation** for **Aggression** Has **Strengths** and **Weaknesses**

Strengths

1) Aggression **does** occur as a fixed action pattern in some animals, e.g. sticklebacks.
2) This theory could explain why humans **kill each other** relatively often — without weapons human fighting isn't usually lethal, so we haven't evolved to **back down**. Now that we have access to weapons, fights are more likely to kill.

Weaknesses

1) This theory doesn't explain aggression which isn't an immediate response to an environmental stimulus, for example **premeditated murder**.
2) **Arms et al (1979)** found that watching aggressive sport **increased aggression** in participants, rather than dispersing it.

Ethological and Evolutionary Explanations

Evolutionary Explanations Say Aggression is an Adaptive Response

Evolutionary psychology explains aggression as a strategy that has evolved as an **adaptive response** to problems. The argument is that using aggression helped individuals to **survive** and **reproduce** in the past — so aggression is a trait that modern humans have **inherited**.

Evolutionary psychologists have outlined various **adaptive functions** which aggression may have served in the past:

1) To **gain status** or **dominance** in a group.
2) To **gain resources** from others (e.g. territory, mates).
3) In **defence** (against losing resources or status, or being injured or killed).
4) To **deter infidelity** in long term mates.

Evolutionary explanations have been criticised because they don't explain cross-cultural or individual differences in aggression, and they don't take social factors into account.

Sex Differences in Aggression May Have Evolved

1) **Wilson and Daly (1985)** studied murders in Detroit and found that the majority of **perpetrators** and **victims** were **young men**. 29 of the cases they looked at were murders that had resulted from '**escalated showing off disputes**', and **only one** of these murders resulted from a dispute between **women**.

2) **Evolutionary psychologists** argue that **men** (and **young men** in particular) are more aggressive because they faced the most **competition** for mates in the past. The main limit on men's reproduction was access to **fertile mates**, so competing successfully for mates was important.

This is related to intra-sexual selection (see p.146).

3) Women, however, were mainly limited by their access to **resources**. Evolutionary psychologists argue that these different pressures have led to different **psychological responses** evolving in men and women.

Buss et al (1992) — Sex differences in jealousy

Method:	This was a **cross-cultural questionnaire study**. Participants were presented with the **hypothetical scenario** that someone they were in a serious, committed romantic relationship with had become interested in someone else. They were asked what would distress them more — imagining their partner forming a deep **emotional attachment** to that other person, or enjoying passionate **sexual intercourse** with the person.
Results:	Across all studies, **more men** than women reported **sexual infidelity** to be most upsetting. On average, **51%** of the men versus **22%** of the women chose this to be more distressing than **emotional infidelity**.
Conclusion:	Men's jealousy is innately triggered by the threat of uncertainty over the **paternity** of children produced within the relationship. However, women are more threatened by **emotional involvement** as it could mean being left for another woman, and so reducing the resources available to her children.
Evaluation:	The fact that the evidence was **consistent** across **different cultures** suggests that these different responses are **innate** rather than learned. However, the fact that the questionnaires were based around a **hypothetical** situation, and the responses available to the participants were **multiple choice**, means that the **validity** of the results is questionable — they may not accurately reflect what participants would actually do if they found themselves in that situation.

Evolutionary theories are very difficult to provide evidence for (or against) — they're effectively impossible to test on humans.

Warm-Up Questions

Q1 What is an innate releasing mechanism?

Q2 How did Buss et al (1992) explain sex differences in jealousy?

PRACTICE QUESTIONS

Exam Questions

Q1 Briefly outline evolutionary explanations for human aggression. [6 marks]

Q2 Describe and evaluate the ethological explanation of aggression. [16 marks]

Forget infidelity — it's people with no exams that make me jealous...

The thing to remember about evolutionary arguments is that they're not saying that people think to themselves 'I'll be aggressive so I'm more likely to pass on my genes'. They're saying that because this behaviour had that effect in the past, it was more likely to be inherited. And it still affects people's behaviour today, even if they're not aware of it. Spooky.

Social Explanations of Aggression

Just when you thought there couldn't possibly be any more explanations for aggression... Next up, social psychological explanations. These theories are all to do with how we interact socially with our environment.

The **Frustration-Aggression** Model Says Aggression **Comes From** Frustration

1) **Dollard et al (1939)** proposed the **frustration-aggression hypothesis**, a social psychological explanation for aggression.

2) They argued that aggression is **always** a result of frustration (defined as interference with attempts to reach a goal), and that frustration **always** leads to aggression (this could be aggressive behaviour, or just feeling aggressive).

3) The **strength** of this aggression is determined by the **degree of frustration**, which depends on how much you **want** to reach the goal, how **close** you were to achieving it, and how much you've been **set back** by the interference.

4) **Fear of punishment** may **inhibit** aggressive behaviour towards the source of the frustration. If this aggression is weaker than the fear it will be **displaced** onto something (or someone) other than the cause of the frustration.

Strengths

1) **Buss (1963)** found that frustration can **increase** the occurrence of aggression — students in groups who had been **frustrated** (e.g. by being prevented from winning money) were slightly **more aggressive** than the control group.

2) **Harris (1974)** studied people's responses when a confederate pushed in front of them in a **queue**. People displayed **more aggression** when they were **close to the front** of the queue than when they were near the back. This supports the suggestion that being **frustrated** causes **more aggression** the **closer to your goal** you are.

Weaknesses

1) **Berkowitz (1965)** argued that frustration alone **isn't enough** to trigger aggression — **environmental cues** to release aggression are also needed. There's more about this below.

2) The suggestion that frustration **always** leads to some form of aggression is widely disputed. Evidence for this claim is **contradictory**. For example, **Buss (1966)** found **no link** between frustration and aggression (contradicting his earlier work).

3) It could be that frustration only leads to aggression if the frustrating behaviour is seen as an **attack**. **Mallick and McCandless (1966)** found that participants responded much **less aggressively** to being frustrated by a confederate if they were given a **reasonable explanation** for the frustrator's behaviour.

Environmental Triggers May Be **Necessary** For **Aggressive Behaviour**

1) **Berkowitz (1965)** proposed a **revision** of the frustration-aggression hypothesis, known as the **aggressive cues hypothesis**.

2) He argued that frustration doesn't usually **directly** produce aggression, instead it creates a '**readiness to aggress**'. For aggressive behaviour to occur it must be **triggered** by the presence of **environmental cues**.

Berkowitz and LePage (1967) gave participants **electric shocks** to make them feel angry. Afterwards, levels of aggression were tested with either a **weapon**, **badminton racket** or **no objects** present. They found that people behaved **more aggressively** when the aggressive **cue** of the weapon was present, than in the other two conditions.

Social Learning Theory Says **Experience** Explains Aggressive Behaviour

1) The **social learning theory of human aggression** says that aggressive behaviour is **learned**.

2) People learn aggression by **observing** and **imitating** the behaviour of **aggressive models**.

3) Reinforcement (behaviour being rewarded) affects **how likely** somebody is to imitate an observed behaviour.

4) This can be **positive reinforcement** (something good happening), or **negative reinforcement** (something bad stopping).

5) Reinforcement can also be **direct** (being rewarded yourself), or **vicarious** (observing the model being rewarded).

Make sure you've learnt the social learning theory stuff on pages 58-59 — you need to be able to apply this to aggression. (You also need to be able to evaluate the theory, and Bandura's research.)

6) Bandura's (1961) **Bobo doll study** (see page 59), showed that children can learn aggression through imitation. In a similar experiment, **Bandura (1965)** found that **vicarious reinforcement** affected imitation:

Bandura (1965) got children to watch a video of a model **behaving aggressively** towards a Bobo doll. The model was either **rewarded**, **punished**, or **neither** (in the control condition). When the children played with the doll, those in the **reward** and **control condition** behaved **more aggressively** than those in the **punishment** condition.

Social Explanations of Aggression

Deindividuation Theory Says Being Anonymous Encourages Aggression

Another **social psychological** explanation of aggression suggests we're **disinhibited** when we're an **anonymous** part of a **crowd**. When they're part of the group, people may feel less **personal responsibility** and less fear of **public disapproval** than when they're clearly identifiable as an individual. **Festinger et al (1952)** coined the term **deindividuation** to describe this state of reduced self awareness.

There's some **real-world evidence** for this effect:

1) **Mullen (1986)** analysed newspaper reports of **lynch mob violence** in the US. The **more people** there were in the mob, the **greater** the level of violence.

2) **Mann (1981)** analysed 21 reports of **suicides** and identified ten cases where a crowd had **baited** the person threatening suicide (e.g. shouting 'jump'). Baiting was more likely to happen **at night**, when the crowd was **at a distance** and when the crowd was **large** (more than 300 people).

Research studies have also supported deindividuation:

1) **Zimbardo (1969)** showed that **anonymity** affects behaviour. Participants in his study believed they were administering **shocks** to another participant in a learning experiment. **Individuated** participants wore normal clothes, large name badges and were introduced to each other. **Deindividuated** participants wore coats with hoods, were instructed in groups and weren't referred to by name. The **more anonymous** participants administered more and longer shocks.

"Hands up if you're deindividuated!"

2) **Diener et al (1976)** observed 1300 trick-or-treating children in the US. If they were **anonymous** (in costumes, masks or large groups) they were **more likely** to steal money and sweets.

This evidence supports the idea that deindividuation **increases** aggression. But there are also examples of it having **no effect** or even **reducing** aggression. For example, individuals in crowds at religious festivals often express goodwill to others. It could be that being in a group means that you **conform to group norms**. If group norms are **prosocial** (rather than anti-social), the individual may behave that way too.

Conformity to group norms is covered on page 2.

Warm-Up Questions

Q1 Describe the results of Berkowitz and LePage's (1967) study.

Q2 What did Bandura's Bobo doll studies show?

Q3 What is deindividuation?

PRACTICE QUESTIONS

Exam Questions

Q1 Which of these processes is **not** part of the social learning theory of human aggression?
  A Observation   **B** Reinforcement   **C** Deindividuation   **D** Imitation   [1 mark]

Q2 Read the item below and answer the question that follows.

> A media report following the UK riots in 2011 described otherwise law-abiding people who engaged in destructive and criminal behaviour, as having been 'swept away with the crowd'.

Using your knowledge of social explanations of human aggression, outline how being part of a large crowd may have affected the behaviour of the rioters.   [4 marks]

Q3 Describe and evaluate the frustration-aggression hypothesis.   [16 marks]

Aggressive cues — the smash-hit competitive-snooker movie of the year...

As ever, make sure you can explain all these theories, and come up with some strengths and weaknesses of each of them. It's really important that you've got all the social learning theory stuff on pages 58-59 down too — you need to know all of the grisly details of this for aggression. Once you've got it all you can celebrate with a cup of tea, or some light aerobics.

Aggression in the Real World

These pages are really interesting. Not that the whole book isn't, obviously. Violent media and prison violence always seem to crop up in the news — learn these pages and you can wow everyone with your knowledge of the issues of the moment.

Violence in the Media Has Been Linked To Aggression

1) The two students who carried out the Columbine High School massacre in the US in 1999 were both alleged to be fans of **violent computer games**. Some people have linked this to the killings.

Not everyone agrees that there is a link — other causes have been suggested too.

2) It's since been suggested that violent computer games have played a part in causing other recent **American school shootings**.

3) Seeing characters in computer games being **rewarded** for violent behaviour could encourage aggression in the players themselves through **vicarious reinforcement**.

4) **Correlations** between aggressive behaviour and violent computer games have been shown by some studies, but the relationship isn't necessarily **causal** — it may just be that more aggressive individuals have a **preference** for more violent games — not surprising really...

	Paik and Comstock (1994) — Media violence and aggression
Method:	Paik and Comstock conducted a **meta-analysis** investigating the impact of **media violence** on behaviour. They analysed the results of **217** different studies dating from **1957 to 1990**.
Results:	The results showed that there was an overall **significant correlation** between **watching violent television** and **films** and **violent behaviour**. The correlation for **men** was slightly **stronger** than for women, and those who watched violent cartoons and fantasy programmes also showed more aggressive behaviour than people who watched other types of films and programmes.
Conclusion:	There is a **correlation** between **aggressive behaviour** and watching **violent media images**.
Evaluation:	Although this review was **large** and included many studies, lots of the experiments took place in **laboratories** and may therefore have lacked **ecological validity**. The results also only show a correlation, and not a **causal relationship** — it might just be that people who are more aggressive are also more likely to **choose** more violent and aggressive media.

5) Some studies have found **no link** between media violence and aggression. For example, **Charlton et al (2000)** looked at the **long term effects** of TV being introduced to an island population, and found little change.

Charlton et al (2000) studied children in **St. Helena** (a remote British territory in the South Atlantic), **before** and **after** television was introduced to the island in 1995. They observed children **aged 3-8** in the school playground before television, and children of the same age **5 years** after TV was introduced. The results showed a very slight **decrease in anti-social behaviour** in the **post-television** group.

Anti-social behaviour includes things like shouting at or shoving other people.

Violence in the Media May Cause Desensitisation, Disinhibition and Priming

There are several ideas about **how** seeing **violence in the media** might lead to aggression in **real life**.

Desensitisation

People usually have an **anxious reaction** to violence and aggression — we respond **emotionally** to it. Repeated exposure to violence in the **media** may reduce this response, making people **desensitised** to violence.

Disinhibition

Most of the time people have **inhibitions** about **behaving aggressively** — it's seen as **unacceptable** behaviour. Seeing violence repeatedly in the **media** may mean it begins to seem **acceptable**, making people **disinhibited**.

Cognitive Priming

Cues associated with violence in the **media** (e.g. guns), may **trigger aggression** in us when we see them in real life. The violent material we see in the media is **stored** as a memory, connected to other **violent memories**. We're **primed** to retrieve these memories if we come across anything **associated** with them, which may **prompt aggressive behaviour**.

Aggression in the Real World

Institutional Aggression in Prison Has Two Explanations

Institutional aggression is the term used to describe aggression within an **institutional environment**, like a prison. There are two main approaches to explaining institutional aggression in **prisons** — the **dispositional** and **situational** explanations.

> An institution is an organisation governed by some sort of authority, usually with strict social guidelines. Schools, hospitals, and the military are other examples of institutions.

The Dispositional Explanation

Dispositional explanations argue that institutional aggression stems from the characteristics of the **individuals** in the institution (their disposition).

The Importation Model	**Irwin and Cressey (1962)** suggested that the characteristics and social norms that inmates bring with them when they enter prison are the main factors that lead to institutional aggression. This is called the importation model — inmates import characteristics from their life outside. E.g. they bring in the norms of criminal gangs, where aggression may be a respected trait.

Harer and Steffensmeier (1996) looked at data from 58 male prisons in the US. They found that levels of **violent behaviour** in prison were significantly higher among **black inmates**, whereas **drug offences** in prison were significantly higher among **white inmates**. Harer and Steffensmeier concluded that this supported the **importation model**, as these results mirror trends in American society outside of prison.

However, this research has been criticised for being **androcentric** (see page 136), as it didn't include female prisons.

The Situational Explanation

Situational explanations claim that institutional aggression is caused by the **environment** in the institution.

The Deprivation Model	The **deprivation model** states that the **conditions** in prison (e.g. overcrowding) cause **stress**, which results in aggression. **Sykes (1958)** described the particular deprivations that inmates experience in prison as the '**pains of imprisonment**'. These include loss of autonomy, loss of liberty, loss of security, and so on.

Megargee (1977) studied inmates in an American prison for young offenders over a period of **three years**. He found that **crowding** levels in the prison were significantly correlated with levels of disruptive behaviour.

Research Suggests Both Explanations Are Important

1) Research evidence for the **dispositional** and **situational** explanations of institutional aggression in prisons is often **contradictory** — in practice **both types of factor** probably play a part.

2) **Jiang and Fisher-Giorlando (2002)** looked at disciplinary reports from a prison in the US. They found that the **importation model** was best suited to explaining violence towards **other inmates**, whereas the **deprivation model** best explained violence towards **prison staff**.

Warm-Up Questions

Q1 What is cognitive priming?

Q2 How does Harer and Steffensmeier's (1996) study support the dispositional explanation of aggression in prison?

Exam Questions

Q1 Distinguish between the dispositional and situational explanations for institutional aggression in prisons. [4 marks]

Q2 Discuss media influences on aggression. [16 marks]

I blame my aggressive behaviour on playing too much snap as a child...

A few key things you need to learn here — how violence in the media may lead to aggression through desensitisation, disinhibition and cognitive priming, and the dispositional and situational explanations for institutional aggression in prisons.

Offender Profiling

Now you're onto the really fun stuff. Solving crime and saving the world from convicts, criminals and thieves.
Forensic psychology uses psychological principles to try to explain why people might commit crime.

The Police Use **Offender Profiling** to Help Them **Identify** Suspects

The aim of profiling is to create an idea of the offender's **likely characteristics**. This helps the police to focus their resources on more likely suspects, and can create new leads within an investigation.

There are different styles of approach in offender profiling.

The American 'top-down' approach

The **FBI** began by **interviewing** 36 convicted serial killers and sex murderers to gain an insight into their thinking and behaviour. They were classified into two groups, **organised** and **disorganised**. **Organised offenders** were intelligent, socially and sexually competent, lived with somebody and planned their attacks. **Disorganised offenders** were less intelligent, socially and sexually incompetent, were loners and were more likely to behave impulsively and not plan the attacks in advance. These groups are used to compare information from **new crime scenes** to make judgements based on past experience. However, based on **self-report interviews** and a **restricted sample**, the categories devised by the FBI lack validity and can't be generalised to the wider population.

The British 'bottom-up' approach

This approach was developed by **David Canter** and uses **investigative psychology** (applying psychological research and theories to criminal investigations) more than the FBI approach. Canter's **geographical profiling** saw the **crime scene** as a source of information — the behaviour of the offender at the crime scene would reveal information about their everyday life and characteristics (see below). Although Canter also analysed behaviour of convicted offenders, this is a much more **bottom-up approach**, as the focus is on the unique circumstances of an individual offender.

Several Factors Are Considered When **Developing a Profile**

Douglas et al (1986) reported that the **FBI** use **four** main stages when building a profile:

1) Assimilating **data** — collecting all the information available about the crime scene and victim.
2) **Classifying** the crime — identifying the **type** of crime committed.
3) **Reconstructing** the crime — this includes the behaviour of both the **offender** and the **victim**.
4) Creating a **profile** — making judgements about possible physical and lifestyle **characteristics** of the offender.

Geographical profiling uses a crime scene to predict the characteristics of a criminal's profile.
Canter (1994) identified **five** main characteristics that should be included in a profile:

1) **Personal** characteristics — e.g. personality traits.
2) **Criminal** history — types of offences they may have committed in the past.
3) Residential **location** — e.g. if a circle is drawn around an offender's crime scenes on a map, the offender is often found to live in the middle. This is known as **circle theory**.
4) **Domestic** and **social** characteristics — e.g. if the person is likely to live alone or have a family.
5) **Occupational** and **educational** history — likely type of employment and level of qualifications.

There Are a Number of **Biases** and **Pitfalls** in Offender Profiling

1) Profiles can only be used for a **limited** range of crimes such as murders or rapes. They've been used to identify stalkers and arsonists but aren't suitable for use in crimes motivated by **material gain** such as robbery and theft.
2) **Douglas et al (1986)** suggest that the aim of offender profiling has been **misrepresented**. Profiling is not intended to identify a specific person, but instead aims to focus the investigation on a particular **type** of person.
3) Research into the effectiveness of offender profiling shows that it is **limited**. **Holmes (1989)** reported that in **192** cases where offender profiling had been used, arrests had been made in **88** cases. However, the profile only contributed to **17%** of these arrests.
4) **Copson (1995)** found that only **14%** of senior police officers felt that profiling had helped them to solve a case.

Offender Profiling

The **Rachel Nickell** Murder Case Was a **Misuse** of Offender Profiling

Rachel was a young woman murdered in front of her two-year-old son during a walk in the park in 1992. An offender profiler called **Paul Britton** developed a profile which was broadcast on TV, and four callers all identified the same person. The man **fitted the profile** although there wasn't any forensic evidence to link him to the crime.

An **undercover** female police officer befriended the suspect (Colin Stagg) and attempted to get him to confess to the crime during their 'relationship'. The suspect **never** admitted to her that he was the killer and denied involvement, but was still arrested and charged. When the case went to court he was **acquitted** and the misuse of the profile and the police tactics were strongly **criticised** by the judge. In 2008, another man, Robert Napper, **pleaded guilty** to Rachel's manslaughter on the grounds of diminished responsibility.

The Case Study of **John Duffy** is a More **Successful Example**

John Duffy is known as the **Railway Rapist** — between 1982 and 1986 he was responsible for 24 sexual assaults and three murders. **Canter** was asked by the police to analyse the details of the crimes to generate a profile, as forensic evidence suggested they were committed by one person (although sometimes with an accomplice).

The profile made Duffy seem a much more **likely suspect** than had previously been thought. The details of the profile Canter had created were very similar to Duffy's actual circumstances and characteristics. Canter suggested that the offender would:

1) **Live close** to the first three crimes — Duffy lived in Kilburn as suggested.
2) Be **aged** in his mid to late 20s — Duffy was in his late 20s.
3) Work in a semi-skilled or skilled **occupation** — Duffy was a carpenter.
4) Be knowledgeable about **railways** — Duffy worked for British Rail.
5) Have a **criminal record** that included violence — Duffy had been interviewed by the police for raping his wife at knifepoint.
6) Be small and feel **physically unattractive** — Duffy was 5' 4" and suffered from acne.
7) **Fantasise** about sex and violence — Duffy had hard-core pornography videos.
8) Be interested in **martial arts** — Duffy was in a martial arts club.

Canter believed that behaviour is generally **consistent**, so analysis of Duffy's behaviour during the crime gave information about his life and general behaviour. Once Duffy was arrested for the crimes it was discovered that he had started to murder his victims because he was once nearly recognised. Canter also discovered that Duffy burned the bodies of his victims to destroy the **forensic evidence** — he had learned about the procedures used by police for collecting evidence when he was arrested for raping his wife.

Warm-Up Questions

Q1 Who developed the bottom-up approach to offender profiling?
Q2 Outline two aspects included in Canter's profiles.
Q3 Describe one problem with offender profiling.

Exam Questions

Q1 Describe **two** different approaches to offender profiling. [8 marks]
Q2 Evaluate the use of offender profiling in criminal investigations. [8 marks]

The offender is likely to be a sweet old lady who likes kittens and scones...

Offender profiling has long been a popular choice for TV dramas, like 'Silent Witness'. Great show, but even before I read these pages I did have a suspicion that perhaps it wasn't realistic for a profiler to conclude from a couple of bloodstains and a shoelace that the killer is a car salesman aged 43 who collects stamps and wears loud ties...

Biological Explanations of Offending Behaviour

As with most topics in Psychology, biology can be used to explain behaviour. But that doesn't mean to say you can nick a chocolate bar from the corner shop, or cheat in your exam, and then blame it on your genes...

Lombroso Linked **Physical Characteristics** to **Crime**

1) **Positivist criminology** says that criminal behaviour results from **physical** or **psychological** features — **no free will** is involved. **Cesare Lombroso (1835-1909)** believed in positivist criminology, though he only focused on **physical** features.

2) During the late-1800s he studied the physical characteristics of criminals (often studying people **after** they had died). He wanted to discover if certain features were **more common** in criminals than non-criminals.

3) Lombroso concluded that criminals were more likely to have **atavistic** (primitive) features than non-criminals. He described the **atavistic form** of a criminal as being characterised by a **strong jaw** and **heavy brow**.

4) Other **features** included drooping eyelids, large ears, lobeless ears, high defined cheekbones, a flat nose, long arms relative to the body, and sloping shoulders.

5) Lombroso thought that criminal behaviour came from **primitive instincts** which had survived the evolutionary process — criminals were a sort of genetic 'throwback' and this could be identified by their **atavistic features**.

6) He later went on to suggest how certain **combinations** of characteristics could describe **different types** of criminals. For example, he claimed **murderers** had **bloodshot eyes** and **curly hair**.

Strengths	Limitations
• Lombroso highlighted the **role of biology** in criminology. • However, he also considered that criminal behaviour was likely to come from an **interaction** between **biological**, **psychological** and **social factors** — an idea which has been highly influential in future theories of criminology.	• Lombroso didn't use a non-criminal **control group** to see if his atavistic features were unique to criminals. • Lots of his sample may have had **psychological disorders** or **chromosomal abnormalities** which may have been a factor in their criminal behaviour.

Criminality Could Have a **Genetic** Basis

There is lots of evidence supporting a genetic cause for offending behaviour:

1) **Adoption studies**
Some adoption studies have shown higher concordance rates of criminal activity between adopted children and their biological parents than with their adoptive parents.

	Mednick et al (1984) — Criminal behaviour in adopted children
Method:	A **concordance analysis** of 14 427 Danish **adoptees** was conducted. Rates of concordance for **criminality** between the adoptees and their **adopted** and **biological parents** were compared.
Results:	**13.5%** of adoptees with parents (adoptive or biological) **without** a criminal conviction had a criminal conviction themselves, compared to **14.7%** of adoptees with at least one criminally convicted **adoptive** parent, **20%** of adoptees with at least one criminally convicted **biological** parent, and **24.5%** of adoptees with at least one convicted adoptive **and** one convicted biological parent.
Conclusion:	A **genetic link** is supported. However, the **concordance rates** are quite **low**, suggesting that there are **other** factors that lead to criminality.
Evaluation:	Adoption studies allow **separation** of the genetic and environmental influences. Just because a person has not been **convicted** of a crime does not necessarily mean that they have never committed one.

2) **Genetic influences on aggression**
Some psychologists believe that **aggression** can lead to **offending behaviour**. Studies have shown a link between **genes** and levels of **aggression**, particularly through the use of twin studies (see page 212).

3) **An extra Y chromosome**
Jacobs et al (1965) found a higher percentage of people from a **prison population** had the atypical sex chromosome pattern, **XYY**, compared to a normal population. They believed the addition of the extra Y chromosome led to increased testosterone and increased violence, resulting in offending behaviour. However, further studies have since suggested that those with such a chromosomal abnormality are more likely to be **hyperactive**, **more impulsive** and have a **lower IQ**, which would be more likely to explain their criminality.

Biological Explanations of Offending Behaviour

There are also **Neural Explanations** of **Offending Behaviour**

Raine investigated the link between brain dysfunction and criminality. He believed that there was an identifiable **biological disposition** for criminal behaviour. Raine suggested that a **biological dysfunction** within the **brain** could cause an individual to commit acts of violence.

Raine et al (1997) — A neural explanation of criminality

Method:	Raine used **PET scans** to create 3-D images of the functional processes happening in the brains of 41 murderers (pleading not guilty by reason of insanity) and 41 control participants.
Results:	The murderers showed **reduced glucose metabolism** in the prefrontal cortex, superior parietal gyrus and the corpus callosum, and **asymmetrical activity** in the two hemispheres. In other words some of their brain processes were **dysfunctional**.
Conclusion:	The evidence **supported** a link between brain dysfunction and predisposition to violent acts.
Evaluation:	The researchers used a **control group** who were matched on variables such as age and sex. However, researchers could not **randomly allocate** participants to the 'control' or 'killer' groups, so needed to be cautious when drawing conclusions about **causal relationships**.

There are **Strengths** and **Weaknesses** to the **Biological Explanation**

Strengths

- A number of studies have provided support to suggest there is some **contribution** from biological factors.
- The biological theories can often be tested **scientifically**, making them more reliable — for example, Raine et al's study above.

When her Mum was Marigold's age, she too nicked flowers from the neighbour's garden*.

Weaknesses

- Since **no** study has shown a 100% concordance rate between MZ twins or biological parents and their children for offending behaviour, biology **cannot** be the only influencing factor. The environment **must** play a role.
- Andrews and Bonta (2006) stated that the concordance rates for criminality between biological parents and adopted children might not be **directly** due to genetics. Criminality could be a result of **inherited emotional instability** or a **mental illness**, which could **indirectly** result in offending behaviour.
- Some people think that biological explanations are too **reductionist** (page 141) and too **deterministic** (page 140).

Warm-Up Questions

Q1 Give three features of atavistic form, as described by Lombroso.

Q2 Describe the method used by Mednick et al (1984) to investigate offending behaviour in children.

Q3 What did Jacobs et al (1965) believe the addition of an extra Y chromosome could lead to?

Q4 Give two weaknesses of the biological explanation of offending behaviour.

PRACTICE QUESTIONS

Exam Questions

Q1 Describe the atavistic form as an explanation of offending behaviour. [4 marks]

Q2 Discuss genetic explanations for offending behaviour. [16 marks]

I was always taught never to judge a book by its cover...

Lombroso's theory was influential for its time, but treat it with a pinch of salt. You can't go accusing all the strong-jawed, lobeless-eared people you know of being criminals. That's just mean. And probably wrong. So don't do it.

* CGP does not condone 'nicking of flowers from the neighbour's garden'.

Psychological Explanations of Offending Behaviour

So the excitement continues. If you've ever wondered why some of us are law-abiding goody two-shoes while others seemingly couldn't give two hoots about the law, then you'll like these next few pages.

Eysenck Explained **Criminal Behaviour** in Terms of **Personality Types**

Hans Eysenck was one of the first psychologists to examine human **personality**. He initially identified **two** main **personality dimensions** (scales) and suggested that everyone fits in somewhere along these dimensions:

1) **Neuroticism-stability** — individuals towards the neurotic end of this dimension show traits such as anxiousness and restlessness. Traits at the other end of the scale include reliability and calmness.

2) **Extraversion-introversion** — individuals towards the extravert end of this dimension tend to be sociable, impulsive and assertive. Those at the other end tend to be quiet, passive and reserved.

Thomas didn't want to come out of his shell. He was a neurotic, introverted soul.

In later research during the 1970s Eysenck added a **third personality dimension**:

3) **Psychoticism** — this scale shows how disposed an individual is to psychotic breakdown. Those who score highly tend to be aggressive, hostile and uncaring.

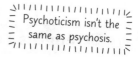

Psychoticism isn't the same as psychosis.

- Eysenck suggested that individuals have a **genetic predisposition** to a particular personality type, but environmental factors play a role too. This leads to particular behaviours, including **criminal behaviours**.

- Eysenck believed that **psychoticism** was a good **predictor** of criminal behaviour. He also thought **extraversion** was a good indicator of criminal behaviour for **young** people, but **neuroticism** a better indicator for criminal behaviour in **older** people.

- Eysenck's theory has been influential across psychology, especially in how it **combines** biological, psychological and social approaches together. However, his theory of the criminal personality was chiefly developed from studies which involved **self-report measures**, meaning his findings **lack reliability**.

Criminals May Have Different **Thinking Patterns**

The **cognitive approach** to offending behaviour suggests that **criminal thinking patterns**, **cognitive distortions** and different **levels of moral reasoning** are all important factors in explaining why people may turn to a life of crime. **Yochelson and Samenow (1976)** looked into criminal thinking patterns:

	Yochelson and Samenow (1976) — Criminal thinking patterns
Method:	A **longitudinal study** over 14 years examined **255 male offenders** from a variety of different backgrounds. The researchers compared two groups, roughly the same size. The first group consisted of offenders at a hospital for 'secure treatment' as they had been found not guilty due to mental illness. The second group consisted of offenders from a 'normal' prison population. Each participant underwent a series of **interviews** over several years.
Results:	Although only **30** participants finished the study, **52 thinking patterns** were found to be common across **all** the criminal participants. These included **criminal thinking patterns** (fear and the need for power), **automatic thinking errors** (e.g. lack of trust, lack of empathy, impulsiveness, manipulativeness) and **crime-related thinking errors** (fantasising about criminal behaviours).
Conclusion:	Criminals **share** common **thinking patterns** and **thinking errors**. The researchers acknowledged that even though these characteristics are not unique in criminals, they are thought to be more likely to exist in criminals.
Evaluation:	Since there was **no control group** in the study, the results are less **valid**. There is also evidence of **gender bias** (p.136) since only males were studied, and so the results cannot be generalised. Since the study was **longitudinal**, it would be difficult and expensive to replicate, but it does have an element of **ecological validity**.

Psychological Explanations of Offending Behaviour

Criminals May Show Cognitive Distortions

Cognitive distortions are irrational thought patterns which give people a distorted **view of reality**, so affect how they behave. **Gibbs et al (1995)** outlined several cognitive distortions which they linked to offending behaviour. They include:

1) Being **self-centred**

2) **Minimisation** — minimising the seriousness of their offending behaviour

3) **Blaming** problems on others

4) **Hostile attribution bias** — believing that others are 'out to get them' and have hostile intentions

Liau et al (1998) found cognitive distortions were **higher** in a group of 52 male '**delinquents**' than in a **control group**. However, studies like this don't show that these thought patterns **cause** criminal behaviour, it could be the other way round.

Criminals Could Have a Different Level of Moral Reasoning

1) **Kohlberg** thought that moral reasoning progresses in **stages**. He argued that your **moral understanding increases** as you grow older because at each stage you take more and more of the **social** world into account.

2) He investigated this idea using a series of ten **moral dilemma** stories. An example of this type of dilemma is the '**Heinz dilemma'**. In the story, Heinz chose to break into a shop to steal expensive drugs to cure his dying wife.

3) The participants had to decide whether these actions were **justified**. Kohlberg was interested in the participants' **reasons** for their decisions.

4) **Kohlberg** used a sample of 72 boys ages 10, 13 and 16. He used his findings to come up with **six progressive stages** of moral reasoning, which fall under **three levels**:

Level 1: Preconventional Reasoning

1) An action is morally wrong if the person who commits it is **punished** as a result (most common in children).

2) The right behaviour is the one that is in **your own best interest**.

Level 2: Conventional Reasoning

Most people tend to fall into Level 2.

3) The right behaviour is the one that makes **other people** think positively about you.

4) It is important to **obey laws** and follow **social conventions** because they help **society** to function properly.

Level 3: Postconventional Reasoning

5) The right course of action is the one that promotes the **greatest good** for the **greatest number of people**.

6) Actions are driven by **abstract**, **universal principles** of right and wrong, which **don't** depend on the situation.

Serious offenders have a **moral outlook** that **differs** from that of the law-abiding majority — they **don't** progress through these stages of moral development in the same way as law-abiding people. **Allen et al (2001)** supported this assumption by showing that criminals tend to have a lower **level of moral reasoning** than non-criminals.

Evaluation

Kohlberg's theory can be considered **gender-biased** — most of Kohlberg's work was carried out on US males, so his findings may not apply to other groups. **Gilligan (1982)** claimed that the theory was **androcentric** and focused too much on **male-oriented ideas** about justice rather than also taking into account other moral approaches that might appeal more to women.

Warm-Up Questions

Q1 Describe Yochelson and Samenow's (1976) study into criminal thinking patterns.

Q2 Name two cognitive distortions described by Gibbs et al (1995).

Exam Question

Q1 Describe how Eysenck's theory of the criminal personality can explain offending behaviour. [4 marks]

I bet examiners are lovely people really — but I'm sure they're out to get us...

Not that I'm showing a hostile attribution bias to all the examiners in the world at all. Never... Ahem. Anyway, time to learn the stuff on these pages. It's all about thinking patterns and cognitive distortions — definite bedtime reading.

Psychological Explanations of Offending Behaviour

Just when you thought things were tailing off, it gets even better. There are more psychological explanations of offending behaviour on these two pages. And this time, Freud is back. Oh yeah...

The **Psychodynamic Approach** May Explain **Criminality**

1) **Freud** claimed that the only way to really understand how people behave is to look at their past.

2) He proposed that offending behaviour was therefore linked to **early childhood experiences**.

3) Several of Freud's **psychodynamic theories** can be used to explain offending behaviour:

1) An Inadequate Superego

Criminality could be due to the **abnormal** development of the **id**, the **ego** and the **superego** which occurs during early childhood. Freud suggested that the **id** provides an **instinctive** drive towards **criminal behaviour**. But the **superego** is there to keep it in line.

There's lots more about Freud's ideas on pages 68-71.

Blackburn (1993) proposed that there are three different types of superego which lead to offending behaviour:

- A **weak superego** — often found in those with **no same sex parent**, as they can't internalise that parent's moral code. As such, they would have **fewer inhibitions** towards conducting antisocial behaviour, and would fully respond to their **id** (the 'pleasure principle').

- A **deviant superego** — usually found in those whose **same sex parent** is immoral. So if a girl had a criminal mother, her **superego** might be **less responsive** to crime than someone without a criminal mother.

- A **strong (or over-harsh) superego** — if the person thinks about acting on the id's desires, they'll end up feeling really **guilty** if they have a strong **superego**. The individual is then likely to feel they should '**get punished**' to relieve their guilt, and so engage in crimes in order to get caught.

2) Defence Mechanisms

Freud outlined different **defence mechanisms** — **displacement**, **repression** and **denial** (see page 69). These could all be used to explain offending behaviour:

- **Englander (2007)** described how **displaced aggression** in offenders might explain their antisocial behaviour. If offenders **cannot control** their aggression (which comes from their **instinctive id**), this aggression may then 'spill out' of their **unconscious**, resulting in violent and offending behaviour.

- Most people can **repress** and **deny** their urges (such as aggression or anger) and keep them at bay. However, the **psychodynamic approach** suggests that a **triggering incident** or **stimulus** might **release** these feelings, resulting in antisocial and offending behaviour.

The **Psychodynamic Approach** to Crime has Several **Weaknesses**

As you've seen, the psychodynamic approach offers a number of explanations for criminality. But in terms of explaining offending behaviour there are a number of **issues**:

- It is difficult to scientifically test the theories because the psychodynamic approach considers unconscious processes — this makes it unreliable and lacking in validity.

- Lots of the data in the psychodynamic approach to criminology is from case studies and is qualitative (page 111), and so it's hard to use it to state laws that can be generalised.

There's more strengths and weaknesses of the psychodynamic approach on page 71.

Psychological Explanations of Offending Behaviour

Sutherland (1939) Developed the Differential Association Theory

The **differential association theory** is used to explain offending behaviour.
Sutherland believed that criminal behaviour could be **learned** in interactions with other deviant individuals.
People not only learn the **techniques** and **methods** involved in certain crimes, but they also pick up the
motives and **attitudes** behind the crimes. He argued that:

1) Criminal behaviour is learnt — in the same way any other behaviour can be learnt.

2) Criminal behaviour comes from interacting and communicating with other people.

3) Criminal behaviour is most likely to be learnt whilst among small groups of people — this is where people are the most influential.

4) Learning about criminal behaviour involves not only the techniques of committing the actual crime, but also the motivation and attitudes towards crime.

5) The law tells a criminal what is right and wrong — the criminal then decides whether an action or behaviour is favourable or unfavourable.

6) Repeated exposure to criminal behaviour is more likely to result in someone committing a crime themself — this is especially true if the crime results in a favourable outcome.

7) The frequency, duration, priority and intensity of interactions between criminals and those learning about criminal behaviour will affect the likelihood of them developing offending behaviour.

8) The general theory of learning by association is also applicable to learning about crime.

9) Anyone can become a criminal — regardless of age, sex, background, etc.

Sammy's dad was a serial bread thief. Says it all really.

Here, 'priority' means how early in their life the interaction occured, not how important it was.

This theory explains why individuals imprisoned for a minor offence often **reoffend** when they're released. Spending time with **other criminals** in the institution (who may have committed more serious crimes) makes them likely to learn further criminal behaviours.

The Differential Association Theory Has Strengths and Weaknesses Too

Strengths

- The differential association theory accounts for **all types** of people — not just juveniles or lower class people who are often described in theories of crime.

- His theory was supported by **Short (1955)** who studied 176 school children, using a questionnaire. Short measured self reported **delinquent behaviour** (e.g. drug taking, petty stealing etc.) and **association** with delinquents or criminals, and found a **positive correlation** between the two measures.

Weaknesses

- Not everyone is influenced by people around them — this theory doesn't consider **individual differences**.

- Problems in defining crime make this theory **hard to test** as it is hard to objectively measure attitudes towards the law and crime.

Warm-Up Questions

Q1 What did Blackburn (1993) propose leads to offending behaviour?

Q2 Give two weaknesses of the psychodynamic approach to criminality.

PRACTICE QUESTIONS

Exam Questions

Q1 Outline the psychodynamic explanation of offending behaviour. [4 marks]

Q2 Discuss the differential association theory of offending behaviour. [16 marks]

Personally, I find Freud quite offensive...

The psychodynamic theory of forensic psychology isn't the most popular, but you still need to know your stuff. You might not agree with what Freud said, but you have to hand it to him... he certainly made an impact on psychology.

Imprisonment

So, the jury's reached a verdict — they've decided the defendant is guilty and needs a spell in prison. But there's debate about whether or not this will change the criminal. Cue two handy pages on imprisonment.

There are Several **Aims** of **Custodial Sentencing**

People aren't locked up and thrown in jail 'just because'. Custodial sentencing (sending someone to prison) has a **purpose**. In fact, it has lots of **different** purposes:

1) **Retribution (punishment)** — the offender should rightfully 'pay' for their crime, and deserves the punishment.

2) **Rehabilitation** — reforming and offering offenders the chance to get their lives back on track.

3) **Incapacitation** — protecting the public by removing the offender.

4) **Denunciation** — showing the public that the offender's actions were wrong.

5) **Deterrence** — stopping future crimes by the criminal themself (specific deterrence), or stopping the public committing the same crime by showing them the punishment (general deterrence).

Imprisonment Can Have a **Big Effect** on **Criminals**

There are lots of different psychological effects of custodial sentencing.

Mental Health Problems

It's thought that prisoners may be more susceptible to problems with **depression** and more likely to attempt **suicide** than other people. **Dooley** studied suicides in prisons in England and Wales.

	Dooley (1990) — Depression and suicide risk in prison
Method:	The **case notes** of **295** of the 300 suicides that happened in prison between 1972 and 1987 were studied.
Results:	Prisoners serving **life sentences** and those convicted of **violent** or **sexual** offences were most at risk. There was an association between suicide and **guilt** over the offence. There was a history of **psychiatric problems** in about a third of cases and **self-harm** was common.
Conclusion:	**Depressive illness** is likely to be a contributing factor to suicides in prison. Dooley thought that better **communication** between staff and prisoners is needed to reduce suicide rates.
Evaluation:	Prisoners **don't** form a **random sample** of the general population — as a group they differ in terms of ethnicity, age, psychiatric history, socio-economic status, and marital and employment status. This makes it hard to measure exactly how much **more susceptible** to depression and suicide prisoners really are.

Zimbardo's prison study (page 5) also showed the 'prisoners' experiencing high levels of **emotional distress**, further emphasising the **psychological effects** of custodial sentencing.

Although studies have shown prisoners to have depression, it is difficult to determine **cause** and **effect** — prisoners may have had psychological problems, such as depression, **before** they were imprisoned.

Institutionalisation

Being kept in a prison often **strips** offenders of their **autonomy**. Studies such as **Zimbardo's** have shown that prisoners are quick to **conform** to given roles and become dependent on others within their environment.

Reinforces Criminal Behaviour

Putting people who've committed crimes all together in one place might seem like a good idea. But it can become a **breeding ground** for crime. Prisons can **reinforce** the criminal lifestyle and **support criminal behaviour** as a result of inmates teaching each other about crime. This can result in high recidivism rates (see next page).

Psychological effects of imprisonment don't have to be negative — there can be positive effects too. Inmates can experience remorse, benefit from new opportunities and undergo treatment to rehabilitate their lives.

Labelling

When offenders are released from prison, they still hold the **stigma** of having been 'inside'. They may find it **difficult** to get a job or **maintain** their **social network**, which in turn increases the likelihood of recidivism (next page).

Imprisonment

There are **Good** and **Bad** Things About Imprisonment

- There are lots of arguments **for** custodial sentencing — it **can** fulfill its aims whilst having positive psychological effects, such as having a new outlook on life, and giving prisoners the opportunity to **reform** and become better people.

- But some people argue that custodial sentencing **doesn't really work**. It only exists to **please** the public, as a sign of 'justice' being served. Some argue that if it **did** really work as a deterrent, there wouldn't be any criminals today.

Bruce really wasn't a fan of prison — his hat gave him the most awful hat hair.

- Putting money and resources into **prevention** might be more efficient. This could **eliminate** labelling and other detrimental consequences of imprisonment.

- There are many **other types** of custodial sentences — imprisonment doesn't suit all. For example, **community service** might be better for those who have committed small crimes. This would enable **low-risk offenders** to keep their social contacts and jobs — important for when they finish their sentence.

Lots of Criminals **Continue** to Commit Crimes **After** Being in Prison

Recidivism is just a fancy word that means **repeating** an undesirable behaviour after you've been punished for it. In the case of criminals and prison there are many factors which influence this:

1) Length of **time** spent in prison.
2) **Supervision** after conditional release.
3) **Disciplinary** reports.
4) **Education** level.
5) **Seriousness** of crime committed.
6) Prisoner **ethnicity**.
7) Individual **experiences** in prison.

> Conditional release is where a person is released early from prison under specified conditions, e.g. they may be monitored or supervised.

In the UK, rates of adult recidivism have slowly decreased over time. In **2012**, nearly **27%** of criminals re-offended. However, in the same year, there was a reported rise in the proportion of re-offenders who served **less than 12 months** — this was reported as happening in **over 50%** of cases.

Studies have also shown a link between **employment** after imprisonment and the likelihood of reoffending. For example, **Gillis et al (1998)** found that offenders who found employment within six months of being released had fewer convictions than offenders who didn't take up employment during this time. **However**, this link doesn't necessarily show **cause and effect**.

> Recidivism costs the economy a great deal — so reducing these rates would benefit everyone.

Warm-Up Questions

Q1 What is reparation?
Q2 Describe Dooley's (1990) study into suicides in prisons.
Q3 Give two factors which could affect recidivism.

Exam Questions

Q1 Which term is used to describe the repetition of undesirable behaviour after punishment?

   A Incapacitation   **B** Denunciation   **C** Recidivism   **D** Retribution   [1 mark]

Q2 Outline the aims of custodial sentencing.   [6 marks]

What did the policeman say to his stomach...?

Whilst you're pondering the answer to this very important question (hint: it involves a pun on the word 'arrest'), perhaps make sure you've learnt these pages back-to-front, inside-out and upside-down. It's gripping stuff...

Behaviour Modification in Custody

Even though recidivism rates may be dropping in the UK, they're still very much there — criminals are still reoffending. Lots of studies have shown that sending a criminal to prison may not do anything to change their behaviour. But that doesn't stop people trying. These pages will tell you all about the methods used to try to modify criminal behaviour.

The **Token Economy Programme** is a **Behaviourist** Treatment

1) The **token economy programme** has been used with various groups, including prison inmates.
2) It's a form of **behaviour modification** based on the behaviourist idea of **operant conditioning**.
3) Operant conditioning deals with the modification of behaviour through **consequences** — rewards which reinforce behaviour, and punishments which discourage the behaviour from happening again.
4) The token economy programme reinforces good behaviour by rewarding subjects with '**tokens**' for meeting their behavioural '**goals**'.
5) Tokens are saved up and can be **spent** to gain 'treats' or 'rewards'.

Token economy programmes must be adhered to in order for them to work. No other rewards can be given to the inmates or the token system will become pointless. Also, several things need to be established in order for the system to be set up:

1) The behaviour that is desired from the inmates must be clearly defined.
2) A variety of rewards must be given to encourage participation.
3) The reasons for token allocation must be clear.
4) What a token is worth must be clearly established, e.g. how many tokens equal a chocolate bar, etc.
5) The rate of earning tokens must also be established, i.e. how many a particular behaviour will earn.

Token Economy Programmes have Strengths and Weaknesses

There is evidence that token economies can **improve inmates behaviour** while they're in prison. For example:

Milan and McKee (1976) studied the effect of using a token economy in a cellblock of an American male prison. They compared the inmates behaviour between several conditions, including normal prison methods, a system of behaviour monitoring and encouragement without issuing tokens, and a full token economy. They found that the inmates' performance for the monitored behaviours (e.g. getting up on time, keeping a tidy cell) was best when the full token economy was in place.

However, the positive effect of token economies **may not last** once people leave the programme.

Kirigin et al (1982) studied the effectiveness of a programme for 'delinquent' youths, which included a token economy. They found that rates of criminality and of behaviour like truancy were reduced during the programme, but returned to the same rate as the control group after the programme.

Token economies can be considered **unethical** — it can be argued that to work properly they need to involve withholding access to basic things like food and drink, which should be a **right**, not a **privilege** that is earned.

Anger Management is a Therapeutic Programme

1) **Anger management** is a **therapeutic programme** often used with convicted violent criminals.
2) This approach assumes that violent behaviour is caused by **anger** and **frustration** — it's hoped that if individuals can learn to **control** this anger then their violent behaviour patterns will decrease.
3) Anger management is based on **cognitive behavioural techniques** and a specific programme has been designed for use in penal institutions.
4) The main aims of this treatment are to **reduce** the amount of **violence** within the prison and to improve individuals' **self-awareness** and **control**. It's hoped that it will still make a difference **after** release.
5) Courses usually involve a **two-hour session** each week for **eight weeks**. Participants are encouraged to **monitor** their own behaviour patterns and emotions so that they become increasingly aware of their own emotional changes. It's thought that this will help them to control their own emotions.

Behaviour Modification in Custody

Anger Management Isn't Effective for Everyone

Studies looking at how **effective** anger management is at reducing inmates anger have had mixed results. This may be because it's **only helpful for certain offenders** — not all crimes are committed through anger. **Howells et al (2005)** found in a study of Australian offenders that a short course of anger management **did not have a significant effect** on self reported anger. However, some studies have found that it can be effective:

	Ireland (2000) — The effectiveness of anger management
Method:	Aggression levels of **50 inmates** in a young offenders' institution were measured two weeks **before** an anger management treatment programme was started. A **record** of each prisoner's aggressive **behaviour** over one week was kept, and they each completed a **questionnaire** and had a **cognitive-style interview**. A treatment programme of twelve one hour sessions over three days was started, and eight weeks later the measurements were **repeated**.
Results:	There was an **improvement** in **92%** of participants. **8%** of prisoners were **worse** after the treatment.
Conclusion:	The anger management programme was **useful** for treating aggressive behaviour in the short term.
Evaluation:	It will have been difficult to **control other variables** that may have had an effect on inmates' anger, such as news from friends and family, interaction between inmates and relationships with staff. Also, all the participants in this study were young offenders in an institution, so the results can't be **generalised** to other groups, e.g. offenders in prison, released offenders, etc.

Restorative Justice is About Criminals Making Amends

Traditional justice is all about being **punished** for committing crimes. The **restorative justice programme**, on the other hand, focuses on criminals **making amends** directly to the people they've harmed with their behaviour. This helps the criminal to **take responsibility** for their actions, and makes them aware of the **real damage** they've caused.

1) It can be used for various offences from antisocial behaviour (e.g. **vandalism**) to serious offences like **assault**.
2) The victim must **volunteer** to use the approach and the offender must have **admitted responsibility**.
3) The process may involve the victim and offender **meeting** face-to-face or communicating by **letter**.
4) It can also involve offenders working to **undo** the damage they have caused, e.g. by removing graffiti.

A study by the Smith Institute (**Smith Report 2007**) found that the restorative justice programme has many advantages:

1) It **reduced post-traumatic stress** in the victims, and they were **less likely** to want **violent revenge**.
2) Both criminals and victims were **more satisfied** with this approach than with traditional justice solutions.
3) It decreased the **costs** involved.

One of the main **problems** with the restorative justice programme is that people are **reluctant** to use it. A report by The Ministry of Justice in 2012 also highlighted the **lack of awareness** by the public and their **confusion** over what restorative justice really means.

Warm-Up Questions

Q1 What is a token economy programme?

Q2 Give a weakness of token economy programmes.

PRACTICE QUESTIONS

Exam Questions

Q1 Briefly outline how restorative justice programmes work. [4 marks]

Q2 Discuss how anger management can be used to deal with offending behaviour. [16 marks]

Kev woz ere — restorative justice sucks...

You've probably just read the stuff on token economy programmes and realised they ring a bell. That's because they crop up in other areas of Psychology too. Take a look on page 184 where you can read about them again. Hoorah.

Addictive Behaviour — Smoking

Loads of people smoke, even though it causes all sorts of illnesses. A big part of this is that it's addictive — once people start smoking, they can find it very difficult to stop. As usual, psychology has come up with reasons for this.

Addictions Can Be **Physical** or **Psychological**

1) **Physical dependence** is where your body becomes dependent on a drug (e.g. the **nicotine** in cigarettes). You get **withdrawal symptoms** (see below) if you don't take the drug. This is your body's way of telling you that you need more of the drug to feel 'normal' again.

2) **Psychological dependence** is more of a **mental state** than a physical need. For example, you believe that you need the drug to stay relaxed — and are drawn back time and time again to take it.

Addictions Involve **Tolerance** and **Withdrawal Symptoms**

Addictions, including addictions to drugs such as nicotine in cigarettes, involve **tolerance** and **withdrawal symptoms**.

Tolerance

Tolerance happens when the body becomes **used to** a substance — taking the same amount of a drug no longer has the **same effect**. You need to take **larger quantities** to feel the same effect.

Withdrawal Symptoms

Withdrawal symptoms are uncomfortable **symptoms** that occur when a person **stops taking** the substance they're addicted to, or **reduces** the amount they take. These are removed by taking more of the drug again.

Many People Are **Addicted** to Smoking

The chemicals in cigarettes can cause diseases such as **cancer**, **emphysema** and **bronchitis**. Despite this, many people smoke and some continue to smoke after being diagnosed with one of these conditions — this is because smoking is **addictive**. Even though many smokers want to quit, the **success rate** of those who attempt it is **very low**.

As with most things in psychology, addiction to smoking can be explained in more than one way.

Smoking Can Be Explained in Terms of **Brain Neurochemistry**

1) There are many chemicals in cigarettes but it's the **nicotine** that causes **addiction**.

2) Nicotine stimulates the release of **dopamine**, increasing the level of dopamine in the brain and stimulating dopamine receptors on neurons. This provides feelings of **pleasure** and **relaxation**.

3) Once the dopamine has been removed from the synapses (reuptake), this feeling **disappears**. In order to regain it, the person wants to take **more** of the substance.

4) If nicotine's taken **regularly** the body **expects it** and **reduces** the amount of dopamine that's released naturally.

5) In order to maintain **normal dopamine levels** and the effect that they have on the body, nicotine needs to be taken regularly. This **reinforces smoking behaviour**, leading to more frequent smoking and **addiction**.

6) **Quitting** smoking is very difficult as the body becomes used to nicotine and **relies** on it to stimulate dopamine release. Quitting deprives the body of nicotine, leading to **low dopamine levels** until the body readjusts.

7) This can lead to **withdrawal syndrome**, which may result in **symptoms** such as anxiety, sleep disturbance and nausea.

	Olds and Milner (1954) — The effect of dopamine in rats
Method 1:	Rats had an electrode connected to the **hypothalamus** in their brain. When the rats pressed a **lever**, the electrode stimulated the hypothalamus, leading to the release of **dopamine**.
Results 1:	Rats voluntarily **chose** to press the lever.
Method 2:	In a second experiment, the rats had to walk over an area with a **painful electric current** running through it in order to get to the lever.
Results 2:	Rats **chose** to walk over the area which would shock them in order to press the lever.
Conclusion:	As rats pressed the lever voluntarily, even if it meant being shocked, it suggests the feeling associated with the release of dopamine was **rewarding** and the stimulus that caused it was **addictive**.
Evaluation:	Although it was a laboratory study and therefore highly **controlled**, the experiment was carried out on **rats** and so the results can't be **generalised to humans**. The procedure also has **ethical issues**.

Addictive Behaviour — Smoking

The Brain Neurochemistry Explanation has Strengths and Weaknesses

Strengths

1) Research, such as that by **Olds and Milner (1954)**, has provided **support** for the idea that **dopamine** is involved in addiction.

2) Studies into **biochemical factors** involve **laboratory experiments** where the **variables** are strictly **controlled**. This means that it should be possible to establish **cause and effect**, because it's less likely that the results were caused by an **extraneous variable**.

3) **Zhang et al (2012)** also provided support that dopamine is involved in smoking addiction, finding that levels become **abnormal** if an addict gives up smoking. They studied mice which had been given nicotine for several weeks, and found that when it was suddenly **stopped**, production of dopamine became **lower** than normal.

Brain neurochemistry is a biochemical explanation.

Weaknesses

1) Explaining substance misuse in terms of neurotransmitter levels is **reductionist** (see page 141) because it **ignores psychological factors**.

2) Focussing on brain neurochemistry ignores the impact of **genetics** — it could be that **inherited tendencies** influence substance misuse. For example, **Doweiko (2002)** looked at **adoption records** for over 3000 people and found that **children** of **alcoholics** were much **more likely** to grow up to be alcoholics themselves. Being raised by **adoptive** parents who **weren't alcoholics** seemed to have **little effect**. This suggests that there's a **genetic influence** in **addiction**.

3) There are problems with **generalising** results from **animal** research to **humans**.

Smoking Can Be Explained Using Learning Theory

Learning through observation is explained by social learning theory (see pages 58-59).

1) New behaviour (in this case smoking) can be learned through **observation** or **modelling**. Whether the behaviour is imitated depends on the perceived **consequences**.

2) Through **operant conditioning**, if smoking is **positively reinforced**, e.g. by **benefits** such as fitting in with peers, it's likely to be **copied**. Seeing **role models** (e.g. parents or celebrities) smoking also encourages people to smoke.

3) Once someone has started smoking they will experience withdrawal symptoms if they stop. These encourage people to start smoking again (to remove the symptoms). This is known as **negative reinforcement**. Drug users may also want to **avoid** feelings of stress or boredom, or negative **social** factors like being the 'odd one out'.

4) Often, smoking becomes **associated** with other activities and objects, which makes it difficult not to smoke in certain **environments**. This is known as **cue reactivity**, and can be explained by **classical conditioning**.

5) For example, repeatedly smoking in the same environment could lead to **associations** forming between smoking and **other stimuli** in the environment, such as alcohol, other smokers or cigarette lighters. When these stimuli are present, the body **expects** to receive nicotine, and will **compensate** in advance for certain effects of the drug — the person will then develop a **craving** to smoke.

Studies have provided **support** for the **learning theory** approach to addiction. For example:

	Akers and Lee (1996) — The effects of social learning over time
Method:	A five year **longitudinal study** of 454 secondary school students was conducted using **self-report questionnaire surveys**. These measured how frequently the students smoked and 'social learning variables'. These were things like whether friends smoked, how often friends smoked, and perceived attitudes of friends and parents towards smoking.
Results:	Significant **positive correlations** were found between the social learning variables and smoking.
Conclusion:	Social learning can partly account for whether smoking begins in adolescence.
Evaluation:	Methods relying on self report may be **unreliable**, and correlation doesn't prove that social learning causes smoking to begin. Also, the effect of social learning wasn't analysed to show the relative influence of different **variables**, e.g. gender or parental vs. peer influence.

Addictive Behaviour — Smoking

Using **Learning Theory** to Explain Smoking has **Strengths** and **Weaknesses**

Strengths

1) Studies of learning theory usually use human participants, so they avoid the problems of generalising from animal experiments encountered in much biochemical research.

2) The learning approach can be used to explain physical addiction as well as psychological addiction to substances that don't cause unpleasant physical withdrawal symptoms, e.g. cannabis.

3) Moolchan et al (2000) found that 75% of teenage smokers have at least one parent who smokes. They also feel that smoking helps them to fit in with their peers. These findings support social learning theory, as the subjects were imitating their parents. They also support the operant conditioning explanation — the social approval that subjects got from their friends for smoking acted as positive reinforcement.

4) A meta-analysis of fMRI (see page 86) studies by Engelmann et al (2012) provided support for the idea of cue reactivity. They looked at studies that had compared fMRIs of smokers shown smoking-related cues compared to neutral cues, and found that the smoking-related cues caused a larger neural response.

David was going to have to find a new hobby. Seeing the cue would be too much for his chocolate addiction.

Weaknesses

1) The learning approach is too nomothetic because it assumes that everyone can become addicted in the same way. It ignores individual differences, and doesn't place enough importance on other explanations such as biochemical or genetic factors.

2) The learning approach doesn't explain how free will (see page 140) plays a part in behaviour such as smoking. It doesn't take into account the idea that people can make their own decisions about what they do or don't do, e.g. whether they smoke or not, based on what they know about the dangers.

It's likely that a **combination** of **biological** and **psychological** factors contribute to addiction to smoking. For example, it might be that **brain neurochemistry** plays a big part, but that it also depends on the **environmental variables** (e.g. exposure to role models) that people come into contact with.

Warm-Up Questions

Q1 Distinguish between physiological and psychological dependence on smoking.

Q2 What is tolerance?

Q3 Outline research that suggests the release of dopamine is rewarding and addictive.

Q4 Describe the study by Akers and Lee (1996).

Q5 Describe the findings of Moolchan et al's (2000) study on teenage smoking.

Exam Questions

Q1 Outline how nicotine addiction can be explained in terms of brain neurochemistry. [4 marks]

Q2 Discuss how learning theory can be applied to smoking behaviour. [16 marks]

My tolerance for this topic is rapidly reducing...

So there you have it. I reckon the neurochemical explanation could also be used to explain my chocolate spread addiction. I can't get through the day without it, and I think I'd happily take a quick electric shock to get my hands on some. Anyway, enough about me — you need to make sure you get to grips with everything on these pages.

Addictive Behaviour — Gambling

Now that you know all about addiction to smoking, it's time to learn about a completely different type of addiction — addiction to gambling. It seems that some people can't help going back again and again for that elusive win.

Gambling Addictions Can be Explained by **Cognitive Biases**

1) Cognitive biases are **mental errors** or **distortions of thinking** that lead to **perspectives** and **judgements** that can be very different to reality.

2) These faulty judgements can come about because we often subconsciously **simplify things** and use **rules of thumb** when processing information and making decisions.

3) Cognitive biases can be like **optical illusions**. Even when you're aware of the mistaken thinking, it still seems right. Because of this, they can be pretty difficult to overcome.

4) Cognitive biases appear in **gambling**. For example, people often believe that the **probability** of a future event, such as tossing a coin, is dependent on **past events** (see representative bias below).

5) **Wagenaar** (1988) identified 16 rules that gamblers commonly use when making decisions. These include:

- **The illusion of control** — gamblers think of gambling as **skill-based**, and believe that they have some control over the outcome. This creates superficially high expectations when, in reality, the outcomes are often determined by chance alone.
- **Representative bias** — gamblers believe that **random events** should **look random**, e.g. 'tails' seems increasingly likely the longer a run of consecutive 'heads' lasts.
- **Gambler's fallacy** — many gamblers believe that the longer a losing streak lasts, the more likely a win will follow.
- **Illusory correlations** — gamblers have **superstitions** which they believe help them succeed, e.g. blowing the dice for a 6.
- **Fixation on the absolute frequency of successes** — gamblers can **recall many past wins**, just because they gamble so much. This creates a false image of how often they win.
- **Sunk cost bias** — gamblers put a lot of money into gambling and so there's the belief that they'll eventually get a return. They don't like to stop gambling just in case they lose out on the win.

There's **Evidence** for **Cognitive Bias**

Griffiths (1994) — Cognitive bias using fruit machines

Method: 30 participants who only **occasionally** used a fruit machine volunteered to take part in a **field study** with 30 **regular gamblers**. Each participant was given £3, which gave 30 gambles on the fruit machine. Participants were asked to try to stay on the machine for at least 60 gambles. If they reached 60, they were given the choice of keeping any winnings or carrying on gambling. Participants were asked to **think aloud**, which required them to say their thoughts out loud during the task. The total number of gambles each participant made was recorded, along with the amount of winnings and the outcome of every gamble.

Results: Regular gamblers were more likely to reach 60 gambles than non-regular gamblers. However, they were also much more likely to play until they had **lost everything**. Some regular gamblers **objected** to gambling on the fruit machine chosen for the study. Regular gamblers also made **more irrational verbalisations** than non-regular gamblers, such as personifying and talking to the machine whilst gambling (e.g. "the machine likes me"). They also tended to refer to losses as '**near misses**' or '**near wins**'. In a later interview, the regular gamblers saw themselves as more **skilful** than occasional gamblers.

Conclusion: There is evidence for the existence of **cognitive biases** in gambling. For example, the fact that some gamblers opposed to using the fruit machine selected for the study indicates that an **illusion of control** exists, where they believe that if they are familiar with a machine they will win more. Also, the fact that many regular gamblers **talked to the machine** shows that their behaviour was not in line with **reality**.

Evaluation: The experiment took place in a natural setting, increasing its **ecological validity**. However, this also means that the results could have been affected by **extraneous variables**. Only one of the regular gamblers was **female**, so the results may not have been **representative** of the whole population. Also, thinking aloud might have an effect on the **cognitive processes** taking place, making the study **invalid**.

Addictive Behaviour — Gambling

The Cognitive Theory of Gambling has Strengths and Weaknesses

Strengths

1) Studies like Griffiths (1994) have shown that there is a **difference** between the **cognitive processing** in occasional gamblers and in regular gamblers.

2) Other studies have supported the idea of cognitive biases. For example, in a study by **Henslin (1967)**, it was found that gamblers playing craps (a dice game) in a casino were likely to adjust how they rolled the dice depending on what they wanted to score. If they needed a **higher number**, they tended to throw the dice **harder**.

3) **Strickland et al (1966)** also found evidence of cognitive biases in gambling. They showed that people would make **higher bets** and were **more confident** that they'd win if they were able to throw the dice **themselves** rather than having someone else throw for them.

"Is there one there that you're happy with, sir?"

Weaknesses

1) **Not everyone** develops cognitive biases which lead them to become addicted to gambling. So the cognitive explanation can't be the **only** explanation as it doesn't take **individual differences** into account. There may be other reasons why some people are more likely to become addicted to gambling than others, e.g. genetic explanations.

2) It is difficult to separate **cause and effect** — it might be that the cognitive biases don't cause the addiction, but rather that they are a **result** of the addiction.

3) The approach can help to explain gambling addictions, but it can't be **generalised** to **other types** of addictions, such as smoking or drug addictions, as they seem less linked to faulty processing mechanisms.

Learning Theory Can be Applied to Gambling Addiction

Both classical and operant conditioning can be used to explain gambling addiction:

Classical Conditioning

1) Classical conditioning (see page 55) explains gambling addiction in terms of the person becoming **conditioned** to the **excitement** and **arousal** they feel when they gamble.

2) The **unconditioned stimulus** in this situation is the **gambling win**, which produces **excitement** and increases **heart rate**, which is the **unconditioned response**. If wins and excitement repeatedly happen together in a typical **gambling environment**, other stimuli associated with gambling (e.g. packs of cards, dice) become the conditioned stimulus and will also cause excitement, the **conditioned response**.

3) This feeling of excitement could then be **temptation** to have a go at gambling.

Operant Conditioning

1) Gambling could also be explained by operant conditioning (see page 56) in terms of **reinforcement**.

2) However, unlike some operant conditioning situations, when someone gambles, they are not rewarded at every go — a lot of the time, they **lose**. So, only **partial reinforcement** is present.

3) One type of partial reinforcement which is important in the explanation of gambling is **variable reinforcement**. Gambling wins **don't** follow a **pattern**, and so the pattern of **reward** and **reinforcement** is also **irregular** — it **varies**.

4) Research has shown that variable reinforcement is enough to maintain a **gambling addiction**. Even if you don't know when you're going to win, you **keep trying**, because it could be on the next go and you don't want to miss out.

Addictive Behaviour — Gambling

A **Big Win** Must Come **First** Though

1) Not everyone who gambles develops an addiction.
2) **Skinner (1953)**, believed that this was down to whether they'd had a **big win** early on.
3) His reasoning was that people who have had a big win will have been **positively reinforced**, and will be more likely to **continue their behaviour** to try to achieve the same again.
4) **Custer (1982)** supported Skinner's (1953) ideas that reinforcement could come about as a result of a big win.

This is the same Skinner that you met on page 56.

Social Learning Theory Can Explain Why People **Start Gambling**

1) **Bandura's (1977)** social learning theory (see pages 58-59) can be used as an explanation for how people become **involved** in gambling in the first place.
2) People might initially start gambling after **watching** someone make a win and seeing the positives that come from it — in other words, they learn to start gambling through **vicarious reinforcement** (see page 58).
3) If they themselves go on to make a win, **classical** and **operant conditioning** (see previous page) could then explain why they **continue** to gamble and become addicted.

The Learning Theory Approach to Gambling has **Strengths** and **Weaknesses**

Strengths

1) Learning theory can explain why people continue to gamble even when they lose, by showing that reinforcement can be just as effective even if it is **irregular**.
2) **Meyer et al (2004)** found that **heart rate** and other signs of excitement **increased** when gamblers began playing a betting game, and that problem gamblers had significantly higher heart rates than non-problem gamblers. This provides support for the suggestion that **excitement** acts as an **conditioned response** to gambling.

Weaknesses

1) Learning theory can't explain why only a **small number** of people who experience a win at gambling become addicted to gambling. This means that there must be **other factors** involved too. For example, genetic factors may play a part.
2) Skinner's ideas of conditioning and reinforcement were based on research using **pigeons** and **rats**. This makes it hard to **generalise** the theories to **humans**.
3) Learning theory can't explain the **cognitive biases** that some people who are addicted to gambling hold.

Warm-Up Questions

Q1 Name three cognitive biases.
Q2 Outline the three cognitive biases that you've named.
Q3 What type of study did Griffith's (1994) carry out?
Q4 How can classical conditioning be used to explain addiction to gambling?

Exam Questions

Q1 What is a cognitive bias in relation to gambling? [2 marks]

Q2 Outline one limitation of using cognitive theory to explain gambling addiction. [2 marks]

Q3 Briefly explain how learning theory can be applied to gambling addiction. [4 marks]

To order chocolate cake or apple crumble — it's a gamble...

I need to put in an order for tonight's birthday meal. Whichever one I order, I'll want the other one when it's put down in front of me. Anyway, I suppose that's not your concern. Make sure you can explain gambling using both cognitive theory and learning theory, and make sure you can evaluate them both. Then go and eat chocolate cake. No, crumble.

Risk Factors in Addiction

Not everybody becomes an addict. Behaviours such as drinking and gambling remain controllable pastimes for many people, so there must be individual differences at work. And, surprise surprise, you need to know what they are.

Stress Could be a Factor in the Development of Addiction

1) **Sinha (2007)** used **brain imaging** to investigate the relationship between **stress** and **drug addiction**. She found that the **same part of the brain** was activated during stress as during drug craving.

2) Sinha suggests that stress makes people more **vulnerable** to reacting to **cues** associated with drugs. This could make them **more likely** to develop an addiction.

3) This research shows an **association** between stress and addiction — but it **doesn't explain** it. Drug use might cause altered brain function, or altered brain function might encourage drug use — or there may be **another cause**, and drug use and altered brain function are both results of this.

I'm stressed just looking at them — pass the chocolate.

4) **Operant conditioning** (page 56) could explain why stress might make people more vulnerable to addiction if the pleasurable effects of the substance **reduce the symptoms** of stress. For example, alcohol is a **depressant** so it can make a stressed person feel **more relaxed**. This acts as **positive reinforcement** and so they're more likely to **repeat** the drinking behaviour.

Behaviour of Peers is a Factor that Seem to be Linked to Addiction

1) **Martino et al (2006)** carried out a **longitudinal study** to look at the social factors that affect the **drinking habits** of adolescents. They concluded that the norms for drinking behaviour are learned through **social observations** and **interactions**. The **perceived approval** or **use** of alcohol by **parents**, other important adults and **peers increased the likelihood** of future decisions to drink and get drunk.

2) Research has shown that although being **socially withdrawn** can be negative for other reasons, such as loneliness, it actually **protects** young people from the **influence** of their **peers** in relation to addiction:

> • **Fergusson and Horwood (1999)** found that children who were **socially isolated** from their peer group at the age of **10** because of **social anxiety** were **less likely** to use drugs or drink alcohol when they were **15**.
>
> • **Shedler and Block (1990)** found that **18-year-olds** who hadn't tried drugs were more likely to be **socially isolated, over-controlled** by others and **anxious**.

Younger People are More Affected by Peer Pressure

Sumter et al (2009) found that a person's **age** affects their ability to **resist peer pressure**.

	Sumter et al (2009) — Age differences in resisting peer pressure
Method:	**464 children and adolescents** were given a questionnaire that assessed their ability to resist **pressure** from their **peer group**. The questionnaire was written in a **style** suitable for all ages and used hypothetical **everyday situations**.
Results:	The participants' answers showed that they were **more vulnerable** to being influenced by their friends when they were **younger**. The participants became **more resistant** as they got **older**.
Conclusion:	As adolescents become **more mature** they are **less influenced** by others. This could explain why early experiences with substances have **long-term effects**.
Evaluation:	This was a **cross-sectional study** (one which tested different people of different ages) so individual differences could have affected the results. Carrying out longitudinal research avoids this design flaw, but it takes longer to collect the data. Peer pressure can be both **positive** or **negative** when it comes to abusing substances. You're less likely to do it if your friends aren't — but more likely if they are.

Risk Factors in Addiction

People Can be Influenced By Their Family

Becoming addicted to something can be down to your **family environment**:

- **Adesso (1985)** thought that children develop **expectancies** about the **effects** of **alcohol** through **observing** friends, family and role models. This supports **social learning theory** — it suggests that people learn how to behave when they're **drunk** by imitating others.
- **Christiansen et al (1982)** found that these expectancies are **modified** as an individual's **personal experience** with alcohol **progresses** — their **generalised** expectancies become more **specific**.

- **Baer et al (1987)** found that adolescents were **more likely** to use **alcohol** if they experienced **family conflict** or **stressful life events**. This suggests that they were using alcohol as a way of **avoiding negative things** — **negative reinforcement**. Learning this behaviour at a **young age** means it's likely to **continue** into **adulthood**.
- However, because this was a **correlational study** it's difficult to establish **cause and effect**. It could be that people are **more likely** to experience **family conflict** because they **drink alcohol**.

Personality Can Affect Addictive Behaviour

Personality Dimensions

You can read more about Eysenck's personality dimensions on page 226.

1) **Eysenck and Eysenck (1976)** outlined three main personality dimensions:

- **P** for **psychoticism**, which includes being egocentric, aggressive and impulsive.
- **E** for **extroversion**, which includes being outgoing, happy and sociable.
- **N** for **neuroticism**, which includes being anxious, moody and irritable.

Eysenck suggested that some personality characteristics make a person more prone to addiction.

2) **Francis (1996)** found that people with nicotine, heroin and alcohol addictions scored more highly on N and P scales on psychometric tests compared to the E scales.

3) The exact relationship between addiction and personality is unclear. Being irritable and impulsive could mean you are more likely to use substances such as alcohol or drugs. Or it could be that these personality characteristics make you less able to control your use of the substances.

4) Alternatively, it could be that having an addiction leads a person to be moody and impulsive, and makes them less likely to be happy and outgoing.

Self-Efficacy

1) **Bandura (1977)** came up with an alternative theory based on **personality** for what makes people prone to addiction.

2) He proposed that **self-efficacy** is a big indicator of whether or not someone will **change their behaviour**, for example, whether or not they'll succeed in giving up smoking.

3) Self-efficacy is how **strongly** someone believes that they are **capable** of doing something. So, if someone has **high self-efficacy**, they're more likely to **succeed** in changing their behaviour, and vice versa.

4) **DiClemente (1981)** carried out a study which found support for this idea.

5) Self-efficacy was measured in participants who had recently given up smoking. They were then followed up five months later to see if they'd managed to **abstain** from smoking.

6) It was found that those who had managed not to smoke had **significantly higher** self-efficacy than those who had returned to smoking.

Risk Factors in Addiction

People Might Be at **Higher Risk** of **Addiction** Due to Their **Genes**

There's a **genetic explanation** for addiction — it's been suggested that some addictions are **inherited**.

1) A review of studies by Sayette and Hufford (1997) concluded that **identical (MZ) twins** showed a **higher rate of concordance** for **alcoholism** than **non-identical (DZ) twins**, suggesting that alcoholism is controlled to **some extent** by **genes**.

2) This can explain why, despite the fact that many people drink alcohol on a regular basis, only a **small proportion** develop an **addiction** to it.

3) However, there must be an **environmental aspect** to alcoholism as the MZ twins didn't show 100% concordance.

4) It's also not clear whether the result is just **specific to alcoholism**, or can be generalised to addiction as a whole.

1) **Goodwin et al (1973)** found that adopted males whose biological parents had an **alcohol addiction**, were **four times** more likely to become alcoholics themselves than adopted males whose biological parents didn't have alcohol addictions.

2) This implies that there is a **genetic factor** in alcohol addiction.

1) Slutske (2010) studied whether gambling addiction has a genetic basis.

2) In a study of approximately 5000 participants, she looked at concordance rates in MZ and DZ twins.

3) The results showed that concordance rates in MZ twins were twice as high as the concordance rates in DZ twins.

4) Slutske concluded that although there is a clear genetic component, there must be other factors at work. She believed that carrying certain genes makes people vulnerable to gambling addiction, but that whether or not this happens also depends on other social factors such as the presence of a role model who gambles.

The true cost of his addiction only hit Andy when he was asked to settle his tab.

Warm-Up Questions

Q1 What technique did Sinha (2007) use when investigating the relationship between stress and addiction?

Q2 Identify the relationship that has been established between age and resistance to peer influence.

Q3 Identify the factors associated with drinking alcohol in the Baer et al (1987) study.

Q4 Give the personality characteristics outlined by Eysenck and Eysenck (1976) that P, E and N stand for.

Q5 What were the results of Slutske's (2010) study?

Exam Questions

Q1 Read the item and then answer the question below.

> Mark has moved to a new school and is worried about making new friends. He tries to make friends with a group of students, many of whom smoke. He is keen for them to like him so that he can settle in quickly. Mark is soon a regular smoker.

Using your knowledge of risk factors in addiction, explain why Mark becomes addicted to smoking. [4 marks]

Q2 Discuss risk factors associated with the development of addiction. [16 marks]

I don't stand a chance...

These psychologists are coming up with risk factors here, there and everywhere. How am I meant to avoid become addicted to everything I see? Come to think of it, maybe I haven't... I can't do without my morning cuppa, and then there's the afternoon biscuit craving, and the bedtime hot chocolate. Oh, moody and impulsive, you say...?

Reducing Addictive Behaviour

Because there are lots of different explanations for addictive behaviour, it means that many different ways to combat addictions have been developed. There's a lot to cover here, so take it slow and it'll all be alright on the exam day.

Addictions Can be **Reduced** Using **Drug Therapy**

1) The biological approach to reducing drug and alcohol addictions involves a **gradual detox**, where the **quantity** of the substance used is **reduced over time**. **Medication** may be prescribed to stop addictive behaviour. However, any medication prescribed has to be carefully controlled so it doesn't become an addiction itself.

2) Drug therapy can involve using **agonists** to help addicts cope with withdrawal symptoms when they stop abusing certain substances.

> *Agonists are a type of drug that trigger a response by binding to receptors on cells. Some agonists can replace and replicate the effects of addictive drugs, but with much less harmful side effects.*

> For example, methadone is used as a biological intervention to help heroin addicts become 'clean'. This drug works by stimulating the opiate receptors, which slows down the nervous system, creating similar effects to heroin but in a less dangerous way. Research has found methadone to be an effective way of allowing addicts to wean themselves off heroin. For example, Newman and Whitehill (1979) found methadone to be significantly more successful than a placebo drug when used by a group of heroin addicts.

3) **Antagonists** are also used in drug therapy to reduce addictive behaviours. They stop the addictive substance from creating pleasurable feelings after someone has taken it, preventing reinforcement.

> *Antagonists reduce the effect of addictive drugs and substances by blocking receptors.*

> For example, naltrexone is a drug which stops pathways in the brain from transmitting feelings of pleasure. It's commonly used to treat heroin and alcohol addiction by ensuring that neither drug produces positive side effects for the user. This means there's no longer an association between pleasure and the drug, so no reinforcement or conditioning can take place.

4) However, one **problem** with drug therapy is that there's the risk that the medications can cause **side-effects**.

5) Drug therapy is often only **effective** as long as the drugs are taken — people may **relapse** if they stop treatment.

Behavioural Interventions Can **Reduce** Addictive Behaviour

1) One type of behavioural intervention is called **aversion therapy**.

2) This is where addictions are broken by forming **negative associations** with the addictive behaviour.

3) For example, Antabuse® is prescribed to alcoholics. It causes nausea if it's combined with alcohol, discouraging alcoholics from drinking. The addict will form an **association** between **drinking** and **nausea** — this will continue even when they stop taking Antabuse®.

> **Meyer and Chesser (1970)** carried out a **repeated measures experiment**. A group of alcoholics who were prescribed Antabuse® were compared to a **control group**. Around **50%** of those taking Antabuse® stayed **teetotal** for at least a year — significantly more than in the control group. From this study they concluded that an **unpleasant response** can be **conditioned** to an **addictive behaviour**.

4) Aversion therapy can also take the form of **covert sensitisation**. This is where the person forms negative associations with the addictive behaviour using just their **imagination**, rather than actually experiencing negative consequences.

5) For example, for someone with an alcohol addiction, the aim would be to associate thoughts of drinking with negative consequences. This would be done by them imagining a **horrible experience** in great detail, such as being ill, at the same time as having **cravings** for alcohol.

> **Kraft and Kraft (2005)** studied the effectiveness of **covert sensitisation** using six participants with different addictions — alcohol, nail biting, cigarettes, cannabis, overeating and chocolate. They found that the technique was **effective** for **all** of the addictions, and was successful after only **2-4 sessions**. However, the very small **sample size** means that the results can't reliably be generalised to the population.

6) One problem with aversion therapy is that it has **ethical issues** surrounding the use of the aversive stimuli.

7) Aversion therapy can take a **long time**, and in the case of Antabuse® it relies on people continuing to take the drug for long enough to form the negative association — addicts may just **stop taking it** so that they can drink again.

Reducing Addictive Behaviour

Cognitive Behaviour Therapy Can Also Reduce Addictive Behaviour

1) **Cognitive behaviour therapy (CBT)** aims to change the way an addict **behaves** by changing their **thought processes**. It identifies the thoughts that cause the behaviour, e.g. 'I can't cope without cigarettes', and then changes this thought process. This is known as **cognitive restructuring**.

2) Cognitive behaviour therapy has had some **success**, e.g. it has enhanced the effectiveness of nicotine replacement treatment for quitting smoking.

3) **Carroll et al (1994)** conducted a study which showed CBT to be **effective**. They compared two different intervention practices using two groups of cocaine users. Group One were given a series of **CBT sessions** whilst Group Two received an alternative form of **non-specific psychotherapy**.

4) Both therapies **reduced** the depressive symptoms of all participants, but **CBT** was **more effective** in stopping the addictive behaviour, and was more **successful** in a **follow-up** one year later.

5) Although there is support for CBT, such as the study above, it has some **weaknesses**:

- CBT can take a **long time**, so the person needs to be willing to **invest time** in the process.
- It can be **difficult** for a person to change their thought processes, so they need to be **committed** and **motivated** to complete the therapy.
- CBT requires a lot of **focus**, **attention**, and **thinking**. People struggling with **substance addiction** may have trouble achieving this without receiving other treatment or help first.

Theories of Behaviour Change Can Be Applied to Addiction

These theories are used to find ways to support people to **change their behaviour**.

The Theory of Planned Behaviour

1) **Fishbein and Ajzen (1975)** initially developed the **theory of reasoned action (TRA)** model of behaviour.

2) It states that an individual's behaviour, e.g. whether they will give up alcohol, can be **predicted** by their **intention** to perform it. Intention is determined by two factors:

- The person's **attitude to the behaviour** — this is shaped by their **beliefs** about the **outcome** of the behaviour, e.g. 'I'll save money', and their **judgement** of whether the outcome is **positive or negative, likely or unlikely**.
- **Subjective norms** — this describes their **expectations** of the **social consequences** of the behaviour, e.g. 'My friends will think I'm boring', and their **motivation to follow these norms**, e.g. 'I want to be popular'.

3) Sheppard et al (1988) carried out a meta-analysis and found that the TRA had a **strong predictive use** — it was pretty good at predicting intentions and behaviour. It's also a useful model for knowing how to **alter** an individual's intentions and behaviour. However, it's been criticised for **neglecting factors** such as **habits** and **emotional aspects**, which are also important when intentions are being formed.

4) **Ajzen (1991)** then added a third factor to the TRA — a person's **perceived behavioural control**, e.g. 'I don't have the will power to give up alcohol'. This factor **increases** the model's **predictive power**.

5) This theory is known as the **theory of planned behaviour (TPB)**. It suggests behaviour is influenced in two ways:

- Indirectly — if a person believes that the behaviour is too difficult they don't form the initial intention to carry out the behaviour.
- Directly — if the perception of their own level of control is accurate, e.g. they don't have sufficient willpower, they won't succeed.

6) In contrast to the TRA, the TPB takes into account the fact that people **don't always have complete control** over their behaviour, as there may be obstacles that stand in their way.

7) Norman et al's (1998) study found that **perceived behavioural control** was a strong predictor of binge-drinking. The TPB could therefore be used to develop **intervention strategies** and **prevention programmes**. For example, programmes that involve **convincing** an individual that they **are in control** of their drinking behaviour.

8) Both models ignore the fact that there may be **discrepancies** between **attitude** and **behaviour** and that a person's behaviour is not always a reflection of their **intentions**. People's actions aren't always rational and based on deliberate decision making processes. This is especially true for **addictive behaviour**, which is often **irrational**.

Reducing Addictive Behaviour

Prochaska's Six-Stage Model

1) **Prochaska and DiClemente (1983)** came up with a model of **behaviour change**.
2) The model has **six stages**. At each stage, the person is given **encouragement**, but it's ultimately down to them to work through the stage and decide for themselves when it is time to **progress** to the next.

Stage	Characteristics	Support Given to the Person
Precontemplation	The person with the addiction **isn't ready** to change. They don't see their behaviour as a problem, and are good at **rationalising** this to themselves.	People show **concern** about the person's behaviour and try to **discuss** the problem.
Contemplation	The person is starting to **consider** that they have an addiction and that it is a problem. They're not yet committed to making any changes though.	The person is encouraged to **weigh up** the pros and cons of their **addiction**, and the pros and cons of **change**.
Preparation	The person has **accepted** that their addiction is a problem and they're **ready** to change. They begin to make **commitments** and to put **goals** in place.	The person is **encouraged** to take their **first steps** to make **changes**.
Action	The person is **actively** working towards changing their behaviour. They've made changes to their **lifestyle** and they're following a **plan**.	The person is given **help** in the changes they're making and is given **social support**.
Maintenance	The person is **focused** on sticking to the lifestyle changes they've made and **avoiding** a return to the addictive behaviour.	The person gets **continued support** to prevent relapse.
Relapse	This is where the person **goes back** to the addictive behaviour after having successfully been free of the behaviour for a while.	The person is shown to treat the relapse as a **learning opportunity** — for example, they can evaluate why it happened, and how they can avoid it happening again.

3) The model has been successfully applied to **addictive behaviours** such as smoking, drinking and drug-taking.

Warm-Up Questions

Q1 Outline one drug therapy used in the treatment of addiction.

Q2 Describe the main findings of the study by Meyer and Chesser (1970).

Q3 What is 'precontemplation' in Prochaska's model?

Exam Questions

Q1 Which of these isn't a stage in Prochaska's six-stage model of behaviour change?
    A control   **B** contemplation   **C** maintenance   **D** preparation   [1 mark]

Q2 Briefly outline how cognitive behaviour therapy is used to reduce addiction.   [2 marks]

Q3 Outline the application of the theory of planned behaviour to addictive behaviour.   [6 marks]

I need an intervention to sort out my TRA — tremendous revision anger...

Phew, that's a whopping amount of information on reducing addictive behaviour. You're just going to have to take it bit by bit, until you know it all. Don't move on until you've got it firmly wedged in your brain. Sorry, there's simply nothing else for it. Still, this is the last page of the very last section you need to learn, so it's not worth giving up now...

Summary of the Exams

Here's what you can expect to see in the AS and A-Level Psychology exams.

AS and A-Level exams are linear, so that means you'll do all the exams at the end of the course.

The Exam Papers are **Broken Down** into Sections

AS Psychology has Two Papers

This table shows you how **AS Psychology** is examined:

Paper	Section	Topics Covered	Marks	Total Marks	Time	% of Total Qualification
Paper 1: Introductory Topics in Psychology	A	Social Influence	24	72	1 hour and 30 minutes	50
	B	Memory	24			
	C	Attachment	24			
Paper 2: Psychology in Context	A	Approaches in Psychology	24	72	1 hour and 30 minutes	50
	B	Psychopathology	24			
	C	Research Methods	24			

For both papers, in each section you'll get **multiple choice questions**, **short answer questions** and at least one **extended writing question**.

A-Level Psychology has Three Papers

This table shows you how **A-Level Psychology** is examined:

Paper	Section	Topics Covered	Marks	Total Marks	Time	% of Total Qualification
Paper 1: Introductory Topics in Psychology	A	Social Influence	24	96	2 hours	33.3
	B	Memory	24			
	C	Attachment	24			
	D	Psychopathology	24			
Paper 2: Psychology in Context	A	Approaches in Psychology	24	96	2 hours	33.3
	B	Biopsychology	24			
	C	Research Methods	48			
Paper 3: Issues and Options in Psychology	A	Issues and Debates in Psychology	24	96	2 hours	33.3
	B	One from: Relationships, Gender, Cognition and Development	24			
	C	One from: Schizophrenia, Eating Behaviour, Stress	24			
	D	One from: Aggression, Forensic Psychology, Addiction	24			

For Paper 3, in Section A you'll be asked questions on one compulsory topic. In Sections B, C and D you get to choose which topic you answer questions on from a choice of three.

For each paper, in each section there'll be **multiple choice questions**, **short answer questions** and at least one **extended writing question**.

Assessment Objectives

You can get loads of clues about your answers from the exam paper.

You Need to Meet Certain **Assessment Objectives**

There are three **assessment objectives** — **AO1**, **AO2** and **AO3**.

AO1 is about the facts and theories

Questions containing **AO1** marks cover your **knowledge and understanding of science**, its **processes**, **techniques** and **procedures**. You get marks by **recalling** and **describing** psychological knowledge, such as theories, studies and methods. What you don't need to do is evaluate the theory (unless the question tells you to) — that'd just be a **waste of time** that you could use elsewhere, and you **won't get any extra marks**.

AO2 gets you to apply your knowledge

Questions containing **AO2** marks are slightly different in that they get you to **apply your knowledge and understanding of science**, its **processes**, **techniques** and **procedures**. Rather than just recalling stuff, e.g. listing relevant experiments, you've got to **apply your knowledge** to the different situations or contexts.

You might have to apply your knowledge:

- to a **made-up example** given in the question — e.g. you might be given some information about a person suffering from depression and have to outline behavioural, cognitive or emotional characteristics from the description.
- to a **practical** situation — e.g. you might be given the results of a study about how different reinforcements lead to different behaviours and be asked to explain how these results show evidence for conditioning. So you'd need to apply your knowledge of conditioning to the information given.
- in a situation with **qualitative data** (see page 111).
- in a situation with **quantitative data** (see page 111).

AO3 is about analysing, interpreting and evaluating

In questions containing **AO3** marks you could be given scientific information, ideas or evidence and be asked to analyse, interpret and evaluate them. You might need to evaluate a study or theory, or draw conclusions from the results of an experiment. You could even be asked to give suggestions on how to make a study better. You'll also need to be able to design psychological procedures.

Watch out — a question could contain more than one assessment objective. You need to read the question carefully and work out what you're being asked to do. See the next page for more on this.

Each Paper Has a **Different Weighting** of Assessment Objectives

There aren't a set number of **AO1**, **AO2** and **AO3** marks in each paper.
For AS and A-Level, in **Paper 1** there are **more AO1 and AO3** marks than **AO2** marks.
For AS and A-Level, in **Paper 2** there are **more AO2** marks than **AO1** or **AO3** marks.
And in A-Level **Paper 3**, there are **more AO3** marks than **AO1** or **AO2** marks.

AS-Level		Assessment Objective		
		AO1	AO2	AO3
Weighting (%)	Paper 1	19–22	12–15	15–18
	Paper 2	14–17	18–21	13–16

A-Level		Assessment Objective		
		AO1	AO2	AO3
Weighting (%)	Paper 1	11–14	6–9	12–14
	Paper 2	7–10	16–19	7–9
	Paper 3	9–12	5–8	15–17

At least **10%** of your grade will come from questions involving some **maths**. It won't be super hard maths, so don't panic, but it will cover maths you've learnt at GCSE. As long as you're comfortable with **basic arithmetic**, **handling data**, **algebra** and **graphs**, then you'll be fine. (And don't worry — you can take your calculator into the exams.)
25–30% of your grade will come from questions on **research methods**. These questions won't just appear in **Paper 2** — they could crop up **anywhere** (see page 252), so make sure you know your stuff really well.

Do Well in Your Exams

Assessment Objectives

The **Wording** of the Question Can Tell You What to Do

Exam questions contain **content words** and **command words**. The content words give away what the **topic** of the question is. A command word gives you an **instruction** of exactly what you need to do to answer the question. It's really **vital** that you know what they mean so that you can write the **correct** things in your answer. For example, if the question simply asks you to '**describe**' or '**outline**' something, you don't need to go into evaluating or explaining stuff.

Command words that you might find in the exam include:

Command word	What it means
Give/Write	Give a brief answer from memory or from the information in the question.
Name	Use a technical term to identify something.
Identify/State	Give a brief one or two word answer, or a short sentence.
Draw	Illustrate your answer with a diagram.
Label	Name parts of a diagram.
Calculate	Use maths to work out the value of something.
Analyse	Break down into characteristics and features.
Comment	Give a backed-up opinion.
Describe	Give details of something — it might be a theory, concept, process or study.
Outline	This requires less detail than 'describe' — it's more of a brief summary of something. Just give details of the main or important features. You don't need to go into too much depth.
Choose/Select/ Which is/What is	Pick from a range of answer options.
Explain	If a question asks you to explain, you need to give reasons for it and say why it is the case.
Discuss	This is a bit like a debate. Give evidence and examples for what you're saying, and support your points with explanations. These questions tend to be worth quite a lot of marks.
Evaluate	Weigh up the advantages and disadvantages, positives and negatives, or strengths and weaknesses. Keep your answer balanced — don't just concentrate on one side.
Compare	Outline the similarities and differences between two things.
Distinguish	Explain the differences between two or more things.
Complete	Finish the question by filling in the missing information.
Suggest	Present a solution or better way of doing something.
Design	Give details of how to carry out something, e.g. a study.
Justify	Give reasons for your answer, providing evidence to back up your ideas.
Consider	This is quite similar to 'evaluate' — your answer will involve weighing up the point that you've been asked to consider. Again, keep your comments balanced.

Command words can sometimes be **combined** together in a question.
For example, examiners will often ask you to 'outline **and** evaluate' or 'describe **and** explain' something.
Don't let this put you off — just break the question down into bits.
Start your answer with the **outline** or **describe** bit, and then **move on** to your **evaluation** or your **explanation**.

Do Well in Your Exams

What You Need to Write

The **Number of Marks** Tells You **How Much to Write**...

1) The number of marks that a question is worth gives you a pretty good clue of **how much to write**.

2) You get **one mark per correct point** made, so if a question is worth four marks, make sure you write four decent points.

3) There's no point writing a massive answer for a question that's only worth a few marks — it's just a **waste of your time**.

4) For the longer extended writing questions, make sure that you've written **enough** to cover the right number of marks, but don't just waffle.

Martha suddenly realised that the question was worth 8 marks, not 88.

...But You Can't Just Write About **Anything**

1) It's important to remember that it's not just a case of blindly scribbling down **everything** you can think of that's related to the subject. Doing this just **wastes time**, and it doesn't exactly impress the examiner.

2) You only get marks for stuff that's **relevant** and **answers the question**.

3) So, make sure you read over the question a couple of times before you start writing so that you really understand what it's asking.

An **Example Answer** to Show You What to Aim for...

> The model has three features, and the question's worth 6 marks. So, you'd just need to write enough about each feature to get you two marks. The answer might look short, but it's all you'd need to write.

This is the sort of answer that would get you full marks.

1 Outline the features of the multi-store model of memory. **[6 marks]**

> The multi-store model proposes that memory is made up of three stores. These are the sensory register, the short-term store and the long-term store. Sensory memory holds the information that is constantly being taken in from the environment, such as visual and auditory information. If you don't pay attention to this information, it will be lost from the sensory register. However, if you do pay attention to it, it will pass into short-term memory. Short-term memory has a limited and temporary capacity, but if the information in it is rehearsed, it will be transferred into long-term memory, which theoretically has an unlimited capacity and duration.

Make sure the information in your answer is relevant, and keep it concise.

Don't open with a general or meaningless sentence — get straight into gaining marks.

Stop writing once you've answered the question — don't add irrelevant detail to fill up the space.

...And an **Alternate Answer** to Show You What **Not** to Write...

I repeat... What **NOT** to write...

1 Outline the features of the multi-store model of memory. **[6 marks]**

> Atkinson and Shiffrin proposed the multi-store model. They thought that memory is made up of three stores — a sensory register, a short-term store and a long-term store. The sensory register holds information from the environment. If you don't listen to this information, it gets lost. If you do listen to it, it will pass into short-term memory. It's then turned into long-term memory.
> The primacy effect supports this model. You can remember the first few items on a list well. They have been better rehearsed and have moved to long-term memory. Also, if rehearsal is prevented, memory gets worse.

This first sentence is a bit irrelevant — it won't get you any marks.

You'd only need to give this detail if the question had asked you to evaluate the model — writing it is just a waste of time.

This could do with more detail to explain that STM only has a limited capacity, and rehearsal is needed to move information to LTM.

The second answer lacks the **detail** of the first — it only sketches over the features of the model. It wouldn't earn all the possible marks. Also, there's quite a bit of **irrelevant information** that wouldn't get you any marks.

Do Well in Your Exams

Worked Exam

Over the next six pages we've given you some examples of the different styles of exam questions that you might come across. You'll get a mix of multiple choice questions, short answer questions and extended writing questions — so make sure you're familiar with them all.

Some Questions Will be **Multiple Choice Questions**

These questions give you some **answer options** and you just need to pick the right one.

2   Answer the questions on learning approaches below.

2.1   Complete the following sentence about Pavlov's research. Tick **one** box only.

Pavlov's experiments provided evidence for:

> Read through all of the options before you choose your answer.

A   Operant conditioning ☐

B   Classical conditioning ☑

C   The cognitive approach ☐

D   The biological approach ☐   [1 mark]

2.2   Which of the following is **not** used in operant conditioning? Tick **one** box only.

A   Positive reinforcement ☐

B   Negative reinforcement ☐

C   Rewards ☐

D   Imitation ☑   [1 mark]

> Watch out — the question might ask you to find the wrong answer.

You could even be asked to select **two** answer options.

> Make sure you read the question carefully. You wouldn't want to get the parasympathetic nervous system mixed up with the sympathetic nervous system.

3   Which **two** of the following occur as a result of the activation of the sympathetic nervous system? Tick **two** boxes only.

A   Muscle tension ☑

B   Decrease in perspiration ☐

C   Increase in pupil size ☑

D   Increase in salivation ☐   [2 marks]

> You'd get two marks for this question — one mark for each correct answer.

In Some Questions You Might Need to **Complete** or **Label** a **Diagram**

4   Complete the diagram of the working memory model by filling in the boxes.

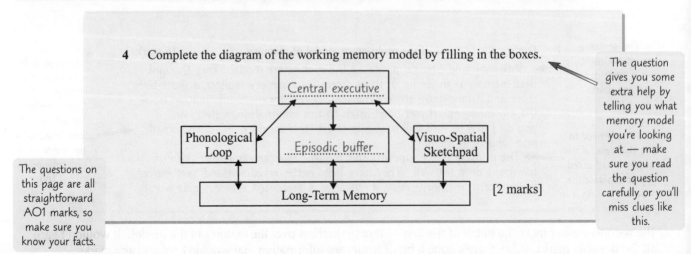

> The question gives you some extra help by telling you what memory model you're looking at — make sure you read the question carefully or you'll miss clues like this.

> The questions on this page are all straightforward AO1 marks, so make sure you know your facts.

Do Well in Your Exams

Worked Exam

You'll be Given Questions Where You Have to Apply Your Knowledge

For example, you could be given a **scenario**, and be asked to use your **knowledge** of psychology to explain it.

5   Read the item below and then answer the questions that follow.

> Roz is talking about her baby son, Charlie, to her friend.
>
> "It's wonderful how he knows I'm his mother. If he's crying, he always calms down as soon as I hold him. It's as if he knows I always feed him."

5.1 Give a brief definition of attachment.   [2 marks]

> Attachment is a close emotional bond formed between two individuals. Attached infants show a desire to be close to their primary caregiver and will show distress when separated.

This is a good, full answer that would get both of the marks.

5.2 Explain how learning theory can be used to explain attachment. Refer to Charlie and Roz in your answer.   [6 marks]

> Learning theory uses conditioning to explain attachment. In classical conditioning, Charlie would learn associations between things in his environment. For example, being fed gives Charlie pleasure and his desire for food is fulfilled when Roz is there. In this way, an association is formed between Roz and Charlie's food. When Roz is close, Charlie will feel pleasure, so he'll desire to be close to her and form an attachment.
>
> In operant conditioning, Charlie's behaviour is reinforced. Charlie will feel discomfort when he is hungry. He may discover that if he cries, his mother, Roz, will come and provide food, removing the discomfort. This is negative reinforcement. Roz becomes associated with food and Charlie will desire to be close to her, again showing attachment.

Use clear explanations of the two types of conditioning.

Use psychological terms, e.g. 'conditioning' and 'reinforcement', where possible.

It's no good just explaining what learning theory is — you won't get very many marks. You need to talk about learning, associations and reinforcers in relation to Charlie and Roz.

You might have to apply your knowledge to a scientific **study** or **procedure**.

6   Read the item below and then answer the question that follows.

> A psychologist wanted to investigate obedience levels. She set up an experiment where participants were asked to complete a mindless task which involved writing out the numbers 1-100, then ripping up the paper and starting again. She found that when instructions were given by a fellow participant, obedience levels were a lot lower than when they were given by a psychologist who was dressed in a white coat.

Outline how the legitimacy of authority can influence obedience levels and explain how it has been illustrated in the procedure above.   [4 marks]

> We are socialised to recognise figures of authority, such as police officers, parents, teachers, etc. They are legitimate authorities. This means we are more likely to obey them because they have a social role, in which they are respected.
>
> In the procedure, the person giving the instructions was seen as a more legitimate authority figure when they were a psychologist dressed in a white coat, compared to a fellow participant. As a result, people were possibly more likely to trust the instructions from the psychologist as they believed that the psychologist had more knowledge than a participant.

Outline legitimate authorities first. Then you can go on to apply your knowledge.

You'll get two marks for outlining and two marks for explaining and applying your knowledge.

Worked Exam

Remember, Research Method Questions Could Appear Anywhere...

7 Read the item below, then answer the questions that follow.

> A study investigated the impact of a 'quit smoking' programme on a group of 10 participants. Participants were asked to record the number of cigarettes they smoked each day before and after engaging with the programme.
>
> The mean and standard deviation of the number of cigarettes smoked by participants each day before and after the programme are shown in the table.
>
> | | **Before programme** | **After programme** |
> |---|---|---|
> | **Mean** | 32 | 8 |
> | **Standard deviation** | 5.43 | 0.26 |

Here, you've been given the mean and standard deviation, but you could be given the raw data and asked to work out the mean, median, mode or even percentages using the data.

When you're given a results table, make sure you understand what it's showing. In this case it's the mean number of cigarettes smoked by participants each day, along with the standard deviation of each condition.

7.1 State the type of design used in this study. [1 mark]

The study used a repeated measures design.

Take a look at page 98 to remind yourself about the different experimental designs used in psychology.

7.2 Give **one** advantage of using this experimental design. [1 mark]

Since the same participants are used in both conditions, participant variables shouldn't affect the results.

Repeated measures designs also need fewer participants.

7.3 Identify the dependent variable used in this study. [2 marks]

The dependent variable is the number of cigarettes smoked each day by participants.

You'd only get one mark if you wrote 'cigarettes' — you need to say it is the 'number of cigarettes smoked each day by participants'.

7.4 Write a hypothesis for this study. [3 marks]

There will be a significant difference in the number of cigarettes smoked each day by participants before and after engaging with the 'quit smoking' programme.

Because the question doesn't specify, you can choose to write either a directional or non-directional hypothesis, or a null or alternative hypothesis.

7.5 Outline the advantages of using the mean rather than the mode when reporting on a set of results. [3 marks]

The mean value uses all of the scores in the data set, which means it is more likely to be representative of the sample. The mode provides the 'most common' score, therefore, it might not accurately represent the data from the sample. With such a small sample, the mode might only involve the same scores from two people, or there might be no mode at all.

7.6 Outline the conclusions that can be made from these results. Include references to the mean **and** standard deviation. [4 marks]

As the mean number of cigarettes smoked daily by participants reduced after the 'quit smoking' programme, the results support the idea that the programme helps people to reduce their level of smoking. Since the standard deviation for the results after the participants engaged in the programme is much smaller than the standard deviation score before the programme, the number of cigarettes smoked is much less varied between participants after the programme. This suggests that individual cigarette consumption is more similar for participants after the programme.

You'll get AO2 marks for making a correct conclusion, and AO3 marks for justifying your conclusion with the data.

7.7 Give an appropriate inferential statistical test which could be used to investigate the differences found in the study above. Justify your answer. [4 marks]

The sign test could be used to analyse these results. This is because the data collected can be converted into nominal data, and the data comes from a repeated measures design.

You need to explain clearly why the test you've chosen is appropriate to get all of the marks.

You could get a question asking you to draw a graph from some given data. Look at pages 121-122 to remind yourself of all the different types of graphs.

Do Well in Your Exams

Worked Exam

You Could be Asked to **Design** Your Own Study

It's time to pretend you're an actual psychologist and **design your own** study. The examiners will give you a helping hand in how to structure your answer — so make sure you address **all** the bullet points:

> This question is really open-ended, and gives you the chance to be creative. But keep it simple, and make sure you explain it well — you'll be more likely to get the marks that way.

8 Design a laboratory experiment to investigate the relationship between eating breakfast and memory performance within Sixth Form students.

In your answer, you will need to include:

- details of how the sample will be selected,
- a description of the task involved,
- a description of how the data will be recorded and analysed,
- any ethical issues which may arise. **[12 marks]**

> This question just contains AO2 marks. You can get 3 marks for each of these bullet points.

This laboratory experiment will investigate the effect of eating breakfast on memory in Sixth Form students. The alternative hypothesis is that there is a relationship between eating breakfast and memory performance, and the null hypothesis is that there is no relationship between the two. This study will use an independent groups design, where each participant only takes part in one condition.

The independent variable is whether the participants eat breakfast or not, and the dependent variable is the number of words each participant gets correct on a memory task.

A systematic sample will be used to select participants. Within a Sixth Form, every 5th person on the register will be asked to participate in the study. This will continue until there are 20 males and 20 females.

Participants will be asked not to have any breakfast at home before coming to school the following day. When they arrive at school, half of the sample (10 males and 10 females) will be given a standardised breakfast, and the remaining participants won't be given anything to eat. All participants will then be asked to learn the same list of twenty random words. Two hours later, following normal lessons, all participants will be asked to recall all the words they can remember from the list.

The number of words each participant remembers will be recorded in a table. The mean number of words recalled by those who ate breakfast and those who didn't will be calculated and displayed in a bar chart to show the differences between the two groups. Since this is an independent groups design using ordinal data, a Mann-Whitney test will be used to analyse the data, and to determine if the null hypothesis can be rejected.

To make sure the study is ethical, all participants will have to give their consent to participate at the start of the study. They won't be told that this is a study investigating memory, so there is an element of deception involved. But, all participants will be given enough general detail, and will be fully debriefed at the end of the study. Finally, all participants will have the right to withdraw from the study at any time, and all results shall remain confidential.

> Here you need to explain what type of experimental design you're going to use. It could be an independent groups design, repeated measures design or a matched pairs design.

> Try to describe your study in as much detail as possible — your study should be able to be replicated accurately.

> The data is ordinal because you don't know if all the words are equally hard to remember. If you can remember the table on page 133, it'll make it easier to decide which inferential statistical test you could use to analyse the results.

> Ethics are really important. Luckily, the things you need to remember are similar for most studies — all participants have to give consent, cannot be harmed, have the right to withdraw at anytime and should be debriefed at the end of the study.

Keep an Eye on the **Time**

- Time management is one of the most important exam skills to have.

- How **long** you spend on each question is really important in an exam — it could make all the difference to your grade.

- It doesn't matter if you **leave** some questions out to begin with.

- For example, if you're stuck on a question that's worth only a **few marks**, don't spend ages trying to answer it — you can always come back to it if you have time.

Tasha really wanted to answer her exam but it hadn't started ringing yet.

Do Well in Your Exams

Worked Exam

You'll be Given Some **Extended Writing** Questions Too...

Take a look at this **describe** and **evaluate** question...

For describe and evaluate questions, you'll get a mix of AO1 and AO3 marks.

Before you start writing, it might help to make a plan of what you want to say.

Referencing the type of study Baillargeon used shows that you have an in depth knowledge of her research.

Make sure you evaluate any theories you talk about to gain AO3 marks.

Round off your answer with a conclusion — it'll help tie all your points together.

9 Describe and evaluate Baillargeon's explanation of early infant abilities. [16 marks]

Developmental psychologists have tried to explain early infant abilities. One influential psychologist, Piaget, developed a theory outlining the stages of development that infants progress through. He stated that they develop a concept of object permanence (the understanding that just because something can't be seen, it doesn't mean it's not there) at around 8 to 12 months.

Baillargeon disagreed with Piaget's theory about when object permanence appears in infants. She believed that it developed much earlier, and that the apparent lack of it was actually a lack of motor ability to be able to search for an object.

Baillargeon believed that infants are actually born with a set of expectations about objects. These expectations develop as they interact with the world and learn to predict the outcome of events.

In order to test object permanence in early infants, she carried out 'violation of expectation' (VOE) research. Rather than relying on infants physically moving to find hidden objects, she focused on recording the time that infants spent looking at impossible and possible events. In VOE research, when the infant is presented with a new stimulus, it is assumed that they will look at it until they become used to it — they will then look away. This shows that they have become habituated to the sight. So when infants are shown two new stimuli — one which is possible and one which is impossible, if they do have object permanence, they'll look at the impossible event for significantly longer than the possible event.

Baillargeon et al (1985) provided support for her theory by showing that infants as young as five months old could understand object permanence. She showed infants a box blocking a drawbridge. The infants looked significantly longer at the drawbridge when it passed through the box (an impossible stimuli) than when the drawbridge stopped on contact with the box (a possible stimuli). Further support came from another study in 1987, involving a truck passing through a box (impossible event) or a similar, but possible event. From these results, they concluded that 3-month-olds understand object permanence.

However, Baillargeon's research has been criticised. Whilst it does provide lots of evidence that early infant abilities may be greater than Piaget had stated, her conclusions have been questioned. Some psychologists have claimed that the infants are just noticing the difference from the stimuli they have been habituated to. Since the infants cannot talk, data analysis relies on the psychologists and researchers interpreting their behaviour, and so could be subjective. Her methodology, whilst providing good control by using laboratory experiments, lacked ecological validity by creating artificial situations.

Finally, Rivera et al (1999) carried out similar VOE research but didn't find any differences between how long infants looked at possible and impossible events, suggesting that perhaps Baillargeon's results cannot be supported.

In conclusion, Baillargeon did provide evidence for her explanation of early infant abilities using a set of controlled, laboratory experiments. However, despite the support for her findings, other theories still exist as to how early infant abilities develop, and how they can best be explained.

It's a good idea to start your answer by briefly describing the background to Baillargeon's research.

Rather than just mentioning that a study was used to test a theory make sure you go on to explain why or how it does this.

Don't waste time going into lots of detail for each study. You're just using it to provide evidence of support here, so a brief summary will do.

There'll usually be studies that support or refute a theory. If you know one or two, they'll help you to pick up those AO3 marks.

1) You'll have gathered that to write a good answer, you need to show **detailed** and **accurate** knowledge.

2) Basically, you need to show the examiner that you **understand** stuff really well.

3) Picking out studies and theories to **support** your answers is great — but keep it all **relevant** to the question.

Worked Exam

Some **Discuss** Questions Allow You to Write in **Detail**

In extended **discuss** questions you get to show the examiner how much you know about a topic.

In this discuss question there are both AO1 and AO3 marks up for grabs.

10 Discuss the cognitive approach to explaining depression. [16 marks]

Start by outlining what cognitive psychology is — and move on to defining depression. Then link them both together.

The cognitive model assumes that behaviours are controlled by thoughts and beliefs. So irrational thoughts and beliefs create abnormal behaviours. Depression is a mood disorder which involves abnormal behaviours. Two types of depression include major depression and manic depression. People with depression can exhibit a range of behavioural, cognitive and emotional symptoms, such as decreased appetite, persistent negative thoughts and feelings of sadness and despair.

Before you start writing, it might help to draw a quick sketch of the ABC model so you remember all the parts.

Several models exist which explain how faulty cognitions may be to blame for depression. Ellis's (1962) ABC model outlines that mood disorders often begin with an activating event (A), which leads to a belief (B) about why such an event occurred. This belief could be irrational, or rational. The belief then leads to a consequence (C). Rational beliefs lead to appropriate consequences, whereas irrational beliefs lead to inappropriate consequences (such as depression). Beck (1963) described a 'negative triad' of automatic thoughts which results in depression. These include people holding negative views about themselves, the world and the future.

In some discuss questions, you'll have to talk about an approach and compare it to other approaches in psychology — so make sure you know your stuff about the different approaches (see Section 5 — pages 52-75).

Hollon and Kendall (1980) created an Automatic Thoughts Questionnaire to assess negative thinking in those with depression. Harrell and Ryon (1983) then used that questionnaire to compare the negative thinking patterns in those with depression and those without. They found that those with depression showed more negative thinking than those who didn't have depression. These findings provide support for the cognitive approach to explaining depression.

Don't forget to criticise the approach too. No explanation is ever perfect.

There are some limitations of the cognitive approach in explaining depression. For example, some people think that faulty cognitions may be the consequence of depression, rather than the cause of it. Another issue is that it could cause the person to feel that they're to blame for their problem.

When talking about treatments, you'll get more marks when you use it to discuss the contribution CBT has made, rather than describing what it is, so make sure you focus on that.

The cognitive explanation for depression is useful because it considers thoughts and beliefs, which are key symptoms in depression itself. The cognitive explanation has led to the development of treatments such as cognitive behaviour therapy (CBT). CBT has been found to be effective by empowering patients, and putting them in charge of their own treatment by getting them to identify and attempt to change their faulty cognitions. Brandsma et al (1978) found that CBT was particularly effective in those who often put pressure on themselves, and felt guilty about how inadequate they felt. Hollon et al (2005) found that it was more successful than drug therapy in preventing relapse after the treatments had ended.

Issues and debates is a topic that it's worth knowing really well. You can talk about things like holism and reductionism in many 'discuss' questions.

You can mention ecological validity when evaluating pretty much any psychological study. It either has it or it doesn't.

A strength of the cognitive approach is that it looks at mental processes often overlooked by other approaches. However, it often involves carrying out research in artificial settings, which means the findings can lack ecological validity. The cognitive approach is also fairly reductionist — it breaks behaviour down into basic processes, which some people argue is too simplistic. The effectiveness of drug therapy in treating depression suggests that, whilst the cognitive explanation for depression is useful, it may not be the whole story — other things such as biochemical factors could be more important.

Make a **Plan** Before You Start Your Answer

- The **quality** of your writing will also be assessed — so make sure you use **good English** with **specialist psychology vocabulary** where appropriate.

- Try to **structure** your answer in an **organised** way. Your answer needs to be **clear** and **coherent**. Before you start, it's worth jotting down a quick **plan** of what you want to write so that you don't just end up with a really jumbled answer full of **irrelevant information**.

Do Well in Your Exams

Index

Index

Index

Index

Index